The Many Faces of Murukaṉ

The History and Meaning of a South Indian God

Religion and Society 6

GENERAL EDITORS

MOUTON PUBLISHERS · THE HAGUE · PARIS · NEW YORK

The Many Faces of Murukaṉ

The History and Meaning of a South Indian God

FRED W. CLOTHEY
University of Pittsburgh

With the Poem
Prayers to Lord Murukaṉ
by A. K. Ramanujan

MOUTON PUBLISHERS · THE HAGUE · PARIS · NEW YORK

Jacket photo by Rijks museum voor Volken kunde, Leyden
Murukan̲ riding on a peacock, bronze statue from South India.

ISBN: 90 279 7632 5

Photoset and printed in Malta by Interprint (Malta) Ltd

For Ann
who has shared
the pleasure and pain
of this venture throughout

Acknowledgements

This book has been more years in the making than I am happy to confess. Most of its data, however, has been gathered during two separate visits to India. Most important was the research I was able to do in 1966–67 under the auspices of the American Institute for Indian Studies. Then in 1971–72 while serving as resident co-ordinator in Madurai, Tamil Nadu, for the Great Lakes Colleges Association's Year in India program, I was able to update my data and enlarge its scope.

Yet this study has been evolving over the course of many years starting long before 1966 and lasting to the present. More people have helped to shape it and me than can be mentioned in a single paragraph. Not least of those to whom I owe much are my parents who made it possible for me to spend a boyhood in India. I am especially indebted to several teachers, colleagues, and friends: Kamil Zvelebil, who first sparked my interest in Murukaṉ; S. Agasthalingam Pillai who made the study of Tamil pleasurable; A. K. Ramanujan who gently disciplined by enthusiasm for things South Indian; Mircea Eliade, Charles Long, and Joseph Kitagawa who conveyed the excitement of studying things religious phenomenologically; V. Raghavan who was patient and exceedingly generous in advising me in much of my research.

Among those who have read this manuscript in whole or in part and have made helpful suggestions are Kees Bolle, K. V. Raman, A. S. Gnanasambandan, and N. S. Subrahmaniam. Another host of people has helped me in the preparation of the text. Of these special thanks is due Ms. Virginia Cassell Buckley who pared and reworded the manuscript to relative readability. And, of course, in the last analysis, the manuscript would not have been completed had not my wife, Ann, not only typed it more times than either of us like to remember, but also been adaptable and supportive especially in the early stages of the study. To all these some credit is due for whatever of merit appêars in this book. Of course, I, not they, bear responsibility for any of its misstatements.

A word on abbreviations is in order. Classical Sanskrit and Tamil works are often abbreviated when mentioned in the bibliographical references. While Sanskrit works will be recognized by most readers, the following listing should clarify the less familiar abbreviations used for Tamil sources:

Ainkuṟu.	Ainkuṟunūṟu	Pari.	Paripāṭal
Aka.	Akanāṉūṟu	Puṟa.	Puṟanāṉuṟu
Cila.	Cilappatikāram	Tiru. *or* Tirumuru	Tirumurukkaṟṟuppatai
Kuṟun.	Kuṟuntokai	Tirup.	Tiruppukaḻ
Kuṟiñci.	Kuṟiñcipāṭṭu	Tol.	Tolkāppiyam
Naṟṟ.	Naṟṟiṇai		

Transliterations from the Tamil follow the Tamil Lexicon, except for some names of persons and places which have commonly accepted Anglicized forms.

Fred W. Clothey
Pittsburgh, Pa.

Contents

Prayers to Lord Murukan̲*

I

Lord of new arrivals
lovers and rivals:
arrive

at once with cockfight and banner
dance till on this and the next three
hills

women's hands and the garlands
on the chests of men will turn like
chariotwheels

O where are the cockscombs and where
the beaks glinting with new knives
at crossroads

when will orange banners burn
among blue trumpet flowers and the shade
of trees

waiting for lightnings?

* Reprinted with permission from A. K. Ramanujan, *Selected Poems* (New Delhi, Oxford University Press).

II

Twelve etched arrowheads
for eyes and six unforeseen
faces, and you were not
embarrassed.

Unlike other gods
you found work
for every face,
and made

eyes at only one
woman. And your arms
are like faces with proper
names.

III

Lord of green
growing things, give us
a hand

in our fight
with the fruit fly.
Tell us,

will the red flower ever
come to the branches
of the blueprint
city?

IV

Lord of great changes and small
cells: exchange our painted grey
pottery

for iron copper the leap of stone horses
our yellow grass and lily seed
for rams'

flesh and scarlet rice for the carnivals
on rivers O dawn of nightmare virgins
bring us

your white-haired witches who wear
three colors even in sleep.

V

Lord of the spoor of the tigress,
outside our town hyenas
and civet cats live
on the kills of leopards
and tigers

too weak to finish what's begun.
Rajahs stand in photographs
over ninefoot silken tigresses
that sycophants have shot.
Sleeping under country fans

hearts are worm cans
turning over continually
for the great shadows
of fish in the open
waters.

We eat legends and leavings,
remember the ivory, the apes,
the peacocks we sent in the Bible
to Solomon, the medicines for smallpox,
the similes

for muslin: wavering snakeskins,
a cloud of steam.
Ever-rehearsing astronauts,
we purify and return
our urine

to the circling body
and burn our faeces
for fuel to reach the moon
through the sky behind
the navel.

VI

Master of red bloodstains,
our blood is brown;
our collars white.

Other lives and sixty
four rumoured arts
tingle,

pins and needles
at amputees' fingertips
in phantom muscle.

VII

Lord of the twelve right hands
why are we your mirror men
with the two left hands

capable only of casting
reflections? Lord
of faces,

find us the face
we lost early
this morning.

VIII

Lord of headlines,
help us read
the small print.

Lord of the sixth sense,
give us back
our five senses.

Lord of solutions
teach us to dissolve
and not to drown.

IX

Deliver us O presence
from proxies
and absences

from sanskrit and the mythologies
of night and the several
roundtable mornings

of London and return
the future to what
it was.

X

Lord, return us.
Bring us back
to a litter

of six new pigs in a slum
and a sudden quarter
of harvest.

Lord of the last-born
give us
birth.

XI

Lord of lost travelers,
find us. Hunt us
down.

Lord of answers
cure us at once
of prayers.

Introduction

Murukaṉ as an Expression of Tamil Religion

Murukaṉ is a name which evokes many images for Tamil Hindus. Though a celibate, he is the husband of two consorts. He has been hunter, warrior, philosopher. He is teacher and inspiration for literature and the arts. He is the eternal child, as old as time itself, yet as young as every new beginning. He is the handsome hero and lover, the Wise, Primordial One. His exploits have been extolled in both Sanskrit and Tamil literature, including the mythology of Epic India and the oldest known Tamil poetry. Known and loved in early Tamil civilization, he has adapted to virtually every significant cultural change in South India, even to the present day, so that his history reflects in large measure the history of South India itself. Known also by such names as Skanda, Kumāra, Subrahmaṇya, Kārttikeya, and Vēlaṉ, Murukaṉ is one of the most persistent and significant deities of South India.

1. Contemporary Tamil religion

Even the most casual observers of Tamil Nadu, India's southernmost state, are struck by the current popularity of Murukaṉ. Three of the six busiest and wealthiest temples in Tamil India are dedicated to Murukaṉ. Each of these temples has an annual income of over one million rupees and at least half a dozen others have an annual income of over a half million rupees.[1] Countless other temples dedicated to the god, on hilltops and in villages and cities throughout the state, attract huge numbers of worshippers for auspicious occasions. In addition, the name Murukaṉ has been adopted by a variety of commercial agencies and the god has become the subject of several popular songs and at least one highly popular film, entitled *Kantaṉ Karuṇai*, 'The Grace of Skanda'.

It is clear that the cult of Murukaṉ reflects, in significant measure, the mood of contemporary Tamil Nadu, even in the face of change and encroaching secularism. There are several reasons why this is so, not the least of which is that the god is riding the crest of a Tamil self-consciousness which has come to new focus in the minds of many Tamilians, at least since Bishop Caldwell's publication of a comparative Dravidian grammar in 1856. This self-consciousness has been fed by a variety of factors: the discovery of early non-Āryan cultures in India; the rediscovery of classical Tamil poetry of considerable literary merit, and the regional and cultural pride of such Tamil poets of this century as Subramanya Bharathi. The cult of Murukaṉ is, in some respects, an expression of Tamil self-consciousness, for many Tamilians recognize that Murukaṉ has been identified with the Tamil cultural heritage for centuries and feel he is an embodiment of their heritage. To be sure, to speak of a 'purely Tamil' Murukaṉ is a fiction, yet it cannot be denied that the god has been a part of Tamil history for centuries.

The celebration of Murukaṉ's divinity is consistent, therefore, particularly in the minds of some Tamil purists, with an increasingly strident and proud regionalism. In the god's regional mythology, Tamil Nạdu is seen as the god's domain; his major pilgrimage centers, said to be six in number, are, in effect, *cakras* which sacralize the region. Some of his devotees find in stressing Murukaṉ's Tamil heritage something of their own identity as Tamilians. The god embodies not a few of the aspirations of religious Tamilians both for themselves and for their region – eternal youthfulness, productivity, unconditional freedom. In a similar way, the deity epitomizes the Tamilian's growing image of his own Tamil culture – its age, its persistance, its relative sovereignity in the face of accretions and modifications from non-Tamil sources, and its vigorous and youthful potentiality. In short, the Murukaṉ cultus helps many Tamil adherents answer the question: 'Who are we?'

But Murukaṉ is not a purely Tamil god. His cult is an eclectic one, which suggests another reason the cult is popular in Tamil Nadu and reflects the contemporary Tamil mood. The cult's syncretic nature is such that Tamilians of varying perspectives can be comfortable in its ranks. It is an eclecticism that makes the cultus a prism reflecting the cultural, historical, and sociological facets that comprise Tamil Nadu.

The cultus shares in the mythological and ritual heritage of classical Śaivism and in that philosophy's pre-suppositions, to the extent that traditional Śaivites accept the cultus as an authentic expression of Hindu orthodoxy. As a son of Śiva, Skanda-Murukaṉ is a young and concrete embodiment of many of the powers, attributes, and motifs which characterize Divinity in the Śaiva tradition. In addition to embodying Śaiva motifs, Murukaṉ has been linked in certain ways with the Vaiṣṇava tradition. In the *Bhāgavata Purāṇa* XI. 4. 17, for example, Skanda is said to be an incarnation of Viṣṇu. In the *Skanda-Purāṇa,* he is depicted as the son-in-law of Viṣṇu for his consorts, Devasenā and Vaḷḷi, were said to have been daughters of Viṣṇu in a previous life. Moreover, a number of motifs commonly associated with Viṣṇu – for example, motifs, of celestial warrior, kingship, and divinely-initiated grace – can be found in the mythos of Murukaṉ. Thus, Skanda serves to integrate and bring into focus important aspects of both these religious traditions in South India. There is, in fact, an occasional point where the Murukaṉ cultus has accomodated itself to Muslims. A case in point is the pilgrimage center of Tirupparaṅkuṉṟam, one of the 'six' important ones of the cultus, where, on top of a hill associated with the temple, Muslim pilgrims visit a shrine to 'Sekunder', whom Muslims equate in a still obscure way to Murukaṉ.

While Tamil purists insist upon Murukaṉ's Tamil character, it is evident that the god was extolled in Sanskrit literature fully as much as in Tamil literature, and that he was worshipped in city-states of North India; in fact, much of his mythology is derived in large measure from Epic sources. Moreover, the ritual life of the cultus is so varied as to attract worshippers from all walks of Tamil life. The orthodox and the thoughtful may participate in traditional forms of *pūjā* and meditation. For urban folk there is an occasional accomodation, such as a New Year's Eve musical convention at Tiruttani. At the same time, the rural and the illiterate are present in the Murukaṉ temples in large numbers participating in spontaneous and colorful expressions of folk worship from the *Kāvaṭi* dance to the fire-walking ceremony. The cultus' symbolism is rich and multifaceted. It reflects aspects of generic Tamil and Sanskrit symbolism together with diversified local nuances. The symbol-system has accrued meanings from most of the cultural sources that comprise Tamil civilization. So even though the cultus of Murukaṉ finds itself in the middle of the Tamil-Sanskrit, brāhmaṇ-non-brāhmaṇ disputes, there is a sense in which the cultus is truly democratic and attractive to a significant cross section of Tamil life. The integration and democratization represented in the cultus of Murukaṉ appears to be of fundamental concern for a number of Tamilians today. This concern has come to focus as part of the Tamil Self Respect movement during the last fifty years and represents the coalescence of a variety of influences: the attempt to recover early Tamil social stratification which is believed to be based on occupational differences rather than caste; the influence of such men as Thomas Paine, Karl Marx, and the nineteenth century American free thinker Robert Ingersoll (Irschick 1969:345); and the whole emergence of the common man seeking self-expression. An increasing number of Tamilians are committed to some process of democratization. The Murukaṉ cultus, in its own way, reflects something of that commitment.

To a summary of the reasons why this cultus is significant as a contemporary South Indian phenomenon, one may add only that there is something self-affirming about participating in the religious life of this cultus. The cultus is a celebration of man's humanness. It has an appeal to the totality of the devotee's person – his emotional and intellectual self, his highly private and his social instincts, his mytho-poetic and his conceptual modes of expression. This is true, of course, of much genuine religion. The Murukaṉ cultus, for its part, affords some meaning to the life of many participants who are otherwise still groping for purpose. The cultus gives to many devotees a sense of idenity with their own Tamilness, on the one hand, and, on the other, a sense of participation both in the past and in the Indian whole. The apparent paradox between provincialism and nationhood is in some measure resolved in the person of Murukaṉ.

2. The history of man in South India

2.1 *History and the Tamil consciousness*

There are dimensions to the study of the god Murukaṉ that go far beyond its significance for understanding something of the contemporary religious mood in Tamil Nadu. Murukaṉ is also a god of no little historical significance. Indeed, as we have suggested, part of the reason Murukaṉ reflects the contemporary Tamil mood is that he also reflects the history of Tamil culture. We are fortunate in Murukaṉ to have a god, who in at least a rudimentary form, was worshipped in very early strata of Tamil society prior to any brāhmaṇization of the South, but who at the same time persists and changes through virtually all the cultural changes that occur in the South. The symbol system and ritual life of the god reflect a long history of cultural change and religious modification that is consistent with the history of Tamil religion itself. In fact, it would be inadequate and misleading to describe and pretend to understand the cultus from the standpoint of what can be seen in the present, without having any sense of the historical context from which present interpretations of this cultus are drawn. In the history of this cultus are illustrated some aspects of the historical process by which religion persists and changes in Indian history. Also, in the history of Murukan̲ are a few clues as to the ways religion is a creative language of the human spirit, related in significant measure to other creative expressions of man in history.

Because we shall detail some of the implications to which the history of Murukan̲ has led us in later discussion, it will be enough, in this context, to make one or two preliminary suggestions. In the first place, it is important for the cultus that its contemporary character and identity be linked to an *arché*, an ancient past. On the one hand, Tamil chauvinists – those who are wont to see little or no valuable Sanskritic influence in Tamil culture and religion – popularly see Murukan̲ as having existed from the oldest known Tamil moment – the period of the so-called *Caṅkam* literature – which, in legend, though not in actual fact, is said to be primordial. In a similar way, some orthodox brāhmaṇs who, in contrast, are inclined to see the Murukan̲ cultus as almost entirely Sanskritic, insist that Murukan̲ has Vedic roots, even though, as we shall argue, Skanda is more nearly a product of the Epic period and is only *post facto* ascribed Vedic attributes. Relating the contemporary cultus to an original moment, whether on the basis of fact or fancy, gives the cultus a sense of authenticity and eternality.

This is not to say that Murukan̲ cultus is now all it was believed to be in that original moment. But the community of Murukan̲ devotees understands itself to have derived from some primordial moment – from *illo tempore*. This presumed antiquity – and the older the better in the popular imagination – gives a sense of identity and authority to Murukan̲'s devotees in a manner that is consistent with the mood of contemporary Tamil Nadu. In present day Tamil India the conviction is widely shared that history, be it actual or mythical, gives meaning and is authenticating. Much that is meaningful for Tamil religion now, therefore, must have some explicit link to the past.

A case might be made that this is true not only for the Murukan̲ cultus but also for some of the apparently non-religious movements of contemporary Tamil Nadu. The *Tiraviṭa Mun̲n̲er̲r̲a Kaḻakam*, for example, the party which came to majority political power in the state in recent years, and which epitomized much of the Tamil self-respect movement, in no small measure, stressed the degree to which it (the DMK) recovered the significance of early Tamil culture and language in all its alleged pre-Sanskritic pristinity. The DMK adopted a language as free as possible from Sanskritizations and a symbol-system that frequently borrowed from early Tamil poetry. Like the Murukan̲ cultus, the DMK associated itself with an authenticating *arché*, for that is part of the mood of the contemporary Tamil movement.

2.2 *Religion in history*

Even if our research does not permit us to conclude that Murukan̲ is as old as the cultus chooses to believe, the history of the god is important for other reasons. Most importantly, perhaps, it enables us to trace the process by which a religion may survive and adapt itself to a series of cultural changes. The cultus of Murukan̲ is an apt illustration of the history of symbol-systems, a history which suggests something of how man's symbols serve, at the least, as commentaries on the human condition. There are a number of symbols in the Murukan̲ cultus which illustrate this phenomenon – and we shall examine several of them – but, of course, the most central and basic of all such symbols is that of the god Murukan̲ himself. The history of the god epitomizes the flow of religion in history and the process by which history changes religion and is changed by it. This interaction between the development of a god and the history of culture is one that has interested historians of religions at least from the time of those nineteenth century anthropologists who sought for the 'origins of religion'. There is neither the space nor the need to review here the train of scholars who have offered either monographs or general hypotheses on the subject. It is enough to note that research in recent years illustrates both the importance of the problem and its complexity. The work of Raphael Pettazzoni and Mircea Eliade, in particular, demonstrates how the history of gods significantly reflects the history and culture of man's eco-systems.

Pettazzoni made important studies into the kinds of gods that occur in hunting, agricultural, and pastoral societies. He affirmed the presence of a lord of animals and of a sky creator-god amongst many hunter societies, past and present. On the other hand, it was amongst agriculturalists that goddesses most frequently appeared, representative both of the ambivalence of the cosmos and the fertility and cyclicality of the agricultural process. Moreover, pastoralists tended to worship sky gods who were generally omniscient and able to know and affect the cosmic process from on high (Pettazzoni 1956:441ff.). Pettazzoni believed monotheism to be a later development which resulted from the reaction of reformers to polytheistic milieu. For him, the gods of a people reflected largely their existential situation – they were personalizations of man's understanding of himself and his cosmos. Pettazzoni's method and conviction is illustrated in his comparison of the gods of agriculturalists and of pastoralists:

> The sky is extended equally over all the peoples of the world, but the sacral experience of the sky is profoundly different where the sky is conceived as a cosmic complement of earth or eventually generated by the earth (Ouranos in Hesiod), from where the heavens are felt as a diffuse, immanent presence that intrudes on man in every place and in every instant, without escape or refuge from an all seeing eye. The earth is always and everywhere the theater of human life; but the sacral experience of earth is different where the earth tilled by man is the Mother, the nurturer, the giver of fruits and flowers for man's sustenance and joy; from the experience of the earth where it is sterile, the boundless extension of steppe whose fascination has inspired in modern times the narratives of Chekhov (The Steppe), the music of Borodin, and indirectly the poetry of Leopardi . . . (1959:66).

Considerably indebted to Pettazzoni, Mircea Eliade added certain dimensions to this discussion about the history of gods. In his discussion of sky gods (1964:40ff.), it is clear that for Eliade the history of gods is not unilinear or evolutionary as Pettazzoni tended to believe, but more complex and dynamic. If there is a discernible process involved, it is a movement from the remote to the concrete, from the old to the new, from the irrelevant to the relevant.

Gods tend to reflect the cultural milieu of man, as Pettazzoni argued, and when the cultural context changes, the imageries by which gods are understood change. Thus a god, like the *urheber* of the early hunters, can become 'otiose' or useless as a change in the cultural context causes a change in the religious vision and imagery of man. Sky gods themselves could reflect differing cultural situations: for agriculturalists and some post-agricultural societies the sky god was frequently a fertility god, virile storm god and consort to the mother goddess. Such was the case, Eliade suggests, with such gods as the Babylonian Marduk and the Mesopotamian deities El, Min, Baal, Bel. On the other hand, in certain pastoral contexts the sky god was often a sovereign god responsible for the conduct of the cosmic order. Such was the case with the Vedic Varuṇa. In those instances where these two types of sky god coalesced, the gods often tended to persist and become supreme; otherwise, they were replaced by more concrete gods, younger in the national consciousness but often having ancient roots in the folk elements of the society. The functions of these 'new' gods tended to subsume the functions of many of the gods which preceeded them. Thus, Eliade tends to see the cycle of Varuṇa, Indra, and Viṣṇu or Śiva in India as a series of 'younger', more concrete and dynamic gods, each in turn rooted in ancient strata of folk society and/or literature, but each coming to prominence largely because of the exigencies of cultural change. In succession, each god replaces the gods of earlier generations in importance and in function.[2]

These theories shed some light on the various faces of Murukaṉ, but do not tell the whole story, for the god reflects no single culture. Rather, his history illustrates the history of the human spirit in South India, and suggests something of how a god can reflect many of the forces – cultural and psychic – that make religious man what he is in history. Why, how and to what extent the god's character in the various periods of his history reflects the total cultural-historical milieux through which Tamil India has passed are questions which will be explored in greater detail in ensuing chapters.

For now, it is enough to record a preliminary – and perhaps even self-evident-hypothesis: a god, at the least, is a commentary on the nature and condition of man. The ways in which a people apprehend the divine is in large measure a statement about the way they see themselves and their context in a given moment. It follows then that the gods which are most persistent are those that have been adapted to changing cultural or historical situations and are in some measure understood in terms of that change. As the present cannot be divorced from the past, the god of a particular cultural moment is not unrelated to nor discontinuous with the gods of earlier cultural-historical moments. It seems more nearly true that the imageries of a god are informed not only by the mood of a particular cultural moment but by the history that precedes that moment. There is, in short, an historical process – or perhaps more accurately, several historical processes – operative in the development of any god. At certain times in the Murukaṉ tradition, myth-makers and interpreters consciously adapt the god to changing cultural circumstances while, at the same time, seeking to link him to an authenticating past either of his own or of other gods from whom he inherits authority and power. At other times, the shift of imageries appears to be more nearly unconscious.

While it may be impossible to know for certain what factors contribute to the historical persistence (and concomitant transformation) of gods, our study suggests several possibilities. One is surely the similarity of vision which arises in cultural/ecological situations which, though separated in time (and sometimes in space) nonetheless share certain common realities; for example, warriors of one period may find meaningful and revivify the religious symbolism which was operative for warriors of an earlier time or another place. In all likelihood, a similarity of symbolism is encouraged by the commonality and limitedness of man's emotional and intellectual possibilities. There may be a similarity of human need, and of psychic response to those dimensions that transcend man yet which impinge upon him.

Whatever the factors in this historical process or processes, it is clear in the history of Murukaṉ that there is a certain basic persistence to the god which even cultural change does not disrupt. Of course, at still other times and often at the same time, the historical process includes the adaptation and change, otiosity and decay of many old symbols and beliefs and the rise of new ones. For example, in the mythos of Murukaṉ, the lance evokes for medieval philosophers a different sort of religious understanding than it did for warriors or hunters in earlier moments of the god's history. Though the processes are complex, the conviction that grows from the study of Murukaṉ's history is that the god is not entirely understood in any one historical moment (including the present one) if that moment is not seen in the context of the whole historical process. Murukaṉ, then, is a suggestive statement about the history of man in South India.

3. Divinity in Tamil India

Murukaṉ, then, is a many-faceted symbol. He is a commentary on history and the human condition. He has integrated in his own person a variety of polarities: lover and celibate, Śaiva and Vaiṣṇava attributes, etc. As visual theology, he embodies most of the cultural and religious whole that comprises South Indian Śaivism. As with all symbols, in fact, he conveys more than is easily summarized in word, analogy, or rational interpretation.

Not the least important of Murukaṉ's symbolic roles is that he represents Divinity and man's attempt to comprehend and relate to it. It goes without saying that those for whom Murukaṉ is god are religious persons; the god gives form to their faith and meaning to their values. He embodies at various levels of apprehension some aspect of Ultimacy or Otherness, and makes possible for his devotees the kind of understanding and relationship which are central to man's being religious. It is this Otherness that appears to religious man to be the true 'stuff' of the world – its creative source, its order, its ultimate meaning. We cannot give this Otherness a single name which speaks for all men, for in the history of human society it has received many names – or none. Yet historians of religions have used varying terms to identify it: Rudolph Otto speaks of it as *numen*; van der Leeuw speaks of a 'Somewhat'; Joachim Wach of the 'Ultimate Reality'; and Mircea Eliade of the 'Sacred'. It has of course, been debated whether this dimension exists at all. However, devotees of Murukaṉ throughout history have assumed that such a Reality exists, that Murukaṉ is a manifestation of it, and that to relate to him is to relate in some way, however unarticulated, to the Ultimate Ground of one's existence.

The ways in which this Dimension is apprehended are, of course, varied, in Tamil India as elsewhere. In Tamil literature and thought several terms are used that illuminate different modes of understanding the Divine available to Tamilians. Four terms, in particular, illustrate the variety of forms as well as levels of abstraction and concreteness through which the divine is believed to be manifest. These terms suggest the various ways in which Murukaṉ himself is apprehended and the symbolic levels of abstraction and concreteness at which he is meaningful to his devotees.

One Tamil term descriptive of the Divine Dimension is *teyvam*. This is a somewhat abstract neuter word, embodying all that constitutes Divinity. It is Otto's *numen*, except that it is not limited to the moment it is experienced. It is the Sacred; all other forms of divinity are manifestations of it.

The term is clearly borrowed from the Sanskrit (*div* – to shine), and therefore we can assume it was not current prior to the Sanskritization of Tamil. Nevertheless, it does appear at least nine times in the *Caṅkam* poetry, the earliest body of Tamil literature, where it connotes 'divinity' or 'a divinity'. Later, in the *Tirukkural* (619:1), a work of perhaps the fourth or fifth century, the term seems to convey the idea of fate or destiny (N. Subrahmaniam 1966:452), and in literature of the fifth to eighth centuries, it is used sparingly to indicate that specific gods embody *teyvam.*[3]

It appears that *teyvam*, though it is used for quite concrete deities in early Tamil literature, became the most comprehensive and conceptual term denoting divinity in later Tamil literature. There is little indication that there were any serious attempts to conceptualize divinity in abstract terms in pre-Sanskritic Tamil literature, for the *Caṅkam* literature generally tends to be concrete and earthy rather than abstract and philosophical. The term *teyvam*, therefore, is more nearly apropos to the theological discussions of the medieval period, when in the context of Śaiva Siddhānta, for example, divinity is seen in philosophic and aniconic terms. But even in early Tamil religion, as I shall argue later, there is an awareness of Otherness, not so much in a transcendent, ethereal sense as in a sense of a mystique or power inhering in the land and the cosmic process itself. In that sense, *teyvam* already implies an awareness of 'more-than-ness' in early Tamil religion as the Divine Dimension to which religious man responds.

Teyvam is embodied in the god Murukaṉ, explicitly, in certain passages of the second century (cf. Kalitokai 39:26) and in such traditions as Śaiva Siddhānta, and, implicitly, in the understanding of most devotees. Even more appropriately, *teyvam* is embodied in *muruku*, the abstract, neuter term associated with Murukaṉ. *Muruku* connotes much that describes divinity in Tamil Nadu – beauty, fragrance, eternal youthfulness, and even Divinity itself. *Muruku* is *Teyvam.*

A second Tamil term connoting divinity is *Kaṭavuḷ*. Literally, *kaṭavuḷ* means 'beyond the mind' (*kaṭa* – to pass, cross; *uḷ* – the within). It is a Dravidian term, slightly less abstract than *teyvam*. *Kaṭavuḷ* tends to be personalized, connoting the god above gods or the totality of Godhood. The term appears in over thirty senses in Tamil literature before the seventh century A.D. Its most common usage in the *Caṅkam* literature is to denote the 'transcendent god' (Subrahmaniam 1966:199). At least three times in early literature *Kaṭavuḷ* connotes Divinity in the abstract (Aka 125:14; Kuṟun 252:4; Pari 4:63). In several instances, the term refers to the god resident in the hillside or in particular trees.[4] Five times *kaṭavuḷ* is associated with Murukaṉ by name; four times with Śiva; once with Tirumāl; and four with a goddess.[5] Elsewhere the term is given even more concrete connotation as the god in stone or iron, a village god, a domestic god, and a demon.

Murukaṉ is appropriately designated *Kaṭavuḷ* in the *Caṅkam* literature, for he is the 'supreme' deity for the *kuṟiñci* in the hill tract (or *tiṇai*) even as a different deity serves as the *kaṭavuḷ* for other of the five poetic modes. Later Murukaṉ is *Kaṭavuḷ* in another sense, for he is ascribed attributes of many other gods and becomes for members of his cultus, at least, the supreme god of all, *Kaṭavuḷ*.

A third Tamil term for divinity is *tēvaṉ*, which is derived from the same root as *teyvam* and connotes not an abstract neuter reality, but a specific masculine deity. The term appears late in Tamil literature. In fact, prior to the seventh century, it appears only in the two Tamil epics; twice in the *Cilappatikāram* where it means simply a 'god', and again in the Buddhist epic *Manimēkalai* where the term seems to mean 'supreme god' (Subrahmaniam 1966:461, citing Cila 6:12 and 10:180).[6] *Tēvaṉ* generally connotes a particular god who has specific functions and embodies specific manifestations of the Divine Reality. Like the Sanskrit *deva* and the Greek *theos*, the Tamil *Tēvaṉ* is any particular god who has meaningful symbolic significance for a particular community. Murukaṉ is a *Tēvaṉ* insofar as he embodies aspects of divinity meaningful to the community of his devotees.

A final term signifying Divinity in its most concrete form is the term *iṟaivaṭivam*. A Dravidian term, *iṟaivaṭivam* literally means a concrete form of the Divine (*iṟai* – the divine; *vaṭivam* – form, shape). The *iṟaivaṭivam* is an hierophany, a visual theology, and refers to the whole range of iconography and theological art. An *iṟaivaṭivam* is a manifestation of the Sacred in a concrete but symbolic medium. It might be noted incidentally that the term *iṟai* itself means the Divine only in a derivative sense. In its earlier usage, the word seems to have connoted kingship, or simply dignity, greatness, or chieftainship (*A Dictionary Tamil and English* 1933:94). But *iṟaivaṭivam* comes to denote any apparently ordinary object in which the Divine is manifest. As such, Divinity has many *iṟaivaṭivaṅkaḷ*; and all deities have their *iṟaivaṭivaṅkaḷ*. Murukaṉ's *iṟaivaṭivaṅkaḷ*, apart from his various iconographic representations, include the peacock, the lance, the rooster, and a number of other manifestations.

In summary, Murukaṉ embodies divinity in several different ways and is apprehended at several levels of understanding; he shows to the devotee many faces from the most abstract to the most concrete. Murukaṉ is seen, on the one hand, as the philosophical and abstract representation of the Tamil view of Otherness. At the same time, for some devotees, he is Personal Being with whom relationship and devotion are possible. He is also *Tēvaṉ*, a specific god with manifold symbolic connotations; and he is made manifest in theological art with an iconography and aesthetic heritage that is proliferate. It is as though every one of the faces religious man in Tamil India uplifts in search of Divinity finds in Murukaṉ some kind of response.

Murukaṉ in the Early South

1. The early context of South India: a cultural sequence

In order to follow the development of Murukaṉ in South Indian history it is necessary to begin with the allusions found in the earliest known Tamil literature, generally called the *'Caṅkam'* poetry because Tamil tradition insists it was collected by a *'Caṅkam'* or academy of poets. This literature reveals a civilization that has already accumulated a variety of cultural nuances. The poetry and its times, and especially the cultus of Murukaṉ, are best understood if seen in the context of the cultural history which they inherit. The sweep of that history begins in the prehistoric era and continues through several cultural epochs which apparently contribute to the Murukaṉ mystique, though the precise contribution of each era is tantalizingly imprecise. An historical survey, nevertheless, gives us a sense of the cultural heritage which informs the cultus of Murukaṉ as we see it in the so-called *Cankam* period.

However, to reconstruct the prehistory of South India is still difficult, not only because archeological findings in South India are still rather inconclusive, but because the fragmentary findings of archeology, anthropology, and linguistics have not been coordinated with any finality into an intelligible whole. It is evident that South India is comprised of a diversity of cultural and racial strands which are at times difficult to isolate. What follows, therefore, is a summary reconstruction of South Indian prehistory based on the work of specialists.

1.1 *The Paleolithic era*

The first period in South India's past is a Paleolithic culture of hunters and food gatherers. Cammiade and Burkitt first noticed Upper Paleolthic elements in South East India in 1930. Recent research by such men as

H.D. Sankalia on the banks of the Pravara River, a tributary of the Godavari in Gujerat; V.D. Krishnaswami near Madras; and SoundaryaRajan near Giddalur in Āndhra confirms the existence of an earlier Paleolithic industry. However, there have been very few Paleolithic finds in the deep South, that is in Tanjavur, Tiruchirapalli, and Madurai districts, though a few stray remains have been found in the Vaigai basin (Raman 1970:500–01). The tools of this industry include handaxes, cleavers, flakes, discoids, hammer stones and burins (SanKalia 1950:40; cf. Krishnaswami 1938:58–90, and Soundarya Rajan, 1952:66–92).

The earliest Paleolithic culture seems to have appeared in much of Peninsular India by 150,000 B.C.[1] These people generally lived along rivers on the edge of forests up to 2000 feet altitude. They were mainly hunters and food gatherers who seldom lived more than forty years. Archeologists are reluctant to speculate on the origin of these people, but H. D. Sankalia concedes that physically and culturally they were probably related to early man in East and South Africa. More willing to guess from fragments of available evidence, such non-archeologists as B. S. Guha, S. K. Chatterji, and Nilakanta Sastri assume Paleolithic man in India was Negroid and migrated eastward from Africa into India and throughout South East Asia (Chatterji 1954:142; cf. Sastri 1966:58).

Following the early Paleolithic culture was a middle Paleolithic starting around 25,000 B.C. and apparently extending down the Southeast coast. While N. R. Banerjee and Bridget Allchin think this culture evolved from earlier man, H. D. Sankalia thinks it resulted from external cultural influences, probably from Africa but possibly from Central Asia (Sankalia 1962:123). The era of Upper Paleolithic man followed and is generally dated around 5000 B.C. Too little is yet known about Paleolithic man to be certain what lasting influence, if any, he had on later cultures of the South.

1.2 *The Mesolithic era*

The nature of the development of culture from the Upper Paleolithic era until the Megalithic period is not altogether clear. There is definitely a Mesolithic stage in the South, for the use of microlithic instruments associated with a Mesolithic era has been noted in several places. In fact, there seem to have been at least two distinct stages of Mesolithic culture. The first, often found along streams and foothills, is noted for its use of flaked and core tools; the second, though characterized by similar microliths, is also recognizable by the abundance of geometric forms, blades and scrapers (K. V. Raman 1970:503). According to D. H. Gordon, the microlithic and protomicrolithic industries, appeared at such places as Tuticorin; the Mangalore area on the West Coast near Bombay; and in the Southern Deccan, particularly in the Godavari and Krishna regions, by 8000–6000 B.C. In some cases they apparently persisted through the Mesolithic hunting and food-gathering stage into a Neolithic hunting and food producing stage (Gordon 1950:67–77)[2] during which the microlith users may have come to use pottery and some agricultural skills, but H. D. Sankalia believes the microlith using culture may have evolved out of the earlier blade and burin culture and represents the coming of a drier climate and environmental change (Sankalia 1962:151).

1.3 *The Neolithic era*

The Neolithic era is generally dated from 3500 B.C. to 2000 B.C. (Sankalia 1962:152). It is characterized by a people who made pottery, were settled, developed agricultural techniques and domesticated the cow, the sheep, the pig and the dog. There is no single Neolithic culture in India. In fact, H. D. Sankalia classifies the Neolithic culture into three: the Northeast, where there is the use of polished stone, but no pottery; the Southeast, where are found polished stone tools, lithic blades, and pottery made by hand (though in the deep South there are no evidences of the blade); and the West, particularly central and Northern India, where the lithic blades are the major tool rather than polished stone instruments, and where pottery is made with a wheel (p. 153).

The relationship between these cultures is not clear, but recent excavations at Paiyampalli suggest the Neolithic culture of what is now northern Tamil Nadu (that is, of Salem and North Arcot districts) is contiguous with that of the Southern Deccan and formed a single homogeneous whole with it.[3] This Southern Neolithic culture developed in at least three stages. An early stage is characterized by the ground stone axe, forest cattle stations, settlements on hills, handmade pottery, and the domestication of cattle, sheep and goats. This stage, as studied, for example, at the Utnur site in the

Deccan, is dated about 2300–1800 B.C. The second stage, observed at Hallur and the lower layer at Tekkalakota, is dated 1800–1500 B.C., and is characterized by the use of mud floors and wattle in building, an increase in stone blades, and the use of perforated vessels. A third stage, such as can be seen in an upper layer at Tekkalakota and perhaps at Paiyampalli, is marked by the use of copper and bronze tools, harder grey and buff pottery, cattle raising, the cultivation of millet and grain and even by the practice of inhumations with grave goods (Allchin and Allchin 1968: 161–67).

There is reason to believe that the Neolithic culture of the South was somewhat independent of that of the Indus Valley. The Neolithic culture of Brahmagiri and Maski in the Southern Deccan is dominated by the use of blades, made of stone, primarily chert, agate, carnellian, and opal), whereas along the Indus Valley the Neolithic culture is characterized by the use of copper axes. D. H. Gordon notes that no stone axes have been found at all in Sind or along the Indo-Iranian border and adds that there is as yet 'no evidence for any extension of the culture eastward of the Punjab (Gordon 1950:77). The use of metal in the Indus Valley links that civilization with those extending to the Mediterranean where the discovery of metal preceded the development of polished stone axes (p. 84). The use of metal tends to rule out the possibility that the Indus culture is the same as that which appeared in the South, as L. D. Barnett and others thought (Barnett 1922: 593), even though some contact between the Northern settlements and such Southern settlements as Brahmagiri and Maski cannot be ruled out entirely. Indeed, that there was intercourse between the Indus and South Deccan villages is suggested by finds in Southern sites, particularly of copper-bronze ribbon flakes and other evidences of chalcolithic culture which may have been influenced by northern industries (Thapar 1957:21).[4]

Whatever the sources and racial composition of the Southern Neolithic peoples, we know that they were settled in the hilly regions of North Arcot and Salem districts and Southwestward into the Pal̲ni range, and that they had developed agricultural and rudimentary pastoral skills. It is possible as K. V. Raman, Stuart Piggot, and K. N. Sastri have suggested, that such tribes as the Veddas of Ceylon, the Pulaiyans of Coimbatore area, the Kadars of Cochin, the Karumbas of North Arcot, and the Chenchus of Andhra are descendants of this Southern Neolithic people. It is also possible that the *kur̲iñci*, the people of the hills mentioned in *Caṅkam* poetry, of whom Murukaṉ is known as the chief god, were related to this Neolithic people, although we cannot rule out the possibility that Paleolithic peoples lingered in this area as well.

1.4 *Chalcolithic culture*

The early history of the South seems to consist in a non-traumatic development from a Paleolithic stage through the Mesolithic to a Neolithic stage. A chalcolithic culture developed, at least in the Deccan, at such sites as Brahmagiri and Maski in North Mysore. This chalcolithic industry did not necessarily supersede the Neolithic stage, but seemed to bring the Neolithic stage to greater sophistication, continuing the use of some earlier tools, and adding the use of copper. For at the chalcolithic sites at Maski several unearthed fossils suggest the people had domesticated such animals as short horn cattle, buffaloes, sheep and goats (Thapar 1957:12).[5] Yet in the same stratum with these fossils spherical balls used in hunting have been found which suggest that hunting persisted into this cultural epoch when food-production and tending of herds had developed (p. 13).

1.5 *The Megalithic culture*

The chalcolithic industries in the Deccan appear to have developed by 1800 B.C.,[6] but, by the time of the Aśokan inscriptions cut in their vicinity, had been superseded by the coming of an iron-using megalithic culture. The megalithic culture became pervasive in the Southern part of the peninsula. Artifacts of the culture have been unearthed at such diverse sites as Trichur District in Southwest Kerala, at Adichanallur at the Southeastern tip of the peninsula, in Chingleput District, in Madurai District, and in the Southern Deccan. Though we have had access to megalithic remains for over a century, relatively little is known about the culture and its origin. As the name suggests, the culture was characterized by the use of huge rock monuments akin to those found elsewhere in the world. The rocks are used to mark burials, usually in sarcophagi and urns. The Megalithic culture appears to be well advanced in irrigation techniques, for the megaliths are often found on rocky hillocks near arable land, bunded and cultivated. The megalith-builders were also iron-users; an impressive number of the iron remains are of implements of war – for example, iron lances at Adichanallur, long and short daggers in Trichur district, and lances, arrowheads, and dagger blades at Maski – affirming that the megalith-builders were a war-skilled people. Excavations in the Megalithic stratum at Maski indicate the development of wheel-turned pottery, the tending of such animals as sheep and humpless cattle, a relatively sophisticated agriculture with a bias for urban life, and the persistence of hunting as an avocation (Thapar 1957:13). While South Indian megaliths have been found widely scattered throughout the peninsula, they seem especially abundant along river banks (Srinivasan and Banerjee 1953:109).

The megalithic findings at Brahmagiri and Maski are clearly stratified from the earlier soil layers, suggesting that some elements of the culture were not indigenous (Thapar 1957:13). Who the builders were and from whence they came is still a matter of speculation. The fact that megalith-building people migrated from the West is generally accepted by most archeologists. The Allchins suggest the culture is comprised of several cultural bases. They believe that elements of the culture associated with burial customs in the Deccan may have developed indigenously in a Neo-Chalcolithic era. Yet the influence of Central Asia, Iran, and Caucusus is suggested by the types of graves evident; other artifacts suggest an influence from the Mesopatamian Valley and the Persian Gulf (Allchin and Allchin 1968:229). It is generally assumed that the South Indian megaliths are akin to those found in West Europe, dated 2000 B.C., and those found in the Anatolian plateau in Iran dated about 1500 B.C.[7]

Fürer-Haimendorf, Gordon, and most other archeologists tend to believe that the megalithic culture was basically Dravidian, an extraneous intrusion into a Neolithic culture, and that the language of this people prevailed in the South for they were a more vigorous, war-skilled people. However, few scholars agree on the theory that the megalithic culture was the major component of the Dravidian peoples. In 1956, A. Ghosh, for example, suggested that the Dravidian culture may be related, not so much to the Megalithic complex, as to the pre-megalithic Chalcolithic culture (Ghosh 1956:3). Similarly, the Allchins believe that evidence is mounting to point, not to the Megalithic culture, but to the Neolithic one as the basic component of Dravidian society (Allchin and Allchin 1968:326).

While archeologists once believed that remains of the megalith-builders in the South could not be dated earlier than 300 or 400 B.C. (Thapar 1957:19), more recent studies would date the cairn burials and the megalithic complex in the South around 800–700 B.C. This would allow enough time to elapse for the development of the sophisticated Tamil language found in the *Caṅkam* literature after the start of the Christian era.

The Megalithic Era came to an end around the first century A.D. In the Southern Deccan, along the frontier where Southern and Northern elements confronted each other, pottery and coins characteristic of the Āryanized 'Andhra' period have been found in a stratum dated from the first century A.D. and lasting until the third century (p. 17). However, there is evidence that some aspects of the Megalithic culture persisted into the period when much of the *Caṅkam* literature is written. The Pāṇṭiyaṉ kings, who governed the area in which Adichanallur (the Southernmost extension of the megalithic culture) is located, apparently perpetuated some of the practices associated with the megalith-builders. For example, inhumation, cist burial, and urn burial are mentioned along with cremation and exposure as means of disposal in the *Maṇimēkalai,* a Tamil Buddhist epic of a relatively late period; indeed, urn burials, which were used even for kings in the *Caṅkam* period, may not have died out until the Pāṇṭiyas were finally overcome by the Cōḻas in the eleventh century A.D. (Srinivasan and Banerjee 1953:111–12).[8]

1.6 *'Āryanization'*

The final cultural complex in the early South is ascribed to the Nordic racial type and is more commonly known as the Āryan migration. When 'Āryanization' of the South occurred is a major question.[9] We know that Sanskrit culture influenced Āndhra and the Deccan plateau earlier than the deep South. The earliest recognizable wave of Āryanization was apparently Prākritic and related to the Mauryan era. Kauṭilya's *Arthaśāstra* suggests that trade was occurring between North and South in the time of the early Mauryas. The second and thirteenth rock-edicts of Aśoka mention such Tamil states as the Cōḻas and Pāṇṭiyas who were independent of Aśoka's territory but had commercial intercourse with it. The Southern inscriptions of Aśoka's era differ from the Northern ones, suggesting that a Southern

Brāhmī script was developing which combined features of Southern and Northern language. Inscriptions dated between the second century B.C. and 50 A.D., though Southern Brāhmī in script, use a language which is a combination of early Tamil and Prākrit.

The Sātavāhanas, who succeeded the Mauryas, reigned for four and a half centuries, from about 230 B.C. They were of Āndhra origin. After a temporary rise of the Śakas to the west, the Sātavāhanas under Gautamīputra Sātakarṇin (ca, 80–104 A.D.) revived and extended their kingdom westward into the Deccan. Under this dynasty Buddhism flourished in the Deccan during the first two centuries of the Christian era; Brāhmaṇism also flourished, as the kings performed a number of Vedic sacrifices. Shortly after the fall of the Sātavāhanas, the Pallavas came to power. They first used Prākrit characters (275–350 A.D.), then Sanskrit (350–550), and finally Tamil, until the tenth century. The Pallavas, like the Kadambas who later came into the South (345–550 A.D.), though Northern in origin and language, adapted many Southern traditions. The Pallavas participated in various aspects of Vedic and post-Vedic religion. It is particularly interesting to us that the early kings, in at least eight instances between 300–550 A.D., were named for Skanda or Kumāra. The Kadambas, significantly, declared their devotion to the Kadamba tree associated with the Murukaṉ tradition in the South and were devotees of Swami Mahāsena, a name associated with Skanda.

There is sufficient historical and archeological evidence to indicate that Northern culture was influential on the Northern fringes of the deep South (i.e., north of what is now Tamil Nadu) by the first century A.D., and had penetrated the deep South in large measure by the third and fourth centuries. Evidence of Northern influence in the deep South prior to the first century A.D. is still fragmentary, however. As noted above, there was some level of trade between Northern and Southern peoples in the time of the Mauryan dynasty, and there is evidence of the migration of Jain, Buddhist, and Brāhmaṇic mendicant–teachers into the Southern Deccan in the time of Aśoka.[10] In addition to the influences of Jain, Buddhist, and brāhmaṇic settlers from North India, it is possible that stimulus toward Prākritization also came from the South – that is, from Ceylon. How early this impetus from Ceylon came and what its effect was is still open to question however.[11] At any rate, in the earliest *Caṅkam* poems, composed probably by the first or second century A.D., there are allusions to and hints of brāhmaṇic influence in the deep South. Nonetheless, the bulk of the early poetry has a stronly non-brāhmaṇ flavor.

The available evidence indicates that early South Indian culture was a mixture of diverse elements. While many scholars assume that the megalithic people were the major contributors to Dravidian culture, none can assume that the earlier cultural layers did not persist in the cultural complex of the early South. Indeed, one of the most striking features of the early Southern culture is the persistence of forms from one era to another and the relatively non-traumatic fusion of cultural layers. There is no evidence that 'Āryanization' in the early centuries of the Christian era superseded earlier culture *in toto*, nor can it be argued that the Sanskrit impetus was violent or revolutionary in character. Rather, the South was characterized by a subtle and relatively slow mixing of racial and cultural features – so subtle that to distinguish the cultural roots of many phenomena is virtually impossible. Similarly, the development of the religious apprehension in the South reflects a related process of persistence and admixture of early with later elements. The history of Murukaṉ demonstrates how this is so, even if it is not always possible to isolate the historic and cultural bases of many of the elements found in the tradition.

2. The early Murukaṉ

2.1 *An introduction to the Caṅkam poetry*

We must wait until the literary period to find substantive evidence that helps us reconstruct the early character of Murukaṉ. The earliest Tamil literature is a body of poetry believed to have been written under the aegis of the so-called *Caṅkam* or 'academy'. It was written by a loosely-related group of poets patronized mainly by the Pāṇṭiyaṉ, and Cēṟan chieftain-kings. The *Caṅkam* poetry consists of a number of poems or poetic collections, most of which were edited and collected by the eighth century and republished as two anthologies within the last century.[12] The anthologies are known as the Eṭṭutokai (Eight Anthologies) and the Pattupāṭṭu (Ten Idylls). The bulk of these poems is now believed to have been written in the space of five or six generations, dating somewhere between the middle of the first century and the late third century (S. Vaiyapuri Pillai 1956:29 ff.)[13]

However, as the poetry was collected and edited, textual additions, such as invocatory stanzas, were apparently added. This seems to have been the case with the invocation to Murukaṉ prefacing the Kuṟuntokai, one of the earliest of the collections. It is difficult, therefore, to sort out and date the cultural sources of the allusions in the poetry.

At least three of the poetic collections included in the anthologies may be dated considerably later: the Paṟipāṭal and the Kalitokai, two anthologies in the Eṭṭutokai; and the Tirumurukāṟṟupatai, the last idyll of the Pattupāttu, (S. Vaiyapuri Pillai 1956:56 ff.).[14] This division of the material is important. The earlier poetry, despite later accretions, allusions to Northern ideas and religion, and the occasional use of Sanskritic terms, may be designated pre-Āryan in spirit and content. It is fair to say that it reflects primarily the amalgamation of pre-megalithic and megalithic cultural strands under the aegis of Southern chieftainship. If one assumes that the megalithic culture is Dravidian, this early poetry may be understood as illuminating the cultural fusion of pre-Dravidian and Dravidian elements. The later poems, on the other hand, reflect a marked Sanskritization of Southern culture. The Murukaṉ of the early poetry, then, is apprehended differently than the Murukaṉ of the later poetry. We shall look at the Murukaṉ of the early *Caṅkam* poetry and suggest an hypothesis regarding the cultural sources which have come together in the god by that time.

Murukaṉ in the early *Caṅkam* poetry is most often associated with the *kuṟiñci,* the hill tract which comprises one of the five allegorical arenas *(tiṇai)* into which Tamil poetry divides the land. In addition to the *kuṟiñci,* there is the *marutam,* the cultivated land, the center of which is generally the city and which represents a relatively advanced civilization; the *mullai,* the forest, pastoral land thought to be between *marutam* and *kuṟiñci* both geographically and in sophistication; the *neytal,* the seashore tract, given to fishing and commerce; and the *pālai,* the wilderness or desolate land generally symbolizing the area beyond the reaches of civilization. Each tract had its own poetic moods, its own characteristic flora and fauna, its own *tēvaṉ* or diety. For example, the god Māyōṉ inhabited the *mullai*; Cēyōṉ, the *kuṟiñci;* Vēntaṉ (or Intiraṉ), the *marutam;* and Varuna, the *neytal;* while the *pālai* is said to be the territory of the malevolent goddesses.

Tamil poetry of this era is further subdivided into two basic types of subject matter: *akam,* the subjective element, usually referring to love; *puṟam*, the objective element, referring to life in general, and especially war and affairs of state. Each poetic *tiṇai* has its dominant motifs of *akam* and *pur̲am*. The dominant *akam* of *marutam* (fields) is *ūṭal* – sullenness and quarrelsomeness (sometimes feigned) between lovers; its *pur̲am* is *ul̲iṉai* – siege. The *akam* of *neytal* (seacoast) is *iraṅkal* – wifely pining and selfpity; its *pur̲am* is *tumpai* – outright war or battle. The *akam* of *mullai* (forest) is *iruttal* – wifely patience; its *pur̲am* is *vañci* – invasion (for purposes of annexation). The *akam* of *pālai* is *pirital* – separation; its *pur̲am* is *vākai* – victory. In the *kur̲iñci* tract the dominant *akam* motif is *puṇartal* – the union which often climaxes the full range of love's emotion, representing the joyous, if often secret, tryst or embrace of lovers. The *pur̲am* motif in the *kur̲iñci* tract is *veṯci*, representing the cattle raid (Tolkappiyam:Porul, 1–76; cf. Ramanujan 1969:107).

The fact that each of these *pur̲am* words is the name of the flower worn by the king or chieftain to symbolize his attitude toward his enemy typifies the character of early Tamil poetry. It is replete with the verve, color and fragrance, and fertility of the land; it portrays the full range of human emotion. The poetry is predominantly committed to the concrete and the present, to the immanence of the cosmic process and the humanness and earthiness of life.[15]

In this early poetry references to rituals and gods are relatively few and incidental. There is virtually no attempt to philosophize about religious or metaphysical problems and there are very few allusions to myths. One gets the feeling that the poets describing the early Tamil people saw a people for whom life in the present was a consuming passion.

However, we hesitate to call the poetry areligious, for, in a sense the business of life itself is perceived and understood in religious terms. In the early Tamil context, religion has to do with the way one orders his life in a cosmos that manifests an inherent quality of Otherness.

2.2 *Murukan̲ in the early Caṅkam literature*

Given the human- and nature-oriented character of early Tamil poetry, it is not surprising that references to Murukan̲ are relatively few, even in those poems describing the *kur̲iñci* mode. Nevertheless, a fairly consistent picture can be reconstructed from the poetic reservoir of imagery, even if a number of questions remain unanswered.

The Murukaṉ of this period is clearly associated with the hills and the hill peoples. The hills are his domain and the hill peoples have a kinship with him. He presides over the hunt; he is hunter (and later warrior) par excellence; he is a lover and possessor of beautiful girls. His enemy is the *cūr* (soor) who roams the hillsides malevolently seeking to possess girls. Murukaṉ can cause as well as dispel *aṇaṅku* (fear and distress, sometimes personalized as an external force that causes suffering). He can be involved through the frenzied dance (*veṟiyāṭal*) of the high priest (*vèlaṉ*). An open field covered with sand or an enclosure (*kòṭṭam*) appropriately arrayed, is the place where he is worshipped and his dance is performed. At some point in this period he is identified with redness and is known as *cēyōṉ* (red one). He has a kinship with much of the flora and fauna of the hills, and with their fragrance and color; the flowers particularly associated with him are sometimes yellow but more often red, and include the blossoms of *kāntal, vēṅkai, kaṭampu,* and lotus. The elephant and the peacock by virtue of their presence in the hills are indirectly his. Priest and priestess have the power of divination by virtue of Murukaṉ's visitation; through the tossing of *kaḻaṅku* nuts they can determine the nature of an illness and prescribe corrective measures. Murukaṉ is worshipped with the strewing of water, the juice of paddy or cocoanut, saṅdal paste, red millet, rice, honey, blood, and red, yellow, or white flowers. Noble hunters, warriors, chieftains, and lovers are likened to Murukaṉ.

This composite picture of Murukaṉ can be reconstructed from the rather unsystematic allusions to him made in what we presume to be the earlier poems. In a few instances more details are provided. For example, the Kuṟuntokai, one of the earliest collections, alludes to an observance which is recorded in several other poems, as late as the Cilappatikāram. A young maiden is pining for her secret lover who is separated from her. Her distress (*aṇaṅku*) is such that she becomes sickly and emaciated. Her mother, not knowing the cause of her distress and worried for her health, approaches *Vēlaṉ*, the priest of Murukaṉ. Apparently intoxicated with toddy, carrying a staff in his hand, and wearing a garland of *kaṭampu* blossoms, the priest dances the frenzied dance of possession (*veṟiyāṭal*). He divines by tossing *kaḻaṅku* nuts into the air that Murukaṉ is indeed the cause of the anguish and prescribes that the family dance a *veṟiyāṭal* that night and provide an offering of rice and smear young lamb's blood on the forehead. The maiden, hearing of the *vēlaṉ's* diagnosis, scoffs at the priest's incompetence and hopes her lover does not return that night lest the priest and her family become confirmed in their belief that Murukaṉ was indeed the cause of the illness (Kuṟun. 360, 362; cf. Cila. canto 24; Naṟṟ. 34:1) and that their antidote is successful.[16] This fascinating anecdote appears to represent a disarming skepticism either on the part of the young or on the part of the poets toward the naïveté or excesses of the exorcist, if not toward the early religious tradition itself.

There is evidence in the early poetry that religious practices associated with Murukaṉ were fairly widespread, at least among the hill tribes. In Naṟṟ 288 a priestess *(kaṭṭuvicci)* is asked for a diagnosis of a maiden's languor. The diviner, be it priest or priestess, is believed to be possessed of the god and thus have access to the god's will (Tol. Poruḷ. 115). The place where this divining takes place is the *kōṭṭam* – the sacred place. This place could be set up in a house, on a river delta or before a *kaṭampu* tree decorated with creepers or garlands.[17] In one such ritual of divination, the site is spread with sand and decorated (if in an enclosure) with red *kāntal* flowers. Before the dance the priest offers an invocation to the hills. The dance is accompanied by musical instruments and songs. The priest elevates a puppet designed to take the illness from the maiden; a ram is sacrificed, and its blood offered to Murukaṉ. The staff of the *vèlaṉ* is then held up over the *kaḻaṅku* nuts as if in benediction. The priestess, as described in later literature, is dressed in two colors. She is given paddy which she throws into the air. She perspires, shivers, smells her palms and starts her rapturous singing in praise of Murukaṉ. The paddy is counted by four's. If one, two, or three paddy grains are left over, Murukaṉ is believed to be the cause of the malaise; if the count is even, something else is the cause (Thangavelu 1963:79, citing Tirumuru. 230 and Ciriyatirumardēl 20:22).[18]

Apart from the *veṟiyātal*, worship of the deity was also conducted in other ways. At some point during this period, a *kantu* (small crude pillar) came to be used as a representation of the god. It was usually set up under a *kaṭampu* tree. The *kantu* was apparently set on a pedestal over a dais and over it, a crude roof was supported by wooden pillars and cross bar. The ground around the *kantu* was soaked with blood (pp. 166, 171, citing Aka. 167:14–16,309:4–6).

Maidens could also be possessed by Murukaṉ. In the early poetry, this possession seems to have ambivalent features. On the one hand, women are apparently not allowed to touch things associated with Murukaṉ, according to Puṟa. 299:6–7, for fear they will be possessed and given anguish by the gods. On the other hand, such possession appears to be a joyous occasion, an act of worship and union with the god as, for example, in the dances described later in the Tirumurkāṟṟupaṭai (lines 280–90), wherein lovely damsels, wreathed in flowers and fragrantly perfumed, dance his praises (cf. Maturaik. 673–648; Cila. canto 24).[19] In fact, some poets suggest that Murukaṉ's possession is not the cause of suffering at all.[20]

The character of Murukaṉ is ambivalent in this literature. He is fearsome when angry; he is virulent and heroic and punishes bad people (Maturaik. 180–181; Puṟa. 16:12; Aka. 158:16–18; Naṟṟ. 225:1–2; Kuṟun. 87; et. al.). He causes and dispels *anaṅku*, distress and anguish. Hunters, chieftains, and eventually kings are compared to him (Aka. 1,28; Malaipatukatam 651; et. al.). But Murukaṉ is not all cruel – he is a benevolent protector, to be praised and adored (Puṟa. 106, 158). He provides rain and keeps the earth fertile (Puṟa. 143). He is a god of justice and virtue *(arakkatavul)* (Puṟa. 35:14).[21]

Something more of Murukaṉ's character is suggested by his relation to other divine agencies in this early literature. Murukaṉ is explicitly identified with *Kaṭavuḷ* in the early *Caṅkam* poetry. The identity is implicit in passages where *Kaṭavuḷ* is characterized in terms usually associated with Murukaṉ. *Kaṭavuḷ* resides on branches of a red *kaṭampu* tree, where he instills fear (Kuṟun. 87:1–2); he climbs the colorfully flowered *vēṅkai* tree (Naṟṟ. 216:6) and has hosts under him (Naṟṟ. 358:6). He is worshipped by mountain folk with the perfume of sandal wood (Aka. 13:3–4); his worship center is on a hillock near a sepulchral stone or bushes; it is decorated with peacock feathers; a lamb and the fermented juice of paddy is offered to him (Aka. 35:7–9). The identity drawn between Murukaṉ and *Kaṭavuḷ* opens up the possibility of Murukaṉ's being associated with the *Kaṭavuḷ* of other areas.

Murukaṉ is also associated with Cēyōṉ (red one). Indeed, the term Cēyōṉ is used interchangeably with the term Murukaṉ. Tolkāppiyanar, Tamil's earliest grammarian, whose work may be slightly older than the earliest Caṅkam poetry, identifies Cēyōṉ as the god of the *kuṟiñci* (Tol. Akattiṉai 5). Why the two terms were fused is not altogether clear. A clue is provided by an unnamed commentator on the Tolkappiyam who notes that 'black and red are symbols of anger' (Tol. Col. Uṟai 74), implying that Cēyōṉ and Murukaṉ are linked by an association with anger and redness. Also, the color of the hills and their foliage seems to be red – and this colorfulness is caught up in both terms for deity. Eventually both Cēyōn̲ and Murukan̲ are associated with the sun (cf. Tirumuru. 1).[22] This association also opens the door for a number of later accretions, for the term *Cēy* eventually comes to mean 'good', 'correct', or 'beautiful', while the related noun *cey* means 'redness', 'juvenility', 'a child', 'Skanda', or 'Mars' (*Tamil Lexicon* 1928:446).[23] Thus, this identity of Cēyōn̲ with Murukan̲ occuring in the *Caṅkam* poetry is continued and elaborated in the post-*Caṅkam* literature.[24]

Murukan̲ is also linked with *Neṭu vēl* in at least one passage (Nar̲r̲. 288:10). The precise meaning of this term is not clear, but it appears to have meant a tall or long (*neṭu*) man, possibly a chieftain-king (Thangavelu 1963:30). The definition is so uncertain that we would drop the inference were it not for the fact that in other contexts in the *Caṅkam* poetry, Murukan̲ is at times held up as a standard of comparision for the chieftain or hero-lover (*talaivan̲*) (e.g., Cir̲uppān̲. 340–352). Also, it appears that at least two Tamil words used for the divine derived from usages connoting chieftain or ruler: *ir̲ai*, discussed earlier, and *kō* (*n̲*), which apparently meant tribesman, cowherd, great man, leader or chieftain in its early connotation and by the latter part of the first millenium came to connote the divine (Burrow and Emeneau 1961:146; cf. Eliade 1964:87; Srinivasan 1960:145).[25] The inference is that the Murukan̲ of the early *Caṅkam* literature may have derived some elements of his character from the role of a tribal chieftain or culture hero, though this is by no means documentable.

Murukan̲'s character in this early period is further illuminated by his relationship to the malevolent forces of the hills – the *cūr* and the *anaṅku*. In several *Caṅkam* passages, *Anaṅku* is used in an impersonal sense to connote fear or suffering, or the source of fear (Subrahmaniam 1966:29, citing Aka. 21; Nar̲r̲. 12; Ainkuru. 8; Kur̲un 1.; et. al.). The term can also connote a personalized force, ghost or god causing fright (Kur̲iñci. 1; Perumpāṅ 3; Pur̲a; ii). At least once in the early poetry (Nar̲r̲. 155:5–6) it refers to a girl or demonees who enchants or bewitches. As previously noted, Murukan̲ was believed to be able to dispel *anaṅku*, and the priests believed he could cause it as well. It appears that Murukan̲ controlled *anaṅku*, an interpretation which is strengthened by a later reference in the Cilappatikāram where the term *anaṅku* is used twice to refer to the young god himself (25:48, 29:66) (Subrahmnian 1966:30).

The term *cūr* (soor), though somewhat ambiguously used, occurs at least twenty times in the *Caṅkam* literature. In the earlier poetry, *cūr* is a somewhat personalized demonic force that causes terror. The *cūr* terrorizes the mountain slopes that are of difficult access so that even the mountain goats are afraid to gambol on them (Naṟṟ. 359:7–9). The *cūr* infests the mountain passes (Kuṟun. 376:2); Naṟṟ. 359:9 and 373:5; et. al.), the springs (Naṟṟ. 268:1) and the waterfalls (Naṟṟ. 34:4). It often appears in the form of a woman (*cūrmakaḻ*: Aka. 198:17; Naṟṟ. 34:4; et. al.). These references to the *cūrmakaḻ* in the early poetry indicate either that *cūr* is feminine or that it possesses women who then impersonate it.

In general, *cūr* in early references is a troublesome force on the mountains. Increasingly, *cūr* is identified in the *Caṅkam* literature as the *cūra* whom Murukañ overcomes in battle. (Patiṟṟupāṭṭu 11:5). In this context, *Cūr* is a male demon whom Murukaṉ slays, at first with a shining sharp leaf (Aka. 59:10–11) and eventually with a leaf-shaped lance. An obvious question arises: what is the relation between the *cūr* and the *asuras* so well known in the Sanskrit tradition? At first it appears there was no interchangeability of the terms.[26] The term *asura* is apparently used only twice in Tamil literature prior to the seventh century, once in each of the Tamil Epics (p. 25). It is clear, however, that the elaborate mythology of the demon *asuras* associated with the Skanda tradition in Epic India eventually adapted easily to the malevolent *cūr* of the Southern mountains.

In addition to these divine agencies, several phenomena of nature are associated with Murukaṉ indirectly, if not explicitly, in this early poetry. In a sense, all that abounds in the hills is Murukaṉ's, but certain natural phenomena are especially associated with him. We have already noted that such elements as sandal paste, flowers, fruit, honey, millet and the fermented juice of paddy or cocoanut – all elements found in the hills – are used in worship of Murukaṉ. Rice and the blood of the ram are also used. Two trees – the *kaṭampu* and the *vēṅkai* – are especially associated with Murukaṉ, and both seem to persist into later times and become interchangeable. The *vēṅkai* (*pterocarpus bilobus*, also known as the Kino tree) is associated with Murukaṉ in Aka. 288. Its yellow blossoms are used in the wedding ceremony to adorn the groom (Aka. 118:1–5). The blooming of the *vēṅkai* tree is thought to be auspicious, especially for young lovers, for its ripening signals the ripening of their love to overt marriage. Indeed, marriage takes place when the *vēṅkai* blooms (Kuṟiñci. 358; Kol. 34, 41). Centuries later, in the Kantapurāṇa, Murukaṉ is said to have become a *vēṅkai* tree in his love affair with Vaḷḷi. Similarly, the *kaṭampu* tree (*anthocephalus cadamba*), associated with the hills near Madurai bearing red blossoms, is explicitly associated with Murukaṉ several times in the early literature.[27] Murukaṉ's worship center and the place of the *vēlaṉ's* dance are associated with the *kaṭampu* tree (Aka. 382:3). Later (Paṟi. 4:67), the *kaṭampu* tree is associated with Tirumāl, the god of the pastoral tract. This association may assist in the identity which takes place between Murukaṉ and Tirumāl. In fact, a myth in which Tirumāl destroys the *kaṭampu* tree in the ocean is frequently mentioned[28] and may have been part of the basis for a similar myth involving Murukaṉ's slaying of the demon Sūrapadma in the form of a mango tree in the ocean.

Why these particular trees are associated with Murukaṉ is not clear. The colorfulness of their blossoms must be part of it, and the *vēṅkai* has leaves shaped like the head of the leaf-shaped lance. Murukaṉ's eventual association with kingship suggests he may, like Tamil kings, have a tree to protect *(kāvalmaram)*. Murukaṉ is apparently linked to the *vēṅkai* – the tree bearing the flowers used by grooms – because he is a lover and later a bridegroom. Associated with the *vēṅkai* tree is the *vaḷḷi* (creeper). In the earlier literature, the term *valli* appears to refer to the creeper almost exclusively. But in Naṟṟ. 82:4 Vaḷḷi is personalized as Murukaṉ's consort. An elaborate and popular tradition is developed later around the courtship and marriage of Murukaṉ and Vaḷḷi. But in the early *Caṅkam* period it is only intimated – for example, in the clandestine love affairs of the hero (often compared to Murukaṉ) and his beloved, and in the frequent comparison of girls to creepers.[29] The creeper's entwining itself around the tree is analogous to the mating of lovers and the dependence of a 'weak' partner on another.

Fauna related to the hills which are associated with Murukaṉ in the early literature include the elephant, the peacock, and the rooster. The elephant's ferocity and fighting skill are equated with that of Murukaṉ, both implicitly and overtly. Naṟṟ. 225:1–2, for example, notes that the elephant fights with increasing anger and with a strength similar to Murukaṉ's; its tusk is like a 'banana blossom' – that is, red and white (covered with blood). The elephant's tusk is analogous to a spear. This comparison is particularly appropriate in the period when 'kings' used the elephant in battle and for a mount (e.g., Maturaik. 761–765). The analogy is explicit in the first stanza of the Kuṟuntokai, probably a somewhat later interpolation, where the elephant with red colored tusks which has just slain the *asura* on the battle field is associated with the lord of the hills who shoots red arrows. By the time of early kingship, the elephant is a mount and ally of the king, and in the post-*Caṅkam* poetry it is one of the royal insignias, which Murukaṉ has adopted (Pari. 21:1–7; cf. Thangavelu 1963:174).

The pea fowl is mentioned over seventy-five times in the *Caṅkam* poetry and is associated with Murukaṉ (Subrahmaniam 1966:645). In several passages, the peacock *(mayil)* dances as if possessed, particularly when it rains (Naṟṟ. 264:1–4; 357; 105:1–4; kuṟiñci. 169) and thus appears to symbolize fertility. Murukaṉ was also believed to bring rain and hence fertility. In at least one such passage (Naṟṟ. 24:1–4) the peacock is also linked with the snake, which, while the fowl likes to dance in the rain, is afraid to come out of its hole in the rain. The peacock roosts in the trees (the traditional abode of the gods), including the *vēṅkai* and *kaṭampu* (Subrahmnaiam 1966:645). Its feathers are used to decorate the small pillar *(kantu)* used in the worship of Murukaṉ; the lance victorious in war or used in worship is decorated with peacock feathers (Aka. 119:11–13; 369:17–20). By a later period, the peacock is offered in worship (Paṟi. 8:97–101). Eventually, as recorded in later passages (Puṟa. 56:9–10; Tirumuru. 247; Pari. 5:2; 17:49; Cila. 24:53). the peacock *(piṇimukam)* becomes the mount of Cēyōṉ or Murukaṉ.[30] It seems that the peacock's colorfulness and association with fecundity serve as a symbol of the tenor of early Tamil poetry and life – the beauty and joy and earthiness of life symbolized in Murukaṉ himself.

Another fowl associated with Murukaṉ, though less clearly at this early period, is the cock *(cēval)*. The word is used over thirty times in *Caṅkam* poetry and may denote the male of any fowl species, though when the term is associated with Murukaṉ, it connotes the rooster. N. Subrahmaniam notes that the cock is associated with both Murukaṉ and Tirumāl in the early Caṅkam period (Subrahmaniam 1966:392). The cock has two functions which link him symbolically with Murukaṉ: he is a fecundator; and he is a protector of the grain crops, for watchers of the millet wake up when the cock crows (Puṟa. 28:8–10). These two functions are associated with Murukaṉ who provides for the fertility of the earth and is forceful in protecting his own. The invocatory stanza of the Kuṟuntokai (lines 5–6) alludes to a phenomenon which is common in the Murukaṉ cultus in a later period of Southern kingship; Murukaṉ bears a banner inscribed on which is the cock. The cock is eventually associated with the sun, but this is a relationship only dimly intimated, at best, in the earlier literature.

An additional word should be said about the lance *(vēl)* which brings together allusions already mentioned. The lance of Murukaṉ with head shaped like a leaf, becomes a predominant symbol in the period of kingship. The lance as an instrument of war brings to focus several images mentioned in the earlier poetry, particularly the lance-like leaf of the *vēṅkai* tree, the blood-soaked tusk of the fighting elephant, and the arrows or spear of the hunter-chieftains. The lance of Murukaṉ is described in the Akananuru (119:11–13; 369:17–20) as having a pointed *(vēṅkai)* leaf-like face, a neck plate with small bells attached, the whole bedecked with peacock feathers (Thangavelu, 1963:182). It should be remembered that the term *vēlaṉ* (literally 'bearer of the lance') refers in an early period to the priest of Murukaṉ, for reasons not made clear in the *Caṅkam* literature. Later the term is used as another name for Murukaṉ himself, no doubt because the *vēlaṉ* in raiment and function personified the god.

2.3 *A later stage of the early Tamil Murukaṉ*

A slightly later stage in the development of Murukaṉ is also reflected in the early *Caṅkam* poetry. It is a stage that might be called intermediate when, under the aegis of the chieftain-kings of the South, certain motifs of the *kuṟiñci* peoples are 'universalized' to a degree. In general, two things seem to be happening: (a) motifs from various 'tracts' are 'brought into' the city and, in some cases, are associated with one another; (b) several such themes are adapted into forms appropriate to poets patronized by kings and chieftains. This is not exclusively a later occurrence, for it does begin in the early poetry. Yet its happening presupposes the existence of a *kuṟiñci* tract with its own poetic motifs. This process probably takes place in the second and third centuries, for it appears to be basically a Southern development. That is, it does not necessarily represent fusion of Northern elements with Southern, though it undoubtedly received some impetus from Sanskritization or Prākritization. It is this stage to which the term 'period of kingship' used above refers; it might also be called 'urbanization'. This development of the Murukaṉ tradition in the South makes it even more amenable to the Northern influence.

An illustration of this development is the few hints which associate

Murukaṉ with Māyōṉ and Tirumāl, who are generally depicted as deities in the pastoral, forest *(mullai)* tracts and who, later in the Paripāṭal and Cilappatikāram, are identified with Viṣṇu, especially as the cowherd Kṛṣṇa. We have noted how the *kaṭampu* tree is linked to both Tirumāl and Murukaṉ and how anger and ferocity link Māyōṉ and Murukaṉ. Tirumāl also is a dark god, associated with intoxication (Subrahmaniam 1966:434). Tirumāl and Murukaṉ are referred to as *Kaṭavuḷ* and in the Paripāṭal become the two major gods of the South.

Murukaṉ is referred to as a 'universal' god at a relatively early stage (Pattiṉ. 183; Malaipatukatam 728; cf. Pari. 5:17–21; 8:64). A clue to the developing universality of the god is in the spread of his worship. We have evidence that there were sanded areas where a *vēlaṉ* danced in worship of Murukaṉ not only in the hill areas, but along the seacoast (*neytal:* Kuṟun. 318) and in the area of cultivated fields (*marutam:* Kuṟun. 87). A good example of the spread of his cult into the cities is the frenzied dance to him of the women in festive spirit. In the first half of the night, the women wearing *kāñci* blossoms, dance in the streets and temple courts of Madurai, zealously adoring him who wears the *kaṭampu* blossoms. While instruments play, they join hands, embrace one another and indulge in noisy songs and cries (Maturaik. 673–684). It appears that, at least by the time of the Tirumurukāṟṟupaṭai, the *vēlaṉ* representing Murukaṉ, dances with the girls in the hamlets. He is wearing purple and is wreathed in *veṭci* flowers; he plays on a flute or horn, leads a ram, rides a peacock, and carries a cock-banner. He wears anklets, an armlet, and a shawl; he embraces the girls and clasps them in his strong arms (lines 280–308).

Perhaps the most obvious and important thing happening to Murukaṉ in the city state is that he is becoming identified with chieftains and warriors. Here some Epic influence cannot be denied. In the hills hunters and hunting chieftains are compared to him, while more and more of the poets patronized by warrior chieftains compare their patrons to Murukaṉ: the chieftain looks like Murukaṉ, by now the god of war (Malaipatukatam 651). The chieftain or 'king' attacks his foes with large troops as does Murukaṉ (Maturaik. 171).[31] The anger of Karikalan, Cōlaṉ 'king' and of other kings is like that of Murukaṉ (Porunaṟṟupaṭai 158–160; cf. Puṟa. 16:11; 158:16–17; 189: 5–6). The elephant takes its place in the entourage of the chieftains as a fighter and becomes part of the retinue of Murukaṉ. Murukaṉ is the standard by whom kings are compared (Puṟa. 16:2), and by the fourth or fifth century, buttressed by the Epic contribution, he has accrued most of the ten insignia associated with Tamil kingship: weapon, banner, umbrella, war-drum, horse, elephant, chariot, garlands, crowns, capital city (Thangavelu 1963:174, citing Kanta Kāli vēṇpā).

Finally, the *naṭukal* – the stone erected over the dead, especially those heroes and warriors felled in battle – begins to assume a role not unlike that ascribed earlier to the *kantu*, or early *Caṅkam* worship center. Contributed by the megalithic culture, the tombstone, at least by the time of the Caṅkam chieftains, was decorated with garlands, peacock plumes, a shield, a lance, and liquor and was apparently worked on with paint and brush (Srinivasan 1960:134 citing Aka 69:9; Ainkuru 352, 2). The *naṭukal*, in fact, came to be identified with the dead hero (Srinivasan 1960:134, citing Puṟa. 221:11–13; 265:1–5; Malaipatakatam 394–396). Not infrequently the *naṭukal* asserts its departed hero is divine.[32] This implied relationship of stone structures – *kantu* and *naṭukal* – suggests there was an understood association between the stone, the god, and the warrior.

These hints suggest that during the *Caṅkam* period, under the patronage of the Southern Chieftain-kings, Murukaṉ became associated with kingship, began to take on the character of a war-god and was worshipped by many groups in urban as well as rural settings. The stage was set for the grand coalition.

3. An hypothesis about the early Tamil development of Murukaṉ

It is impossible to trace precisely the sources of the god Murukaṉ which have emerged by the time of the early *Caṅkam* literature. There is little historical evidence that gives us certainty about the early character of the god. Archeological evidence in the South is still scanty. Anything that is suggested, therefore, in regard to the early development of the god is done on the basis of structural possibilities and must be seen as an hypothesis.

It seems more than likely that the god of the *kuṟiñci* described in the early *Caṅkam* poetry has a pre-megalithic heritage. The *kuṟiñci* appear to reflect a persistence of pre-megalithic culture. They are predominantly hunters and food-gatherers with some agricultural techniques at their disposal. The probability that they had pastoral skills need not disprove their pre-megalithic heritage, for, as we have seen, pastoralism had apparently developed in the South prior to the coming of either the megalith-builders or Āryanization. Perhaps we may assume, therefore, that the *kuṟiñci* embody an admixture of prehistoric cultures which had settled in forests and hills by the time the megalith culture built its cities. This would imply the *kuṟiñci* are either a remnant of the Paleolithic era, and thus largely comprised, perhaps, of Negrito stock, or, more likely, because very few remnants of Paleolithic man have been found in the Southwest, a product of those Neolithic peoples who were known to have settled in the hilly regions of Tamil Nadu and who were apparently proto-Mediterranean or proto-Australoid in racial composition. It is not yet possible to confirm any of these assumptions archeologically and historically, but from the frequent references to the *kuṟiñci* as hunters-farmers and rural hill-dwellers in the literature, that they represent one or the other cultural layer, or a combination of both, is at least plausible.

Caṅkam references would lead us to believe that Murukaṉ was known, by whatever name, amongst the early hunting societies as a lord of the hunt, a mythic hunter-chieftain, and the presiding spirit of the hills. As agriculture developed, the god's hunting attributes seemed to persist while characteristics associated with vegetation and fertility came to be ascribed to him. This process may have been one through which a variety of separate primitive dieties, both hunting and vegetative, came to be associated under the name Murukaṉ by the time of the *Caṅkam* period. Or, it is also possible that the primitive hunting god (or gods) persisted, as did other aspects of the hunting culture in South India, through agricultural and pastoral stages, accumulating functions appropriate to the successive stages, and that this god received the name Murukaṉ by the time of the early *Caṅkam* poetry. Whichever of these possibilities is more likely, it seems that the megalithic or post-megalithic peoples adapted the deity (or deities) already present in the South, possibly ascribed to him some of the more advanced agricultural attributes, brought him into their cities, began to think of him as a deity with whom their chieftains and 'kings' could be compared, and provided the name Murukaṉ.

Some detailed study of the religious practices of such contemporary tribes as the Pulaians of the Anamalai range near Combatore, the Kadars of Cochin, and the Karumbas of North Arcot might be productive in this context. As observed earlier, K. V. Raman and others suggest these tribes may be vestiges of the Neolithic peoples of the early South and that certain of their religious traditions may be similar to descriptions of worship of Murukaṉ by the *kuṟiñci*. Initial studies, however, have not been too conclusive. There is some evidence to suggest that the Karumbas, Kadars, and even the Chenchus, may share a common heritage, that includes a forested food-gathering peoples. Together with the Pulaiyans, they are a dolicephalic people (Thurston 1909: Vol. II, p. 43). Each of these tribes do use stone in their worship, in such a way, in fact, as to suggest there may have been some megalithic influence in their background. Edgar Thurston, for example, reported that the Kadars believed a stone set up under a teak tree, marked with ash, could protect the people from sickness. Interestingly, the deity associated with this stone is Iyyapaswamy (Vol. III, p. 21), a deity which has become part of the orthodox tradition in Kerala as Aiyappa, and is currently said to be a brother of Murukaṉ. To avert illness, the Kadars offered camphor, fruit, betel, and rice cooked with honey, apparently to this stone. Exorcism of evil spirits was also practised (Vol. III, p. 22). V. R. Ehrenfels reports that the Kadars believed in 'spirits' of nature, and especially of trees, and in *picācu* and *muṇi* (forms of demons) which caused illness and misfortune (Ehrenfels 1952:188–89). Yet Ehrenfels insists, for reasons not clear, the use of stones in worship is unlike that of other hill tribes in Tamil Nadu where stones are set up, vermillion is applied and a food-sacrifice made (Ehrenfels 1952:190).

Similarly, the Karumbas of the Nilgiri hills include a hill folk who are expert woodsmen and collectors of wax. While their religious life, like that of other tribes, evidences borrowing from the orthodox tradition, it still includes vestigial elements of a people or culture perhaps homologous to the *kuṟiñcis*. There is some 'worship' of rough stone, set up in a cave or circle of stones to which a goat and cooked rice is sacrificed (Thurston 1909: Vol. IV, p. 167). Harkness reported in 1832 of an instance when a Karumba, before starting to plow, set up a stone, decorated it with flowers, prostrated himself, offered incense, sacrificed a goat, ploughed ten to twelve paces, then made off with the head of the sacrificed animal.[33] Yet as with the Kadars, there is some evidence that the tribe was also influenced by the Megalithic culture, for they have been known to erect dolmens, which led one early researcher named Fergusson to identify them as descendants of the megalithic peoples (Vol. IV, pp. 169–70).

These tribes, descendents, it seems, from the hill folks once peopling

Tamil Nadu, apparently have retained some elements of a ritual life associated with this earlier culture and influenced to varying degrees by the megalithic culture. Yet evidence is still too scanty to suggest that these tribes have retained any form of deity that is unmistakably related to Murukaṉ. Somewhat more suggestive in that regard are the studies made of the Veddas, a contemporary hunting people of Ceylon, done over half a century ago by H. Parker and the Seligmanns, that reveal striking parallels between Veddoid religion and that of the *kuṟiñci.*

The forest Veddas [35] in the interior of Ceylon continue to acknowledge *Galē-Yākā* ('demon' of the rock) as chief deity. The Tamil Veddas along the Northern coast call him by several names: *Malei Pei* (hill demon); *Kallu Pei* (rock demon); Maleiyan (He of the hills); and *Maleiya Swami* (lord of the hills) (Parker 1909:134–35; Seligmann and Seligmann 1911:188). Legend among Veddas has the god coming from *Malawara-desa,* that is Southwest India (literally, Malabar country) (Parker 1909:177). The interior Veddas associate Galē Yākā with two hills on the northern coast and with Kataragama, the sacred hill of Ceylon. The Tamil Veddas claim that when he came into the interior 'he told us the names of things, trees, and animals, and how we should make offerings and dance to him when going into the jungle to hunt, and at other times. He told us everything we know' (p. 179). The Veddas believe that he attends to hunting requirements, provides game and food, assists in 'medical' aid by protecting from epidemic and misfortune, and sends the rain (pp. 155, 182).

That Galē Yākā is associated with the hunter chief is suggested by several things. There are known instances in the community of household-chieftains becoming spirits or Yakas who make themselves known through a possessed soothsayer (pp. 152–53). Also there are at least three related and virtually interchangeable deities of hill and rock. Aside from the Galē-Yākā or Galē Deviya there is the Galē Bandara (Chief of the Rock), and Kande Bandara (Chief of the Hill) 'p. 144). The term Yaka itself apparently derives from the term *iyaka* (users of the arrow), thus suggesting its relationship to the hunter (pp. 15–22).[36]

That the hill god was deity of the hunt is confirmed by ritual dances still performed by the Veddas (pp. 182 ff.). The deity is worshipped prior to the hunt under a Velan tree, a tree whose wood is used to make arrows. A shrine is laid out with red lotus and the yellow flowers of the Danawara bush. A dancer with a staff of flowers in his hand invokes the god's help in the hunt for sambar deer. The dance is also used by the forest Veddas to cure or avert illness. To arrest an epidemic a dance is done once or twice a year under a blossoming ironwood tree or a banyan. The dance could also be performed on rock crags near the auspicious hills of the district. A professional dancer also known as a 'devil priest' or *anumaetirala,* becoming possessed, holds a stick in his hand shaped like a large arrow or short spear believed to have efficacy in warding off harm or 'aude' (Seligmann and Seligmann 1911:137). He may hold a short-handled sickle-like bell-hook in addition to or in place of the arrow-spear. When the dancer becomes possessed he is believed to speak for the god or Yaka who possesses him (pp. 209 ff.). The *anumaetirala* also holds flowers of the arekapalm, wears bangles, a conical white hat and an ornamental jacket. The priest is ritually purified three days prior to the dance and remains *tabu* until three days later. During that period he must refrain from eating pig, monkey, peafowl,[37] or other fowls, shark, eels, turtles or large king fish.[38]

The Veddas' tradition has it – and Parker believed it to be true – that their god of the hills is the same as the hill god of early South India. Indeed, the similarities are too numerous to be coincidental or merely structural. The Veddas appear to be a basically pre-megalithic people, as do the *kuṟiñci.* Parker believes the people and their deity came to Ceylon prior to the Buddhist civilization which was established in the Aśokan era – that is, probably before the fourth century B.C. (Parker 1909:15–22, 134–35). This would be about the same time that the megalithic people came into South India, suggesting the possibility that the hill peoples were scattered by the more advanced migrants.

The hypothesis that the primitive form of Galē–Deviya is the same god as the hill god of the *kuṟiñci* is also suggested by the fact that the tradition of Skanda is grafted into this god in Ceylon. The village Veddas occasionally worship Skanda as the god of the hill known as Kataragama, and the northern Tamil Veddas periodically worship him as Kumāra Tēvaṉ along with Ganeṣa his brother, who is known as Pulikāra Tēvaṉ or Pilleiyar (p. 133). As god of Kataragama, Skanda is said to marry Vaḷḷiammal, in Ceylonese myth the daughter of a Vedda chief (Seligmann and Seligmann 191:156). Skanda's importance is eventually superceded by that of Aiyanar (Ayiyanar in Sinhalese), who appears to have the same heritage.[39] The Ceylonese believe Ayiyanar.to have come from Madura and to have been originally the god of the Nayars, an aboriginal forest-hill peoples, now extinct. Amongst the Wanniyars, a pre-hunt ritual similar to the one described above is performed to Ayiyanar, known there as Wanniya Bandara (Chief of the Wanniyas).

The evidence from the *Caṅkam* poetry and the Veddas of Ceylon leads us to believe that the South Indian sources of Murukan̲ include a hunting people. He was apparently a lord of the hunt who provided game, warded off evil, was an ancestral hunting chieftain, and presiding spirit of the hills, and who was reflected in the color and fertility of the hillsides. Because these hill peoples also depended on agriculture, the god was seen as provider of food, the giver of rain and the source of fertility. There must have been an intermingling of hunting and agricultural motifs around the deity even before the coming of the Megalithic peoples.

The development of agriculture in the South can be attributed, as we have seen, to many sources. Some aspects of agriculture may have developed indigenously; some may have been contributed by Neolithic migrations from the Northeast, which S. K. Chatterji calls the 'proto Australoid' people. It is also probable that some aspects of Southern culture, including some agricultural skills, may have come from the Mediterranean area. As noted earlier, there are those who believe that early Neolithic elements in the South may reflect a Mediterranean background. Most scholars believe the Megalithic migration had West Asian roots.[40] In addition, there is abundant evidence that trade between South India and the Mediterranean existed, certainly by the first century A.D., and perhaps as early as the third century B.C.[41] Some archeological finds in the South are strikingly similar to those found in the Mediterranean area: rock cut tombs in Malabar are like those found in Israel; tripod vases are found in Malabar and Syria; bronze bowls have been found in the Nilgiris and Assyria; similar iron hoes occur in the Tinnevelly District and in Pheonicia and Palestine; gold mouth pieces have been found in Trichinopoly District and amongst the Hurrians, etc (Nayar 1963:129–32). To be sure, similarities in diverse cultures do not prove historical contact as the nineteenth century diffusionists assumed; but archeologists no longer doubt the probability that South India received some cultural influence from the Middle East, if not by a Neolithic migration, then by Roman merchant–traders or the megalithic builders.[42] It is at least possible this was the route by which some of the agricultural elements associated with Murukan̲ came to South India, particularly those attributes sometimes called Dionysiac.

By the time of the *Caṅkam* literature, as we have noted, the Murukaṉ cultus manifests certain aspects that have striking parallels in the Dionysian cult of the Middle East. The early Murukaṉ is particularly similar to the agricultural Dionysos of a pre-Greek era before he became 'Āryanized' (Guthrie 1950:148ff.).[43] Murukaṉ is of the hills, as was Dionysos – and the hills in both cases were at first very much of the earth – whereas, the mountain with which both are later associated has a more celestial character. Both have roots amongst hunters but come to preside over vegetation. Both are associated with intoxicating drink and the life-giving sap of vegetation. Both are associated with tree and creeper. Both are worshipped in frenzied dance by women who have left their traditional functions so to dance:[44] At least one scholar, N. Gopala Pillai, believes the *kāvaṭi* (which, in one of its forms, is a sling on a pole in which offerings are brought to Murukaṉ) is related to the *liknón* (winnowing basket) in which Dionysos is cradled (Gopala Pillai 1937:987). Murukaṉ and Dionysos at a later period are 'Āryanized'; both become associated with warrior and celestial motifs and become a son of the presiding deity of the mountain at the center of the world. Both are found in the thickets and suckled by the heavenly maidens, though in Murukaṉ's case, this occurs as part of the Northern epic tradition.

There are admittedly several possibilities as to how these apparently Middle Eastern motifs came into the South Indian tradition of Murukaṉ. It is possible that these developments occurred independently in the South and are related to Middle Eastern motifs only structurally, insofar as both traditions develop as part of an agricultural world-view. Another alternative, suggested by N. Gopala Pillai, is that the Dionysiac tradition came into India with Alexander. Pillai argues that the Skanda tradition originates with the Alexandrian invasion, for Alexander was known as Iskandar in Asia and was associated with Dionysos in an Arab myth (1937:958ff.). Clarence Maloney picks up this suggestion and goes on to speculate that the Skanda cult was brought to the South with those migrants from Gujerat who founded the Pāṇṭiyan chieftainship in the Indo-Ceylon straits. Interesting as these suggestions are, they fail to recognize the agricultural stage of either Dionysos or Murukaṉ, a stage which is more obvious in the Southern *Caṅkam* Murukaṉ than in the Northern Epic tradition of Skanda. Whether or not the Skanda Northern Epic tradition was influenced by Greek motifs is a question which need not detain us here.

We suggest only that it is tempting to see some Mediterranean influence in the agricultural aspects of the early Southern Murukaṉ.

Whether or not the megalithic peoples contributed some of these agricultural themes associated with Murukaṉ and the rather sophisticated agricultural society reflected in the *marutam* tract, it is likely that the cities built and the chieftainships (and eventually kingships) developed by the time of the *Caṅkam* poetry influenced the Murukaṉ cult. The city culture, over which the Pāṇṭiyaṉs presided, helped to 'universalize' the cult and bring it into the cities; poets patronized by kings tended to think of the god in terms appropriate to a context familiar with regal and warrior values. That the Pāṇṭiyaṉs patronized Murukaṉ in the deep South is evident from allusions in the *Caṅkam* poetry and from bits and pieces of archeological evidence which suggest there may have been shrines to Murukaṉ at such Pāṇṭiyaṉ towns as Tiru Alaivay (later associated with Tiruchendur) and Tirupparaṇkuṉṟam.

One question that remains is: How did the name Murukaṉ come to be associated with this god? A number of theories have been suggested, all of which are speculative.[45] The term *muruku* is given the following meanings: an ear-ring for the upper part of the ear; tenderness, youth or tender-age; honey; beauty; a festival; flower–salver; fragrance; toddy; dancing under possession; a kind of sweet-scented wood from the agil tree; sour lime; divinity; Skanda, the younger son of Śiva; elevation or height (Tamil Lexicon 1928:3279). Of these definitions, the first has nothing to do with the deity, while the concept of Murukaṉ as son of Śiva is relatively late, as we shall see.

Conspicuous by its absence in the early Tamil poetry is any striking reference to Murukaṉ's youth or childhood, except in the indirect sense in which he is strong and virile and represents the freshness or tenderness of plant life. Thus, the earliest usage of the term *muruku* seems to have had the connotation of fragrance, beauty, festivity, etc. The *Tivakāram,* a Tamil lexicon dated perhaps between the sixth and eighth centuries, defines *muruku* as youth, enthusiasm, agilwood, firewood, and festival; and *Pinkalantai*, a lexicon of the same period, defines the word as meaning beauty, toddy, or lime fruit (Rajamanickinar 1964:3, citing K. Srinivasan Pillai, 'Tamil Varalaru', 240). Later, in the *Sulāmaṉi (Náṭṭupaṭalam)*, a tenth century work, the word *muruku* is used to denote a festival intended for the god Murukaṉ, and in the sixteenth century *Naiṭatam (Maṉampūrip-*

aṭalam 23*)* the word means 'honey' (Rajamanickiniar 1964:4). In the early *Caṅkam*, the word has diverse meanings: for example, the *vēlaṉ's* frenzied dance (Kuṟun. 362); fragrance (Pattin. 1:37); the divine – *Teyvam* (Puṟa. 259). Similarly, the Murugiyam is a kind of drum used at the *vēlaṉ's* dance Tol. Poruḷatikāram: 18 commentary).[46]

These etymological clues lead us to believe that the term had basically to do with the atmosphere in which the hill god was worshipped. If the Dravidian language was contributed, as Gordon and Fürer–Haimendorf believe, by the megalithic people, we would have to assume that they associated this word with that which could be observed around them, or perhaps derived the term from a word already in oral use by the hill tribes. The word seems to describe the beauty, fragrance and festive character of the hills and life in the early South, and thus is appropriate for the deity who reflects (and whose worship reflects) that atmosphere and vivacity.

The Early Sanskritic Tradition and the Southern Sequel

We turn now to that tradition generally called the 'Āryan', 'Sanskritic', or 'great' tradition, whose contribution to the Skanda-Murukaṉ mythology as it is known in the South today is substantial. Although it is difficult to date precisely the historical developments in the Sanskritic main stream, the materials in it relating to the emergent Skanda motif, particularly those of the Epic period, are numerous and can only be summarized and illustrated here. In general, in this discussion the term 'Sanskritic tradition' refers to that developing stream of culture, thought, and mythology purveyed by the literati for centuries (primarily the brāhmaṇ communities) whose roots were in the 'Āryan', Vedic tradition. The priestly community of succeeding generations sought to ascribe to their changing religious perspectives an orthodoxy and authenticity by relating their teachings to motifs evident in or ascribed to the Vedic and post-Vedic literature. In turn, this main stream incorporated into itself elements and motifs that were rooted in the religion and culture of peoples with 'non-Āryan' origins. Precisely which elements in this stream are 'non-Āryan' is still a matter of conjecture; to what degree the stream developed as it did because of its fusion with non-Āryan traditions and to what degree its development was rooted in 'Āryan' motifs themselves are still matters of debate.[1] Without attempting to enter this debate in this context, it is sufficient here simply to term this developing orthodox stream as the 'Northern' or 'Sanskritic' tradition.

1. Vedic and post-Vedic motifs

The Skanda mythology came to prominence in the North during the periods of kingship sometime between 200 B.C. and 500 A.D., but the motifs caught up and elaborated in this mythology did not develop in a vacuum. There were suggestions of these motifs in the orthodox tradition itself before historical circumstances brought them to focus in the figure of Skanda.

By way of illustration, we shall point out some of these continuing motifs.

An obvious motif in the Skanda mythology that appears in earlier literature is that of divine sonship. There is no lack of reference to sonship in the Vedic literature. Indra is said to be the son of strength (*sūnuḥ sahasaḥ*) (ṚV. VI:18:11; VI:20:1). Parjanya (rain) is the son of Dyaus, the sky (ṚV. VII:102:1), as are the Maruts (ṚV. X:77:2) and Sūrya (ṚV. X:37:1). Varuṇa and Mitra are the sons of *dakṣa* (ability, adroitness, skill) (ṚV. VIII:25:5). Of special interest to the Skanda tradition is the fact that Agni is understood to be a son – the son of *dakṣa* (ṚV. I:95:6) and of *sahas* (strength) (ṚV. VI:48:5; I:27:2).

It should be noted that sonship in these contexts is not necessarily related to physical generation. Rather, fatherhood refers to a source of authority, fullness and power (Gonda 1959:6); the father represents experience and an older generation; he grants wishes to the 'son' and bestows vigor and strength upon him. This qualitive rather than biological character of generation is connoted in several Vedic allusions: for example, the four quarters of heaven are generated from the earth, the sun is the son of heaven and earth (ṚV. I:160:3), and the existent is formed of the non-existent (ṚV. X:72:2). The role of the son then is as a 'manifestation or realization of that being or idea which is called . . . father' (p. 10). That is, the father is embodied in the son, and the son is a representation of the father. This idea is explicit in the Mahābhārata (I:159:11): 'The son is the very self of a man' (p. 10). Elsewhere (Bṛ. Up. I:5:11) the son is explicitly understood as a manifestation and fulfillment of the idea represented by the father, and the father is said to be poured forth in manifestation in the son (p. 13; cf. Śatapatha Brāhmaṇa X:4, 5, 6; VI:1:1,8).[2]

The son is like the father and the father continues to exist in the son. In this sense the offspring saves the father (Mbh. I:159:4; V:118:7; VII:173:54). Sonship is often related to 'salvation' – fulfilling the function of the father, doing the father's work with the father's blessing. This is also to suggest that sonship is, in the orthodox tradition, often associated with the work of a creator. The son becomes a demiurge, a creator. Thus, we are confronted with the paradox that Agni, the son, is a father who gives power to his own fathers, – i.e., to those deities and/or priests who bring him into being (ṚV. I:31:11; II:5:1). In one of the creation stories of the Śatapatha Brāhmaṇa (X:2:1, 2) Agni is identified with Prajāpati, the pre-eminent creator and Father. Similarly, Rudra, who is frequently identified with Agni in several respects,[3] and is known as the father of Skanda, is son and father. He begets Hiraṇyagarbha and he is Hiraṇyagarbha (Aiyangar 1901:30).[4]

To speak of the son as father, creator, or demiurge is to speak of the son's primordiality – that is, as the origin and substance of the world. The generation of the son was 'in the beginning' (Kaṭha Upaniṣad II:4:6; IV:6). That which is generated is sometimes called Hiraṇyagarbha, and sometimes called Vāc. Both the Hiraṇyagarbha and Vāc in varying cosmologies are thought to be primordial demiurges from which the world was born: Vāc generated of Brahmā as the asexual primordial mass from which the original reed emerged (Vājasaneyi Samhitā XXIII:20; Kaṭha Upaniṣad IV:6; cf. Heras 1956:151ff.); Hiraṇyagarbha as that golden germ or egg which became the world (Śatapatha Brāhmaṇa VI:3:1–20; VIII:1:4, 10; cf. Agrawala 1962:6–13). So the son in early Sanskritic motifs is in some sense not only the generator of the world but the substance of which the world is formed. He is thus akin to the world, created even as the world is created while at the same time being the world's creator.

Sonship is also related in some Vedic and post-Vedic contexts with 'wisdom'. The created one is termed the fruit of the intellect (manasā asahāya) and later 'son of the mind' (*manodbhuta*) (Mahābhārata, Śānti-parva, 12005) or 'generated by brooding' (*tapasā jātam*) (Kaṭha Upaniṣad II:4:6). This process is illustrated in the name Vāc which comes to connote first 'thought' and then 'speech', for as the Aitrēya Āraṇyaka puts it (III:1:1): 'The mind (thought) is the earlier form, speech is the later form' (Heras 1956:153). Vāc is the 'second self' of the divine (Bṛ. Up. I:6:3) and is eternal knowledge (Śaṅkara, Bṛhadaraṇyaka Upaniṣad Bhāṣya III:19:28, 7). The wisdom of sonship is personified in Sanatkumāra (eternal son) who appears by the Upaniṣadic period, when he is pictured as enlightening the Brāhmaṇ Nārada on the doctrine of the Ātman (Chāndogya Upaniṣad VII:1:4) (p. 161).

Another motif associated with Skanda, but which is common prior to his emergence is that of the warrior. Indra had been the fecundating warrior god of the Vedic period; his thunderbolt slays Vṛtra, the dragon, thereby permitting the rains to fall and fertilize the earth. Agni and Rudra were also depicted as warriors. Agni is a typical leader of the vanguard of the army (ṚV. X:84:2; AV. III:1:1; III:2:1; et al.). Later he is known as Senāgni (army fire) (Mukhodhyay 1931:315). Rudra led the gods against the three enemy cities and Agni led them against the *asuras* (ṚV. III:15:1; VII:15:10;

VII:23:13–14). Rudra put the *asuras* and Rākṣasas to flight (ṚV. VIII:6:2). He demolished cities and performed other feats; he waged war for the gods (ṚV. I:59:5). He was hero of one thousand engagements (I:188:1); he saved the gods from disaster (ṚV. VIII:13:2) and became known as Senāni (Śatapatha Brāhmaṇa V:3:11) (Venkataramanya 1941:75).

The role of the warrior is to preserve the world or the *dharma*. Hence, the warrior is both destructive and creative: by destroying the enemies, he saves the cosmic order for which he is responsible. In this sense, the warrior is a 'creator', for by preserving the old order, he brings about a new order and propels himself into the role of dominant deity. This aspect of the warrior's role makes it quite common in early brāhmaṇic speculation that the motifs of warrior and son are linked.

Another motif associated with Skanda but evident in the earlier Sanskritic literature, is that of the sun. Of particular interest is the way in which the sun motif is caught up and linked with the mythological development of the son and warrior motifs. V. S. Agrawala summarizes suggestively a cosmogonic basis for this process: the ocean, the cosmic womb or water principle receives the seed deposited by the sky. The primordial seed is a fiery principle. This cosmic egg is the golden egg or golden germ which emerges from the ocean as the eternally energized force of cosmic pulsation. The sun is equated with this golden germ, for it is the red or golden one springing from the womb of the great Mother Goddess Aditi, once concealed in the ocean, now thrown up by the force of the universal laws of creation (Agrawala 1962:18–24; cf. ṚV. I:160:3). The sun, then, is the fecundated and the fecundator; it is generated and it generates. It is the Hiraṇyagarbha, the primordial substance and demiurge. Its coming dispels the forces of darkness and chaos. The sun is in this sense related to the sacrificial fire. The performance of the sacrifice and the bringing into being of the fire was to re-create the world ritually, not only because Prajāpati's primordial sacrifice brought the world into being – and the sacrifice re-enacts this mythical event – but also because the fire, like the sun, was intended to dispel spiritual darkness and become the Hiraṇyagarbha, the microcosm of the universe.

These motifs of son – sun – and warrior coalesce in Skạnda but also in several of the gods who precede Skanda but are associated with him. They come together in the figure of Indra who, as we have seen, is the 'son of strength' (ṚV. VI:18:11; VI:20:1) and is born of the sky, Dyaus (Bṛ. Up.

VI:4:22). Indra is golden in color and rides a golden chariot; he is Lord of the gods (*Devapati*) and leader of the Celestial Hosts (*Jiṣṇu*) (Danielou 1964: 107–09). Likewise, these motifs come together in the person of Rudra, the red storm god and warrior who, at some historical moment, both is Hiraṇyagarbha and begets Hiraṇyagarbha. Similarly, this complex of symbols comes to focus in the figure of Agni, who is fire born of two sticks (ṚV. I:177:1); the heat generated by the primordial pair; the golden seed which gives life to the world; and the sun, Sūrya, which governs the heavens, yet is born of the ocean (*apām napāt*) (Agrawala 1962:6–9). Agni is the warrior son, the fertilized and fertilizing seed.

The historical process by which these cosmological and mythological developments occurred and the historical factors they represent are obscure and virtually impossible to reconstruct.[5] The essential point is that the Skanda mythology embraces motifs that had already developed in earlier Vedic mythology. In fact such attributes as those of son, warrior, and sun had been earlier ascribed to deities like Indra, Agni, and Rudra, all of whom are eventually associated with Skanda. Skanda coalesces and perpetuates, theologically much that had preceded him.

2. The development of Skanda-Kumāra in Sanskrit literature

2.1 *The myths and literary references*

The name Kumāra is apparently first used to describe Agni. In ṚV. V:2, Agni is Kumāra held close to his mother; in the Śatapatha Brāhmaṇa VI: 1–3, Agni is described as Kumāra whose parent is Uṣas, the dawn, impregnated by the lord of beings. Later, Kumāra (child, son) is used to refer to Skanda. The name *Skanda* is apparently derived from the past participle of the verb *skandṛ* (to attack, leap, rise, fall, perish, burst, be spilled, ooze) and literally means 'that which is spilled or oozed, namely "seed"' (Monier–Williams 1951:1256). Kumāra and Skanda are explicitly equated in the seventh chapter of the Chāndogya Upaniṣad where Sanatkumāra (eternal son) is said to be the same as Skanda. The Sanatkumāra of this chapter is particularly associated with the wisdom that knows the mysteries of existence. The wise Brāhmaṇ Nārada is taught the essence of Ātman by the eternal youth, Sanatkumāra. The implication is that because the youth is from the beginning of existence he is aware of its meaning. Skanda the philosopher is frequently linked to Skanda the warrior, implicitly in the myths of Skanda's birth to Agni, and in other respects during the Epic period. The relationship is particularly explicit at a later period in the south in the character and iconography of Subrahmaṇya.

Relatively minor references to Skanda appear in the Taittirīya Āraṇyaka (X:1) where a mantra is addressed to Ṣaṇmukha, together with other gods. And in the Baudhāyana Dharmasūtra, libations of a householder offered to Gaṇapati and Skanda are described. Here also Skanda is equated with Sanatkumāra.[6]

In another relatively early account, we find described a household ritual to Skanda, addressed as Dhūrta.[7] This account is found in a rather obscure passage known as the Skanda-Yāga in the Atharva Veda Pariśiṣtas. In this passage, the god is thought to be surrounded by many mothers, accompanied by a thousand maidens, associated with the peacock and such other animals as the partridge, elephant, tiger, and lion. He has six faces and eighteen eyes; he is called Kārttikeya, is the brother of Viśākha, and yet is identified in the same passage with Viśākha. He has an army, a large following, a chariot, and he wears a bell. He is the son of Śiva, Agni and the Kṛttikas[8] and is associated with Rudra, Indra, and Paśupati. He is called incomparable and inimitable; he likes red flowers, red ointment and red cocks. The worship center consists of garlands, bells, wreaths, an amulet, and mirrors. The deity is offered sour milk, rice and sugar, mixed grain and sweetmeats, fragrances, flowers, and fruit.[9] As part of the ritual, the Kāmasūkta is to be recited, suggesting the deity has an amorous and virile character. The worship is intended to free the worshipper of malevolent influences, for the worshipper wears an amulet on the arm, duly blessed by Aśvins and Āditya, which can free one from trouble and demons. Prayers are offered for the attainment of position, jewels, servants, wealth, grain, herds, enjoyments of various kinds, speech and knowledge.[10]

It is in the Epics that we find extensive accounts of the birth and exploits of Skanda, and we must assume it was in the Epic period that the mythology of the god came to a focus and his worship became prominent. The longest and most complex account appears in the third book of the Mahābhārata (Vana Parva), chapters 223–232, where Skanda is primarily the son of Agni.

In the first book of Vālmīki's Rāmāyaṇa (the Bālakāṇḍa), chapters 36 and 37, Skanda is described as the son of Agni and Gaṅga, the river, and then as the son of Rudra. In the ninth book of the Mahābhārata (Śalya Parva), chapters 46 and 47, Skanda is depicted as the son of Maheśvara, and his coronation and victory over the demons are described. In the thirteenth book (Anuśāsana Parva), chapters 84–86, in what is presumably a later passage, Skanda is the son of Śiva, who is sporting with Pārvatī. Finally, a work connecting the Epic to the Purāṇic period, the Kumārasambhava, puts into poetic form the basic story of Kumāra's birth to Śiva which is generally consistent with the mythology that abounds in the Purāṇic material. The salient features of these accounts will be summarized as they provide much of the basis for the Skanda tradition as it later develops.

2.1.1 *The basic myth*

The myth in Mahābhārata III:223–232 can be summarized as follows. The Devas are battling the Danavas (*asuras*) and are often defeated. One day near Mt. Mānasa, the distressed general of the *devas*, Indra himself, rescues a beautiful damsel called Devasenā from the Daityas; she tells him she was the daughter of Prajāpati, that her sister Daityasenā loves the *asura* Keni who carried her off, but she wants a suitable husband who could protect her. The sun is rising and Agni is carrying offerings to the sun, while, at the same time, the moon (*soma*) is also entering the sun.[11] Indra thinks Agni or Soma would be able to generate a son fit to be Devasenā's husband, so he goes to Brahmā to see what can be arranged. He and the gods go to the abode of seven *ṛṣis* to drink soma; the *soma* is offered in sacrifices being performed by the seven *ṛṣis*, who are accompanied by their wives. Seeing these wives, Agni falls in love with them. But he leaves disappointed, for his love is not reciprocated. Yet Svāhā loves Agni and, being a clever woman, she assumes the form of one of the wives of the *ṛṣis* and tells Agni the wives have learned of Agni's interest and will come to him one by one in private. So one by one, Svāhā assumes the form of each of six of the *ṛṣis'* wives.[12] However, she could not assume the form of Arundhatī, the especially virtuous wife of Vasiṣṭha. After each session, Svāhā assumes the form of a garuḍa bird (so no suspicion would fall on the impersonated wives) and carries Agni's semen (*retas*) to Mt. Śvēta, where she puts it into a golden pot at a place overgrown with *śara* reeds.[13] Born with six heads (one that of a goat) set on one neck and twelve hands, Kumāra, within six days, has grown to a strength sufficient for battle.

In his childhood the prodigious Kumāra plays with a cock which he makes part of his banner; his arrows split Krauñca Mountain (son of Himavat), from which eagles and flamingoes fly to Mt. Meru. The rumors of Kumāra's exploits spread, and the *ṛṣis*, hearing their wives were involved in infidelity, divorce them. Visvāmitra learns of the wives' innocence and comes to do obeisance to the child. The *devas*, fearing the child will surpass Indra in greatness, plead that Indra slay him. Indra declines, saying he should not fight a mere child. So the *devas* send the malevolent goddesses who bear diseases to kill Kumāra, only to have the child adopt them as his mothers. Agni in a goat-headed form has played with Kumāra and protects him. Then the *devas*, led by Indra, come to fight Kumāra. But Kumāra burns the armies of the *devas* with flames from his mouth. Indra seeks to slay Kumāra with his *vajra*, (thunderbolt) but only slices off a portion of Kumāra's right side from which Viśākha springs into being bearing a *śakti* or lance. Indra then trembles and surrenders, and the *devas*, given fearlessness by Kumāra are made glad. From the same blow by which Viśākha is born a host of children come forth to serve in Skanda's army.[14] Skanda thus comes to be known as a father, and persons wishing children are exhorted to worship him. The girls so born become mothers, some claiming Skanda as their own child;[15] these mothers in turn bring forth a red-eyed goat-headed child, homologous to Skanda's goat head.[16]

The brāhmaṇs (*ṛṣis*) come to Skanda, addressing him as Hiraṇyagarbha, all golden and red in his attire, and ask that he become Indra. Kumāra refuses, granting to Indra the right to be himself; for this he is appointed general of the *devas* and is married to Devasenā.[17]

Rudra then visits Kumāra to give a golden necklace. At this point the story alludes to Rudra's fatherhood of Skanda. The brāhmaṇs are reported to say that Rudra is Agni and Umā is Svāhā, and that Rudra's seed entering Agni was cast on Mt. Śvēta and the Kṛttikas made the seed to be Kumāra.[18]

The six divorced ladies then come to Kumāra and beg for a heavenly place. Skanda declares them to be his mothers and sends them into the sky to be the constellation Kṛttikas whose god is Agni. Vinatā is celestialized, also claiming to be Skanda's mother. The mothers request that they replace the older mothers (Brahmī, Maheśvarī, etc.) in worship. Skanda makes them the protectors of children, and confers the privilege of possessing his *śakti* and assuming fierce forms to tease youngsters under sixteen.

Skanda declares Svāhā to be his own mother; then, at Brahmā's advice, he pays his respects to Rudra, who is again identified as his father. Rudra comes in procession to greet him together with all the gods, including Indra, Varuṇa, Yama, and others. As Kumāra is leaving, a fierce Deva-Danava battle ensues, Mahiṣa, chief of the Danavas, puts the Devas to flight and is about to smash Rudra's chariot. But Rudra calls on Kumāra who immediately comes in a beautiful chariot, dressed in red, and kills Mahiṣa with his *śakti*. That same day he conquers the three worlds and Rudra tells the Devas to regard Kumāra with the same respect as they do himself.[19]

This account also records the six day life span of Skanda. The god is conceived on the first day of the fortnight; he becomes visible on the second day; on the third he takes the form of the child; on the fourth, his limbs grow and he becomes Guha, general of the army; on the fifth, he takes Śiva's bow, performed other heroic deeds, and is worshipped by all the *devas* as the one born to save their cosmos; and on the sixth day he takes his arms and emblems of war, especially the lance called *śakti*, the cock, and the ram; then, roaring with power, he shatters the *krauñca* mountain, has his religious initiations from the sage, leads the divine hosts into battle and destroys the demons.[20] The sixth day, Ṣaṣthi, is still especially sacred to Skanda's devotees.

There follows, in chapter 233, a long list of Skanda's names, apparently added to the account later.

2.1.2 *Variations to the myth*

a) *The Rāmāyaṇa account.* We turn now to the Rāmāyaṇa where a somewhat different account of Skanda's birth appears. In the first book of the epic, Bālakāṇḍa, chapters 36 and 37, the sage Vālmīki narrates to the two young princes, Rāma and Lakṣmaṇa, the story of the young war-god Kumāra, his exploits as a youth and his conquests over the *asuras*. The intent of the narration appears to be to inspire the young princes to heroic aspirations. At first (chapter 36) the sage narrates this account:

Mt. Himavat marries his daughter Umā to Rudra of great austerity. No son is born after one hundred years. The *devas*, fearing a son born to Rudra would surpass them, beg Rudra not to have a son. Rudra complies, but as he stood, his seed (*tejas*) remains on the ground. Only Dhārā, the earth, could bear it. At the request of the *devas*, Agni and Vayu entered the seed, whereupon the seed becomes Mt. Śvēta. It was there in a forest of reeds that Kumāra is born. Umā, deprived of the opportunity to become a mother, curses the *devas* not to have sons of their wives, and curses *Dhārā*, the earth, to become the wife of many (Aiyangar 1901:68–70).

In the next chapter, the sage continues the story with adaptations:

Rudra becomes a *tapavasin*, given to meditation, leaving the *devas* in need of a general since he, so appointed by Brahmā, had 'retired'. At their request, Agni gives his seed (apparently the same as deposited by Rudra) and the river Gaṅga, elder sister of Umā, bears it. But she can not contain the flood of the golden seed, and spills over, causing everything which it touches to become gold – trees, plants, creepers, grass. By its heat, the metals are formed in the earth. In that golden forest Kumāra is born. The Kṛttikas, finding him, accept the child as their son; with his six mouths he sucks their milk for a day and eventually conquers the army of the Daityas (p. 73).[21]

The Rāmāyaṇa account also notes that those who become devoted to Skanda will attain long life, happiness in the family, and ultimate union with the god. It also records how the god received some of his names: Gaṅgeya because he was born of the Gaṅges water; Kārttikeya, because he was attended by the Kṛttikas or Pleides; and Ṣaḍānana because he had six faces. Elsewhere, the Rāmāyaṇa describes Kumāra as the embodiment of heroism and physical beauty and frequently describes the heroes Rāma and Lakṣmaṇa with the simile of Kumāra (Raghavan 1964:2).

b) *Mahābhārata, ninth book.* In a later account of the Mahābhārata, the ninth book (Śalya Parva), chapters 46 and 47, the whole story of Skanda is retold. Significant variations in the story include the following:

The seed of Maheśvara is dropped into the fire (Agni), which, unable to contain it, throws it into the Gaṅges, which in turn, sends it to Himavat where it is deposited in a clump of reeds, The child, when born, is suckled by the six Kṛttikas; Gaṅga and the earth wait on him; Bṛhaspati, the celestial priest, performs the usual rites (*jātakarmādikah kriyāḥ*) – Rudra, Umā, Agni, and Gaṅga prevail on Brāhmaṇ to make the child a generalissimo.

Kumāra is so installed on the banks of the Sarasvatī by Brahmā and the gods. Bṛhaspati, Himavat, Indra, and Brahmā duly anoint him with water (even as Varuṇa was) signifying his right to sovereignty. The gods then give him companions who are also warriors and devotees. He is given an entourage of goddesses to be his companions and mothers, beautiful damsels whose abodes were in the trees, open areas, the crossings of four roads, caves, crematoria, mountains and springs. In addition, all manner of beasts, reptiles, and birds surround him.[22]

Four persons – Rudra, Parvatī, Agni and Gaṅga – appear before Skanda, each claiming to be his parent. There is suspense to see whom Skanda would embrace first. But the god assumes four forms: Śākha, Viśākha, Naigameya, and Skanda. Skanda goes to Rudra; Viśākha to Pārvatī; Naigameya to Agni; and Śākha to Gaṅga.

The gods then give Skanda special gifts: Indra gives a dart and banner; Śiva gives an army protected by 30,000 warriors. Viṣṇu gives a garland; Umā gives cloth; Gaṅga, a celestial waterpot produced of *amṛta*. Garuḍa presents its favorite son Citrabarbin, the peacock. Aruṇa, the charioteer and harbinger of the sun, gives the cock; Varuṇa gives a snake; and Brāhmaṇ, a black deer skin.[23] All the gods praise Kumāra.

Skanda then kills all the demons, of which Tāraka is the head and Mahiṣa an aide. But Bali's son, Daiteya Bāna, takes refuge in Krauñca Mountain, so named because its sound is like the cry of the krauñcas bird (heron). Skanda pierces the mountain with his dart and thus destroys the last demon. The celestial ladies shower him with flowers. Some in acclaiming him refer to him as Sanatkumāra, the son of Brāhman; some call him son of Maheśvara; others son of Agni. Gaṅga, Umā, or Kṛttikas. He is conceived as one, as two, as four, as one hundred, or as 1000 in forms.[24]

c) *Mahābhārata, thirteenth book.* Later, in the thirteenth book of the Mahābhārata, chapters 84–86, another variation is added to the story.

In this account, Śiva is depicted as sporting with Pārvatī while Tāraka troubles the *devas*. This love play and its setting offer many parallels to the account in the Kumārasambhava of Kālidāsa to be discussed below. The gods eventually persuade the Kṛttikas to bring up the seed, which is six in number, the one seed having become six. The child is called Kārttikeya because he is reared by the Kṛttikas: he is called Skanda because he is from the seed spilled by Śiva; he is called Guha because, though he was secluded and brought up in the thicket, he becomes a general of the gods. Gods and sages visit the child with six faces, who had been lying in the thicket. Each god gives him playthings and birds and animals: the Garuḍa gives the peacock; the Rākṣasas give the pig and buffalo; Aruṇa gives the cock; the moon gives the goat,[25] and the sun gives its splendor; Agni gives the ram; Illa, fruits and flowers; and Varuṇa, elephants, lions, tigers, and clawed animals. The demons crowd around, trying to kill him. The gods ask him to become their commander. With the *śakti*, Kumāra kills Tāraka; he then restores Indra to his kingdom and becomes Senāpati. The passage notes that the process by which Skanda is born is the same as that by which gold (*gaṅgeya*) is brought into being.[26]

d) *Kumārasambhava.* Finally, we come to the poem *Kumārasambhava*, which contains an extensive account of Skanda's birth and exploits, and most certainly represents the period of transition from late Epic to early Purāṇic times. The account portrays the more or less final and orthodox form of the myth, poetically embellished, to be sure (Kale 1913:Preface; cf. Aiyangar 1901:76, citing K. T. Telang).[27] The poem must be divided into two sections: the first eight cantos are clearly the work of Kālidāsa, while the last eight, most scholars agree, are by another, later hand.[28] The story of Skanda's birth and exploits in the *Kumārasambhava* includes the following features:

Śiva sits in austere *tapas* (meditation) on Mt. Himavat, the measuring rod of the earth, whose daughter Pārvatī each day comes to pick flowers. Pārvatī is Umā who in a previous birth was Satī, wife of Śiva, who 'died' as the result of intense yoga (1:21). Tāraka, the demon, given a boon by Brahmā, torments the world of the gods.[29] The gods go to Brahmā to ask for a general urged on by Indra. They are told that Śiva is the supreme spirit, greater than Brahmā, or Viṣṇu and only his energy can stop Tāraka. In other words, only a son of Śiva and Pārvatī could save them from Tāraka (II:57–61). The *devas* plot to have Śiva fall in love with Pārvatī. At their request, Kāma, the god of love, accompanies Pārvatī one day into Śiva's presence and shoots his arrows into Śiva. Momentarily stirred from his *tapas* by the arrows and by the beauty of Pārvatī, whose limbs are as beautiful as the blooming Kadamba flowers (III:68), Śiva recovers and with sparks from his forehead consumes Kāma. Pārvatī is so humiliated she retires to do *tapas* the rest of her days. But Śiva, mo ́ed, appears before her as a religious mendicant to talk her out of her infatuation with him. She defends Śiva, only to have the god reveal himself and ask for her hand. Modestly she requests him to ask her father. The *ṛṣis* mediate and the wedding takes place. Meanwhile Kāma is resuscitated and rejoins his wife Rati, who had bitterly bewailed his loss. The final canto of Kālidāsa's work describes the love play of Śiva and Pārvatī.

In the cantos added later, we find that no son is born for many years, so the *devas*, becoming impatient, send Agni to the couple during their love play in the form of a dove. Pārvatī discovers the dove is Agni and retires lest her privacy be invaded. But Śiva's seed (*tejas*) is carried away by Agni, and from it Kumāra is born in a manner similar to that stated in the Rāmāyaṇa.[30] Kumāra's appointment as general of the gods and his conquest of Tāraka and the other *asuras* are then retold.[31]

2.2 *What do these myths mean historically and religiously?*

If the mythological material is rather easily summarized and its symbolic significance at least occasionally transparent, it is nonetheless impossible to date it accurately and reconstruct the historical setting it reflects. When Skanda first emerged and came into prominence is particularly difficult to ascertain. Patañjali, in the Mahābhāṣya written about the middle of the second century B.C., commenting on a remark by Pāṇini in the Aṣṭādhyāyī V:3:99, mentions that images of Skanda and Viśākha were being made for worship during the time of the late Mauryas (Banerjea 1956:85).[32] It seems that the dual deity Skanda-Viśākha was, at some relatively early point, conceived to be twin deities, apparently analogous to sun and moon, for so they are mentioned in the Vaṃsa Brāhmaṇa of the Sama Veda (Raghavan 1964:2).[33] That these gods were increasingly identified is apparent, and Bhandarkar (and implicitly Nilakanta Sastri) believes the first myth of the Mahābhārata reflects a stage in this identification. This would suggest that the myth was known about the time of Patañjali. V. Raghavan also notes this progressive identification of Skanda and Viśākha but declines to date the myth on this basis (p. 2; cf. Sastri 1964:21).[34] Some scholars think it likely that the Mahābhārata myth is the earliest of the accounts, reflecting a period or at least a community in which Skanda was replacing Agni in importance. This would presumably mean that the references to Rudra as father and possibly even the account of Skanda's military triumphs were interpolations added to the story by a later editor. Other scholars assume the Rāmāyaṇa account to be earlier because the Mahābhārata version alludes to the Rudra myth found in the Rāmāyaṇa.

Whatever the date of these narratives, the tenor and intent of the Agni myth are strikingly different than those evident in the story of Rudra's parentage. The Skanda born of Rudra seems to be predominatly a warrior-god. The Skanda born of Agni is characterized by the symbolism of fire, sacrifice and sun and represents astral and ritualistic motifs that are of less importance in the Rudra myths. For example, Agni's Skanda is associated with *ṛṣis* conducting the sacrifice; with *śara* reeds, the grass used in making the sacrificial fire; and with gold, the color of the fire and sun. On the other hand, the Rudra myths change the role of Agni in the birth accounts from that of a father to a transferer of the sacred seed, and incorporate the role of Gaṅga, the river, who is not mentioned in the myth of Skanda's birth to Agni. It is difficult to resist the conclusion that these two accounts reflect varying, if related, religious structures. If this assumption is correct, the historical relationship between the two accounts is not clear, but two possibilities are suggested: (1) The Rudra myths are later than the Agni myths and incorporate the Agni motif into their accounts; and the earlier Agni myth is editorially amended at a later time to incorporate the Rudra motif. (2) The myths, more or less contemporaneous, reflect the religious heritage of two distinct communities – the one presumably a more or less independent, sacrifice – performing brāhmaṇic community; and the other community more nearly associated with growing *kṣatriya* dominance. It is likely that these myths were reconciled in the centuries during which Skanda became dominant.[35] On either of these bases, it appears that Skanda's sonship of Śiva is a slightly later development, presumably around the time of the Gupta kings, and represents the coalescence of Rudra and Agni into the person of Śiva. More will be said on this relationship later.

The later accounts appear to be those found in Mahābhārata IX, Mahābhārata XIII, and the *Kumārasambhava*, possibly in that order. The *Kumārasambhava* is more than likely the last of these accounts, for the poet (or poets) appears to be familiar with the later Epic versions and, as we have noted earlier, possibly with the Śiva Purāṇa accounts as well. Whether or not Kālidāsa lived during the reign of the early Guptas, we know there was a general veneration of Skanda-Kumāra by the Guptas. This is reflected in the names a number of the Gupta kings were given, and by the discovery of coins and seals attributed to the Guptas on which were stamped the image of the god. One coin, attributed to Kumāragupta I, for example, shows Kārttikeya riding a peacock with a spear in his left hand (Banerjea 1956:144).[36]

The fact that Skanda was particularly associated with kingship even earlier in this period is attested by the discovery of other coins and seals. Archeologists have discovered a silver coin and several copper coins attributed to the Yaudheyas of the second century A.D., on which the six-headed Kārttikeya is inscribed. Some of these show the god with six heads, two arms, and bearing a spear. Tell-tale inscriptions appear on the coins: on one appear the words: 'Of Brahmānuja Skanda, the divine lord of the Yaudheyas'; and on another: 'Of Kumāra, the divine lord Brahmaṇya deva' (pp. 140–41). In Rohitaka, still in Yaudheya country, a seal dating from the third or fourth century shows Kārttikeya, the tutelary deity, as a one-faced war god; his right hand holds a spear, his left hand rests on his hip and to his left is his *vāhana*, the peacock (p. 140).[37] K. A. Nilakanta Sastri adds that the Śakas, who came to power in the Deccan in 40–80 A.D., minted coins attesting to their allegiance to Skanda. He notes also that, at a later point, the Ikṣvākus, who ruled over the Krishna-Guntur region in Andhra for some fifty-seven years during the third century, constructed shrines to Skanda in the Nagarjunakonda Valley.[38]

There is numismatic evidence that Skanda worship was practiced in the North prior to the second century A.D. For example, on one of two controversial Kuṣāṇa coins the deity stands with two other persons; inscribed on that coin are the names 'Skanda, Kumāra, Mahāsena, and Viśākha'. The deity is clad in an undergarment, his sword in a sheath; in his right hand, a standard is mounted by a bird (p. 145). Nilakanta Sastri refers to 'certain Ujjain coins of the third or second century B.C.' which bear the legends Brāhmaṇya and Kumāra (Sastri 1964:21).

The literary and numismatic evidence suggests, therefore, that the Skanda mythology captured the imagination of kings as well as the poets and religious apologists patronized by them. It appears that this occurred at least by the first century A.D. (and possibly as early as the post-Aśokan Maurya period) and lasted at least until the end of the Gupta dynasty, covering a period dating roughly between 200 B.C. and 450 A.D. It is possible, in fact, that myth makers in the era of kingship fashioned a Skanda mythology, based on earlier motifs, which propelled Skanda into a place of prominence amongst the gods and provided the warrior-kings a divine prototype which gave their kingly roles a sacral character.

What additional factors contributed to the emergence of Skanda at this time is difficult to ascertain. It is possible that the emergent mythology reflects certain 'non Āryan' influences. Nilakanta Sastri concedes this possibility and suggests that the cult may have roots in the Gaṅges Valley. Indeed, this is a possible basis for the role of the river as the bearer of the fetus and of fertility itself in the myths of Skanda's birth (Sastri 1964:20).[39] It seems inevitable that there was some popular and folk (possibly Southern) influence on the mythology that appears in the Epic literature. It has generally been assumed that most of the North-South interchange was one way – religious mendicants migrating South and Northern dynasties extending their borders southward. Nevertheless, some of the themes in the Epic myths of Skanda may reflect motifs that appeared originally in Southern, or, at least, 'non-Āryan' form – for example, the malevolent goddesses, the train of fauna, the use of fruits and flowers in worship, and perhaps others.

Nor can we rule out altogether the possibility that in the post-Alexandrian period some Greek and Middle Eastern influences came into North India by way of the Northwest. The Kuṣāṇa dynasty, one of the early ones to pay obeisance to Skanda, was known to have nurtured Greek influences. Yet, substantive evidence to document such an influence is lacking.[40] Considering the possibilities, it nonetheless is probable that the most important single cultural factor in the development of the Skanda mythology in Epic India is the growing importance of kingship and the city-state.

In the Epic period, then, Skanda's role as warrior-king comes to the fore, replacing or surpassing for his devotees a similar role formerly played by Rudra and Indra. It is also evident that, at some point, Skanda the warrior is fused with the brāhmaṇic Skanda – the god associated with astral and sacrificial phenomena, reflected in the myth of his birth by Agni. The bringing together of the Agni and Rudra genealogies by the myth-makers is facilitated by several factors: the fact that Agni and Rudra are identified in earlier literature; motifs appropriate to each lend themselves to coalescence with the other; the practice of brahmāṇic myth-makers in universalizing a phenomenon by the familiar process of consciously integrating apparent polarities; and, the fact that *kṣatriya* and brāhmaṇic motifs seem to be mixed under the aegis of the kings of this period – for example, the use of brāhmaṇic myths and sacrifice to sacralize their kingly role. The merger of these two aspects of Skanda could also represent an attempt to bring together the symbolism of the temple and the palace, the two major foci of the city in the kingly era. Finally, it is possible, perhaps even likely, that the *ksatriyas* by the late Upaniṣadic period had come to influence philosophical and mythological development, a factor which would further help link Skanda the warrior with Skanda the philosopher.[41]

The religious implications of this mythological coalescence are several. As considerable space will be given later to interpreting motifs, the implications need only be summarized here. Skanda is a relative late comer to Indian mythology. His name is given to a god who represents a 'new' generation of deities, and also a new cultural epoch; yet motifs are ascribed to him which had long been present in the mythological heritage, thereby making the god part of the orthodox stream. Thus, Skanda is a son with two genealogies, embodying all the religious meaning attributed to sonship. In the genealogy of Rudra, he is primarily a warrior and inheritor of the virile skills needed to destroy the enemies of the *dharma*, whether that *dharma* represents the function of the gods and the cosmos, the king and the state, or the devotee and his world. He becomes a sovereign of the cosmos duly anointed in the tradition of Varuṇa.

Skanda's functions as a warrior-god are linked in this era of his eminence with the functions associated with the genealogy of Agni. The younger god has solar features. He is born of the fire and the sacrifice, and he is the fire and the sacrifice. As such, he is the *hiraṇyagarbha*, the microcosm of the universe. He presides over the stars and the ordering of time. He becomes identified with particular celestial bodies and is ascribed the characteristics often attributed to such bodies, particularly wisdom or omniscience and sovereignty. He is thought to be at the beginning of creation, to be the essence of creation, and, hence, to know the meaning of creation. Further, as a son of Śiva, Skanda seems to represent the coalescence of earlier genealogies; he inherits the characteristics of the high god and thereby becomes a high god in his own right. The myths of his birth explicitly depict how the power and role of Agni, the sacrifice; Rudra, the warrior; and Maheśvara, the cosmic ascetic are vested in Skanda – indeed, are revitalized and magnified in Skanda's very youthfulness and concreteness. In coming to concrete personalized form he presides as a 'high god' during this era, embodying for those who are his devotees much of the totality which the orthodox tradition calls divine.

3. The Southern coalescence

The fact that the Sanskritic mythology of Skanda reflected in the Epics was at least partly known in the South by the fourth and fifth century is attested by the Tamil literature written in that period. The god had by that time become a virtually pan-Indian god – in the North, as we have seen, as Skanda, inheritor of earlier Sanskritic motifs and a product of a kingly era; and in the South, as Murukaṉ, a fusion of Southern, early Tamil and Sanskritic motifs. We have noted that Sanskritic religious elements were brought into the South by migrant mendicants and that dynasties sympathetic to or patronizing Skanda also influenced the South. On the Northern fringes, the Śakas, Ikṣvākus and Cālukyas were apparently patrons of Skanda; the armies of such rulers as Gautamīputra Ursadhaja of Bhita, a devotee of Kārttikeya, had penetrated south of the Vindhyas; and dynasties in the South, like the early Pallavas and the Kadambas, combined Southern and Northern elements particularly with respect to the Skanda-Murukaṉ tradition. This indicates that at least by the fourth of fifth century there was undoubtedly a considerable Sanskritic and Northern influence in the South. The picture of Murukaṉ which had developed in the minds of Southern poets by that time can be reconstructed from references in the Paṟipāṭal, Tirumurukāṟṟupaṭai, and, to a limited degree, in the Cilappatikāram.

3.1 *Early evidences*

There are allusions even in the early *Caṅkam* poetry that indicate the poets were familiar with the presence of brāhmaṇs in the South and certain aspects of brāhmaṇic religion.[42] In the Puṟanāṉuṟu, for example, the Vedas are termed 'old work' (*mutunūl*) and are said to be of four kinds and to have issued from the mouth of the Ancient One (presumably Śiva) (Puṟa. 166:1–4). An early poet pays his respects to brāhmaṇs (*pārppār* – literally, seers)[43] who have read the Vedas (Aiṇkuru. 387). The hero of another stanza asks a seer (*pārppāṉ*) if any cure for a pair suffering because of their separation is mentioned in the Vedas (Kuṟun. 156). Brāhmaṇs and even parrots residing in the brāhmaṇ quarters recite the Vedas (Maturai. 654–656; Perumpāṉ 300–301). Reference is made in Patiṟṟuppattu 24 to the six duties of the brāhmaṉs – teaching, learning, sacrifice, helping others to perform sacrifices, giving charity, and taking presents (Subrahmaniam 1966:555, citing Tol. Porulatikāram 75:1). Sacrifices having Vedic roots performed by a Pāṇṭiyaṉ chieftain are described in Puṟa. 15:17–21. Those learned in the four Vedas attend the sacrifice performed by a Pāṇṭiyaṉ chieftain (Puṟa. 26:12–15). Another Pāṇṭiyaṉ chieftain patronizes scholarly seers (Puṟa. 221:6). Another 'king' gives presents to those priests who officiated in sacrifices (Patiṟṟu. 64:3–6). Cōḻa 'kings' refrain from doing things detested by brāhmaṇs (*pārppār*) (Puṟa. 43:13–15). Penance is done in the hills with matted hair (Naṟṟ. 141:3–5). The performance of sacrifice and ritual related to the brāhmaṇic community is mentioned rather frequently (Puṟa 2:22–24; 99:1; 122:3; Paṭṭiṉ. 200; Patiṟṟu 18–19; 21:5–7; 74:1–2; Aka 220:608; Perumpāṇ 315–16). Sacrifices performed by a Pāṇṭiyaṉ 'king' and several Cōḻa 'kings' are described in the Puṟanāṉuṟu (Puṟa. 15:17–21; 224:4–9; 367:12–14; 44:19).

The early Tamil literature also alludes to some of the gods of the orthodox mainstream, but they are seldom, if ever, mentioned by name. Brahmā's four faces and his origin in a lotus from the navel of Viṣṇu are apparently referred to in Perumpāṇ 402–404. Rudra's exploits are mentioned quite often in the later literature, but occasionally even in the earlier material. In the Puṟanāṉuṟu allusions are made to him with the crescent in his hair (91:5); whose throat is blue (56:2); with the third eye in his forehead (6:18). In later works, allusions to Rudra include a reference to him who wears the sacred thread (Kali. 38:1); on whose head falls the Gaṅges (Kali. 38:1); who destroyed the three cities with the help of Brahmā and Viṣṇu (Pari. 5:22); who holds the trident (Kaki. 103:15); who sits under the banyan tree (Tirumuru, 256); and who prevents the demon from lifting the mountain on which he and his consort are sitting and enjoying the scenery (Kali. 38:1–5).

It is possible that some of these references are later interpolations, but there is convincing evidence that a brāhmaṇ community was present in this early period and was beginning to add its heritage to the religious life of Tamil Nadu. A result of this interchange, evident by the fourth or fifth century, is an amalgamation of imageries in the person of Murukaṉ, reflecting the persistence of early Southern hill motifs and the addition of elements of brāhmaṉic mythology.

3.2 *Literary references to Murukaṉ in this period*

3.2.1 *The Paripāṭal*

In the Paripāṭal there is evidence of familiarity with the mythology of Skanda as it appears in the two Sanskrit Epics. Eight cantos are addressed to or about Murukaṉ; fewer are related to Tirumāl who by this time is equated with Viṣṇu. In the fifth canto, there appears an extensive description of Murukaṉ's birth to Rudra on the mountain similar to the Rāmāyaṇa account. A number of the god's youthful exploits mentioned in the Epics are mentioned in the work: he splits the *krauñca* mountain (5:9–10); he fights Indra and bends Indra's *vajra* (18:39); he destroys the Sūra (18:II–6; 19:95–105).[44] He leads his hosts into battle, mounted on an elephant (21:11–15 et al.). The fact that he has six heads is mentioned in these cantos, apparently for the first time in Tamil literature (5:9–10; 14:18–28). He is dressed as a warrior (21:11–15). The gods, led by Agni, Indra and Rudra come to pay homage to Murukaṉ and give him gifts (8:1–5 et al.). Interestingly, the gifts are of a different nature than those mentioned in the ninth book of the Mahābhārata, for each god gives a part of himself in the form of a vehicle or instrument that can be useful to Murukaṉ. Agni gives a portion of himself in the form of a vāraṇam;[45] Indra gives a peacock; Yama a ram; others give a tree, a sword, a lance, an axe, a garland, jewels, etc.

In a number of ways, the Paripāṭal shows a mingling of Tamil and Sanskritic motifs in the figure of Murukaṉ. Murukaṉ soars atop the peacock (18:22–29); his splendor is like the sun for his garments and garlands are red in color as is his weapon. He abides in the *kaṭampu* tree (19:95–105); the drum is used in his worship, but stringed instruments are also used (19:5–7). The Pāṇṭiyaṉ king and his entourage are said to have visited the mountain of the god on a pilgrimage (19:19–29). His mountain is encircled by the *cūr* damsels (*cūraramakaḷīr*) (apparently now a part of Murukaṉ's retinue), and its caves echo with the sound of thunder of the elephant and the cock (8:15–20). Yet Murukaṉ's mountain is like the pool in which he was born of a lotus (8:10–13). Moreover, Murukaṉ is said to have the freedom to love two girls (8:81). Indeed, he is married to both Devasenā, the daughter of the 1000 eyed Indra, and to Vaḷḷi, the hunter maiden (8:8–9). His relationship to Vaḷḷi is made explicitly analogous to that between the lovers in the hills idyllized in the early poetry (8:8–9).

Murukan̲'s universality is illustrated in other ways in the Paripāṭal. He is the nephew of Viṣṇu, for his 'mother' Umā is understood to be Viṣṇu's sister (19:57).[46] He is often referred to as the supreme, the excellent or the ancient one (e.g., 5:3–4; 14–19–32) who is renowned and exalted (5:9–13). He is the absolute who is charitable (14:28). He is to be worshipped and praised with awe and reverence (14:29–32; 19:104–105), for he dispels opposition and darkness (e.g., 21:66–70). To worship him is said to enable the worshipper and those around him to attain 'golden dawns' (*ēma vaikal*) (17:53). In another suggestive passage (19:1–7) Murukan̲ is said to live as much on earth as in heaven. He provides for the 'common man', as the poet expresses the belief that all may have the happiness that only sages had been able to attain. In fact, there is an implication in this passage that the Red God's dual habitation – earth and heaven – is represented in his two brides – Devasenā is a heavenly girl and Vaḷḷi an earthly girl. Murukan̲'s marriage to the latter tends to have made the god 'immanent'. There is also a growing sense of attachment to the deity in some passages of the Paripāṭal, a foretaste, as it were, of a bhaktic tradition to come later. Such a hint occurs in line 18:51, where the poet expresses the hope (as I translate it) 'Let us [god and worshipper] remain unseparated'. Again, in 8:81–85 the devotee expresses an affection for and attachment to Murukan̲, while in 21:66–70, there is an expression of desire to be 'joined with' the god.

3.2.2. *The Tirumurukār̲r̲upaṭai*

The suggestive references to Murukan̲ that appear in the Paripāṭal illustrate a new stage in the process by which Murukan̲ emerges as a high god in the South. The Tirumurukār̲r̲upaṭai illustrates this development equally well, if in a slightly different way. We shall note particularly those references which describe the more universal character of the worship of Murukan̲ in the South.[47]

Murukan̲'s splendor is like the sun at Mt. Meru (1–4).[48] His light is felt both by those who see internally and those who see only externally (4–8). The fragrant garlands on his chest are shaped like a chariot wheel (12). Lovely damsels, fragrantly perfumed, bedecked in colorful flowers, and sporting the cock banner dance on the hills in praise of the god. He is said to have slain with his red lance the *cūra* who took the form of a mango tree.[49]

The demoness dances wildly on the battlefield laid waste in Murukaṉ's triumph over his foes.[50] The deity is said to honor the desire of devotees who after performing good deeds in a previous birth, wish to attain freedom from consciousness of self (96–101). The city of Madurai, capital of the Pāṇṭiyas and a nearby hill on which stands a shrine to Murukaṉ are described (102–118).

In the second section the god is described in some detail, bedecked in jewelled splendor and mounted on an elephant. Each of his six faces is given a function – one face sheds light on the world's darkness; one looks upon and grants a boon to his devotees; another watches and guards the brāhmaṇ priests as they perform the appropriate ritual sacrifices; another enlightens the minds of sages; another destroys his foes and celebrates victory thus gained; the sixth face enjoys the consort Vaḷḷi. As each face has a function, so does each arm: one protects the *ṛṣis*; one rests on the waist; another plies the goad; another rests on his lap; two more whirl the disc and lance; another lies on his breast; another adorns the wreath on his breast; another with bangled wrist, signals the battle; another holds a bell; still another causes rains to fall; and the last rests on his heavenly consort.[51] Carrying a peacock banner to the accompaniment of drums, trumpets and conches, the god travels to Tiruccīralaivāy home of another shrine.[52]

The third canto describes the procession of gods and *ṛṣis* who come to do homage to the god. Murukaṉ is with his chaste wife Devasenā. The *ṛṣis*, clad in bark, eminent in wisdom and comprehension, freed of desire, and well-disciplined in their behavior, are part of the procession. The procession is led by the three great gods: the one who bears a garuḍa on his banner (Viṣṇu); the one who has a bull on his banner and Umā springing from his side, who burned the three cities of the asuras (Rudra); and the thousand-eyed one who achieved victory over his foes (Indra). They come to plead for Brahmā, whom Murukaṉ is said to have imprisoned.[53] The three gods are accompanied by bands of lesser gods, who shine like stars and move as swiftly as a storm, and whose voices sound like a clap of thunder. Wreathed musicians, playing on their *yāls*, are also in attendance.

The next brief canto describes the austerity of brāhmaṇs at another shrine. The brāhmaṇs perform their six duties, recite the sacred texts, tend the three sacred fires, perform appropriate rituals and sacrifices[54] and worship the god.

The next canto returns to the forested hills where intoxicated hunters of the jungle make merry in the *kuravai* dance. Dancing with them are the lovely damsels. The Red God (or the priest impersonating the god) dances with the girls, in a manner described in earlier Tamil literature.

In the final canto the ubiquitous character of the god is noted, for he appears at festivals, where his cock banner is unfurled, at woods and groves, rivers and lakes, crossroads and in the shade of *kaṭampu* trees. He is worshipped by rustic folk with red millet, flowers, ram flesh and blood, with ghee, white mustard, white rice, turmeric, sandal-paste, garlands, incense, and music. The reader is exhorted to offer praise to the god, who will honor that praise by granting salvation and making his presence beneficial to the worshipper. The poem ends with a vivid description of the verdant hills, with its waterfalls and its foliage – the bamboo, sandal, the akil, the palmyrah and fruit trees like the jack, plaintain and cocoanut. Also mentioned are the fauna – particularly, the elephant, monkey, bear, wild buffalo and peacock.

Included in this final canto is a benedection to Murukaṉ which succintly summarizes the kind of god he has become. The benediction, as translated by J. V. Chelliah, reads:

O Blessed one whose forms are six. Thou born
of women six, and taken up in the palms
Of one of the Five in meadow overgrown
With *kusa* grass on summits of Himalayas!
Thou offspring of the god that sits beneath
The banyan tree! Thou son of the daughter born
Of the king of mountains, where big bamboos grow!
Thou death to foes! Thou son of Kotravai[55]
Victorious over foes in battlefields!
Thou child of the Ancient One resplendent with
Bright ornaments! Thou captain of the hosts
of heaven equipped with the curved bow! Thou lord
Whose breast is decked with wreaths! Thou sage
Well-read in books;[56] Thou peerless hero brave!
Thou warrior bold to whom great victory comes
Without much strain! Thou wealth of Brahmin priests!
Thou object of exceeding praise of seers!
Thou husband of celestial dames! Thou best

Among the heroes great! Thou well-renowned
For the arm of thine that wields the spear! Thou lord
Of *kuṟiñci* hills that reach the skies that host
The undying fame of cleaving the mountain great!
Thou lion so brave, among the learned men
Much praised for words of wisdom! Muruka god!
Salvation's goal so hard to reach! O Lord
Beyond all praise that *moksha* grants to those
Who yearn for it! O Cey that grants thy grace
To those distressed, and golden jewels wear
Upon thy breast exposed to battles fierce
Achieving victory! Muruka well-esteemed
That doth protect those who desire thy gifts!
O god of mighty name adored by the great!
Thou that doth bear the name of Madavalli,
As thou didst kill the brood of giants huge!
O victor waxing strong in the battlefield!

(J. V. Chelliah 1962:357).[57]

3.2.3 *The Cilappatikāram*

The Cilappatikāram, that Tamil epic well-known even to casual Western readers also refers to the god Murukaṉ.[58] While these references add few new insights about the god, they do help illustrate his 'universality' in the South at the time and are worth recording. Near the outset, Kōvalaṉ, the hero and lover of the tale is likened to Murukaṉ, the god of youth and beauty (canto 1). Shortly thereafter, in a delightful analogy, Kōvalaṉ praises his wife, noting that the gods themselves gave up attributes to adorn her. The contribution of Murukaṉ, the beauteous, young, and six-faced god of war, are the fiery arrowheads which have become the red corners of her eyes and keep away the 'dark clouds of her hair' (canto 2).[59] In canto 5, there is a reference to the young girls doing a frenzied dance, as if possessed, like that which 'Krishna had performed with the cow girls' (Danielou 1964:19).[60] During the festival to Indra, described in the same canto, rituals are performed in the shrines of gods, including that of Murukaṉ, the beauteous youthful god. In canto 6, reference is made to the dance of Murukaṉ, which can be seen in Parhar, along with the dances of other gods. Murukan̲'s dance is a dance of triumph, wherein the god of youth uses the ocean as his stage, for it was in the ocean he finally killed the *sura*. At another point, Murukan̲ is mentioned as the source of wisdom whose words are used by monks to recite to gods and other monks (canto 11). Early in the morning the sounds of worship can be heard in Madurai from temples, including that of Murukan̲, 'whose banner bears a cock' (canto 14). Finally, in canto 24, in a part of the epic sometimes attributed to a later source, there is a small collection of folk songs sung by the *kur̲iñci* damsels, in praise of Murukan̲, including the one mentioned earlier in which the exorcist is mocked.

3.3 *Implications of this development*

T. P. Meenakshisundaram, referring to the title of the Tirumurukār̲r̲upaṭai, says something about what is happening in the Murukan̲ tradition during this era of Tamil history, even if he does read into the literature more than the poet intended:

> God is named Muruku by the poet. This reminds us of the earliest known popular deity of the Tamils, which a later generation has identified with Subramaṇya. Writing, as he does, in the Tamil country and in Tamil, this is but natural; but the implication of his description of God is indeed universal. The Ancient Dravidian God has been known as Murukan̲ in the masculine gender. Our poet, however, uses the abstract form of that word, Muruku – without the masculine suffix – reminding us there of the 'It' – The Absolute. This word Muruku means honey, beauty, fragrance, divine music, the magnetic touch of youth and eternity, all combining to denote the divinity underneath all these pleasures. This name as signifying the eternal feast, to the eye of the colour and form, to the ear of the music of harmony, to the nose of the charming aroma, and to the body, of the magic touch, is appropriate enough, when the poet tries to turn the attention of the worldly, hankering after pleasure, inward to the fundamental basis of all their varied goals – the Eternal Divine Bliss. The Bliss of Truth and Knowledge, arising from atonement or submission to His will, as opposed to the ephemeral and illusory self-

> delusions, in this world of ignorance, death and misery (Meenakshisundaram 1957:312).

It is unlikely that the poet himself was as explicit as Meenakshisundaram in discussing the nature of the absolute; nor does the spirit of this period encourage us to believe that the poet intended the philosophical or theological insight which devotees, looking back on his material from the vantage point of centuries, see in it. Nonetheless, there can be little doubt that the poetry of this period, particularly the Tirumurukāṟṟupaṭai, became a springboard for considerable theological speculation at a later date, when the poem was apparently rediscovered and editorially enhanced. Nor is there any doubt that Murukaṉ had become a 'universal' deity by this time, though in a limited sense. Murukaṉ became a 'universal' god in the sense that his worship could be found throughout the South, in cities as well as in rural hill places; and in the sense that people from various walks of life found religious meaning in the deity – the hill folks with their festive, almost sensual, worship, as well as intellectuals with their conception of how the god was linked mythologically to the orthodox tradition. The brāhmaṇ who saw in Murukaṉ the personification of the sacrifice by which he sought to recreate reality; the chieftain-warrior who saw in him the prototype of his own role; the *ṛṣi* whose meditation and austerity were embodied in the god, seen as the source of wisdom and integration – all found some meaning in the worship of the deity.

The god is also 'universal' in the sense that, by this time, he represents an amalgamation of many Southern and Northern motifs. One aspect of this fusion is particularly striking. The god Skanda in the Sanskritic tradition is entirely mythological – that is, he is believed to have lived and performed his exploits in the 'beginning of time' in the world of gods. It is a celestial world – the mountains are in a celestial realm, his birth is celestial; he is linked symbolically with the stars and the sun. As a celestial god he is understood to be a heavenly model, a mythical possibility, the re-enactment of whose work is a ritual. That re-enactment could take several forms: for example, the construction of a ritual fire and the performance of a sacrifice were a ritual bringing the god to birth again. This re-enactment was intended to bring about a new order, a new cosmos. The re-enactment could also be performed in the work of the king or chieftain, whose task was to save his state and protect it from encroachment. Because the chieftain had a divine prototype, whose example he could emulate, his work and the state he sought to preserve were given a sacral character. The immortality afforded by the god was equated with release, liberation, and entry into a celestial realm.

The early Southern Murukaṉ, on the other hand, is very much of the earth. He presides over the fertility and productivity of the forests and the land. His hills are replete with the color and fecundity of life. Worship of him seems to have been an affirmation of life – an extension of a joyous humanness, rather than an endeavor to enter a new order. It seems that he was believed to afford an eternal youthfulness, a freshness, a loss of care and anxiety basic to life itself.

The merging of these two traditions in the person of Murukaṉ makes his popularity comprehensible. The fusion is explicit in the hills associated with him, inasmuch as these are said to have both earthly and heavenly attributes. The hills reverberate with the sound of the elephant and the peacock; and are lush with the verdancy by which man is sustained. They are festive, red, vibrant – on the one hand; and, on the other, the mountain is the home of the gods, the center of the celestial world, the place of divine birth. This integration of motifs, perhaps still awkward and self-conscious in this period, characterizes the remaining history of the god in the South. In the medieval period, when there is a revival in the Murukaṉ tradition, the fusion has more subtlety, implicity, and sophistication.

It seems appropriate, as a result of this coalescence, to call Murukaṉ a 'high god' during this period. Certainly, together with Tirumāl (who integrates early pastoral roots with Vaiṣṇava motifs) Murukaṉ receives considerable attention from poets, kings, and general populace. The fact that Murukaṉ and Tirumāl assume a certain ascendancy in the period says something about the time period and the god. On the literate, 'state', level the god has assumed the character of a celestial warrior with many of the characteristics often attributed to Viṣṇu and other warrior gods. This god is nonetheless the god of the rural peoples who persist in their worship of him in a manner appropriate to them, though somewhat modified by the exigencies of urban, courtly life.

The catalyst in this process is presumably the city culture with its warrior chieftain who patronizes the arts and religious practices. In particular, it would appear to have been the Pāṇṭiyas and early Cōḻas, in contact with the Pallavas, the Kadambas and dynasties on the Northern fringes, harboring within their gates the stream of brāhmaṇic settlers, under whose aeges this development of religion and myth occurred. Nor need we be surprised at this development in the life of a god in South India, for we have seen a similar phenomenon in the Middle East. Marduk, the 'urban god' of Babylon, with the character of a virile warrior-creator, comes to ascendency in an era of military urbanity, wherein the king dominates city life and has a prototype in the god. Perhaps even more comparable is what happens to Dionysos when the agricultural god of the hills is adapted to the Olympic family and is given an urban respectability.

The Medieval Period

1. Period of transition

The centuries between the sixth and the tenth were centuries of relative silence as far as the Murukaṉ tradition in South India is concerned. In North India, after the Gupta period, we hear comparatively little of Skanda, save as he has persisted to this day in the form of Kārttikeya, son of the Kṛttikas. In the South, during the five or six centuries immediately following Murukaṉ's early prominence a great deal occurs but very little can be reconstructed of the development of the god in this period.

Toward the end of the late *Caṅkam* era, by the middle of the fifth century, there is a shift in the spirit and tenor of the South. There is an apparent ascendancy of Jainism and Buddhism which, though present in the South since the Aśokan era, now becomes more pervasive. It is in this era that the epics Cilappatikāram and Maṇimēkalai were probably written. Of this age Nilakanta Sastri has written:

> The joyous faith in good living that generally animates the poems of the Sangam age gradually gives place to the pessimistic outlook on life that is, in the last resort, traceable to the emphasis laid by Buddhism on the sorrows of life and its doctrine that the only way of escape was the repression of the will to live. This note of sadness, already noticeable in some poems towards the close of the Sangam age, becomes more pronounced in the setting of the *Maṇimēkalai* which contains a round denunciation of the fools who, not meditating upon the ruthlessness of death, spend their time in the blind enjoyment of carnal pleasures (Sastri 1966:144).

It is likely that this growing emphasis on the other world can be traced not to Buddhism alone, but to the influence of other 'Northern' traditions as well. Jainism's call to ascetism; a developing feudalism resulting from Southern chieftain-kings' attempts to assume the role of ordering society in a manner characteristic of *kṣatriyas* in the Epic tradition; the religious professionalism and austerity of the Brāhmaṇic community itself – all may have helped to create a cultural and literary world that expressed less and less of the joy and affirmation of life so explicit in the early Tamil poetry and attitude.[1]

Also contributing to change in the South is a century often called by Hindu commentators the dark period of Southern history. South Indian tradition has it that during the sixth century, an obscure and apparently semi-barbaric tribal people led by a dynasty of chieftains known as the Kalabhras swept across the South. Little is known about the Kalabhras, but Tamil historians generally refer to them as a ruthless cattle-robbing frontiers-people who upset much of the existing order. A Pāṇṭiyaṉ copper plate dated around the ninth century A.D. states that a political revolution had taken place during which several kings lost their thrones, religious endowments were abrogated, and much disorder and oppression occurred. Late literary tradition claims that one of the Kalabhras confined the Cōḻa, Cēṟa, and Pāṇṭiya kings. It seems that the rise of the Kalabhras, whether legendary or historical, represents a 'disruption of the political order and a suspension of state patronage for much of the religious heritage prominent prior to their advent (Sastri 1963:35–36; cf. Sathianathaier 1954:265–66).[2]

A cultural and religious renaissance began in the South after the start of the seventh century. Three dynasties rose to power and contended for dominance in the next three centuries: the Cālukyas, who rose to power in the Southern Deccan and established their capital at Bādāmi under Pulakeśin the First and the Second; the Pāṇṭiyas, whose king Kaṭuṅkōṉ defeated the Kalabhras at the start of the seventh century and who re-established their capital at Madurai; and the Pallavas, who under Simhaviṣṇu and his descendants re-developed a flourishing capital at Kancheepuram (Sastri 1963:146–49). Religiously, this era is characterized by a surge of Hinduism, particularly of Śaivism and Vaiṣṇavism, inspired in large measure by the bhakti poets who lyricized the possibility of personal salvation through a relationship to a personal deity.

The *bhakti* movement gathered momentum in South India in the second half of the seventh century. Yuan Chwang who visited South India in 640 noted with regret the decline of the Buddhist faith but remarked repeatedly that it had yielded to Digambara Jainism (p. 427). It was after this date, therefore, that the *bhakti* movement attained prominence. Poets from a variety of caste and occupational backgrounds wrote in sensual and human terms, different from yet reminiscent of the earthy language of earlier Tamil poetry. Their poetry and faith expressed militant disapproval of the Jain tradition and can be understood as a reaction to the anti-social, feudalistic, life-negating turn society and religion had taken in the centuries immediately preceding theirs. One of the results of the missionary fervor of these poets and the growing popularity of this devotion in the South was the conversion of both Paṇṭiyaṉ and Pallavan kings from Jainism to Śaivism in the second half of the seventh century.

Another religious occurrence of this transitional period is the development and extension of temples and iconography in hard stone. Mahendravarman I, Pallavan king from about 600–630 A.D., claims to be the first king of the South to use hard stone in the building of temples. His claim may be a valid one, though his contemporaries, the Cālukyas, like the Guptas further north had apparently been using hard stone (Srinivasan 1960:139). Nor are there any remnants of stone temples in the South that can be dated prior to late in the sixth century. K. R. Srinivasan believes there was a resistance to the use of stone in worship in the South because of stone's association with funerary characteristics during the megalithic era.[3]

Throughout this era, references to Skanda–Murukaṉ are fragmentary. It is clearly a time in which Śaiva and Vaiṣṇava motifs come to dominance. In virtually every appearance of the Skanda motif, in literature and iconography, the god is a son of Śiva and of relatively minor importance. The deity is mentioned in about forty stanzas of the Tevāram, a collection of the Śaiva Bhakti poets; in virtually every case he is the son of Śiva.[4] The iconographic representations of Skanda, particularly in Pallava sculpture, suggest a similar historical development. Skanda is most frequently depicted in the Somāskanda figure as an infant, situated between Śiva and Pārvatī.[5] There are several such representations in seventh century Pallava art: it appears on at least two panels of the shore temple at Mahabalipuram, the Pallava seaport, and on two middle panels of the rock cut cave known as the Maniṣamardin Maṇṭapa in the same town. These carvings are attributed to the reigns of Mahendravarman I (600–630 A.D.) and Narasimhavarman I (630–668) respectively. Somāskanda also appears in Kancheepuram, the Pallava capital, on a panel in the Kailāsanatha temple, built apparently during the reign of Narasiṁhavarman I, who was also known as Rajasimha (630–668).[6] Interestingly, on an addition to the temple, built several generations later, there appears a panelling depicting the family of Śiva, which includes two sons, with Ganeṣa by then a part of the family. In the same context there is a simple carving of Ganeṣa, complete with pot-belly and elephant head.[7]

Few other sculptures of Skanda have been identified as belonging to this period from the sixth through the ninth centuries. One such cutting is that at a hill-top shrine dedicated to Śiva in 773 A.D. at Tirupparaṅkuṉṟam, five miles from Madurai where Skanda is given one of three subsidiary cells along with Durgā and Ganesa (Sivaramamurti 1961:32).[8] No temples appear to be dedicated solely to Skanda until the Lāṭankōvil is erected at Āṉamalai in Madura District somewhere near the start of the ninth century. This temple, dedicated to Subrahmaṇya and Devasenā, has the cock and peacock inscribed in stone in its doorway (p. 35). C. Sivaramamurti thinks these Pāṇṭiyaṉ shrines are for the most part inspired by Pallava art and are contemporaneous with the Pallavans Rājasiṁha and Pallavamalla – that is, ascribable to late in the eighth century (p. 17).

One iconographic form of Skanda beginning to develop in this period is that of Skanda as philosopher or guru. A sculpting in a cave temple at Pillayarpatti has been described by C. Sivaramamurti, in which Subrahmaṇya (he concedes it could as well have been his father Śiva) is depicted as a guru (plate 28). At Kalugumalai, in Pāṇṭiyaṉ country, Skanda is depicted as a *guru-murti,* although bearing some militaristic insignia. He wears a military cross belt, one arm bears a *śakti*, and a bejewelled crown sits atop his head (p. 26). The implication is that Skanda's militaristic emblems are beginning to assume philosophical meaning. It should be noted, however, that even this portrayal is given a relatively insignificant place in the temple's art.[9]

In general, what appears to be happening during this period of transition when South Indian social and political life is unstable, is a surge toward Hinduization, in particular the establishment of Śiva and Viṣṇu as high gods in the South. Skanda, at least on the official level, is adapted into the family of Śiva and takes a subsidiary role to his father. It is significant that this process had not occurred by the fourth or fifth century in the South – there had been, particularly in the Paripāṭal, occasional allusions to Murukan–Skanda's generation of Rudra, but for the most part, that role of sonship was not dominant. Rather, the god had had an authenticity, a *sui generis* character of his own. But during the period roughly between the seventh and the ninth centuries the god, at least on the official, literate level, is given a subsidiary place as a member of Śiva's family. At the same time Gaṇeṣa emerges into official acceptance. Indeed, he appears to assume some of Skanda's attributes, particularly the role of chieftain of the divine army or attendants.[10] Skanda, now very much affiliated with the Śaiva tradition, has begun to assume the more specific role of teacher–philosopher, while his militaristic role has receded. The implications of this development will be made more explicit later in our discussion.

2. Proliferation and concretization

The middle of the tenth century marked the beginning of a resurgence of the Skanda–Murukaṉ tradition throughout the South. This development coincided temporally, if not causally, with the coming to power of the Cōḻas in the South and the establishment of an era of stability. This new stage in the history of the god represents his attainment of a new *sui generis* authenticity which embodies both much of his own history in modified form as well as the current Indian understanding of divine totality. This development is not necessarily unique to Skanda–Murukaṉ. A similar movement toward proliferation and concretization can be seen in the traditions of Gaṇeṣa and Durgā, the other son and consort of Śiva, respectively. Each member of the Śaiva family, in a sense, comes to represent the Śaiva whole and as such comes to be a 'total god' (or goddess); at the same time, each comes to represent specific aspects of its own history in various iconographic and mythological forms.[11]

2.1 *Iconography*

The Skanda–Murukaṉ tradition in the Medieval period is characterized by the elaboration of a complex iconography; frequent literary references in both Sanskrit and Tamil sources, including a vast proliferation of devotional literature; a growing collection of myths which are primarily modifications and embellishments of motifs present in the earlier period; increased conceptualization and esoteric explanations of historical motifs;

and a subtly continuing fusion of the various sources represented in the god's history, particularly the epic and early Tamil sources.

An illustration of Skanda's emergence into concreteness and prominence in the tenth century is the construction of *svayampradhāna* (standing alone) temples to the god. If the *Lāḷankōvil* at Āṉamalai was the first such shrine, built before the ninth century, it was followed by several others. An example of the *svayampradhāna* temple is the one built in the middle of the tenth century at Kaṇṇaṉūr in Pudukkottai (now part of Tiruchirapalli District). This temple is dedicated to Skanda in his aspect as Bālasubrahmaṇya in which his hand is shown in a *ciṉmudra* pose offering wisdom to his devotees (Srinivasan 1960:176).[12] The Kaṇṇaṉnūr Temple has four elephants on each of the four sides of the temple, and an elephant in front. [Interestingly, the elephant persisted as a representation of Skanda in Tamil Nadu, though it is not associated with the god in any other region. However, by the tenth or eleventh century, the elephant ceases to be seen as the god's mount (Srinivasan 1960:172). The elephant-mounted god (*gajavāhana*) and other representations of the god had often been depicted carrying the cock in the left hand and usually tucked on to the hip (Gopinath Rao 1916, II:435) a pose peculiar to northern sculpturing as, for example, in the Ikṣvāku and Cālukya areas (Srinivasan 1960:173). By the eleventh or twelfth century the peacock is the standard vehicle of Skanda in the South and the cock is almost always depicted on a banner, a form which again is peculiar to the South.]

The shrine to Subrahmaṇya, whether *svayampradhāna* or related to a Śiva Temple, could be built on any side of a town except the east and could face in any direction.[14] The temples could be built in capital cities, towns, villages, on the tops of mountains, on the banks of rivers, in gardens, forests or under large trees.[15] The temples of Subrahmaṇya were to be adorned with either peacocks or elephants placed in the corner of the *vimāṉam* (central tower),[16] just as the *garuḍa* (the sunbird) graces the temple of Viṣṇu and Nandi (the bull) adorns that of Śiva.

The iconographic elaboration of Skanda–Murukaṉ during and after the early Cōḻa era bears further witness to the diversification and concretization that have taken place by this time in the god's history. Appearing for the first time in iconographic form in the early Cōḻa era is the figure of Ṣaṇmukha – the six-faced god riding a peacock. One illustration of this representation can be seen in the Cōḻa addition to the Ihāmbaram Īśvaraṉ

Temple in Kancheepuram. The figure of the god in this representation is faithfully patterned after that of a virile and well-proportioned human torso in a manner consistent with Cōḻa art in general. The god has twelve hands, each bearing an appropriate symbol. These symbols vary with the particular sculpturing, but generally include the lance, the *vajra* (thunderbolt), the noose (*pāca*), the wheel, and, at least in Northern forms, the cock. (Gopinath Rao 1916, II:437). Importantly, the god is astride the peacock, by now his standard mount throughout the South.

Another common representation of the god in the South, as already noted, is the figure of Subrahmaṇya with all its variations. Subrahmaṇya could be depicted seated, usually on a lotus, and either with four arms – two in the common *varada* and *abhaya* poses, and the other two holding the *vajra* (or *śakti*) and, at least in the north, the cock – or with two arms – one in the *abhaya* pose and the other resting on the hip (*kaṭyavalaṃbita*) (pp. 434–35). If the god is standing, he may have two, four, six, eight or twelve arms, each bearing symbols, again varying by locale. Subrahmaṇya as a *gurumūrti* appeared in the South by the seventh century, and by the tenth and eleventh centuries was quite common. Particularly when the figure had two or four arms was it understood to be capable of bestowing *siddhi* (liberating insight) to the worshipper (p. 426).

Another of the god's iconographic forms which developed is the figure of Senāpati. Senāpati has six faces and twelve eyes. One of his arms is around the waist of his consort, Devasenā, who sits on his left thigh (p. 434). A Southern variation of this representation is at Tirupparaṅkuṉṟam, one of the six sacred sites of Murukaṉ in Tamil Nadu, where the mythical marriage of Murukaṉ to Devasenā is said to have taken place. Here the god is represented in an affectionate relationship with Devasenā, whose name, incidentally, becomes *Devayāṉai* (the celestial elephant) in Tamil. In other Southern iconography the god is seen with a consort, but more often it is with Vaḷḷi. One representation of this relationship shows the god being married to Vaḷḷi (Vaḷḷikaliyāṇasundarar) while Brahmā and Viṣṇu officiate. More frequent than either of these in the South is the representation in which the god is depicted with both goddesses, but touching neither, clutching the lance firmly.[17]

Kārttikeya, an especially common northern form of the god, was prescribed to have six faces and six arms or, according to the *Śrītatvanidhi*, an alternate manual on iconography, one face and ten arms. He is generally seen beside the peacock. Two of his hands are invariably in the *abhaya* and *varada* poses, and the others hold, among other things, the *śakti*[18] the *vajra*, the noose, and the wheel (pp. 436–37). Karttikeya is invariably a *brahmacārī*; indeed, in the north where his temples are still found, women are not permitted to enter his temple.

Among the other forms of the god appearing in the medieval period is Kumāra, the young philosopher who has four arms, two generally in the *varada* and *abhaya* poses, and two holding the *śakti* and the cock (p. 437). This is primarily a Northern form. Another form, Brahmaśāstā, already mentioned as having been identified by some scholars in Mahabalipuram carvings, is the aspect of Subrahmaṇya putting down the pride of Brahmā. The figure has one face and four arms. Two of the arms are in the *varada* and *abhaya* pose. The other two hold the *akṣamālā* (beads) and *kamaṇḍalu* (water pot), emblems usually associated with Brahmā. The fact that they are now held by Skanda suggests the younger god took over the functions of the 'humiliated' Brahmā (Raghavan 1939:110).[19]

Bālasāmi is the figure of Subrahmaṇya as a child. He may be depicted standing beside his parents as in the Somāskanda carvings, in which he is supposed to carry a lotus in each hand. When alone, the Bālasāmi has the left hand on the hip and a *padma* (lotus) in the right (Gopinath Rao 1916, II:443).

Subrahmaṇya may also be represented as a *brahmacārī*, the celibate, or as *deśaka*, the teacher of his father Śiva. As a *brahmacārī* he has a tuft of hair on his head, a sacred thread, a grass girdle, and two arms (*ibid*). Subrahmaṇya appears as a *brahmacārī* in the Pa<u>l</u>ani and Vadapa<u>l</u>ani (Madras) Temples, where his chief aspect is that of the celibate *Pa<u>l</u>ani Āṇṭavar* (Lord of Pa<u>l</u>ani). As the teacher of Śiva, Skanda could be depicted in a number of ways. He can be shown sitting on a peacock, with one face and six arms, with his father sitting as a disciple in front of him (*ibid*). Elsewhere, he can be depicted as a child seated on his father's shoulder, whispering the sacred syllable into his father's ear.[20] More rarely, he is seen seated on his father's knee with Śiva bending low (and thus humbling himself even further) to receive the sacred insight. A contemporary molding of this form can be seen at the Tirupporur Temple to Subrahmaṇya outside Madras.

A striking feature of all iconographic representations of Skanda–Muru-ka<u>n</u> is the persistent red color prescribed for the god's complexion. He is generally to be represented in the 'color of the rising sun',[21] and this is varied only slightly in different icons. For example, 'saffron' is the color for the Ṣaṇmukha and Subrahmaṇya representations and the 'red of the lotus flower' is prescribed for the Brahmaśāstā, Bālasāmi and other aspects.

2.2 *Literature*

Turning from medieval iconography, we find prolific references to Skanda–Murukaṉ in both the Sanskrit and Tamil literature of the period. This literature sheds light on the developing mythology of the god and in many cases renders intelligible the symbolism found in the iconography. We shall illustrate this literary proliferation by alluding to a few salient references found in the Purāṇas.

Purāṇic literature abounds with references to Skanda, but many cannot be dated later than the Epic period and differ very little from the Epic sources.[22] There is, however, an increasing degree of speculation about the meaning of Skanda's birth in the Purāṇic accounts. One example is the way in which Skanda's birth to Agni is explained. While Skanda is the son of Paśupati, to be sure, the learned know that Paśupati has Fire as his very self (*vahnyātmā*) (Linga Purāṇa II:13:7–8). Agni carried the semen of Rudra–Śiva for some 5000 years suffering the intense heat as a punishment given by Pārvatī to Agni for peeking while she was with her husband (Vāmana Purāṇa, chap. 57; Brahmā Purāṇa II:10:27). By Agni's swallowing the energy of Śiva, that energy entered the belly of all the gods, for Agni is the mouth of the gods. Being undigested, the energy exploded out in the form of a body of water (Mātsya Purāṇa Chap. 51, as cited by P. K. Agrawala 1966:140). Similarly, from the union of Śiva and Pārvatī, Skanda was born like fire from two churning sticks (*araṇi*) (Mātsya Purāṇa 154:52–53).

Elsewhere (Varāha Purāṇa 25:1–43), Viṣṇu is identified with Siva and is termed Puruṣa; Umā or Śrī is Avyakta. From their union *Ahamkāra* is born in the form of Kārttikeya. And in the Bhāgavata Purāṇa XI:4:17, Skanda is reckoned as an avatāra of Hari or Viṣṇu (P. K. Agrawaha 1966: 141).

The most extensive collection of the mythology of Skanda is found in the Skanda Purāṇa,[23] in which is recorded virtually all the mythology relating to the god. The most salient features of this mythology were translated into Tamil and the collection is known as the Kanta Purāṇa. In order to better understand the medieval development of Skanda–Murukaṉ, we shall look to certain mythic episodes recorded in the Kanta Purāṇa that reflect a modification of the earlier Epic accounts.

Sūrapadma, the *asura* who had obtained the boon of immortality from Śiva, and his two brothers, Siṅkamukaṉ and Tārakan, arrogantly mistreat the gods. At the *devas*' request, Śiva emanates a spark from each of his five faces and another from his inward face. The six sparks permeate the ethereal region, and are carried by Vāyu, the wind, Agni, the fire, and Gaṅga, the river, and deposited on a lotus flower in a pond surrounded by *śara* thickets on the mountain. The journey of the sparks is intended to symbolize divinity's pervasiveness of the five elements: ether, wind, fire, water and earth (Chengalvaraya Pillai 1954:3; Satchidanadan Pillai 1963:15). When a child is born from these sparks, the Kṛttikas want to nurse him. In order to please the Kṛttikas, the child splits into six forms; he becomes one child with six heads and twelve arms.

Several stories of Skanda's youth are narrated in the Kanta Purāṇa, and some are important because they explain the 'origin' of certain iconographic symbols and philosophical motifs. One such episode involves the *ṛṣi* Nāradás performing a sacrifice. From the sacrifice arises a fierce ram which seeks to destroy everything near and terrifies all. Murukaṉ has the ram brought before him and rides it playfully, thereby taming it and making the animal his vehicle.[24]

Another important episode finds the child Murukaṉ humbling Brahmā and teaching his own father the meaning of existence. In this account, Brahmā fails to pay obeisance to Murukaṉ, dismissing him as a child whose own strength is derived from Brahmā himself. Determined to teach Brahmā a lesson, the child asks him the meaning of the sacred syllable *ōm*. The great Brahmā can only stutter. Murukaṉ then imprisons the god and assumes Brahmā's role as creator. Śiva, coming to the child to plead for leniency for Brahmā, is asked if he knows the meaning of the syllable. Śiva asks to be taught its meaning, partially to humor his son but also hoping to be enlightened. Murukaṉ explains to his own father the meaning of existence. Thus Skanda is said to have been called *Takappaṉ Cāmi* (master or preceptor of the father) and *Cāmi nātar* (lord or guru of god). This episode is also said to be the reason that Skanda is called Brahmaśāstā (teacher of Brahmā). In Tamil tradition, this mythical event is said to have occurred at Swamimalai, near Kumbakonam in Tanjore District, one of the six sites sacred to Murukaṉ in Tamil Nadu.[25]

An elaborate account of Skanda's victory over the *asuras* is given in the Skanda Purāṇa. The generally accepted Southern account of the battle includes interesting variations. Three *asura* brothers opposed the young god and his army. First, Murukaṉ slayed with his lance *(vēl)* Tārakan and his associate Kirāvuñcan, in the region of the Himalayas. Then, coming South, Murukaṉ and his hosts finally camped at Tiruchendur on the southeastern coast of Tamil Nadu, considered another of the six sacred sites of Murukaṉ. Murukaṉ sent a messenger to the remaining two brothers, who did not yield. War ensued. Siṅkamūkaṉ (the lion-faced) was slain, and the immortal Sūrapadma, seeing the battle was going against him, turned himself into a mango tree in the middle of the ocean. Murukaṉ split the tree in two with his lance (*śakti*). The split portions appeared as the peacock and the cock. Murukaṉ tamed them both by his benevolence. He then mounted the peacock and rode on it around the world. The god adopted the cock as the emblem on his banner. Thus Sūrapadma was subdued and the afflicted *devas* were free.[26]

Another myth especially popular in Tamil Nadu even today and preserved *in extenso* in a southern recension of the Skanda Purāṇa is the tale of Murukaṉ's marriage to Vaḷḷi. Devasenā and Vaḷḷi are in a previous life the daughters of Viṣṇu himself. Both were destined to be the eventual brides of Murukaṉ. Devasenā was known as Amirtavaḷḷi; she was faithful in her practice of appropriate rituals and austerities and was rewarded by being adopted by Indra in her next life, and married to the heroic Skanda in the traditionally prescribed manner. Vaḷḷi, known as Sundaravaḷḷi, the younger sister of Amirtavaḷḷi, was more frivolous and fun-loving. Hence, her marriage to Murukaṉ came about more circuitously. In her rebirth she was found as a baby under a creeper by a hunter chieftain known as Nambarājan, purportedly at a place known as Vaḷḷimalai near Chittoor in Tamil country.[27] She was brought up by the hunter, and like all daughters of hunters spent most of her adolescent hours protecting the millet fields from birds. Told by a wandering fortune-teller that she would be married to Murukaṉ, she longed for him, determining to love no other. Meanwhile, Murukaṉ, somewhat settled with Devasenā at his hill retreat in Tiruttani – to this day one of the six sacred sites of Murukaṉ in Tamil Nadu – was informed of the beauty of Vaḷḷi, the daughter of the hunter chief. When he went to see her for himself, Murukaṉ was immediately struck by her innocent beauty and charm. He appeared before Vaḷḷi as a handsome young hunter and sought to win her through amorous advances. She resisted. Hearing the girl's father and brothers returning to the field, he became a *vēṅkai* tree, hoping thereby to remain near the girl without being detected. Noticing the tree, the men decided to cut it down, only to have Murukaṉ, at the next opportunity, become an old ascetic. As an ascetic, Murukaṉ received the hunter's permission to have Vaḷḷi remain with him as his handmaiden.[28] However, even as an ascetic, Murukaṉ could not resist making amorous suggestions to the girl. She became suspicious and remained at a distance. Then Murukaṉ remembered he had neglected to ask the aid of his brother Gaṇapati in this enterprise, and realized it was for that reason the obstacles had not been removed. At Murukaṉ's request, then, Gaṇapati appeared as an elephant and frightened Vaḷḷi nearly out of her wits. In desperate need of protection, Vaḷḷi ran to the old ascetic, embraced him, and at his insistence, agreed to marry him. Then Murukaṉ revealed his true self to her and married her clandestinely. When Vaḷḷi's family found the young lovers they insisted on an orthodox wedding. This was duly held in Nambirājan's hut. Murukaṉ took Vaḷḷi to Tiruttaṇi, and then to his abode on *Kanta Mātaṉam* (the celestial mountain of Skanda) where, with Vaḷḷi on his right side, and Devasenā on his left, he is believed to protect the universe.[29]

This charming myth has several implications which have become the basis of various philosophical discussions and interpretations. The myth suggests, for one thing, the wedding of southern and northern motifs, as Vaḷḷi, the hunter's daughter, product of a non-Āryan southern context, is fully accepted and adapted into the popular mythology. Similarly, the myth, as understood popularly, affirms the Tamil character of the god, who by now is fully accepted as part of the Tamil cultural stream. The love affair is consistent with early Tamil poetry's understanding of love, particularly amongst the *kuṟiñci* people. The hunting hero and hunting maiden court; the lovers in the courtship are appropriately symbolized by creeper and *vēṅkai* tree; the love relationship is characterized by separation, uncertainty, overt wooing, and, finally, clandestine union.

At the same time the two consorts of the god come to symbolize a variety of religious realities. On the one hand, the celestial and terrestrial character of Murukaṉ is affirmed, for, in a sense, Devasenā is the heavenly consort, and Vaḷḷi, the earthy, terrestrial consort, by whose wooing Murukaṉ is believed to express his immanence in earth and his mastery over it. The dual marriage may be intended to represent a fusion of Śaiva and Vaiṣṇava motifs, for in the courtship of Vaḷḷi, Murukaṉ typifies the god in quest of the soul in a manner consistent with that exemplified in Viṣṇu's wooing of the *gopis*. That is, the god pursues the soul and becomes attached to it.[30] In the case of Devasenā, the more traditional Śaiva understanding is embodied; the consort, like the soul, is generally more detached from the god – she has her own relative autonomy and, as it were, earns the love of the god by her own merit. Both consorts come to symbolize the soul *(pacu)* freed from the bonds of earthly passion *(pāca)* and clinging to the god *(pati)* in a manner consistent with Śaiva philosophy. But at the same time, each consort symbolizes the bringing together in the person of Murukaṉ aspects of Śaiva and Vaiṣṇava thought. Murukan is no longer the son of Śiva alone: he is the son-in-law of Viṣṇu.

At the same time, and somewhat paradoxically, the consorts may represent passions to which the god is no longer attached. The fact that the god has two consorts suggests he is really bound to neither. Iconographically, in Tamil Nadu, the god is seldom depicted as touching the consorts affectionately.[31] This is quite consistent with the Śaiva understanding of the soul's autonomy from the god and of the need for detachment from all passions to find total release. This is also why for the Śaiva there is little inconsistency between depicting Murukaṉ as the celibate *brahmacāri* and as the husband of two consorts. This interpretation of the role of the consorts is made explicit when it is said that Vaḷḷi represents volition *(icca śakti)*, Devasenā represents action *(kriyā śakti)*, but the lance which the god grasps in lieu of the consorts represents wisdom or discrimination *(jnâna śakti)*.[32] By appropriate use of intelligence and discrimination the god (and the true devotee) is believed to be able to control the passion and action resident in emotion and will. In that control is there freedom for the Śaivite.

2.3 *The development of philosophical speculation*

The medieval period in the South is characterized by a wedding of religion and philosophy that renders the two almost indistinguishable, at least on the orthodox level. Each of the individual deities is woven into a philosophical fabric in such a way that the deity comes to represent abstract divine totality and becomes the basis for speculation and conceptualization. Skanda–Murukaṉ is no exception to this pattern. Indeed, Skanda lends himself exceptionally well to this intellectualizing tendency.

2.4 *Murukaṉ as guru, ascetic and inspirer of literature*

We have already seen some of the forms this process has taken. The most obvious, perhaps, is the stress on Skanda's character as teacher–philosopher. This is not a new development for it was evident in the early Epic traditon in the North. But it is brought to sharper focus and proliferated in the South after the eighth and ninth centuries. Thus, we have the abundant iconography of Subrahmaṇya, the *gurumūrti,* and the increased significance of the mythology relating to Murukaṉ's teaching Brahmā and his own father the significance of the sacred syllable. Similarly, we see an increased emphasis on Kumāra as the child ascetic, the insightful *brahmacāri* who has conquered passion. The Subrahmaṇya enshrined as the god at Paḻani illustrates this development. The mythology at Paḻani narrates that the god as *Pàḻani Āṇṭavar* (Lord of Pàḻani) renounced the world when his father's fruit was given to his brother Gaṇapati. Angered, we are told, he became an ascetic, in full measure the fruit of his own father, the cosmic ascetic. In a similar way Skanda becomes the fruit of each *yogi* or ascetic, who, by renouncing the world, or performing appropriate sacrifices, or practicing *bhakti,* gives new birth to the god.

The role of Murukaṉ as the source of language, the inspirer of poets, and the root of Tamil literature and grammar is stressed at some point in the Medieval period. A few allusions from Tamil literature and mythology can illustrate this phenomenon. Murukaṉ was believed to have taught the Vedas to Agastya, the mythical culture hero said by *brāhmaṇs* to have brought civilization to the south from the north (*Kallaṭam* I, lines 47–49). At Tiruttani Murukaṉ is said to have taught Agastya Tamil and blessed him with Śivañāṉam (the wisdom of the Siddhāntin).[33] It was also at Tiruttani that Murukaṉ is supposed to have taught Nandi Devar the significance of the Śaiva Siddhānta philosophy (Chengalvaraya Pillai 1954:7). Murukaṉ is both the source and the fruit of the best Tamil literature. It was from Murukaṉ the Tamil grammarian Akatiyar is said to have received the essentials of Tamil grammar, and it is of Murukaṉ the greatest Tamil poets are said to sing (*Kallāṭam* I, lines 52–55). Elsewhere, Gnasasambandar, one of the foremost Tamil Śaiva *bhakti* poets, is said to have been an *avatār* of Murukaṉ (*ibid.*).[34] Another myth has it that as a dumb boy at Madurai, named Rudrasvarman, Murukaṉ spoke out to settle a controversy amongst the Caṇkam poets as to whose commentary on *Iṟayaṉar Ahapporuḷ* was the correct one (p. 6, summarizing a myth recorded in the Tiruvilayāṭal Puṟāṇam).

Myths developed which ascribe to Murukaṉ the inspiration of virtually every piece of devotional literature addressed to him in Tamil. Nakkiṟar, the alleged author of the Tirumurukāṟṟupatai, is said to have been saved from the clutches of a demon by Murukaṉ (p. 6, referring to the Tirup-paraṅkuṉṟam and Śrikalati Purāṇas). Another legend notes that Kumā-ragurupara Swamigal, the seventeenth century author of Kanta Kali Veṇpā, a highly philosophical hymn to Murukaṉ, was given speech by Murukaṉ. Despairing for their dumb child of five years, the poet's parents determined to drown him in the seashore at Tiruchendur, a sacred site of Murukaṉ. When the water was up to his neck, the boy of five began to sing the verses of the great hymn.[35]

The legend surrounding the life of the great Tamil poet and Murukaṉ devotee, Aruṇakirinātar, illustrates the pattern of Murukaṉ's inspiration still further. Born at Tiruvannamalai five hundred years ago, Aruṇakiri wasted his youth as a good-for-nothing drunkard, brawler and seducer of women. All despaired of him save his sister. Because of the rise of his violent temper, lack of control, and daring, his health and reputation were ruined. Finally, a menace to society, he determined to commit suicide and threw himself down from the top of the tower in Tiruvaṉṉāmalai Temple. Just then a holy man appeared unexpectedly at the bottom of the tower and caught the falling youth in his arms. The old ascetic was none other than Murukaṉ himself. The god then proceeded, with his radiant lance, to thrust out of Aruṇakiri's heart his threefold craving for earth, gold, and women. Then, with the point of his lance he touched Aruṇakiri's tongue and said *Nī pāṭu!* (Sing!). But Aruṇakiri was unable to sing. So Murukaṉ himself sang the first verse which became the basis of Aruṇakiri's poetry. From that moment, Aruṇakiri was a changed person. His physical features were rejuvenated and his tongue uttered beautiful and complex songs in praise of Murukaṉ, including the collection called Tiruppukaḻ, of which 1367 songs are still extant (Zvelebil 1965:156).

To be sure, the basic pattern of this legend is common in South India and is used in regard to virtually all Bhakti poets, whether they sing praises to Śiva, Viṣṇu, or Murukaṉ. Yet, in the context of the present discussion, it is striking to note how consistent the role of Murukaṉ as source and inspiration of Tamil poetry and poets is with that of his role as teacher–philosopher. These legends and myths serve to bestow a certain sanctity to the Tamil language, a sanctity which gives it a religious, almost ritual, authenticity for the south, equalled only by that ascribed to Sanskrit. Both languages are of the gods, we are told even today, the one for the 'north', the other for the 'south'.[36] Murukaṉ and Tamil are further bound in a relationship, which, already longstanding, becomes almost inextricable in the Medieval period.

2.5 *Murukaṉ as exponent of Śaiva Siddhānta*

Another way in which the philosophical tendencies of the Medieval period are reflected in the Skanda tradition is in the interpretation given at that time to the symbols long associated with the tradition. We have noted how symbols once given a literal militaristic interpretation had been 'spiritualized', becoming symbols of abstract philosophical realities. The lance, for example, came to be a common symbol of wisdom and the discrimination of enlightenment. The orthodox were interpreting mythological motifs in a manner consonant with the philosophical speculation of the era. In particular, Skanda–Murukaṉ became a window through which to view the whole system of Śaiva–Siddhānta. Before discussing the specific implications of this development, it is useful to review the historical basis for the surge of philosophical thought in the Medieval period.

A striking historical feature of Tamil Nadu by the start of the Cōḻa era (ninth and tenth centuries) is the existence of a strong *brāhmadeya* – community of *brāhmaṇs*.[37] The *brāhmadeya* was a nodal institution around which other institutions were clustered, comprised totally of *brāhmaṇs* of broad competence who maintained and purveyed a high level of civilization. The *brāhmadeyas* were powerful, landed institutions with considerable secular influence. Few temples were built outside the context of the *brāhmadeya*, and few warriors or 'kings' could come to power without coming to terms with the *brāhmaṇ* community.

This is to suggest that during the ninth and tenth centuries, and to a certain extent throughout the Cōḻa era, the *brāhmaṇs* rather than the warriors were the powers of the South and the major purveyors of civilization. To be sure, there were famed rulers, Cōlaṉ and Pāṇṭiyaṉ, whose military exploits were extensive and whose wealth and patronage were considerable. Nor is there any shortage of inscriptions which extol the virtue of the chieftains. Especially interesting are inscriptions describing the sacral function of the chieftain as inheritor of the power and functions of the gods, patron and purveyor of the arts, protector of the world, etc. (cf. Dikshitar 1952).[38] However, there is reason to believe that the Southern chieftains, in general, did not attain the cultural finesse, power, or stability which the *kṣatriyas* had attained in the north. For one thing, the Southern kings' social and cultural roots were less constant. According to N. Subrahmaniam and K. K. Pillay, most of the Southern kings even in the time of the *Caṅkam* period were not *kṣatriyas*, but *sudras* (Subrahmaniam 1968:256; Pillay 1965:167). Nor was there a persistent lineage in Southern kingship.[39] It is difficult to resist the inference that the *brāhmaṇ* community of that period may have been the 'kingmakers', legitimating the *de facto* power holders as long as the latter were 'in power'. It is this *brāhmaṇ* community that appears to have been responsible for much of the cultural development and philosophical speculation that occurred throughout much of the early Medieval period.[40]

It appears that philosophical speculation develops around the figure of Skanda before and during the early Cōḻa period. This process seems to be rooted primarily in the Sanskritic tradition and, in a sense, that it occurs in the South is only incidental. Yet, it may be precisely because the orthodox tradition is in the process of coming to grips with diverse cultural elements that it proves to be creative, for this had been the case earlier in the history of the orthodox mainstream. Further, the *brāhmaṇ* community, though largely informed by the post-Vedic literary tradition, may have, by the Cōḻa period, already incorporated Tamil motifs and persons into its ranks. Throughout this period there continued a steady stream of Tamil literature which was not necessarily a product of the *brāhmadeya* but may have been produced in the *ūr* (village), the community which served as a focus of Tamil culture in the Cōḻa era. Despite these qualifications, it appears that, in general, what is happening in the period from the ninth to the thirteenth centuries reflects the continuation and intensification of the Sanskritization of Skanda in Tamil Nadu.[41] This process of Sanskritization is illustrated in the changes made in place names. The Tevāram, in the eighth century, refers to a number of places with Tamil names. Later literature refers to the same places with Sanskrit names. Thus Maṟaikāṭu becomes Vetaranyam, Veṅkaṭu becomes Śvetāvanam, and Paramalai becomes Vṛiddhāchalam (A. S. Gnanasambandan in conversation).

Whatever the impetus for the development of philosophy in the South, it is evident that from the eighth century on Tamil Nadu became the arena for philosophical speculation and controversy. Kumārila, for example, who frequently attacked Buddhist thought in his works, developed a systematic philosophy of ritualism, which came to be known as Mīmāṃsā. Śaṅkara, with intellectual ties to the Upaniṣads and Mahayana Buddhism, developed a monistic system which served to reenforce the philosophical basis of the Hindu tradition rooted in the Upaniṣads. In the eleventh century, Ramānuja, following in the Śrīvaiṣṇava mainstream, posited a philosophy of Viśiṣtadvaita which served to reconcile the bhaktic devotion of a soul to a personal god with the Vedantic tradition by asserting that 'the soul, though of the same substance as god and emitted from him rather than created, can obtain bliss not in absorption but in existence near him' (cited by Sastri 1963:430).

Of particular interest to our discussion is the fact that the Cōḻa era which witnessed the flowering of Śaivism in the South also witnessed the emergence of the carefully-reasoned school of Śaiva Siddhānta. The literature of the Śaiva system is abundant. There were available by this time the ritual 'handbooks' of Śaivism – the twenty-eight *Sivāgamas* – whose relation to the Vedas are described by Tirumūlar in the Tirumantiram:

> The Vedas and the Agamas are true revelations from the same Supreme Lord. Understand that the Vedas are general and meant for men of all grades of spiritual evolution, whereas the Sivagamas are special and were meant only for the advanced souls. Those who read these words of the Lord say that the conclusions reached by each one differ. But to the great ones the conclusions are the same.[42]

Śaivites saw the Sivāgamas with their three divisions of Tantra, Mantra, and Upadeśa as the fulfillment of the Vedas and Śaiva Siddhānta as the fullest flowering of Vedic religion. Kumārakurupara, the seventeenth century founder of the Śaiva *maṭam* at Kāśī and author of *Kanta Kali Veṇpā*, likened the Veda to a tree growing up from the field of *Praṇava*. He speaks of the followers of various schools of Vedic religion as being satisfied with the leaves, tendrils, buds, flowers, or fruits of the tree, but describes Śaiva Siddhāntins as having tasted the honeyed nectar or juice of the fully ripe fruit at the topmost region of the tree (Paṇṭāva Mummanikkōvai 575:23–35).

Quite apart from the Śivāgamas is the devotional literature of Śaivism especially the twelve Tirumurais or collections of the *bhakta* saints and the Tiruttoṇṭar Purāṇa, popularly known as the Periya Purāṇam of Sekkilar all written in Tamil. These works, incorporating (and in the case of the Periya Purāna, describing) the hymns and devotional experience of the *bhaktas* between the eighth and eleventh centuries, begin to reflect philosophical implications more explicitly spelled out in later treatises. The nature of the divine, the soul, sainthood, and human bondage – all find their way into these *bhaktic* hymns.

The philosophical assumptions of Śaiva Siddhānta are sumarized, for the most part, in the fourteen Śiddhanta Śāṣtras, written in Tamil. Of these, two are particularly lucid as expositions of the system. The Śivañāṉa Pōtam by Meykaṇta Teva is by far the most concise of these, condensing an entire system into twelve sutras. The first six sutras, which make up the 'general' part of the treatise, deal with proofs of the existence and nature of *pati* (god), *pāca* (wordly bonds) and *pacu* (soul). The next six sutras, comprising the 'special' part of the treatise, deal with the *sādhanas* (methods and practices) for realization and the benefits of such realization. This part includes such topics as the special characteristics of the soul, the appearance of God as a *guru* before the ripened soul, the methods of obtaining purification of the soul *(ātma siddhi)*, the removal of *pāca,* the realization of *pati,* and the state of *jivan mukti* (S. Satchidanandan Pillai 1952:9). Of this concise treatise, J. H. Piet has remarked: 'This book contains forty lines of Tamil poetry, and is without doubt one of the most closely reasoned religious philosophies found anywhere in the world' (1952:11).

The second important philosophical treatise is the Śivañāṉa Siddhiyar, attributed to Arulnaṇṭi Śivacarya, a disciple of Meykaṇta Teva. This lengthy treatise is intended, in part, to be a commentary on the Śivañāṉam Pōtam and to present the Śaiva Siddhānta philosophy in contradistinction to rival philosophies. The first part of this work, known as Para Pakṣa, states and refutes the philosophies of the Lokāyatās (materialists), the

Buddhists, the Jains, the Purva Mīmāṁsākas, the Māyāvidins, the Nirīśvara Samkhyas, and two other Vedic schools, making a total of fourteen systems. The second part, the Supakṣa, sets out the Śaiva Siddhānta philosophy in considerable detail. The author follows the general outline his master had followed, but also attempts to anticipate and refute the arguments of rival schools in expounding his system (S. Satchidanandan Pillai 1952:8).

These two basic expositions were complemented by many others. Umapati Śivacarya's Śivaprakāśam, following on the heels of the Śiva-ñāṉam Pōtam and Śivañāṉa Siddhiyar, is an important one and was followed by numerous commentaries on these works.[43] While the Sivāgamas were of predominantly Brāhmaṇic authorship, and the devotional literature had a broad spectrum of authors with diverse social and caste backgrounds, Śaiva Siddhānta's philosophical works, although in Tamil and of non-Brāhmaṇic authorship, succeeded in combining Brāhmaṇic or 'Sanskritic' with non-Brāhmanic and Tamil elements in its spirit and character. While the Śaiva Siddhānta system is in many respects distinct from many of the brāhmaṇic traditions and is consistent in many ways with its heritage in Tamil literature, it owes much to the impetus afforded by the process of Sanskritization and the concerns addressed by other philosophical systems.

The basic position of Śaiva Siddhānta is that there are three co-eternal realities: *pati* (god); *pacu* (soul) and *pāca* (the worldly bonds.) *Pati* is the supreme who permeates, dominates and controls the *pacu* and the *pāca*. In its transcendental aspect, *pati* is neither *rūpī* (formed) nor *arūpī* (formless), neither *cit* (sentient) nor *acit* (insentient). 'He does not create or sustain or perform other functions. He is neither a *yogi*, nor a *bhogi*. Though he dwells in everything and pervades all, he remains unaffected by them and retains his own nature (S. Satchidanandan Pillai 1952:13, translating Sivañāṉa Siddhiyar I:90). Elsewhere we read:

> It (*pati*) has no finite attribute or mark. It remains ever free from *mala* (impurity). It is one and eternal. It awakens consciousness in countless souls. It is motionless and indivisible into parts. It has *ānanta* (bliss) for its form. It remains beyond the reach of the perverted, and is the goal of the devout. It is the smallest of the small, and the biggest of the big. Men of spiritual realization call it *śivam* (p. 14, translating Śivaprakāśam 14).

Hence, Śivam the abstract is not one of the 'trinity' – rather, it is thought to be One above them. The gods are but functions of *Śivam.* But the Supreme Being also has an immanent side. In its relationship to souls and the world, it is known as Śivaṉ or *Pati.* He takes suitable forms – *arūpa* (these generally include the formless aspects of Śiva, Śakti, Nāṭa, or Vinḍu) *rūpa* (these include the forms of Maheśvara, Rudra, Viṣṇu, and Brahmā); and *rūpa-arūpa* (that which is both with and without form and is usually symbolized by the lingam). The Supreme's *śakti* is that which furnishes him with forms; *śakti* is the Supreme's attributes which are generally fivefold – *para-śakti* (pure wisdom); *ati-śakti* (the Supreme's energy directed toward the soul); *icca śakti* (the Supreme's desire to help the soul); *ñāṉa-śakti* (the Supreme's recognition of the fruits of the soul's *karma*); and *kriyā śakti* (the Supreme's will to provide the soul with means to enjoy the fruit of its *karma*). These five aspects of the Supreme's *śakti* are usually represented by the divine consort in various forms.[44]

The Supreme, in its relation to souls, has five functions or activities. *Sṛṣṭi* (creation) involves making the bodies, organs, and environments necessary for each soul and making the bonds of *pāca* capable of dissolution. *Sthiti* (preservation) protects created things. *Samāhara* (destruction) enables souls to be rid of bodies and worlds. *Tirobhāva* (concealment) hides the Supreme from the soul until the soul is ready to envision the Supreme. *Anugraha* (revelation) bestows bliss on the soul who has qualified to feel as one with the Supreme.

The *pacu* (soul) is formless and all-pervasive. It assumes the nature of the thing with which it is associated. It never stands alone, but is associated with either the world or the Divine; as such, it assumes something of the character of that with which it is associated. Of the soul we read:

> . . . Souls are countless, eternal, and sunk in spiritual darkness. By the grace of God, they take up bodies suited to work out their two-fold good and evil karmic tendencies, and are born as lower and higher beings. In the course of experiencing the endless fruits of their karma, they commit acts of merit and sin, and have births and deaths. When the season arrives for the dissolution of the dark bond affecting the soul, the light of grace in the inmost soul dawns, and darkness is dispelled. Then the good freed souls reach the Feet of Providence.[45]

Pati and *pacu* are of one category, in that both are intelligent beings, having emotion (*icca*), intellect (*jnāna*), and will (*kriyā*). But God and soul differ in that: (1) the soul is tainted by *pāca*, while God remains untainted;

(2) the soul changes, moving from association with *pāca* to association with the Divine, whereas the Divine never changes; (3) God is ever all-knowing, but the soul can know only with the help of the Divine (S. Satchidanandan Pillai 1952:21).

Thus, *pati* is one with the *pacu*, yet different from it. By his five-fold activity, *pati* guides many souls in consonance with each one's *karma* and his own will. He is in inseparable relation with them, but remains unaffected by their nature and actions. *Pati*'s relationship to the soul is dual but like that of two things which are inseparably connected: music and tune, fire and iron, water and salt, air and space, life and body, sun and crystal, sunlight and lamplight, sunlight and eyesight (p. 26, citing Sivañāṉa Muṉivar's *Dravida Mahā-Bhasya*).

Pāca is the term denoting the bonds of existence, which are three in number, and known as *mala*. *Āṇava mala* (ego-consciousness) is the most persistent and most natural of them. Its character is to conceal reality and truth from the soul. *Āṇava* tends to make the soul take the senses and passions too seriously, including lust, sorrow, covetousness, suffering from material needs, likes and dislikes, pride and satisfaction in oneself. The second *mala* is *māyā;* the primordial matter which clings to souls in the form of various bodies and environments. *Māyā* is like the husk which covers the grain – purity results when it is removed. *Māyā* takes many forms; in its grossest stage, called *Prakṛti māyā*, it is comprised of twenty-four *tattvas* (realities, or evolutes). These *tattvas* include the five elements, the sense organs, the sensations, the mental instruments and the three *guṇas* (*sattva* – truth or reality; *rajas* – passion or attachment; and *tamas* – inertia, torpor). The third *mala* is *karma*, the factor of causation which takes souls through experiences of pain and pleasure, birth and death. It induces the soul to act in ways which are not always beneficial to it. Like the other *malas*, it is co-existent with *pati* and *pacu* (S. Satchidandan Pillai 1952:22–25; cf. Devasenapati 1963:28–38).

Souls may be rid of the *malas* progressively. If they possess all three *malas*, they are known as *sakālars*. If they are bound by only two *malas*, *āṇava* and *karma*, they are in a second stage, and are known as *pralayakālars*. A still higher stage is that of the *viñāṉakālar*, tainted only by *āṇava*. Salvation is to be rid of all *pāca* and to attain blissful relationship with the *pati*.

This is an all – too-skecthy summary of the basic tenets of Śaiva Siddhānta, but it is enough to suggest the philosophical context by which Śaiva deities were interpreted by the twelfth century. In this period, Subrahmaṇya–Murukan̲ becomes a particularly apt embodiment of the Śaiva philosophy. He is the divine totality, transcendent yet fulfilling the five immanental functions of the divine. He is all that Śiva is. Indeed, he is an even more complete expression of the divine, for he is the five plus one. He is the guru who teaches the sacred insight of Siddhānta to the devotee who is ready. He prepares the soul for liberation; he destroys the bonds of *pāca*. He is, in short, all that *pati* is intended to be.

Subrahmaṇya's role as exponent of Śaiva Siddhānta is illustrated perfectly in the seventeenth century poem Kanta Kali Ven̲pā, addressed to Murukan̲, by Kumārakurupara Cuvāmikal, founder of the Śaiva *maṭam* at Kāśī, and the poet of whom legend says Murukan̲ opened his mouth when he was but a dumb child of five. I quote here at some length only the most relevant parts of the poem, as it has been translated prosaically from the Tamil by M. Arunasalam. Particularly striking is the interchangeability of motifs associated with Śiva and Skanda:

> My Lord!
>
> You are the Supreme Knowledge that is beyond the comprehension of Brahmā, the Creator dwelling in the red lotus and of the Vedic hymns, ancient and divine. You are incomprehensible even to the principle *Nadā*, the *Nādanta Yoga* and the faultless human knowledge.
>
> You are without a beginning, middle or end. Your nature is Sat-Citānanta, Omnipresence, Infinite Bliss and Omniscience. You are the Supreme Light that is free from all bondage. You transcend all name, attribute and form. You are the all-pervading *Pārama–Śiva*.
>
> You are beyond the reach of all knowledge. You transcend even the five functions You perform. Your form is beyond the comprehension of the mind and other seats of thought. Through Your own grace, You assume the five forms.[46] Supremely blissful, You are the Matchless Being, the Refuge for all beings. You are the Complete Whole. You are Eternal. You are immanent in all things and so require no going or returning or union. Being the Cause of all things, You have no cause; You are the goal of all.
>
> The magician enchants every one in the world by the spell of his magic, but himself is not entangled in it. So also, though You are the

source of all things, You have no source. You have no form except through the manifestation of Your own grace.

With the three-fold Śakti of volition, knowledge and action. You perform the three functions of involution, enjoyment and evolution. You are One. But You manifest Yourself in Form, Formlessness and Formless-Form. You appear in many shapes as occasion demands.

Souls are of three categories, according as they are engrossed in three, two or one impurity. In order to liberate the countless souls that are entangled in the three bonds, You confer on them the gracious look, so that these impurities are fit for removal. You bind them firmly with the three *māyās*, the pure, the impure and the prakṛti *māyā*, so that they may assume bodies. You unite them with the six *adhvas* both physical and cosmic and cause them to undergo the four classes of births and the seven kinds of existence and assume the eighty-four hundred thousand categories of forms.[47]

When they are born in this manner, you obscure their intellect; they whirl round in the various births, like the kite and the cart-wheel, according to their own ineradicable *karma*. You grant them all experience including that of the terrible hell and paradise. In due course, as they become fit and as the time for their liberation approaches, you initiate them into the dialectics of the various religions and cause them to study their ancient scriptures and feel that the respective gospels are the true gospels.

Ultimately, You guide them to the path of Śaivism and its means to salvation such as *carya, kriyā* and *yoga*.[48] These means are the essence of all penances and other religious observances. When they have pursued these means, You confer on them the corresponding three states of partial liberation, viz., coexistence with You in the same world, nearness to You and similarity of form to You, but restrain them from getting totally immersed in those states.

You watch them tossing about in misery for long, until they attain the state of perfect equanimity with regard to good and evil and their imperfection or ignorance is fit to be dispelled. This stage is the ripe time for bestowing Your grace on those souls.[49]

Thereupon, You appear before them. You are the Supreme Knowledge but they do not perceive You in that state. Therefore, You assume a form through Your own grace and appear before them bodily in the name and guise of the Supreme Teacher. You annul their accumulated *karma* by Your gracious look,[50] reduce to nought the instruments[51] attached to the body, its seven stays and six *adhvas* and tear asunder the film of ignorance that envelopes the soul.

Then you bestow on the souls the true vision, so rare to realize. By this gracious knowledge, You cause them to perceive the real nature of the Ultimate Reality, of all the worlds and of themselves, the souls. You unfold to them Your all-pervasive nature, the state of supreme everlasting bliss and confer on them perfect happiness that knows no abatement or increase, no remembrance or forgetting, no light or darkness.

To the souls of the next class, viz., those that are developed in the two impurities of *āṇava* and *karma*, You vouchsafe a vision of Your celebrated divine Form. You appear before them riding on Your big Bull. There are three lotus-like eyes on Your countenance. Your matted locks are flowing behind. Your hands are holding aloft a battle axe and a deer. Umadevi occupies the left half of Your form. Her slender figure and Your crimson hue appear as though a coral hill with a streak of lightning appeared on the silver hill of Kailas. You present this Divine vision to those souls and sever their bond of *karma*.

To the third class of souls who are enveloped in only one impurity, You grant inward joy, remove the three states of *kevala*, *sakala* and *sudhā avasthas*, place them in the company of liberated souls and confer on them final liberation.

Where 'I' and 'mine' have ceased to exist, there are Your Feet planted. The supreme bliss of silence is Your crown. Knowledge is Your sacred form. Volition, action and wisdom are Your three eyes. Grace is Your lotus-like hand. The wide world is Your temple.

My Lord! You are the Matchless Light that reveals Itself in this manner. You are in all beings, in an inseparable condition.

Your radiant golden crown, bedecked with jewels, is made up of the nine resplendent gems of lightning-like lustre. The beautiful marks on Your six foreheads, smeared with the sacred ash[52] appear like six crescent moons set in line. The twelve benevolent eyes on Your countenance look like lotus flowers in full bloom. The fish shaped rings adorning Your ears are resplendent like many suns shining together. Your lips, red like the crimson lilies in bloom, have a radiant smile lingering in them. Your pleasant words dispel all desire in the souls for births and enjoyment.

One of Your six countenances saw the slaying of cruel Surapadma, celebrated among the *asuras* armed with bows and arrows and the annihilation of foes. Another countenance expounds the ancient Vedas and the Āgamas to the devotees. The next one, resplendent like several suns shining together and soft like a fragrant flower, liberates the souls from their inseparable bonds. The fifth countenance, of moon-like beauty, makes love to Vaḷḷidevi and the celestial nymph, Devayāṇai. The last countenance, divine and lotus-like, grants all boons to those that fall at Your feet with sincere devotion.

Your arms are twelve in number, large like twelve hillocks. They are adorned with the fresh blooms of the fragrant *kaṭampu* and the sweet *kura*. One arm distributes nectar to the celestial beings. A second embraces celestial nymphs. Another showers rains over the world ceaselessly. A fourth arm is wearing floral wreaths in close array. One is on the chest, one on the left waist and another on the thigh. One arm is adorned with the armlet, another holds the *rudrākṣa* beads[53] and yet another holds the goad for directing the elephants in battle. The last two arms are brandishing the thundering shield and the shining sword.

Your broad chest, decked with gems and golden jewels, lovingly embraces Your consorts, of slender figure and red lips. The golden sacred thread, *rudrākṣa* beads, soft silken clothes, a waist cord and a belt round the waist adorn Your body. Many types of the anklet, such as the *Kalal*, symbolic of the *Nāda* principle, the smiling golden *kiṇkiṇi* and the *paripūram* tinkle on Your Feet. Your Divine appearance is dazzling like a million suns shining together.

My Lord!

You are the soul's soul of those that realize You in themselves. You are the Divine Light that shines in the lotus hearts of devotees. You are the Radiant Light that is immanent in the esoteric light of the mystic symbol, *Ōm*. You are the Universal Form that is inseparable from the fivefold functions of evolution, preservation, dissolution, obscuration and liberation.

Your Form is comprised of the six *adhvas*. The irresistible mantra is the blood flowing in the veins. The celebrated *pada adhva* is the

> beautiful crown. The binding *varṇa adhva* is the skin. The *bhuvana adhva* is the hair on the body. The *tattva adhva* is the seven constituent elements of the body. Lastly, the *kalā adhva* forms the various limbs.
>
> The million of worlds all constitute Your form. All the beings therein, animate and inanimate, are Your limbs. The three Śaktis, volition, knowledge and action, are the inner seats of thought. While wisdom is thus imparted to the soul, You cause the five unique functions to be performed. You are the five elements, the sun and the moon and the soul. You are the real penance of the eightfold yoga that confers true wisdom.
>
> Gifted poets sing the glory of the tenfold insignia of Your royalty.[54] Your hill is that mountain of bliss which dwells in the hearts of those that are filled with unceasing devotion. Your river is the joyous and elegant everflowing flood of supreme bliss. Your land is that which confers great happiness on righteous souls. Your city is that beautiful city of infinite joy, transcending all earthly joys. Your steed is that which has no beginning or end in this ancient world, which is all pervasive and which teaches the mystic five letters and operates them. Your elephant is the *Śivañāṉa* that burns out the five impurities in those that are happy in their devotion to You. Your fragrant floral wreath is that garland wherein the fresh blossoms of perfect divine wisdom are strung together by means of true devotion. Your noble banner is that which graciously carries out the five functions, the sign of the Bull. The fresh principle of *Nāda* is Your gemmed drum. Your authority is that which is ever immanent in all things and which causes the universe to function, just as the reflected image in a mirror moves according to the will of the mover.

There follows a recitation of some of the most important elements in the mythology of Skanda and the poet praises the god's exploits. The poem concludes with a plea for release quite typical of medieval *bhakti* poetry:

> Spare me the dreadful numberless births. Save me from untimely deaths. Remove the many obstacles that come in the way of work. Protect me from the many ailments that may afflict me. Save me from the many sins and black magic, from ghosts and fierce monsters, from

the danger of fire, water and the enemy's arms, from terrible poison and from serpents and wild animals.

Whenever I am confronted with these dangers, vouchsafe unto me a vision of Your Divine Person so that all of them cease. Wherever I turn, let me behold You, riding Your green peacock, with Your twelve strong arms, the sharp spear that dispels all fear and the belt round Your waist, Your handsome little feet and fair hands, Your twelve benevolent eyes, six handsome faces and the radiant crown on Your six heads.

Let me behold this vision of You. Grant me all boons. Be You enshrined in my heart to my great rejoicing. Grant me the skill to sing the four types of poems. Grant me the skill to attend to eight things simultaneously. Make me well versed in the classics and in five branches of Tamil poetics. Inspire me with the genius to sing delightful Tamil poetry. Give me the right conduct. Release me in the present birth from the two attachments, 'I' and 'mine'. Remove from me the powerful bonds, *āṇava* (ignorance), *karma* and *māyā* (illusion). Place me in the company of the ancient devotees who always meditate upon You, having cast off all thought of self. Let me experience supreme bliss. Vouchsafe unto me a Divine Vision of Your fragrant red tinged lotus feet. Make me Your servant and be always present before me.[55]

2.6 *Devotion and the personal god*

One of the significant developments in the Skanda–Murukaṉ tradition in the medieval period is that the god becomes the object of an intensely personal devotional experience which finds expression in much Tamil literature. Rather than describe the history and nature of this bhaktic movement extensively, we shall merely illustrate some aspects of this development as it relates to the god Murukaṉ.

The bhaktic tradition in the South clearly had two sources – one orthodox and philosophical, the other unorthodox and cultic. On the one hand, early Tamil poetry informs us of the presence of a 'folk' religious experience in which the worshipper and the god were joyously related. We know of an experience of ecstasy – of momentary immortality, as it were – when in the dance or the frenzy of intoxication the worshipper believed himself to be possessed of the deity. The immortality thereby afforded, as argued in an earlier chapter, was not so much an escape from life as an affirmation of the verve and fullness of life. The moment of relationship with the god was thought to be a moment of rejuvenation, a re-creation serving as a prelude to a return to life. The confrontation with the god seemed to be an affirmation of the worshipper's humanness, for the god was very present and almost human in that moment. The experience was, in a sense, democratic, for it was available to all. It was self-affirming in the sense that the human spirit found some degree of fulfillment in its relationship to the god.

It could be argued that a certain degree of this 'democratic' spirit is reflected in the Tamil *bhakti* experience, especially in the Śaiva tradition. We know, for example, that the Śaiva *bhaktas* from the seventh to the ninth centuries were of diverse backgrounds. Of the sixty-three Nāyanārs, twelve are said to be Vedic *brāhmaṇs*, four Aṭiśaiva brāhmaṇs, twelve kings or chieftains, six merchants, thirteen *vēḷāḷar* (agriculturalists), and ten others from different communities including a hunter, fisherman, toddy-tapper, washerman, oilmonger, shepherd.[56] and at least two Harijans: Nālppaṉar and Naṇṭaṉār (A. S. Gnanasambandan in conversation, 1971). These early *bhaktas*, as Kamil Zvelebil has argued, were attempting to reaffirm the value of human existence and the possibility of a more universal experience of the divine in contradistinction to the anti-social, non-democratic, and ascetic influences which had come into Tamil Nadu. Indeed, in later devotional literature and in the Śaiva Siddhānta system itself, we find an insistence on the autonomy and validity of the human soul. The religion of Tamil *bhakti* and of Śaiva Siddhānta is more 'experiential' than metaphysical in a manner consistent with the Tamil heritage's affirmation of the human and the present world.

On the other hand, the bhaktic experience is gradually seen as a further expression of the orthodox philosophical–religious experience. The Lord, though often manifested in tangible forms, is seen as the embodiment of impersonal Ultimacy. He is understood as that reality which is the essence of the world, irrespective of one's cosmology. *Bhakti* is accepted as a form of yoga; it is ritual sacrifice – the sacrifice of oneself in devotion; it is *jnāna* (wisdom), for it is predicated on that wisdom which perceives the reality of the world. As such, *bhakti* is return to the primordial essence, it is to become one with the Universal one;[57] it is disattachment from the tangible world, release from the bonds of existence and attainment of that Bliss which is found only in the presence of the Divine.

In this context, immortality is understood as release from the inconstancies of existence and attainment of that reality which is beyond experiencing and knowing. Its result if self-effacement, or, depending on one's viewpoint, total fulfillment of the Real Self. This implies that in some bhaktic experience, there is a degree of self-denial or self-mastery, a longing for release from desire and all else that characterizes attachment to the self. Indeed, some scholars have argued that this spirit of self-denial is increasingly the character of Tamil *bhakti* poetry, even, occasionally, that of Śaiva poets, after the ninth and tenth centuries – that is, when the process of Sanskritization was accelerating (Zvelebil in 1967 lecture).

One finds in Śaiva *bhakti* this paradox – or, if one prefers – the attempted reconcilation of these two heritages of the devotional experience. The human soul is affirmed as an authentic entity, participating to a great extent in the character of the Divine, yet distinct from it. Nonetheless, its salvation lies in becoming totally detached from the bonds of the world and totally immersed in a relationship to the Divine. The stages of this release are systematized in Śaiva Siddhānta, in a manner which, in the long run, is as much 'Sanskrit' as 'Tamil' – if one may use these terms as structural categories. There are several steps by which the Siddhāntin is believed to attain Bliss with the Supreme (S. Satchidanandan Pillai 1952:28ff.). The first step, *iyama* (omission) includes the practice of non-injury, truthfulness, non-covetousness, humility, impartiality, hospitality, purity, refraining from drink and lust. The second step, *niyama* (commission) includes compassion; moderation in food; honesty; firmness; abstaining from lust, theft, and injury; study of ultimate problems of life; performance of daily *homas* and Śiva *pūjā*; and faith in scriptural practices. The devotee then cultivates a love for the god and yearns for a vision of him. At this point, the Lord may appear as a *guru* or through a human *ñāṉi* (wise soul) to give initiation (*dīkṣā*), which may take any of a number of forms. Following initiation, each of the four main paths must be followed, in turn, to final fulfillment. The first path, *carya mārga*, consists of a devotee's rendering bodily service in Śiva's temple. Then in the *kriyā mārga* the devotee does loving *pūjā* directly to the Śiva lingam (the god in his aniconic state). The *Yoga mārga* begins with *prāṇāyāma* and involves the practice of inner meditations and concentration on the 'Inner Light Transcendent' (p. 32).

The final stage, *ñāṉa mārga* includes studies of the Siddhāntas and meditation on the formless Śivam and results in *para mukti*, the highest form of god-realization possible while still in the human body. The *jīvan mukti* who attains this state is said to have a relationship to Śivam which is like that of iron to the magnet, or of salt to the water into which it is put, distinct from it, yet inseparable from it.

The devotional relationship envisioned by Śaiva Siddhānta entails a complex series of stages to the ultimate relationship. The ultimate relationship of the god to the soul may take any of five forms, varying in degress of intimacy: (1) master and servant; (2) father and son; (3) friend and friend; (4) master and pupil; (5) lover and beloved (Devasenapati 1963:8). The love of the soul for the god is said to be classified by three degrees: (1) very slow, like wax melting in the sun; (2) slow, like candle melting in the sun; (3) quick, like ghee melting in heat and flowing quickly like oil (p. 64). The relationship of the devotee to the god in *mokṣa* is said to be analogous to the compound Tamil term for devotion, *Tāṭalai*. The word *tāṭalai* is said to be comprised of two terms *Tāḷ* (foot – of god) and *Talai* (head – of devotee) (Seshadri 1959:174). Once again, this stresses the Śaiva conviction that the soul does not become one with the god but remains distinct though inseparable. Invariably, it should be noted, the Siddhāntin is expected to strive to merit the grace of the Divine.

When Murukaṉ is the subject of devotional poetry in the medieval period, the devotee's relationship to him is understood in terms that are consistent with Śaiva Siddhānta. We would expect this to be particularly true of the poetry written in the Cōḻa era or by Śaiva Brāhmaṇs. Yet in some cases, the *bhakti* poetry to Murukaṉ reflects more than a Śaiva sectarianism. For example, the poetry of Aruṇakiri in the Vijayanagar era also expresses a total abandon to the mercy of the divine, with an awareness of the unworthiness of the devotee that seems more consistent with the Vaiṣṇava concept of grace than with that of most Śaiva schools.[58] Further, while the plea of the Murukaṉ *bhakta* is generally for release from the bonds of life, one can also find in the poetry of some Murukaṉ *bhaktas*, that longing to live creatively which is found in earlier Tamil poetry, and in many of the hymns of the *Tevāram*. This at times takes the form of requests for competence in Tamil composition, for companionship, for notable rebirth, for adequate material prosperity or other benefits – which suggest some of the Tamil poets thought that life may not be so bad after all! This is especially true of Aruṇakiri, that sometimes sensual exponent of Tamil poetry and Murukaṉ devotion.

A few samples of the bhaktic spirit as it appears in medieval hymns sung to Murukaṉ follow. In the twelfth century Kallāṭam, poem I, lines 1–65, a hymn to Murukaṉ ends with the Siddhāntin's plea, which I translate prosaically to read:

> Grant today an extended manifestation of thyself to me, who has not the wise words of a sage to praise thee, nor the ability to refrain from lust and passion; separate me without delay from this world wherein I suffer affliction and sorrow, repeat mistakes periodically, and tire of the constant rebirths in paradise and hell.

Three centuries later, the hymns of Aruṇakiri, while voicing this longing for release, strike a somewhat more universal note, combining Sanskritic with Tamil motifs and a yearning for release with an affirmation of life that makes his hymns still popular in Tamil Nadu amongst literate and semi-literate alike. Particularly popular are the hymns found in the collection known as the Tiruppukaḻ. A sampling of some of Aruṇakiri's pleas to Murukaṉ, taken from the Tiruppukaḻ, follow.

> Pray! Grant me these boons: -
> Let me not enter and be entangled in the waves of ceaseless births
> Let me not wander in the path of wordly affairs
> Let me, by following the efficacious teachings of the Guru, be blessed with the sight of thy Holy Feet,
> (J. M. S. Pillai, n.d., p. 350, translating Tiruppukaḻ 1298.)

> Pray! Grant me these boons: -
> Let me not waste my life as one doomed to vilification as an ungrateful wretch
> Let me not associate myself with persons who do not understand thy grace
> Let me be worthy to receive thy Grace by constantly chanting the sacred mantras which you were pleased to impart unto me.
> (*Ibid.*, p. 350, stanza unspecified.)

> Pray! Grant me these boons: –
> Let not my mind go astray lured by the sweet words of prostitutes
> Be pleased to teach me how I can get over the bond of egoism of

'I' and 'mine'.

Let me not be soaked in the womb of a woman and be born again
Let me not wander in this world toiling with a heavy heart!
Be pleased to give me shelter under your Holy Feet blessing me with superior wisdom.
(*Ibid.*, p. 352, stanza unspecified.)

Oh ye! The Dancing Lord of supreme effulgence
Let me not be born again in this world;
Let me not associate myself with imposters:
Let me not tire myself when reading and rereading the three branches of Tamil[59]
Pray, bless me with the attainment of Eternal Bliss.
(*Ibid.*, p. 354 translating Tiruppukal 1280.)

My prayer to you is this–
Please bless me with Wisdom to free myself from my loneliness and to think of your lotus-like feet comparable to the faultless gem of emerald and gold, so that the relentless God of Death may not bind me by throwing his twisted rope around my head and separating me from my relatives, from my home and household, from my dear riches and from my kingdom.
(V. S. Chengalvaraya Pillai in J. M. S. Pillai 1963:28–29, stanza unspecified).

My prayer to you is this–
In case you ordain that I should have another birth – birth which is as terribly deep and dark as the ocean and is comparable to hell itself;
Please let me not be born either deaf or dumb, deformed or poverty stricken even to any small extent;
But be pleased to bless me with a celestial physique, notable birth and high wisdom and be pleased also to kindly and generously take me and my vaccillating mind as your vassal.
(*Ibid.*, p. 29, stanza unspecified.)

Oh ye! The Lord residing on the Palani Hills!
Please bless me with your grace so that the steadfastness of good nature may not be affected or tarnished by worldly ties, by bonds due to human desires, by family ties, by mental affliction and

afflictions due to bodily ailments, such as constipation, urinary troubles, and respiratory troubles.
(*Ibid.*, p. 30, stanza unspecified.)

3. The 'Tamilness' of Murukaṉ

We have noted that the medieval period, and particularly the Cōḻa era, was a period characterized by the intensification of brāhmaṇization in the Skanda–Murukaṉ tradition, but we have also intimated that there was at the same time a persistent relationship of Murukaṉ with the Tamil tradition. There are several historical factors which may have contributed to the persistent association of Murukaṉ with his Tamil heritage. The most obvious, perhaps, is that there was a steady stream of literature written in Tamil, by brāhmaṇs and non-brāhmaṇs alike, which uses Tamil terms and expressions in describing the deity. These Tamil works not only put into Tamil terms Sanskritic ideas and terms but continue the use of Tamil idioms found in the early literature. The probability that the major portion of the Caṅkam poetry was written by non-brāhmaṇs (Pillay 1965:169) as well as a large portion of the Tamil *bhakti* poetry which came later attests to the fact that there was a literate, Tamil cultural stream that was only indirectly related to the *brāhmaṇ* community. What occurs as a result is that both the Tamil and the Sanskrit character of Skanda–Murukaṉ are rendered in Tamil terms.

There is reason to believe that the *brāhmaṇ* community which Burton Stein suggests was the prime purveyor of culture in the Cōḻa era had incorporated into its ranks Tamil motifs and personnel. This seems particularly true of the Śaiva *brāhmaṇ* community. N. Subrahmaniam and K. K. Pillay argue that some non-*brāhmaṇs* had joined the brāhman community as early as the fourth or fifth century A.D. (p. 164).[60] Pillay relates an incident reported to have occurred in the fourth century A.D. in which, because there were not enough brāhmaṇs to perform required sacrifices, a number of non-brāhmaṇs were selected and provided the appropriate instruction (p. 163). During the time of Mayuravarman of the Kadamba dynasty some Andhra brāhmaṇs are said to have selected a number of families from non-brāhmaṇ castes, initiated them as brāhmaṇs and chose exogamous sect names for them (p. 164, citing Thurston 1909:45–

46). Further, in the late *Caṅkam* era, some brāhmaṇs are said to be from the north (*Vaṭamar*) while others (*Bṛihācaranam*) apparently are not (p. 164). To this day, the Aṭiśaivas or Śivacaryas, who wear the sacred thread and often officiate not only in orthodox Śaiva temples, but also in temples of Kāli, Amman, and other deities with particularly transparent indigenous roots, are popularly said to be 'imitation brāhmaṇs', having come into the community by adoption. Pillay suggests there may have been some intermarriage in the South between brāhmaṇs and non-brāhmaṇs inasmuch as such 'brāhmaṇ' figures as 'Ravana, Vali, Sugriva, Maricha, Suhaku, and Kharu' (who may be fictional) are said to be children of non-Āryan mothers, though born of 'Āryan' fathers (p. 164).[61] The inference is that, at least at a certain point in Tamil history, the caste system was not very rigid, and brāhmaṇs may indeed have brought Southern non-brāhmaṇs into their community. There is also evidence that brāhmaṇs adapted certain Tamil customs, and K. K. Pillay lists among these the tying of the *tāli* at marriage, the boring of the nose, and the presenting of a new sari to the bride at marriage (p. 168).[62] If Pillay is correct in his observations, we need not assume that the *brāhmadeya*, apparently so strong in the Cōl̲a era, was purely 'Northern' or 'Sanskritic' in its composition, even if it was undoubtedly influenced in significant measure by the post-Vedic tradition.

It is possible that, at the coming of the Vijayanagar Era, there was a resurgence of democratization and Tamilization. Historian Burton Stein reports that this era witnessed the decline of the *brāhmadeya* and the rise of other power groups in the context of imperial rule. The era was marked by an attempt to clear the forests and to incorporate forest and hill peoples into the main stream of Tamil culture. Consequently, power and culture were diversified and decentralized. A result of this development in terms of religion was the attempt to democratize Vaiṣṇava ritual by permitting non-*brāhmaṇs* to perform certain elements of worship. There was, simultaneously, a Vaiṣṇava resurgence marking the end of Śaiva pre-eminence.[63] It may not be coincidence that Aruṇakiri's poetry, which continues to strike a responsive chord amongst Tamilians of all walks of life, was written in this era of Tamil and democratic resurgence. The poetry undoubtedly reflects a level of popular religion which was in this period reasserting itself.

Whatever the historical factors, available evidence indicates that throughout the medieval period (and especially in the Vijayanagar period), there is a persistent manifestation in the Murukaṉ cultus of its Tamil context. For example, the elephant, a South Indian mount even in the *Caṅkam* period, persists in association with Murukaṉ. The peacock, indigenous to the South and long associated with Murukaṉ in Tamil literature, becomes the standard mount of the god in the South. The rooster appears on a banner in Tamil iconography, and the banner has persistently been one of the insignias of Tamil kingship. The *pāca* (noose) which is cast in the hand of many gods, may, in the hand of Murukaṉ, convey a particularly Tamil connotation, inasmuch as the noose was used by Tamil chieftains to capture and subdue the elephant – a motif which in the later tradition is spiritualized to represent the god's subduing the world.[64] The myth of Murukaṉ's wooing of Vaḷḷi, the Southern hunter maiden, is given a prominent place, even in Sanskrit sources. Similarly, the myth of the *asura*'s transformation in the ocean into a mango tree and then into a peacock and a cock, not found in the epic myths, is common in Tamil literature and, eventually, in some of the Sanskritic Purāṇas.

We have noted how Murukaṉ is inextricably wed to Tamil language and literature – indeed, he is understood to be its inspiration and source. In poetry and in common parlance, Murukaṉ is often called the 'god of Tamil', the 'god of the Pāṇṭiyas', and 'lord of the Palni Hills' and other phrases associating him with Tamil Nadu. Particular sites in Tamil Nadu have become associated with particular aspects of the god's mythology, and have been elaborated in local myths. As a result, most of the god's young life is believed, both in the popular imagination and in the officially accepted mythology, to have been lived out in Tamil Nadu: his teaching of his father (Swamimalai, Tanjore District); his becoming an ascetic (Paḻani); his marriage to Vaḷḷi (Tiruttani); his marriage to Devasenā (Tirupparaṅkuṉṟam); his conquest of the demon (Tiruchendur); and a host of other exploits.

On a more subtle level, in Murukaṉ are affirmed the religious aspirations of both his Tamil and Sanskrit heritages. In Murukaṉ there is an ambivalence of polarities which was reflected in both traditions. For example, Murukaṉ is both creative and destructive – he is thought to 'save' or 'create' the world and to destroy it. By destroying the *asuras*, he is said to save the cosmic order as it is meaningfully preserved in the dharma. By the medieval period, at least, the *asuras* have come to symbolize the involvement in the pleasures of life which destroys the possibility of liberation and union with the ultimate. Thus, Murukaṉ is believed to make possible deliverance from the attitudes and attachments which prevent release; he instills that insight which dispels spiritual ignorance. As such, Murukaṉ is the appropriate object of mystic concentration and bhaktic devotion. Yet, on the more popular level, Murukaṉ is apprehended as dispeller of disease and poverty, and purveyor of health and prosperity. At whatever level of worship, Murukaṉ is universally recognized as the vanquisher of one level of man's existence and the bringer of a new mode of being – one who can destroy that he might create.

The ambivalence of destruction and creation is found in the earlier elements of both Sanskrit and Tamil heritages. In Vedic literature, the sun dispels darkness to bring light; in Epic mythology, the warrior must destroy to save the ordered society. This polarity is also consistent with the functions of the early *kuṟiñci* lord of the hunt and the god of vegetation, who preside over the destruction or decay of animals and plants that the order of human life may be preserved and a new generation of cosmic life come into being. The sophisticated reasoning behind the function of Murukaṉ in the medieval period is, in a sense, a consistent fulfillment of earlier aspirations. That which man sought of the divine, as expressed in earlier literature and ritual, continues to be expressed, if more fully, in the medieval Murukaṉ. Murukaṉ is neither Sanskrit nor Tamil alone; rather, he is both Sanskrit and Tamil, bringing together the polarities within both traditions and coalescing, in a similar way, the polarity represented by each tradition.

Another illustration of the way in which both Sanskrit and Tamil motifs persist throughout this period and coalesce in the figure of Murukaṉ is in the basic attitude which the god's devotees have to the world. There exists within the same poetry and community a spirit of renunciation of the world, on the one hand, and, on the other, an affirmation of the joy, the color, and the fullness of life. This is particularly well-illustrated, in the poetry of Aruṇakiri. On the one hand, the poet describes the deity as one who is beyond life, who liberates from the bonds of life, destroys ego-consciousness and frees man from inane pleasures. The god is the instiller of liberating wisdom and purveyor of the bliss which is beyond earthly ejoyment, or, in other terms – perhaps more appropriate for the Śaiva – the bliss which is both expression and embodiment of total enjoyment. On the other hand, Aruṇakiri's poetry is replete with descriptions of the vitality of life, and Murukaṉ is described as presiding over the present life in a manner that reminds us of the spirit of early Tamil poetry. Kamil Zvelebil has written of Aruṇakiri's poetry that 'it is the poet's reflection of his all-embracing and glowing love for all aspects of life, from inorganic nature to flowers, animals, birds, and finally men – especially women – and from man, of course further, to God'; and even when the poet is lost in praise to his god, 'he is aware of life, of nature, of people, of the beauty surrounding him', and his personal deity Murukaṉ himself 'can only be glorified in terms of radiant rejoicing, extravagant colouration and youthful enthusiasm' (1965:157).

Aruṇakiri's verses, in marked and masterly detail, can describe the gradual decay of the body and the vanishing of consciouness in a manner that makes them appropriate accompaniments to the Siddhāntin in quest of detachment. At the same time, using colorful symbolism, the poet joys in the blueness of the peacock, and the purpleness of Murukaṉ, who by riding the peacock becomes like the sun rising over the sea, and in erotic detail he can describe Murukaṉ's wooing of the delectable Vaḻḻi (p. 157).

All this is to suggest that Murukaṉ is the personification of 'eternality'. Whether the world is itself of ultimate meaning or of only relative importance (or not at all of real significance), Murukaṉ is he who symbolizes ultimacy and eternality. The 'eternality' he is believed to author can be a 'rejuvenation' – an eternal youthfulness and renewal of cosmic fertility – or it can be seen as a complete liberation from the cycle of cosmic succession. Murukaṉ's name 'eternal youth' thus proves to be appropriate for both the Tamil and the Sanskrit aspirations.

Murukaṉ is as fully Tamil in the medieval period as Subrahmaṇya is Sanskrit. It is virtually impossible to say exactly when and how the 'Tamilness' of particular symbols and forms associated with the god are emphasized. Presumably there was in the Vijayanagar era a growing consciousness of the popular and Tamil aspects of the god, as there has been in recent decades. It seems more than likely that, because the Tamilness of the god is part of his early heritage, there was little 'new' in the attempt to recognize him as fully at home in Tamil Nadu.

Because Aruṇakiri's poetry incorporates a number of Sanskrit and Tamil elements of the Murukaṉ tradition, it seems appropriate to terminate this chapter with a few samples of that poetry. One stanza, the fifty-first, taken from the hymn 'Kantaranupūti' demonstrates the poet's free and clever use of Sanskritic and Tamil words, his concise and rhythmic style, and the character of his thought:

> Uruvāy aruvāy ulatāy ilatāy
> maruvāy malārāy maṇiyāy o! iyāyk
> karuvāy uyirāyk katiyāy vitiyāyk
> kuruvāy varuvāy aruḷvāy kukan̲ē
>
> Formed and formless, being and non-being
> Flower and its fragrance, jewel and its luster
> Embryo and its life, goal of existence and its way
> Come, You, as the Guru, and bestow Your grace.[65]

Another stanza, incredible in its composition, is included in the collection called 'Kantarantāṭi'. Legend has it that the collection was written as the poet was engaged in a contest with the conceited poet Villiputhuran to determine who was the greatest. The conceited rival is said to have confidently made the challenge and decreed that the loser would lose his ears. For fifty-three stanzas, the poets matched each other in creativity. But Aruṇakiri's fifty-fourth stanza is said to have won the contest. It goes as follows:

> Titattattat tittat tititātai tātatut tittattitā
> Titattattat titta titittitta tētuttu tittitattā
> Titattattat tittattai tātati tētutai tātatattu
> Titattattat tittatti tīti titituti tītottatē

Even this piece of alliterative fun, it seems, can be interpreted and translated as an expression of praise to Murukan̲. Kamil Zvelebil interprets the stanza thus:

> Oh you first blissful Being, who (are worshipped by) the Father (Śiva) dancing according to the rhythm 'tidattat tattitat', by Brahmā and by the one (Viṣṇu) who has for his mate the snake with spotted hood, and eats the sweet curds from the restless ocean! You (beloved of) parrot-like (Deivayān̲ai, fostered by) elephants! Let my mind adhere to you, my mind which praises you every day, and which burns in the fire of this weak body, between birth and death, a body of bones and arteries (1965:157).

Two brief hymns of Aruṇakiri addressed to Murukan̲ will further illustrate his spirit, and the combining of Sanskrit and Tamil motifs discussed earlier:

Like a child unto the barren womb,
Like a mine of new-found treasure,
Like a floor of diamonds,
So be my songs.

Like the wilful embrace of love's soft bosom.
Like a string of the purest gems
Like a garden of fragrant blossoms
Like the River that descends from Heaven
Even so be my songs.
Like the daughter of the Ocean,
Like eyes unto poets,
Like a stream full to the brim easy to drink of,
Like the taste of the nectar of thy beauty,
So be my wondrous songs of love,
By thy grace, O Lord.

(S. Bharathi, in J. M. S. Pillai, n.d., p. 355).

Murukaṉ, Birthless, deathless Lord,
Who abducted the daughter of the deer,
You took all other meaning from me
When You said: 'Be still; think not'.

Not knowing, despite His grace,
Murukaṉ of the lance is the supreme Guru,
Is not knowing Being is neither formed nor formless,
Existent nor non-existent, darkness nor light.

(Arunakiri, *Kantaranuputi*, stanza 12 and 13.
Translated by A. S. Gnanasambandan and the author.)

Lord of Space and Time

Expressions of Murukaṉ in the Contemporary Cultus

1. The resurgence of Murukaṉ

The resurgence of Murukaṉ in the present century has by no means occurred in a vacuum. There seems little doubt that the poetry of Aruṇakiri had reflected the growing concern for 'democratization' and the involvement of the populace in religious life that was characteristic of the Vijayanagar period. This concern had been expressed by the increased celebration of festivals, the enlargement of temples to include such features as the *kalyāṇa maṇṭapas* or marriage halls and the increased use of lay participants in ritual in both Śaivism and Vaiṣṇavism. Aruṇakiri's poetry had also catalyzed a resurgence of *bhakti* and *bhakti* poetry within Śaivism that served to popularize religion at many levels of society. This new wave of *bhakti* literature, akin to that of the seventh through the ninth centuries, yet cognizant of the systematizations of Śaiva Siddhānta, carried the message of devotion to Śiva and Murukaṉ into later centuries.

Murukaṉ was frequently extolled in the literature of the late Medieval period. Most memorable of this proliferation was the work appearing in the seventeenth century. This included not only a Tamil version of the Skanda Purāṇa, written largely by Kacciyappaśiva, but also the Kanta Kali Veṇpā by Kumārakurupara Cuvāmikal. Also flourishing in the seventeenth century were several forms of Piḷḷaittamiḻ addressed to Murukaṉ as a child. This was a style of devotional hymn that came to full flower in the twelfth century but became proliferate in praise of Murukaṉ after the seventeenth when Kumārakurupara Cuvāmikal wrote an extensive collection of it.[1] The work of Tāyumāṉavar, also appearing in the seventeenth century, is important both in perpetuating the post-Medieval Śaiva *bhakti* tradition and in alluding to Murukaṉ as the full embodiment of the Śaiva view of the Divine.

A significant feature of this post-medieval *bhakti* literature is the Tamil romanticism it espouses. Tāyumāṉavar, for one, is enamored of Tamil as the language of devotion. He sees God as especially attracted to those who weave garlands of Tamil poetry (Sankaranarayanan 1969:54). A similar theme is found in other of the seventeenth century poets. Parañcoti Muṉivar speaks of the Tamil language as divine, the Tamil poets as God's concern; Tamil land as His favorite resort; the same Parañcoti suggested that Śiva had once sat with the Caṅkam poets in order to research on his beloved Tamil language (p. 54). In a similar vein, Kumārakurupara rhapsodized that Tamil was the language of Śiva who, with Umā and Murukaṉ, had become incarnate on earth, to taste the sweetness of the Tamil language (*ibid.*). This is a spirit consistent with that of Aruṇakiri, who had seen Tamil as the language of and for Murukaṉ and his own poetry as a garland for his beloved god (Kantaranupūti Kāppu). It is a spirit also consistent with the regional romanticism of the twentieth century, be it the poetry of Subrahmania Bharathi or the rhetoric of Karunanidhi.

The resurgence of the cultus of Murukaṉ within the last century might be viewed in terms of two distinct but related 'waves' or periods. The first period, starting late in the nineteenth century extends to the time of independence. It is a period characterized by a renascence of Tamil culture and arts. The re-editing and publishing of early Tamil literature first by Swaminathan Aiyar, and more recently by such agencies as the Śaiva Siddhānta Publishing Works stimulated interest and pride in earlier Tamil culture and made available to the public such treatises important to the Murukaṉ cultus as the Tirumurukāṟṟupaṭai and the Paripāṭal. Also, some persons important in the stimulation of regional pride and social change in recent years were devotees of Murukaṉ. For example, Ramalingam Swami, poet and mystic of the late nineteenth century and the father of modern Tamil humanism, was a Murukaṉ *bhakta*. In fact he made the cultus of Murukaṉ the basis for a 'universal religion' in which God was depicted as merciful and light, and in which all were equal. One of his works, the Tiruttaṇikkai Mālai, is, in significant measure, a hymn of praise of Murukaṉ. Subrahmaniam Bharathi, militant regionalist, and reformer of the early nineteenth century, invoked images of Murukaṉ as the modern warrior god who could preserve Tamil Nadu and India from the yoke of external forces. In the 1920's and 1930's, Tiruvi Kalyāṇa Sundaraṉar, a Mudaliar who started the first labor union in India and gave a new florid prose style to Tamil literature to the extent that he is considered the father of neo-classical Tamil prose, wrote some forty-five booklets, among them a tract called 'Muruku allatu aḻuku' (Muruku or Beauty), a booklet seeking to 'universalize' the god Murukaṉ and compare him favorably with other visions of divinity and beauty.[2]

Both stimulating and reflecting this resurgence of Murukaṉ *bhakti* has been a renewed interest in the poetry of Aruṇakiri. This Aruṇakiri revival was sparked on many fronts: A Murukaṉ *bhakta*, V. T. Subrahmanya Pillai in the early part of this century began to collect stanzas of the Tiruppukaḻ from families who had preserved them on palmyrah leaves; his son, V. S. Chengalvaraya Pillai, in a labor of love, became the world's foremost commentator on all the work ascribed to the poet. Several generations of vocalists and pipers, and specially Nayanāra Pillai, his disciple Chittoor Subrahmanya Pillai, and the latter's disciple and a current favorite in Tamil Nadu, 'Madurai Somu' were instrumental in the revival both of Aruṇakiri's music[3] and of devotion to Murukaṉ. These musicians and others popularized Aruṇakiri's poems and made them standard hymnody for non-brāhmaṇic devotees; they also rediscovered and lyricized the wings of song which have been so persistent in the worship of Murukaṉ. But *brāhmaṇs* too came to virtually canonize the hymnody of Aruṇakiri. Most significant of these Brāhmaṇ Aruṇakiri-lovers was Śrī Vaḷḷimalai Sacchidananda Swami, who went about Tamil Nadu from 1908 to the 1940's singing the Tiruppukaḻ and organizing Tiruppukaḻ groups (Parthasarathy 1970).

Another of the ways the Murukaṉ revival manifested itself was in the renovation and increased popularization of temples associated with the god. Renovation of the temple at Tiruchendur, for example, had started as early as 1868 with the concern of one Mouna Swami and his successors and led eventually to a *kumpāpiṣekam* or dedicatory ceremony of the renovated temple in 1941 (J. M. S. Pillai 1948:3, 36). Similarily, at Paḻani, the Taṇṭāyutapāṇicuvāmi Devasthanam has been increasing amenities at the temple and expanding its properties and functions since 1924. The Tiruāviṉaṅkuṭi Temple at the foot of Paḻani hill celebrated its *kumpāpiṣekam* in 1910, while the *astabandha kumpāpiṣekam* was held in 1933 (pp. 12ff.). The increase of pilgrims and income at both Tiruchendur and Paḻani made possible extensive renovations. In a similar way, every major temple to Murukaṉ was undergoing extensive renovation and expansion in the early decades of this century.

The second period of the resurgence has occurred in the quarter-century since independence. Opening of temples to harijans and peoples of the 'backward classes' and the increase of communication and transportation facilities has enlarged the numbers of non-brāhmaṇ middle and lower class worshippers of Murukaṉ, hastened the accessibility of important Murukaṉ temples and enlarged their budgets. The building of choultries for pilgrims; the installation of neon lighting and air conditioning; the repainting of temple *kōpurams* are all evidence both of the temples' popularity and their increasing affluence. In the year 1972 alone *kumpāpiṣekas* for repainted temples were performed at Swamimalai, Tiruchendur, and Vaṭapaḻani.

The character of this resurgent cultus today reflects much of its history, both Tamil and Sanskrit, but at the same time bespeaks the mood of a newly emergent Tamil Nadu. By now the mythology of the deity is largely associated with Tamil country. While much of the cultus perpetuates brāhmaṇic symbolisms of time, space, and ritual and continues to attract brāhmaṇ devotees, *bhakti* has proliferated amongst non-brāhmaṇ communities. This *bhakti* of non-brāhmaṇs has been characterized by a fierce pride in the assumed Tamil heritage of Murukaṉ and a renewed religious self-assurance. The coming to power of the *Ṭirāvita Muṉṉeṟṟa Kaḻakam* in 1967, whose chief minister declared at Paḻani in 1971 that Murukaṉ was the 'god of the DMK', increased the Tamilization of the cultus by its appointing of non-brāhmaṇs as executive officers in temples, its attempt to have all *ārccaṉais* or hymns of praise recited in Tamil and by generally encouraging at the state level a movement away from brāhmaṇic traditions. In the five years immediately after 1967, attendance at the major Murukaṉ shrines and temple budgets had increased manifold.[4]

2. Tamil Nadu as Murukaṉ's domain

One of the interesting manifestations of the contemporary cultus of Murukaṉ is the existence and popularity of 'six' pilgrimage centers in Tamil Nadu. These sacred places serve as 'topocosms' (to use T. H. Gaster's term (1956: 26ff.) where the god is believed to have performed some noble feat and to be especially present today, and where the whole of the world's meaning is embodied. The religious and symbolic significance of these sacred sites suggests not a little about the meaning and intent of the Murukaṉ cultus today, and of the degree to which it is grounded in the historical and mythical past. At the same time they serve in the popular imagination to 'sacralize' Tamil Nadu and to make of the region the special domain of Murukaṉ.

Of course, certain places have been held especially sacred in the Murukaṉ tradition for centuries. The place (*kōṭṭam*) where the *veṟiyāṭal* was danced, for example, was often in a river delta (Kur̲an. 263:1–6). At first an open space, covered with sand and sprinkled with red and yellow flowers, the *kōṭṭam* soon came to be a covered enclosure, and may have been a forerunner to the Tamil temple. Another sacred spot was the foot of a tree (usually a *kaṭampu*, but sometimes a banyan or *vēṅkai*) where the *kantu* (small pillar) was set up and decorated with fragrant and colorful products of the hills. By the tenth century the Śivāgamas suggested where Subrahmaṇya temples could be built (Gopinath Rao 1916, II:421). A capital city was one such site, consistent with Murukan̲'s association with kingship and the fact that the city was one of the ten insignias of Tamil royalty. Other sites for Subrahmaṇya temples included the tops of mountains, the banks of rivers, towns, villages, gardens or forests, and under large trees. Some of these sites have continued to be of particular significance to this day.

Murukan̲ devotees are virtually unanimous in acclaiming the existence of six pilgrimage centers of special sacrality today. However, in the present cultus only five of these sites are accepted as authentic without dispute. These five are Paḻani, at the foot of the Palni Hills some twenty miles from Dindigul Junction; Tiruchendur, on the southeastern coast some thirty-five miles from Tirunelveli; Tiruttaṇi, nestled in hillocks some seventy miles northwest of Madras City; Tirupparankun̲r̲am, a hill five miles southwest of Madurai; and Swamimalai, near Kunbakonam, in Tanjore District. On the identity of the sixth major center there is no consensus, though several local temples claim or are variously ascribed that distinction. The popular opinion, generally undisputed by the tradition's scholars is that the sixth site is every other shrine in Tamil Nadu dedicated to Murukan̲. The Tamil expression is actually *Kun̲r̲āṭal*, which can be translated 'every hill on which the god dances'. The very vagueness of that assertion aptly expresses the god's ubiquity in Tamil Nadu.

The five major pilgrimage centers and the temple complexes associated with them share in common the mythical heritage of the Murukan̲ cultus and a ritual calendar largely consistent with all Tamil Śaivism. Nevertheless, each site has its own myth which gives it a particular place in the cultus. The myth of each site suggests how the god Murukan̲ manifested himself there. Each such manifestation often determines how particular kinds of ritual are especially appropriate for that site and on what special occasions. The myths, taken together, show that all the significant events of Murukan̲'s mythical career occurred in Tamil Nadu.

2.1 *Pa<u>l</u>ani*

The busiest of all these pilgrimage centers is that at Paḻani. Every year its budget exceeds four million rupees (over $500,000), and it is visited by over two million pilgrims. In all of South India this temple's wealth is second only to that of the famed shrine at Tirupati in Andhra Pradesh; Paḻani has become the most popular pilgrimage center in Tamil Nadu despite the fact it is relatively distant from major cities or main transportation lines. Actually some thirty-two shrines are administered by the Sri Taṇṭāyuta-pāṇicuvami Devasthanam in Paḻani; of these two are especially noted: the main one atop the central hill in the town is that wherein Murukaṉ is enshrined as the ascetic Paḻani Āṇṭavar; the other near the base of the hill is the temple known as *Tiru-āviṉankuṭi*,[5] extolled in medieval Tamil poetry and song.

While this temple complex is so popular today, there is evidence that suggests a shrine here was regularly visited at least since the late Pāṇṭiyaṉ era. Inscriptions left on portions of an older shrine indicate that gifts of land were given by Pāṇṭiyaṉ and other wealthy donors in the thirteenth and again in the fifteenth centuries. In addition, tradition suggests that the temple was built and endowed by the Cēṟas of Kerala. Two figures of a king on horseback sculptured outside the main shrine and outside a smaller shrine to Cēṟa Vinayaka are said by local tradition to represent the early Cēṟa monarchs and to support the theory that the temple fluorished early with Cēṟa patronage. Whatever the authenticity of the Temple's historical ties to the Cēṟa region, the temple continues to cater to Malayali pilgrims.

The primary myth of Paḻani is on this wise: At that spot the god's parents, Śiva and Pārvatī, made a promise to Murukaṉ and his brother, Gaṇapati. The brothers were told that to whomever could travel around the cosmos first would be given a fruit symptomatic of Śiva's approval. Gaṇapati, much less agile, merely walked around his parents, saying 'You are the cosmos'. The fruit was given to him. Murukaṉ, meanwhile, circled the globe on his peacock. Upon his return, Murukaṉ discovered what had happened, became angry, and retreated to the top of a nearby hill to become an ascetic. Śiva, trying to assuage Murukaṉ, said to him, 'You are the fruit' (Paḻam Nī). This phrase gave to the town its name and signified Murukaṉ's becoming at this spot the fruit and authentic extension of his father, the cosmic ascetic.[6] The temple stands atop the hill where Murukaṉ is said to have gone in anger.

This myth of Paḻani cannot be found in any of the myths about Skanda in the Epic literature, but variations of it are commonly found in Tamil literature and particularly within the Gaṇapati cultus. At Paḻani the myth is apparently intended to reflect Murukaṉ's superiority over his rival and would-be brother. The main shrine on the central hill in Paḻani, then, is the spot where Murukaṉ is enshrined as a young ascetic. Paḻani is also associated with healing; this tradition is nurtured by local legends about *bhogars* or alchemists who in a prehistoric era wandered in the nearby hills and who, in fact, are said to have constructed the main icon of the temple from a combination of medicinal and immortalizing substances.[7]

Another myth associated with Paḻani and suggestive of the kind of worship expected here is as follows: Agastya went to Mt. Kailās to worship Śiva. The god gave to the devoted sage two hills, Śivakiri and Śaktikiri to take to Poṭikai, the god's mountain abode. Agastya commissioned Iṭampaṉ, his disciple and the preceptor of the *asuras*, to carry them. After appropriately initiating Iṭampaṉ with certain *mantras* and acquainting him with the route, Agastya sent his disciple on his way. Iṭampaṉ carried the mountains like a *kāvaṭi*, letting them hang from a pole strung across his shoulders. The pole was none other than the staff of Brahmā and the ropes used for tying the mountains to the pole were snakes. Approaching the forest near the spot now known as Paḻani, Iṭampaṉ rested and set his burden down. When he tried to lift them again, he found they were fixed to the spot. To see why they could not be moved he climbed the larger hill, the Śivakiri, only to find a youth holding a staff and wearing only an under-garment (*kaupīṉam*). The youth claimed the hills as his own. Iṭampaṉ, seeking to defend the hills, started to fight, only to fall lifeless at the feet of the youth. Both Agastya and Iṭampī, the wife of the fallen *asura*, were instantly on the scene and pleaded to the youth for mercy. Iṭampaṉ was restored to life and to the service of the youth, who, it proved, was Murukaṉ himself. Iṭampaṉ asked to stand ever at the god's portal and requested that whoever should offer vows to Murukaṉ bearing a *kāvaṭi* should be specially blessed. Both requests were granted.

This myth was intended to explain a number of things. The two hills (and there are two hills near Paḻani) were the gift of Śiva himself and were brought from the Himalayas through the agency of Agastya, the mythical civilizer and bringer of culture to Tamil Nadu from the North. The two hills symbolize Śiva and Śakti, the cosmic duality. The hill on top of which the temple now stands is that claimed by Murukaṉ where Iṭampaṉ the faithful *asura* submitted to the young god. All devotees who bring the *kāvaṭi* or submit to the god on the hilltop are thought to be re-enacting the example of that primordial devotee, all of whose malevolence and simple-mindedness was taken from him in that act of worship.

Quite apart from the mythical bases for Paḻani's importance, the site's significance is enhanced by the symbolism of its geography. On one hand, the Paḻni Hills rise not far to the west of Paḻani. The Paḻnis have a special meaning for Tamil Nadu, having often been extolled by the poets as the abode of Murukaṉ. It is possible that the Paḻnis were part of the domain of the *kuṟiñci*, and, if so, would have been the habitat of some of Tamil Nadu's earliest settlers.[8] By being a 'gateway' to the Paḻnis, the town of Paḻani and its two adjoining hills inherit something of the symbolic and historic significance of the Paḻni range. On the other hand, the Ṣaṇmukha river, two miles west of Paḻani is ascribed sacrality not only because it obviously descends from the sacred Realm that is the Paḻnis, but also because it is the confluence of six tributaries – the Palar, Varattar, Porundalar, Suriar, Kallar, and Pachaiar rivers. As such, the river represents the integration of that totality-in-diversity which is so often depicted in the six-in-one symbolism associated with Skanda-Murukaṉ.

The ritual life at Paḻani is rich and colorful and is especially attractive to peasants from Coimbatore, Salem, and Madurai Districts as well as from Eastern Kerala. Not least because of the exigencies of the agricultural calendar, the largest crowds gather in Paḻani for three festivals celebrating aspects of Murukaṉ's career: *Tai Pūcam* in January-February; *Paṅkuṉi Uttiram* in March-April, and *Vaikāci Vicākam* in May-June.

The forms of worship by which pilgrims celebrate the presence of Murukaṉ here include virtually the entire range of ritual appropriate to Tamil Nadu, orthodox and folk. Circumambulation, whether by foot or by prostration, ritual ascension up the hill by steps or winch train, bathing in the nearby rivers, the bearing of vessels of water (often for miles on foot) to be used in *apiṣekam* or anointing of the deity – all are especially common sights in and around Paḻani. Most pilgrims bear offerings: some kind of fruit, milk, money, a rooster, and even an occasional peacock. Not infrequently worship reflects an attempt to identify with the ideal of self discipline embodied in the person of the ascetic Paḻani Āṇṭavar. Thus some pilgrims may be dressed in the garb of an ascetic or appear with a lance piercing tongue or cheek. The giving of hair is a common offering and may serve not only to celebrate a boon granted by the god during the year but also as a form of self-discipline.[9] Most commonly associated with the cultic of Murukaṉ for reasons suggested in the myth of Iṭampaṉ is the bearing of the *kāvaṭi*[10] in praise of the god.

2.2 *Tiruchendur*

Another pilgrimage center for Murukaṉ devotees, almost as popular as Paḻani, is Tiruchendur in Tirunelveli District on the shore of the Bay of Bengal. One of the three busiest temples of Tamil Nadu, its annual budget exceeds one million rupees and its ritual and festive calendar attract over a million pilgrims a year, most of them from the middle and upper classes. Of all the temples associated with Murukaṉ that at Tiruchendur is one of the oldest. References to a seashore shrine to Murukaṉ called Tiruccīralaivāy are to be found even in early *Caṅkam* poems and are traditionally thought to refer to this place. The oldest inscription on the site has been ascribed the date 875 A.D. and refers to a Pāṇṭiyaṉ named Varekuṉa Maraṉ (J. M. S. Pillai 1948:17). It appears the temple was also the focus of struggle in the era of European colonialism. The Dutch, in retaliation for a Portuguese attack, occupied the temple in 1646 and fortified and ravaged it. For two years the Dutch withstood the attacks of ill-organized and ill-equipped local peoples only to finally withdraw and take the main icon with them. The icon was eventually restored and rededicated in 1651.[11]

The temple has been rebuilt in recent years. Starting in 1868, three mendicants devoted their lives to raising funds for the temple's reconstruction: the first of these sanyassins was the silent Mouna Swami who gave *vipūti* to devotees in return for funds for reconstruction. He was succeeded in his commitment by one Kāśī Swami, a mendicant from Vārāṇasī, and then by Āṟumuka Swami, the son of a Pillai. A dedicatory *kumpāpiṣekam* was held in 1941 and another *kumpāpiṣekam* for renovation and completion of a *Kōpuram* was held in 1971.

Tiruchendur is the village of the sacred embattlement. Its mythical heritage has it that it was at this spot that Murukaṉ overcame the *asura* in the ocean. Murukaṉ and his hosts are said to have come here in pursuit of Sūrapadma, by then deprived of much of his army. Seeing the battle go against him, Sūrapadma entered the ocean where he became a vast, fiery red mango tree spreading expansively underwater.[12] With his *vēl*, Murukaṉ split the tree which therewith turned into a peacock and a cock. The *cūra* was not totally annihilated inasmuch as he had been given immortality by Śiva himself because of his austerities. Rather, in the form of the two fowls, he became forever the submissive instrument of the god's purpose.

This basic myth is reflected in a variety of ways in the setting of the temple and its environs. The temple's location, on the shore, in addition to making the site recreational and climatically attractive to pilgrims, embodies the constant polarization between god and *asura*, good and evil, cosmos and chaos. Tamil literature alludes more than once to the cosmogonic dimensions of sunrise and ocean.[13]

Also perpetuating the myth of the cosmic battle is a fresh water spring, situated within one hundred yards of the sea, which local legend maintains was formed when Murukaṉ thrust his victorious lance into the ground at that spot. To bathe in that spring after bathing in the ocean, therefore, affords particular ritual merit for the devotee. Also situated near the temple, in a bank overlooking the sea, is the legendary 'Vaḷḷi cave'. Here, legend avers, Murukaṉ hid his lover, not only to protect her from the enemy, but to afford himself a trysting place with her so that he could come to her and gain 'inspiration' before the battle.[14]

Because technically skilled priests were brought in to conduct the ritual affairs of the temple two or three centuries ago,[15] the Śrī Subrahmaṇya Swamy Temple here is the scene of some of the most aesthetically pleasing and technically precise ritual procedures within Śaivism.

The official ritual of the temple is orthodox and performed with great care, suggesting that one important feature of the modern mood is the careful preservation of tradition. *Apiṣekam* (anointing of the icon) *arātaṉai* (showing the lights to the icon); *vastram* (dressing of the icon) – all common to Śaiva ritual – are performed at Tiruchendur with special sensitivity. Nine of the twelve sacred hours of Śaiva ritual prescribed by the Āgamas for daily observance are meticulously maintained – more than at any other Śaiva temple in South India.

Yet the most common expectation of devotees who sojourn to Tiruchendur is that personal and cosmic malaise may be averted in their behalf. Skanda Ṣaṣṭi, the festival in which Subrahmaṇyan's subduing of the demon is celebrated in October-November, attracts about a half million pilgrims a year. That festival, held at the watershed of the Northeast monsoon, symbolizes in a variety of ways the central concern of this temple for conquest of evil. A gigantic dramatization occurs on the beach on Ṣaṣthī – the sixth day of the waxing moon, re-enacting the destruction of the *asuras*. And thrice on each day of the festival, a special fire ritual, combining Vedic Āgamic, and Tantric themes is conducted by the Mukhāṇiar priests for the express purpose of dramatizing Subrahmaṇyam's identity with the sacrifice and enhancing his power and overcoming the forces of malevolence which infest the cosmos and the person. The lance, once the weapon of the hunting and warrior god and for the philosophers the instrument whereby passions are overcome, has assumed new significance for a wide spectrum of devotees today. The lance has come to symbolize Murukaṉ's capacity to overcome all misfortune – ill health, unemployment, crop failure. The pilgrim who comes to this place expects the power of Murukaṉ to again be made manifest in his own life and in the lives of those he loves.

2.3 *Tiruttaṇi*

On the Northern border of Tamil Nadu, not far from Andhra Pradesh, in rolling terrain some seventy miles northwest of Madras City, nestles the sacred center called Tiruttaṇi. Its importance as a pilgrim center is enhanced by its relative proximity to Madras City which makes it the most easily accessible of Murukaṉ's holy places for Madrasis, and by its locality in a hilly area said to have been Murukaṉ's retreat. No doubt, in recent years, its proximity to the Northern border of Tamil Nadu has also assumed some symbolic significance, making it, as it were, the Northern outpost of Murukaṉ's sacred domain. So, together with Paḻani near the Western edge of Tamil Nadu, and Tiruchendur, on the Southeastern boundary, Tiruttaṇi on the Northeastern boundary completes a triangle encompassing Tamil Nadu.

Tiruttaṇi, in the Murukaṉ myths, is said to be the home and retreat of Murukaṉ, where he repaired after he had conquered the *asura* and had married Devasenā. It was from Tiruttaṇi Murukaṉ's courtship of Vaḷḷi was conducted; it was to Tiruttaṇi that the young lover brought his new bride. It is from Tiruttaṇi Murukaṉ reigns over and tends to his sacred domain, Tamil Nadu. Also associated with Tiruttaṇi is Murukaṉ's role as teacher and preceptor of the best of Tamil literature and Śaiva Siddhānta philosophy. For the local mythology has it that here Murukaṉ taught Tamil to Agastya, the mythical bringer of culture to Tamil Nadu, and endowed him with *sivañāṉa* (the final blissful wisdom of the Siddhāntin). Here also Murukaṉ is said to have taught Nandi Devar the significance of Śaiva philosophy. In sum, Tiruttaṇi is considered the abode of the older and more mature Murukaṉ. This is, in essence, the last major place Murukaṉ is supposed to have come in Tamil Nadu, after most of his youthful exploits were completed.

It is not inconsistent with the spirit of Tiruttaṇi that it is the scene of numerous *bhajaṉais* (musical conventions), when urban pilgrims come in large numbers to worship with music, dance, and recitation. It is also at Tiruttaṇi where the Murukaṉ cultus has made one of its few – and perhaps its only – concession to the Western calendar by which, of course, all the governmental and industrial agencies of urban Tamil Nadu measure time. At Tiruttaṇi, for almost the last half-century, pilgrims, in increasing numbers, arrive on December 31 for an all-night New Year's vigil and *bhajaṉai,* known as *Tiruppaṭi Bhajaṉai* (Concert on Sacred Steps). This event was started in 1914 or 1915 by V. S. Chengalvaraya Pillai, a member of a family committed to the rediscovery of poetry by Aruṇakiri and the extension of the worship of Murukaṉ. A brāhmaṇ, T. M. Krishnaswami Aiyar came to lend his support to the New Year's Eve vigil in 1923. In this festival, pilgrims bearing musical instruments and singing hymns usually from the Tirukkuraḻ, converge on Tiruttaṇi on New Year's Eve. The night is spent climbing the steps to the temple ritually, pausing at each step for worship and the singing of appropriate verse.

2.4. *Tirupparaṅkuṉṟam*

Five miles from Madurai, the old capital of the Pāṇṭiyaṉ chieftains, is the temple at Tirupparaṅkuṉṟam. Tirupparaṅkuṉṟam (literally, 'the sacred hill of the Great God') is one of the oldest and most eclectic of the 'six sacred spots' of Murukaṉ. The hill associated with the temple has at various times in its history attracted Vaiṣṇava, Muslim, and Jain attention. The oldest inscription associated with the site is ascribed to the second century A.D. and refers to a Ceylonese householder (īla Kuṭumbikaṉ) who gave a grant to a cave resort at this spot (Maloney 1970:603ff.). Caves which housed Jain monks in the ninth century and still bear vestiges of

Jain carvings can be seen on one side of the hill. A rock cut panelling of Śiva and his family, ascribed to the year 773 A.D., is to be found near the top of the hill. However, while passages in such Tamil literature as the *Tirumurukār̲r̲upaṭai* refer to Tiruppankun̲r̲am as an abode of Murukan̲, and such medieval poets as Arunakiri sing the hill's praise, there is at least some question whether the present site is the same as that associated with Murukan̲ in the pre-medieval literature.[16]

At any rate, today the site attracts numbers of Murukan̲'s devotees, and members of other religious communities as well. At the very top of the hill is a Muslim shrine dedicated to 'Sekunder', an apparent corruption of the term Iskandar once used to refer to Alexander the Great.[17] Just below the Muslim shrine is the old Pāṇṭiyan̲ panelling, now seldom used in worship. Still lower on the hill a small rock carving of Murukan̲ marks the place where, according to local legend, 'hundreds' of peacocks come in the appropriate season to dance their praises to their god.[18] A similar shrine to Perumāl (Viṣṇu) is said to be attended by monkeys, the living embodiments of Hanumat, Ra̲ma's monkey general.

The present temple to Murukan̲ sits at the foot of the hill. The *sanctum sanctorum* is centered by an old rock-cut cave temple, ascribable to the late eighth century. The center panelling of this original shrine is a sculpting in rock of Durgā. On the left of Durgā, and slightly less indented is Subrahmaṇya; on the right is Vin̲āyakar; on both sides of the panelling is a protruding cell – that on the left, Vaiṣṇava, that on the right Śaiva, the latter containing a rock cut Somāskanda, also ascribable to the late eighth century. The temple surrounding these cells has been recently renovated. Appropriately, the *sanctum sanctorum* is elevated above the rest of the temple, so that the god presides atop a knoll and can be reached only by the climbing of stairs.

The basic element in the Murukan̲ mythos that purports to explain Tirupparaṅkun̲r̲am's sacrality is that Murukan̲ is believed to have come to this spot for a rest after his battle with the *asura*. And it is here he is said to have married Devasenā, given to Murukan̲ by Indra and the gods after he had proven his merit by winning the cosmic battle. This celestial marriage is expressed and remembered in a number of ways in the structure and cultus of the temple. A subsidiary icon, used in festivals, depicts Murukan̲ seated affectionately close to Devasenā. An elephant is kept by the temple, which, in addition to the other functions it performs in the temple (pushing temple carts, serving as a mount for Murukaṉ, bringing 'sacred water' from the tank to sanctuary) also represents Devayāṉai (literally, 'the elephant of the gods'), the Tamil term for the Sanskrit name Devasenā. And *Paṅkuṉi Uttiram*, the festival held in late March (a time considered especially auspicious for the marriages of both god and man) when the highlight of the festival is the ritual re-enactment of Skanda's marriage to Devasenā is celebrated in a major way at this temple.

However, perhaps the most popular ritual event at Tirupparaṅkuṉṟam today is the festival of *Vaikāci Vicākam* in May–June. Peasants from surrounding villages parade through the streets of Madurai toward Tirupparankuṉṟam on the climactic day of the festival, many of them bearing *kāvaṭis*, pulling carts hooked to their backs, carrying vessels of milk or water to be used in *apiṣekam* or walking in a pit of coals on the temple grounds. This festival, while it celebrates Murukaṉ's 'birthday' (on vicākam day) is nonetheless not directly related to the central significance of the temple's mythic *raison d'être*. It may be currently popular as much for commercial reasons as symbolic. The temple authorities find this a profitable counter-festival to the huge Cittirai festival in Madurai and at a time when peasants are relatively free from agricultural chores.

Other legends and literary references add to the mythical lore of Tirupparaṅkuṉṟam. The land itself is said to have become Murukaṉ's because of a trick the god successfully executed. A rich king, Sepu Chakravarty, was said to have given away all his land to one thousand persons. When one of these persons refused his gift, Murukaṉ, appropriately disguised, stood in his place and received this hill and the adjoining land as his own. It was here (or more accurately, enroute to this place) that Nakkirar, the alleged author of the Tirumurukāṟṟupaṭai, was said to have been encaved along with 999 others by a colossal giant who was about to destroy his victims when Murukaṉ appeared to rescue this most favored pilgrim of Tirupparankuṉṟam. It was also here that Murukaṉ is believed to have tested Nakkirar's faith by causing a leaf to fall before the poet's eyes, while the latter rested under a banyan tree, and turning that half of the leaf which fell into water into a fish and that half which fell on dry ground into a bird. Unstirred and undeterred from his intentions, the faithful Nakkirar went on to complete his worship (Santaramurthi 1966:21ff.).

A number of passages in Tamil texts are claimed by temple authorities as referring to the celestial and salubrious character of the hill at Tirupparankuṉṟam. The Tirumurukāṟṟupaṭai is believed to claim Tirupparaṅkuṉṟam as the Southern Himalaya where the gods held a conference with Murukaṉ (pp. 25ff.; cf. Tirumuru. 187–255).[19] Similarly, the Paripāṭal is said to speak of girls without children or husbands bathing in a hilltop 'spring' at Tirupparaṅkuṉṟam in search of fulfillment. In a similarly extravagant way, Aruṇakiri is said to have written that the sun and moon abide on top of the hill at Tirupparaṅkuṉṟam, replete with sweet celestial springs (pp. 27ff.).

And so it is that the Tirupparaṅkuṉṟam temple authorities express in several ways the character and state of the Murukaṉ cultus today. Myth and history are adapted to lend authenticity and continuity to the cultic tradition. This mythic history is recorded in the *sthāla purāṇa* written, published, and distributed in recent years to publicize the identity and character of the temple. Yet adaptations are made to the exigencies of modernity: the necessity for financial support; the schedules of potential pilgrims, be they argriculturally or industrially employed; and the concern to be competitively attractive as over against other temples and entertainment options.

2.5 *Swamimalai*

Swamimalai is a fifth significant pilgrimage center of Murukaṉ. The name literally means 'the mountain of the lord', but for Murukaṉ devotees, who ascribe to their deity the name 'Swami'; the name means 'the hill of Murukaṉ'. Near Kumbakonam in Tanjāvūr District, the shrine is geographically and philosophically set in Cōḻa land. The pilgrimage center is not far from Tanjāvūr, the old capitol of the Cōḻas; its significance is based on a myth that developed particular relevance in the philosophical context of the Cōḻa period. Here, we are told, Murukaṉ the precocious child taught his own father the meaning of the sacred syllable. The god enshrined at Swamimalai, therefore, is depicted primarily as philosopher and *guru*. The primary icon has the child god perched on the shoulder of Śiva imparting the divine wisdom. The syllable *Ōm* in Tamil letters has recently been emblazoned in neon lights on the temple *kōpuram*.

As with other pilgrimage centers, the significance of the Swamimalai shrine is enhanced by its geography. The temple stands virtually on the banks of the Kāveri river. The Kāveri is Tamil Nadu's Ganges; not only does it fertilize the delta of Tanjavur District, but is ascribed significance as a creative and sacralizing agent for all Tamil Nadu both in popular imagination and in literature. Similarly, the 'hill' which is now Swamimalai, while it has no discernible elevation, takes some of its significance from its juxtaposition to the Kāveri. It suggests the fertility and vibrancy that ensues from the river's flow in a way that is consistent with the mood of early Tamil poetry's description of the hills.

Thus at Swamimalai is linked the motifs of fertility, eternal youthfulness, and wisdom. The pilgrim to this site receives of the god the insight which is believed to impart immortality and final bliss. Two festivals assume particular importance at or near Swamimalai. The *vaikāci vicākam* festival in May–June, for all else it commemorates, assumes a particular significance at Swamimalai. Myth says that on that day of the *vicākam* star at Swamimalai, Indra worshipped Subrahmaṇya and received strength to defeat the troublesome *asura*, Arikeśa. The festival at Swamimalai therefore serves to re-enact that mythical event. At Kumbakonam nearby, the *Māci* festival which is climaxed at the conjunction of the full moon and the star Magha, commemorates Subrahmaṇya's teaching of his father Śiva. Tradition at Kumbakonam claims this event occurred on the day on which the star Magha was presiding in the month of *Māci.* Every twelve years, the Mahā-Magha festival, a festival assuming gigantic proportions, is held (P. V. Ayyar 1921:75).

2.6 *Other holy steads of Murukaṉ*

The 'sixth' sacral center of Murukaṉ's Tamil Nadu, as noted earlier, is generally thought to be every place, and particularly every hill, where a temple to the god is erected. There are numerous shrines which have assumed importance for the cultus throughout the state. A description of a few of these will illustrate the extent and variety of the worship places where Murukaṉ's devotees may go to meet him.

Among these temples is that at Tirupporūr, near Mahabalipuram, where Subrahmaṇyam is enshrined in his rare aspect as Bālasāmi. Mailam, on the way to Pondicherry from Madras, is another famous one. Vaidyeśvaramk-ōil, where Murukaṉ is enshrined as Muttu Kumāracāmi, is important. Kalugamalai, in Tirunelveli District, which has a heritage and sculpturing dating back to the Pāṇṭiyaṉ era, and which has been extensively described by C. Sivaramamurti, serves as an important pilgrim center in its area.

Uralimalai, near Pudukkottai, and the *Kumārakōṭṭam* in Kancheepuram serve pilgrims in these districts. *Eṭṭukuṭi Erikam* near Tiruvarūr serves a similarly important function for Murukaṉ devotees. Even the popular Vaiṣṇava temple at Tirupati is claimed by Murukaṉ devotees as a shrine to their god; and, in fact, one of the one hundred and eight names of the presiding deity recited there identifies that diety as Murukaṉ. The 'sixth site' can even be found in other places outside Tamil Nadu, for a Subrahmaṇya shrine in Kerala on the West Coast and the Katirakāman temple in Ceylon are said to serve their respective locales as pilgrim centers and points of break-through to the Sacral Realm governed by Murukaṉ.

All of these temples and sites reflect something of the totality of the Murukaṉ cultus and mythos. At the same time, every such site has its own peculiar mythos which attests its own particular claim to sacrality. These local myths demonstrate that the god visited this place. Some other unusual divine event occurred which renders the site sacred. This pattern can be illustrated by the mythical 'history' to be found behind a few Murukaṉ shrines, selected at random.

Kuṉṟakkuṭi, a small town of Ramnad District, is centered by a Murukaṉ temple constructed atop a rock hill roughly shaped like a peacock. The myth which explains the origin of that rock hill is that which accounts for the site's sacrality. The myth tells us that Brahmā astride his swan and Viṣṇu astride his *garuḍa* came to this place to do homage to Murukaṉ, who resided there with his peacock. During the sessions, the three bird-vehicles started disputing as to which of their three masters was superior. A fight ensued. The peacock destroyed the other two fowls, thereby demonstrating Murukaṉ's superiority over the other gods. But Murukaṉ, to discipline the peacock for its rashness, turned it into rock on the spot. At that spot Murukaṉ has remained and on that peacock hill a temple has been built. The lure of that myth, together with the presence of one of South Indian Śaivism's most charismatic swamis – the Kuṉṟakkuṭi Aṭikal[20] – and the temple's location in the midst of the rural South, serves to bring to the spot hundreds of rural devotees especially on festival days These devotees, in turn, make Kuṉṟakkuṭi the locale for some of the most colorful and spontaneous worship in Tamil Nadu.

Kumāra Vayalūr, in pasture lands seven miles west of Tiruchirappalli, is another temple dedicated to Subrahmaṇya. This is said to be a place where Murukaṉ worshipped Śiva after digging the tank of the temple with his *vēl*. Today, therefore, the tank is called *Śakti Tīrtam* (water consecrated by Śakti), or *Kumāra Tīrtam* or *Agni Tīrtam*. Interestingly, Śiva here is enshrined as Agneśwarar (Lord Agni). It is thought particularly meritorious if devotees re-enact the devotion of Murukan̲ to his father by planting a *vēl* near the tank or in front of the temple. Hence, numerous lances of various sizes continue to stand in the sands in front of the temple ('Kumāra Vayalur' 1966:14).

Andarkuppam or Subrahmaṇyapuram, a village twenty miles north of Madras, is the site of a temple to Balasubrahmaṇya. According to the *sthālapurāṇam* of the temple, the purpose of this manifestation of the god was to emphasize that aspect which gives *abhaya* (blessings) to devotees. Myth has it that a pious brāhman priest, Saṁvardhana, was passing this spot when it was but a thicket. At dusk he wanted to perform *samdhyavanaṇḍanan*, but could find no water. A handsome brāhmaṇ lad appeared and directed him to a small rivulet nearby. To his surprise the priest found the rivulet and completed his rites. But when he returned to thank the lad, the latter had vanished. Realizing this had been the work of the divine, the priest prayed that he might have an opportunity to express his gratitude. At this the Lord appeared as Bālasubrahmaṇya under a tree. At that spot, the priest set up a shrine.

Later, it is said by local legend, a Muslim lieutenant on his way to battle, having heard of the powers of the presiding deity of the temple, came to ask for success in his mission and promised lavish gifts for the temple if he did succeed. He did win the battle and thereafter endowed the temple lavishly and caused its fame to spread (Veliah 1967:12).

In Neyveli township is a small shrine to Murukan̲ in the form of Villutayan̲pati (the lord who has the bow). Here Murukan̲ is in the form of a hunter with a bow and arrow, together with his two consorts. The god and the two consorts are sculptured from a single rock and are said to be *svayambhū* (self-emergent). A natural stream flowing near the temple is perennial and considered by many to be sacred. Legend maintains that Murukan̲ went as a hunter with bow and arrow to court Vaḷḷi. Local myths have it that *devas* came to this place to receive a vision of the god, after granting which, Murukan̲ is said to have gone out of sight. The temple was recently renovated and re-dedicated in 1960 (Krishnamachari 1967:14).

Vaṭapal̲ani, now a suburb of Madras City, has become the site of another increasingly popular temple to Murukan̲. Its name means 'The Northern

Pal̲ani' and it is a frank attempt to duplicate for Madras and environs the aspect of Murukan̲ which appears at Pal̲ani. Despite the fact its popularity is only recent and its claim to mythic fame is apparently unoriginal, this temple site also has a story to attest its sacrality and authenticity. It seems two faithful devotees used to trudge to Pal̲ani from Madras every year on foot to pay homage to their beloved diety. One year, before such a trip, the god appeared to them in a dream saying he would reward their faithfulness by affording a special vision of himself. He told them to look around them and find him in their midst. They turned and, sure enough, an icon of Pal̲ani Āṇṭavar, existent from 'time immemorial', appeared. This aspect of the deity became the presiding god of the Vaṭapal̲ani Temple, now one of the most popular and wealthy temples of Madras City. In a special room in the temple, pictures of the two devotees hang and receive *pūjā* at appropriate times[21].

These illustrations are enough to demonstrate the extent and pervasiveness of the Murukan̲ cultus in Tamil Nadu today. Many Tamilians see the god and the region as virtually inseparable. The god's life has been mythically lived out in Tamil Nadu. Generic elements from both the Sanskrit and Tamil traditions have been fused with local and folk imageries in such a way as to make the god's holy steads attractive to peoples from all walks of Tamil life. His exploits speak to all dimensions of the Tamil imagination – whether he be seen as teacher and philosopher *par excellence*, or the one who dispels misfortune; whether he is giver of joy in life or release from it; be he mischievous lover or ideal ascetic. The full range of human needs and emotions are expressed in the contemporary mythology of Murukan̲. It is not surprising that, for the present at least, praises to Murukan̲ are to be heard in all the arenas of Tamil India.

3. Murukan̲'s moments in the cultic life

It is not only space – and especially Tamil space – that is made holy by Murukan̲. Time is also rendered meaningful by the god's availability and power in special moments.[22] Of course, throughout Hinduism, cultic life has been measured in chronometric units that epitomize the rythm and flow of the cosmic process. The day, for example, throughout Śaiva ritual, is divided into twelve units of sacrality which serve to make the day congruent with the year and the cosmic cycle.[23] Each cycle of ritual time has its 'tempocosms' or sacred moments which make possible awareness of the larger cosmic process, breakthrough from the tedium or tyranny of meaningless time, and new beginning. The devotees of Murukaṉ share many of these sacred moments with other Hindus, and especially with all other Śaivas. Other moments are sacred to Murukaṉ alone. The way these sacred moments are celebrated by devotees today suggests further the character of the god in contemporary Tamil Nadu.

At the outset, it is useful to note that Murukaṉ–Skanda has traditionally had special associations with time and season. Myths and allusions to the deity in both Tamil and Sanskrit literature refer to this association. Tamil references point out that Murukaṉ presided over the coming of the rains and the blossoming of such trees as *vēnkai, kāntal* and mango. The *Paripāṭal* describes in more than one extensive hymn (e.g., *Paripāṭal* 6:7–10) the coming of the monsoon, and the concomitant flooding and fecundation of the earth as the coming of Murukaṉ with his entourage of elephants and army. The association with time is even more explicit in the Epic mythology, and particularly in the myth of *Mahābhārata* III, 223–232. Herein we read that Skanda is born on *amāvāsyā* (the new moon day) when sun and moon are conjoined; his birth is equated to the rising of the sun; he is suckled by the Kṛttika maidens whom he later sends into the heavens to become a constellation by which time would thereafter be measured. Indra declares Skanda to be the lord of time and a new era of chronometry to have been initiated.

However one interprets the meaning of this Epic allusion it does intimate that by the late Epic period the worship of Skanda is cognizant of at least two elements of the *pañcāṅka* or contemporary ritual calendar, namely, the notion of *titis* or stages of the moon's waxing and waning, and of *nakṣatras* or lunar asterisms or regions of the sky through which the moon passes during its orbit. In the Epic mythology and in the cultic life, Skanda is associated with the movement of the sun in the heavens and his career homologized to the cycle of the moon. Yet at the same time, and especially as expressed in Tamil literature and peasant lore, Murukaṉ is associated with the blossoming of certain trees and the coming of the rain, that is, to the agricultural and seasonal cycle. All of these elements continue to be reflected in the ritual times which the contemporary cultus of Murukaṉ celebrates.

3.1 *Murukan̲ and the moon*

There is little doubt that there is a close relationship between Murukan̲ and the moon.[24] Epic myths show the god to be conceived on the new moon day and to grow to manhood in the first seven days of the waxing moon. Inscriptions suggest that forms of lunar chronometry like the *pakṣa* (fortnight) and the *titi* (a stage of the waxing-eaning moon) were being used by the Sātavāhanas and more extensively by the Śakas (Mahalingam 1968:63–67). It is plausible that the Skanda cultus, coming to eminence in the Epic period as it does, was associated with lunar chronometry by that time. There is also some evidence that early Tamil poets used the waxing and waning moon as a measure of time.[25]

Whatever its history, the lunar cycle is an important determinant in the ritual life of Śaivism today, particularly in rural Tamil Nadu, and in the Murukan̲ cultus. Of particular significance is the concept of the *titi* or stage in the lunar cycle. The *titi* is literally a segment of the sun's reflection on the moon as the latter is in orbit. Each fortnight is divided into fifteen *titis* or graded segments of light, though the moon's orbit is actually 29.53059 days (Sastri 1968:46). Three such stages are especially illustrative of the importance of lunar chronometry in temples to Murukan̲ in Tamil Nadu today.

3.1.1 *The new moon*

The first *titi* is the new moon itself (*amavācai* or Sanskrit: *amāvāsyā*).[26] The new moon constitutes the start of a new unit of time. It is said that Brahmā started the creation process on a new moon day, a day which was therefore called a *yugadhi* (the beginning of a *yuga*) (Ayyár 1921:68). The new moon day serves as the beginning of the ritual month in the Telugu year, though, in the Tamil year, the month starts when the sun enters a new sign of the Zodiac. In association with Murukan̲ however, *amāvāsyā* also coincides with the 'birth', of the deity. Certain new moon days become particularly important junctures of the solar year or the seasonal-agricultural calendar.

Tai amāvāsyā in January–February and Āṭi amāvāsyā in July–August are significant new moon days usually accompanied by ritual bathing and other purification ceremonies of a special order. They are the new moons of the first full months after the winter and summer solstices respectively and constitute the lunar beginnings of the bright and dark halves of the solar year. These new moons also relate to the agricultural season as in January–February the winter rice crops have just been harvested and in July–August the summer rains have come and the new crops recently planted. These two new moon days, therefore, are popularly celebrated perhaps more than any other by pilgrimages to sacred waters where ritual bathing and other forms of purification are observed. These ceremonies are observed in *Tai* and *Āti* months in many homes which do not take the other new moon days seriously.

Each year there is a *mahāḷaya amavācai* which falls late in the month of *Purattāci* (September–October) or in early *Aippaci* (October–November). Literally, the term means the new moon of the great immigration and is characterized traditionally by the visitation of the *pitṛs* or manes – that is, spirits of the dead. The start of this lunar cycle is a day of special penitence, falling as it does just after the autumnal equinox and representing the start of the 'winter' and 'nighttime' months. This new moon day is accompanied, in most Śaiva temples, by fasting and exchange of vows, particularly by women. The *Navarāttiri* festival – the festival of nine nights – follows immediately. In this particular cycle of the moon, and no other, the ninth *titi* or *Mahānavami* (the great ninth stage of the moon) assumes importance in Śaiva temples and is marked by consecration of books by the learned and of tools by laborers. Then in the dark fortnight (*mahālaya pakṣa*) of the lunar cycle of this month, originally called Bhādrapada, the manes are said to visit. Lights are lit to show the manes back to their world. It is from this early practice that the festival of Tīpāvaḷi has developed (Sastri 1968:11)[27].

Finally, the new moon of *Aippaci* month (October–November) which immediately follows the *mahālaya pakṣa* (the fortnight of the great immigration) and which follows the last day of *Tīpāvaḷi*, serves an important function in the cultus of Murukaṉ. It precedes the first day of the Skanda-Ṣaṣṭi festival, during which the birth, maturation, and triumph over the *asura* is ritually re-enacted. That new moon day becomes not only the day of Murukaṉ's conception, but, as we shall argue later, becomes a virtual midnight of the ritual year in the cultus of Murukaṉ.

3.1.2 *Ṣaṣṭi*

A second *titi* or lunar stage important to the cultus is *ṣaṣṭi* (Sanskrit: *ṣaṣṭhī*) the sixth stage of the waxing moon. *Ṣaṣṭi* takes its name from the goddess Ṣaṣṭhī mentioned in several Epic texts. Ṣaṣṭhī was one of the malevolent attendants of Skanda and a giver of lingering (*yāspa*) diseases. The *Devibhāgavata Purāṇa* (IX:46) says she is called Ṣaṣṭhī because she is the sixth part of *prakṛti*. The same text suggests she is the presiding deity of children, a spouse to Skanda, also known as Devasenā, and grants progeny to the childless. On the sixth day after childbirth her worship is to be performed in the Sūtikāgrha. The Kāśyapa Samhitā says Ṣaṣṭhī is a sixth form of Skanda. the sister to five Skanda deities (Agrawala 1966:135ff.). Ṣaṣṭhī apparently came to personify all the goddesses and forces believed to cause diseases of the mother and child, and particularly such as whose favor was sought on the sixth day after birth. As a result, she came to personify the sixth day of the child's life. From this background, the sixth day of the lunar cycle on which Skanda conquered the *asura* is known as Ṣaṣṭhī.

This mythical slaying of the demons by Skanda–Murukan̲ is remembered every month on the *Ṣaṣṭhī titi*. It assumes special significance in the festival of Skanda–Ṣaṣṭi. The day and the event re-enacted on it celebrates the triumph of Skanda–Murukan̲ over the cosmic forces of evil and personal malaise.

3.1.3 *The full moon* (paurṇami)

The *paurṇami* or full moon is important in all orthodox Śaiva temples, including those of Murukan̲. In the lunar cycle, the full moon served a variety of functions. It was the full moon, or more specifically, the asterism in whose house the full moon was located that gave to some of the months their names. For example, Caitra and Vaiśākha were names given to months because the star groups known as Citra and Viśākha were those suitable or in appropriate locations when the moon was full in a particular month of the year (Sastri 1968:46). Further, in some parts of Northwestern India the months are still reckoned from full moon to full moon, a practice which apparently occurred even in Vedic times (p. 46). However, in Tamil ritual, and particularly in the cultus of Murukan̲, the full moon connotes completion, fulfillment, and total maturity. It is on or near the full moon that the climactic functions of most festivals occur. Insofar as the lunar cycle is homologized to the cosmic rhythm, the full moon connotes the zenith of the cosmic cycle, and in its association with the Murukaṉ cultus in which the waxing of the moon and the career of the deity are explicitly homologized, the full moon suggests the deity's attainment of full maturity and powers.

As with other lunar moments, full moons assume particular significance when they conjoin with sacred moments in other measures of time. In particular, it is the conjunction of full moon, appropriate asterism, and appropriate portion of the solar year that determines when a festival is held.

3.2 *The cycle of asterisms* (nakṣatras)

Along with the waxing and waning of the moon, a different form of chronometry is used which depends on the movement of the moon in orbit around the earth. This is known as the cycle of asterisms or *nakṣatras*. The *nakṣatras* were determined by observation of the path of the moon in the heavens. It was noted in due time that nearly once in twenty-seven days the moon came to practically the same point in its path, so that the path could be divided into twenty-seven parts marked by prominent stars or star-groups. The precise history of this method of reckoning time is unclear,[28] but *nakṣatras* are mentioned in regnal inscriptions with any frequency only after the eighth century A.D. (Subbarlu 1968:76ff.).

Whatever date the *nakṣatras* become important, some of them were associated with the Skanda cultus in the Epic mythology and are an important dimension of the contemporary ritual calendar. On the day of each 'asterism' a significant event or events is believed to have happened in the life of a god which is remembered and re-enacted each time the day of that asterism returns. These mythical events vary for each deity, so the cultus of each deity may observe certain *nakṣatras* in unique ways. Moreover, each asterism is believed to have certain powers which make its influence on the day of its prominence particularly effective for the occurrence of good or ill.

Kārttikai: Two *nakṣatras* are of particular significance in the Murukaṉ cultus. These are *Kārttikai* and *Vicākam*. *Kārttikai* is the most important of these two, as it is celebrated popularly each month. The third *nakṣatra* in the series, it was this one which was sent into the heavens by Skanda after his triumph over the *asuras*. Mythically, the *kṛttikas* were the six maidens that suckled the six infants who were eventually integrated into the one deity Skanda. Commonly, Skanda is said to be the son of the *Kṛttikas*, as in the name *Kārttikeya*. Celebrations on *Kārttikai* day thus commemorate Skanda's coming into being, his being nurtured into maturity, and his lordship over time. In popular imagination, *Kārttikai* is called the 'birthday' of Murukaṉ.

While *Kārttikai* is celebrated each month, once a year the celebration takes on particularly significant proportions. In the month of *Kārttikai* (November–December) which takes its name from the fact the asterism *kārttikai* falls on or near the full moon, the one day celebration of *tirukkārttikai* occurs. In addition to its association with Skanda's relation to the *Kṛttikas*, there is some evidence that *tirukkārttikai* is associated with an ancient Tamil festival of lights. Miss R. Champalakshmi has suggested that references to the lighting of lamps in such early Tamil works as the *Kār Nāṟpatu* (26:1) *Kaḷavaḻi Nāṟpatu* (17:3); *Akanāṉūṟu* (141:8, 11) and *Jīvakacintamaṇi* is to a practice still observed, not so much at *Tīpāvaḷi* as *Tirrukkārtikai*, for it includes the lighting of lamps on hills in a manner still done, for example, in *Tiruvaṇṇāmalai tīpam* and the lighting of rows of lamps commonly done at *Tirukkārtikai* (Champalakshmi 1968:91).

Vicākam: The asterism *vicākam*, the sixteenth in the cycle, is said to have been presiding on the day of integration when Skanda became one being from several diverse heritages. Therefore, *vicākam* is also said to be the 'birthday' of Skanda.[29] More precisely Viśākha is associated with Skanda in the Epic myths as one who springs from the side of Skanda and is depicted on several seals of the Epic period as standing beside Skanda. Viśākha may have been one of several folk deities of the Epic period who were eventually integrated into the one deity Skanda (D. R. Bhandarkar 1921:22–23).

The observance of *vicākam* is not so universal in Murukaṉ temples as that of *kārttikai*, but some temples do observe the day in each month. But, once a year in the month of *vaikāci*, which takes its name from the asterism, the *vicākam* asterism falls on or near the full moon and the day becomes the climax of the *vaikāci vicākam* festival; in that festival, among other things, the deity's birth and ascendancy to a place of supremacy amongst the gods is re-enacted.

Pūcam: Two other *nakṣatras* assume importance in the cultus of Murukaṉ, as in Śaivism as a whole, but not because of unique associations to Skanda Murukaṉ. The *nakṣatra pūcam* is one of these. Of particular significance is the *pūcam* that falls on or near the full moon in the month of *Tai* (January–February). The asterism *pūcam* is said to be that of *taṇṭapāṇi* (Sanskrit: *Daṇḍapāṇi*). This is a name used for Murukaṉ or for Viṣṇu (and even for Yama) and has two connotations attributable to Murukaṉ. First, *taṇṭapaṇi* can mean one with a staff in hand, as *taṇṭa* can mean staff or walking stick. In this sense, the term suggests the role of an ascetic as the staff is a symbol of the ascetic. Murukaṉ is called *taṇṭa yutapāṇi* at Paḻani (and also at Swamimalai), where he is enshrined as an ascetic. But almost paradoxically, the term *taṇṭa* can also mean 'army' or 'punishment'; hence *taṇṭapāṇi* can connote military prowess. It is this connotation which relates to Viṣṇu and to other deities with a military heritage like Skanda–Murukaṉ; in this sense of the term, allusion is made to the virility and strength of the respective deities. The term *taṇṭapāṇi*, thus, identifies the relationship made explicit within the Murukaṉ tradition between ascetic and military leader. The latter subdues the enemy with an army; the former subdues the passions with a staff. The festival of *tai pūcam*, therefore, while observed throughout Śaivism, nonetheless has more specific meaning when celebrated at Murukaṉ temples and especially at Paḻani.

Uttiram: The asterism *uttiram* is said to be auspicious for marriage. On the day of *uttiram*'s influence, virtually all the gods and goddesses were said to have married, including Rāma and Sitā, Śiva (as Sundareṣa) and Mīnakṣi, and Murukaṉ and Vaḷḷi. According to one myth popular in the Tamil cultus of Murukaṉ, Nambirājan, thought to be the 'first man' and the mythical hunter-father of Vaḷḷi, is said to have believed that the star *uttiram* was especially auspicious for marriage and insisted that his daughter marry Murukaṉ on that day.[30]

When *uttiram* falls on or near the full moon in the month of *Paṅkuṉi* (April–May), a month also believed to be auspicious for marriage, especially in the Tamil tradition inasmuch as such trees as the *vēṅkai* and the mango are blossoming, the day is particularly auspicious for marrying and re-enacting the marriage of the god. The festival that results, the *paṅkuṉi uttiram*, observed in virtually all Śaiva temples, is highlighted, in the Murukaṉ cultus, by re-enacting of Murukaṉ's marriage to Vaḷḷi (or Devasenā). The festival is taken especially seriously in such temples as that at

Tirupparaṅkun̲r̲am where Murukan̲ is said to have married Devasenā, but it is also the busiest festival of the year at such pilgrimage centres as Pal̲ani and Kun̲r̲akkuti.

3.3 *The solar year*

The solar year operative throughout India now and since the Epic period at least is a luni-solar year, a year of twelve lunar units whose names and calculation are based largely on the movement of the moon in relation to the *nakṣatras.*[31] Despite the growing importance of the moon, there is still a cognizance in ritual chronometry of the orbit of the earth around the sun. In fact, the Tamil month begins, not with the new moon or full moon, but with the day on which the sun 'enters' the new sign of the zodiac. Of the twelve zodiacal constellations, each is said to be dominant, by virtue of its position on the Eastern horizon, for the duration of a month.[32] Each entry of the sun into a new zodiacal house is known as a *saṁkrānti.*

More significant for understanding the meaning of the solar year in the ritual calendar is the fact that the year is intended to represent a day in the life of the gods.[33] This relationship is made explicit in the Murukan̲ cultus especially at certain times of the year. In general, it can be said that the start of the month after the winter solstice (*Tai*) represents a ritual dawn. The start of the month after the vernal equinox (*Cittirai*) represents a ritual mid-morning (as well as being the Tamil New Year). The start of the month after the summer solstice represents a ritual noon, and the time of the autumnal equinox is homologous to dusk.[34] The ritual year is given specific nuances of meaning because of this relationship, which though more explicit at certain points than at others, is nonetheless operative in the festival calendar. In effect, the ritual 'daytime' runs from pre-dawn to noon, when the sun is in the eastern skies, while the ritual evening and night runs from noon to pre-dawn – the Tamil term *cayaṅkālam* (evening) encompasses that time from noon to dusk; and *rāttiri* (night) runs from dusk to pre-dawn. Similarly, the ritual year has its 'daytime' (actually 'morning') during the six months falling roughly between winter and summer solstice when the sun is in its northern course, whereas ritual 'evening' is represented by the period falling approximately between summer solstice and autumnal equinox, and the 'night' by the period falling approximately between autumnal equinox and winter solstice.[35]

Given this rhythm of the solar year, it becomes apparent that virtually all major festivals addressed to Murukaṉ, observed in Tamil Nadu, occur during the period we have said was congruent to the hours between pre-dawn and noon in the ritual day. Thus, Skanda–Ṣaṣṭi in October–November becomes the first festival to the god, and, in addition to all else that it represents, in the context of the solar year, represents his rising in the pre-dawn hours and subduing the forces of chaos and darkness. His overcoming of the *asura* thereby becomes a creative act, assuring the coming of a new cosmic 'day' and a new created order. Conversely, the last major festival to Murukaṉ, celebrated universally in Tamil Nadu is the *vaikāci vicākam*, the climax of which falls in May–June on the last full moon prior to the summer solstice.[36] The new moon which starts the Skanda–Ṣaṣṭi festival represents a cosmic midnight, while the full moon of *vaikāci vicākam* is said to represent the cosmic noon.[37] Further, the festival calendar from Skanda–Ṣaṣṭi to *vaikāci vicākam* suggests the six day career of the god is rendered homologous to the growth and maturation of the cosmos from the 'pre-dawn' period of the year to 'noon'. We shall sketch in some of the highlights of this festival calendar which suggest this homology between day, year, and deity's career, remembering all the while that each festival has specific significance quite apart from the solar year, derived largely from the myth which is said to have occurred at the time of the *nakṣatra* and lunar cycle on which the festival falls.

We have observed that the 'nighttime' of the ritual year encompasses approximately that period between autumnal equinox and winter solstice – or, more precisely, the months of *Purattāci* (September–October), *Aippaci* (October–November), and *Kārttikai* (November–December). The festivals of these months are nighttime festivals, starting with *Navarāttiri*, the festival of nine nights, and including Tīpāvaḷi (festival of lights), Skanda–Ṣaṣṭi and *Tirukārttikai*, noted for its lighting of lamps. The lunar cycle in which Skanda–Ṣaṣṭi falls is one of the most significant of the year. That it constitutes the first lunar cycle after the cosmic 'midnight' and a new year of sorts is apparent. Many merchants throughout India celebrate the new year on Tīpāvaḷi day (Sanskrit: *Dīpāvali*), that is the day before the new moon starting Skanda–Ṣaṣṭi (Raghavan 1963:34). That same new moon day is thought to be the day of Viṣṇu's slaying of Bali, a personification of malevolence, and Tīpāvaḷi, in part, celebrates that triumph (p. 14). Further, we have seen that the Tīpāvaḷi season is associated with the return of the spirits from the dead, spirits which are assisted to return to the world of Yama by the light of lamps and firecrackers (p. 14).[38] The nature of this season is further reflected in the purpose of Tīpāvaḷi, a purpose which V. Raghavan summarizes in these words:

> . . . As rejoicings, they [the observances of Dīpāvaḷi] have probably their ultimate roots in the Season, in the passing away of the darkness and the rains and in the break of light the onset of autumn the resumption of cultivation and commerce and the activities of gain and pleasure. The lamps of Dīpāvali not only light the path of our ancestors, but they shine forth as symbols of the eternal prayer of the Soul *'tamaso ma iyoti gamaya'* – 'Lead me from darkness to light'. (p. 14).

Skanda–Ṣaṣṭi, then, for all else it celebrates, marks, for Murukan̲ *bhaktas*, the coming of the diety into existence, the conquest over darkness and evil, the passing of the midnight of the cosmos, and the watershed of the Northeast monsoon. *Tirukkārttikai* which follows in the month of *Kārttikai* (usually in late November), represents the suckling and nurture of the deity by the Kṛttikas and is associated with the lighting of rows of lights on or near the full moon just prior to the 'dawn' of the ritual year.

The month of *Mārkal̲i* (December–January), which follows, when the sun enters the sign of Sagittarius, is a highly significant one; in all Śaiva temples it is homologized to the dawn, *ucakālam* (Sanskrit: *uṣāḥkālam*). On the first day of *Mārkal̲i* the dawn ritual of *tirupaḷḷi el̲ucci* (rising from the bedchamber) is started in a number of temples and continues each day throughout the month. It is a month sacred to Naṭarāja as his *nakṣatra*, *tiruvātirai* or Betelguese falls on or near the full moon day. Kṛṣṇa himself is quoted as saying: 'of the months, I am *markasi*' (Bhagavadgita X:35). *Mārkal̲i* is the prelude to daytime and creation.

The month of *Tai* (January–February) follows. It is homologized to *piratakālam* (Sanskrit: *prathakāla*), the post-dawn early morning hours. Throughout Tamil Nadu, the month starts with the *Poṅkal* festival. Not only does *Poṅkal* celebrate the harvest; it celebrates the sun's entering the sign of Capricon and starting its journey in the northern skies. The start of the sun's apparent northern journey is known as Uttarāyaṇa or Udagāyaṇa, and was mentioned in some Upaniṣadic and Brāhmaṇic texts and in the Gṛhyasūtras (Champalakshmi 1968:87). The festival of *Tai Pūcam*, which follows at the conjoining of the star *pūcam* and the full moon of *Tai*, celebrates, in the cultus of Murukaṉ, the god's conquest of passions and malevolence. Coming as it does at this period in the solar year, the god's youthfulness, virility, and creativity relate it to a similar stage in the waxing of the cosmic cycle, and of the year and the day.

There follows, in some, but not all, Murukaṉ temples, the *Māci* festival.[39] Climaxed on the last full moon day before the vernal equinox, it celebrates, in effect, the total life and youthful exploits of the god, including his slaying of the *asuras*, his conquest of the ram, his fulfilling of the five functions of godhead, and his reigning in triumph. The month of *Māci* (February–March , which comes just prior to the sun's reaching the midway point on its journey in the Northern sky, is congruent to the sacred time preceding mid-morning.[40]

On the full moon day of *Pankuṉi* (March–April) which occurs near the vernal equinox the festival of *Pankuṉi Uttiram* is celebrated in most temples and is one of the most popular festivals in the entire cultus. *Paṅkuṉi Uttiram* is universally observed as the festival of marriage; the month in which it falls, *Pankuṉi*, is congruent to the mid-morning hours of daily ritual, the *mattyacanti* (Sanskrit: *Madhyasāmdhi*). The climatic day of *Paṅkuṉi Uttiram* is said to mark winter's becoming summer and cold's turning hot (Ayyar 1921:59).[41]

This festival's current popularity is evidenced by the interesting paradox that even at Paḻani, where the god is enshrined as a celibate. *Paṅkuṉi Uttiram* attracts almost half a million pilgrims. Several important features of contemporary Tamil life and religion are expressed in the festival of marriage and the concomitant mythology related to Murukaṉ's association with his consorts. Among them are the undoubted significance of marriage as a sociological phenomenon for Tamilians. Also significant is the symbolism implied in the existence of two consorts, especially that of Murukaṉ's expressing two kinds of grace – the one actively seeking 'unworthy' souls, the other more passively being available to meritorious devotees; then too, the consorts express two kinds of love expressed persistently in Tamil literature: Devasenā represents *kaṟpu* or chastity and an orthodox form of marriage; Vaḷḷi represents *kaḷavu* or love outside of marriage, a love lyricized in early Tamil literature and not infrequently given to squabbles of jealousy. In short, with all else *Pankuṉi Uttiram* expresses it is a celebration consistent with ongoing Tamil romanticism.[42]

The Tamil month of *Cittirai* (April–May), which starts the new year, follows when the sun enters the sign of Aries. No festivals to Murukaṉ are observed in this month. It is in *Vaikāci* (May–June) that the final major Murukaṉ festival occurs. The festival *vaikāci vicākam* celebrates the god's reaching his full maturity, his integration into a simple supreme god, and his dominion over the cosmos. It is that full moon day of *Vaikāci* which marks for most temples the zenith of the year, inasmuch as the sun 'starts its journey southward' in a matter of days.[43]

The start of the 'dark half' of the solar year is marked in Tamil temples by the start of the month of *Āṭi* (July–August), when the sun enters the sign of Cancer. The cosmic evening has started, and, as in the ritual day, a ritual kind of abstinence is observed. With one exception, there are no major festivals addressed to Murukaṉ in this period. Not coincidentally, this is that period of the Southwest monsoon which brings to Tamil Nadu light summer rains and causes a shift in the agricultural pattern. Accordingly, most of the significant festival occasions are agriculturally-oriented. The festival of *Āṭippūram* in the month of *Āṭi* is a case in point.[44] The festival may actually begin late in *Āṇi* (June–July) when newly planted paddy shoots appear. The highlight of the festival is the ritual transferring of shoots (even though in some districts of Tamil Nadu transferring of shoots may actually occur a month or two later). Similarly, also in *Āṭi*, on the eighteenth day, the ritual commemoration of the 'overflowing of the Kāveri' occurs. The eighteenth of *Āṭi* marks the traditional date when the rivers crest, swollen by summer rains. Treated as a goddess, the river is offered garments, bangles, winnowing baskets or other paraphernalia appropriate for feminine use. Purificatory bathing is appropriate on that day. It is clear that the festivals of *Āṭi* eighteenth have roots in rather early Tamil civilization, for the *Paripāṭal*, a text which may be as old as the fourth century, has at least three hymns addressed to the river Vaikai, describing it in flood, while people bathe and play in its waters, and celebrate the fertility of the land that rains will bring. Strikingly, the coming of the rains are likened to the coming of Murukaṉ and his host, routing drought and want (Paripāṭal 6, 7, 10).[45]

The one festival to Murukaṉ which does occur in a few temples of Tamil Nadu during these months takes place in the month of *Āvaṇi* (August–

September). Climaxed on the last full moon day prior to the autumnal equinox, this festival is a virtual duplicate of the *Māci* festival in which the total career of the god is re-enacted, including his conquest of the *asuras*, his fulfilling the functions of Divinity, and his triumphal reign over the cosmos. However, this festival is more than likely a vestige of a new year festival in the old Cēṟa kingdom, brought to Tiruchendur (which temple is the primary celebrant of the festival) by *potṛs* from Kerala in the sixteenth or seventeenth century.[46] Therefore, this festival does not appear to fit into the solar scheme outlined above with respect to the Tamil festivals addressed to Murukaṉ.

So the solar year and the day are congruent, though more explicitly so at some points than others. This pattern is also consistent with the rhythm of the cosmos and especially at such moments as dawn and the beginning of a new year, which, like the new moon day, are likened to the creation of the cosmos. Moreover, the career of the god is apparently homologous to the movement of the earth in relationship to the sun. The linking of Skanda–Murukaṉ to the sun in ritual is not surprising in light of the frequent references to Skanda's equation with sun to be found in the Epic myths. In those myths Skanda is like the sun in that he is the primordial demiurge and the creator and sovereign of the cosmos. Like the sun, the god is an embodiment of the rhythm and pattern of the cosmos.

3.4 *Other measures of time's sacrality*

Other dimensions of chronometry have entered into the cultic life of Murukaṉ which are not reflected in the largely brāhmaṇic pattern outlined above. One of these is the significance of certain days of the week for Murukaṉ devotees. There is some reason to believe that the days of the week were borrowed from the Middle East and were not part of the numerical and astronomical systems developed in traditional brāhmaṇic chronometry.[47] Be that as it may, two days of the week have become particularly associated with Murukaṉ: Tuesday and Friday.

Tuesday (*cevvaykkīḻamai*) is literally the day of the planet Mars, or of the 'red one'. The association between Murukaṉ and Mars appears to rest on at least two factors: the fact that both are red (in the case of Murukaṉ, associating him with sun, fire, lotus, etc.), and the fact that both are associated with military prowess. On Tuesdays, in some Murukaṉ temples appropriate rituals are observed. The reason that Friday (*veḷḷikiḻamai*) is associated with Murukaṉ is even more obscure. It is commonly observed that *Veḷḷi* is the term for Venus (and whiteness) but its relationship to Murukaṉ is not clear. Even so, Friday is a 'holy day' not only for Murukaṉ but for many indigenous and folk deities.

Interspersed with the highly formalized chronometric system, preserved and calculated by specially trained brāhmaṇic *śāstris* and astrologers, there is the rhythm of seasonal and ecological time, known even to the most illiterate of peasants. Especially noticeable in the cultic calendar are the coming of two monsoons, the blossoming of certain trees, and the balance of the agricultural cycle with its planting and harvesting. These factors are particularly reflected in such festivals as *Poṅkal* in mid-January and Āṭippūram, the festival celebrating the planting and transferring of summer crops and the coming of the summer rains. In some rural areas certain other festivals are said to be popular (or even scheduled in the first place) because people are relatively free from their agricultural toil and need an opportunity for rejoicing and celebration.[48]

Another factor playing an increasing part in determining the sacrality of time is the growing observance of the Western year. This is particularly evident, of course, in urban centers, where it takes such forms as providing a 'reason' for the early morning and evening *pūjās*. These *pūjās* are held at these times, we are told, to provide working persons an opportunity to worship at the beginning and the end of their working day.[49] Even more striking in this respect is the *Tiruppaṭi Bhajana* (Concert on Sacred Steps) held at Tiruttaṇi on December 31, when the new 'English' year is greeted with song and penitence. A similar combination of traditional and modern chronometry – and of brāhmaṇic and non-brāhmaṇic perspectives – is to be seen in the creation of new festivals to commemorate the lives of saints. For example, a two day festival in August at Tiruvaṇṇāmalai, started in 1954, celebrates the date that Aruṇakiri, fifteenth century Murukaṉ poet and *bhakta*, received grace at that spot. A similar centenary festival held in November, 1970 at Vaḷḷimalai commemorated the birth of Sri Vaḷḷimalai Satchidananda Swami, who helped popularize Aruṇakiri's songs in this century. Both of these festivals, like an increasing number of traditional ones, schedule concerts and lectures less on the basis of appropriate chronometric calculations as on the basis of convenience for devotees. At least one of the factors involved in this process is that executive officers of temples are often non-brāhmaṇs who are sometimes less concerned for the observance of traditional chronometry, with which they are scarecely familiar, at any rate, than with public relations and the availability of the temple's facilities to the public.

3.5 *Time and the present*

In the foregoing we have observed and articulated a sense of what we might call concentric cyclicality. One cycle of time operates within another and beside others. Had we chosen we might have followed this concentric pattern to still smaller cycles: to the cyclicality of ritual observed within one *Tirukālam* or sacred moment, for example, or to the specific ritual acts wherein a certain cyclic structure is discernible: The *apiṣekam* (anointing of the icon), the *arātaṉai* (adoration with lamps) or the *lakṣārccaṉam* (recitation of 108 names). Or we could have pursued the pattern to increasingly large units: the sixty years which comprise a unit in which lunar, stellar, and solar measurements are synchronized; or even to the *Purāṇic* concept of an era or *yuga*, the fourth of which (*kali yuga*) we are said to be experiencing. Almost every astronomically calculated unit in traditional ritual use becomes a microcosm of the cosmic rhythm, waxing to a climax in one half, waning to a new beginning in the other. Further, in at least some instances – at some junctures more than others – the chronometric unit becomes associated with the mythic life of the deity. This is especially explicit during the day at dawn in the *Tirupaḷḷi eḻucci* and *viṣvarūpa*; in the lunar cycle, particularly at new moon, *ṣaṣṭi* and the full moon; and in the solar calendar, particularly at the times of *Skanda–ṣaṣṭi tirukkārtikai*, and *vaikāci vicākam*.

The implications of this cyclicality are several. Suggested is a concept of history which views time as repetitive, homogeneous, perhaps even relentless. Time would be tyrannical if it were not for the fact it can be understood and measured, indeed even ritually transcended, especially at those moments we have called 'tempocosms', when the possibility of breakthrough is dramatized in the conjunction of chronometric units. And more, the very repetitiveness of the cycles suggests the world's eternal renewability.

Further, the role of the priest becomes no less than that of ritually maintaining the cosmos and assuring its constant renewal. Whether or not devotees are present, the priests must perform their functions; like chemists combining elements by precise formulae to make new compounds, the priests are technicians seeking by repeating appropriate formulae, to ritually recreate the world temporally. They preside over each new beginning and endeavor to make each 'tempocosm' an appropriate portrayal of ultimacy. The relationship of the deity to the priest seems ambivalent, for, the priests, on the one hand, are invoking the god's creativity and sovereignty over the cosmos and are re-enacting the god's work. Yet, on the other hand, the god himself reflects the rhythm of the cosmos and his vitality and power is dependent on the instrumentality of the priest. That many priests are nonetheless unaware of these dimensions of their work is clear from their inability to articulate the intricate nuances of the calendar.

If the complex system of brāhmaṇic chronometry we have outlined does indeed have cosmological implications, one can only wonder whether the increasing de-brāhmaṇization of temple and calendar, alluded to at the end of our discussion, also implies that differing conceptions of time and cosmos are becoming increasingly operative. In other terms, for those for whom brāhmaṇic chronometry is no longer applicable either because it is not understood or because it is being deliberately rejected, what views of time and cosmos are operative? Part of the answer to this may be that, for some devotees, re-affirmation of time and cosmos is occurring in a manner not inconsistent with that found in early Tamil literature. In that literature we find little concern for transcendence or ultimacy, little evidence that ritual or chronometry serve as openings to larger temporal realities. Each moment, measured largely in terms of the season – the coming of rains, vegetation, foliage – is itself; it is celebrated as a sign that life and fertility as it is known will continue and flourish. Time, measured in those terms, is less an astronomical unit used to calculate the rhythm of the universe, as it is a biological unit, which affirms that the processes of human growth and agriculture are proceeding in anticipated ways. As such, it is celebrative time; they are moments which affirm the festive, the fertile, and joyous in life. Yet, for still others, living in the context of urban and technological change, where both the astronomical and biological senses of time have become remote even for those middle classes which remain devout, the ritual calendar poses a question: will the calendar invite subtly meaningful combinations of differing visions of time to be found in history? Or will the challenge of suggestive yesterdays be rather to discover new meaning in the potentially homogeneous and tedious present? Whichever be the case, Murukaṉ remains 'Lord of Time' for large numbers of Tamil people whose days and years are affirmed and enriched by their devotion to him.

6

The Many Facets of Murukan̲

If one steps back from the specifics of history it is possible to see persistent symbolic themes in the cultus of Murukan̲ which say a great deal not only about the meaning of the god, but of the nature of religion, especially in South India. These themes or motifs suggest how the god relates to the mythology of Hinduism as a whole; but, more importantly, they suggest how the gods' character invokes human response – or more accurately, perhaps – how the gods' life and attributes bespeak human needs and aspirations. The 'theology' associated with Murukan̲ makes sense for his devotees because it reflects a profound human creativity and vision. The symbolic themes which recur in Murukan̲'s mythic history are interesting also because they embody the cultural and social history of his devotees. It is worthwhile then to reflect on the character of Murukan̲ and on the 'theology' he embodies, especially as that character is expressed in the dominant themes and motifs of his person. We do so in the expectation that they tell us something not only of God, but of man and history.

1. Symbol, persistence and change

Even in the face of a long literary history and the influence of several cultural impeti, there has been a certain persistence to the symbol-system associated with the god Murukan̲. This is not to suggest that the god's history of symbol-system was determined for all time at some primitive moment, nor that there was no change or shifting of emphasis. It does mean that the changes that did occur in the symbolism were not inconsistent with the possibilities inherent in the earlier history of the god. It also means that many of the meanings found early in the history of the god's symbols remained with those symbols even though cultural and historical change brought about a change in the forms and terms by which those meanings were expressed. This persistence is not surprising from the standpoint of what we have seen occurring in South Indian history, even in early times, when hunting motifs persisted into and commingled with an atmosphere in which agricultural, pastoral, and even urban and philosophical developments have occurred. Nor is this persistence surprising from the standpoint of what, from the analysis of several scholars, we have come to expect of a symbol (cf. Eliade 1959:86–107; Ricœur 1962:191–218).

The most elementary – and perhaps the most obvious – form of this persistence is the way in which a meaning or a unit of intelligibility continues to be associated with a symbol throughout the symbol's history. A meaning ascribable to a symbol at an early stage of the symbol's existence may be found in the symbol centuries later – even if that meaning is later modified, garbled, or is not even consciously perceived by the symbol's apprehenders.

In the Murukaṉ tradition, for example, the lance is a symbol which represents the instrumentality of power of the bearer throughout its history, whether that bearer is seen as the mythical hunter, the prototype of the warrior king, or as the god who slays the *pācas* which molest the souls in quest of liberation. Similarly, the god himself is persistently a 'hunter' – whether of life-giving game, 'enemies' of the state, the dharma-destroying *asuras*, or the imperfections of the human soul. In this elementary sense, the god and his related phenomena are symbols which persist throughout their history with a consistent message even though specific connotations may vary in the context of cultural changes. It is as though old symbols never died; they just found new things to mean.

But the symbol does not function that simply. It does not insist on carrying only a particular message. On the contrary, there are moments in the life of the symbol, when a 'coalescence of messages' takes place and related structures of meanings accrue to it. In this sense, the symbol becomes a stick in the stream of cultural history, around which the related flotsam and jetsam of meaning which flow in that history gather, giving the symbol a broad collection of related meanings.

In the Murukaṉ tradition, for example, the peacock undergoes such a series of coalescences. In the early Tamil tradition, the peacock seems primarily to reflect an earth-oriented view of the world – it embodied the beauty and fertility apparent in the hill country; it represented the abundance and color of vegetative life. In it was reflected the dancing gait and colorful affirmation of the vitality and fullness expressive of early Tamil life as depicted in its poetry.

But as South India and the Murukaṉ tradition come in contact with the imagery of Sanskrit, and particularly Epic and post-Epic literature, the peacock more clearly assumed celestial attributes. He has the capacity for flight; he rises like the sun and is brightly adorned like the sun. He acquires some of the attributes associated with the *garuḍa*, the sun bird and vehicle of the heavenly Viṣṇu. By riding the peacock, Murukaṉ soars above the world and masters the celestial realms.

However, by the fifteenth century, the blue-green peacock is equated with the ocean, both in the poetry of Aruṇakiri and in the myth of the wicked *asura* who became a peacock in the ocean. The god 'tames' it, subdues it and makes it his vehicle. The peacock thus represents land, sky and sea – the world's totality. Religiously, it has come to symbolize the subdued world which the god has made into his vehicle. It is not too surprising, therefore, when a commentator tells us that the spread tail of the peacock represents *Ōm* (V. S. Chengalvaraya Pillai in Aruṇakirinātar, n.d., VI:625), the syllable connoting totality, for by the medieval period the peacock has indeed come to represent much of that whole which the history of the tradition incorporates.

So the symbol carries not only a particular meaning persistently, but at certain historical moments accrues meanings related to and consistent with the mood of that moment and with the earlier history of the symbol. The symbol brings into itself meanings which, though they may appear to be in contrast, are related and embodied in a creative synthesis.

Persistence can take another form: the meaning may persist, yet be manifest in changing phenomena or symbols. It is as if the message flitted from one symbol or phenomenon to another, precisely because the symbols or phenomena were similar in appearance or intent. We might reverse the truism offered earlier: some old meanings never die; they just find new symbols on which to mean. Thus, in the context of the Murukaṉ tradition, it is possible for many of the motifs ascribed to Vedic and post-Vedic gods to be transferred to Skanda who emerges into prominence in the Epic period. A similar transference takes place in religious techniques: the religious meaning of the sacrifice, by which the sacrifice as a microcosm of the universe re-creates the world, is transferred to the yogic technique in which the human body is a microcosm, and *ecstasis* re-creates primordiality. Symbolic intent is transferred, in turn, to the bhaktic relation between the god and the soul who, in their relationship, become a microcosm of ultimacy and a re-creation of Reality.

Murukaṉ's history is an illustration of the persistence of religion, and of the tendency of a symbol to bear persistent meanings throughout its history. It illustrates also how related meanings accumulate around a symbol to make it increasingly a reflection of the whole. We must hasten to add that this need not mean that all the meanings are always conscious in the human apprehension of the symbol, nor that each of the meanings is necessarily relevant to each of the historical moments in which the symbol is set. It is also possible that a symbol itself may cease to bear in changing cultures the meanings it bore in former cultures. Presumably this is why old symbols are sometimes replaced by new, and the persisting meanings are transferred from one phenomenon to another.

2. Murukaṉ and his relationships

2.1 *Sonship and divine youthfulness*

A fundamental theme that recurs in the mythology of Murukaṉ, and especially in its Epic and post-Epic stages is his character as a Divine Son. As a mythical device, Sonship serves several purposes. Not the least of them is to link historical and cultural changes with an ongoing authenticating tradition. Skanda's rise to prominence in the Epic period represented the fact that a new cultural and religious era had come, demanding a god which reflected and met the needs and aspirations of that era. The theogony that resulted was a creative religious and cultural event symptomatic of the cultural realities of the age, for in the Epic Skanda is evidenced the emergence of the city-state and the powerful king and the increased influence of the civilization in the Gangetic valley.

Yet, Skanda's being a 'son' means that though he is 'new', he is also depicted as consistent with and inheritor of the orthodox tradition. His relationship to his fathers is not so much a biological one as a qualitative one. He extends the attributes, the power and the strength of the father. Not only is the 'new' god legitimized in that way, the older tradition is also recast and made amenable to the new situation. An authenticating *arché* gives credibility and depth to the new symbol-system.

The role of the divine son then is integrative. It integrates one cultural moment with older cultural moments, assimilating each 'new' situation into a mythic whole. The god becomes a persistent personification of the 'changelessness' of divine reality even in the midst of the fluidity and flexibility of historical change. The divine son also integrates the religious meanings embodied in each of his parents into a new whole. Skanda especially serves to pull together the significance of myth and cult implied in the heritages of Agni and Rudra-Śiva. And as he is adopted by the goddesses Skanda increasingly subsumes into his person the symbolism associated with the mothers as well. Thus Skanda comes to embody attributes that are transcendent and chthonic, orthodox and folk, Sanskrit and Tamil.[1]

Divine Sonship not only personified the authority and energy of the father; it takes them to a higher power. The son, by virtue of being younger, more recently created, and more concrete, is able to perform feats the father had begun to find impossible. The old god tends to be *otiose* and either unable or unwilling to do that which must be done to save the world. This reality is suggested in the myths of Skanda in several ways: Śiva has retired to engage in *tapas* on the mountain top. Rudra and other gods give their weapons to Skanda. It is as though the cause for which the father stood needs the son to perpetuate it with greater vigor. The son, in fact, comes to exceed the father in greatness – at least for his own devotees. This phenomenon is especially well illustrated when the prodigious child Murukan̲ teaches his own father the sacred mysteries and conquers the *asuras* which his father had been impotent to overcome.

Sonship is relatedly associated with creatorship, saviorhood, and fatherhood. The son is generated that he may generate; by his vigor he can bring into being new armies or worlds. Skanda's fatherhood is suggested in his bringing into being the *grahas* who were greater than those beings sent by Indra and fought the latter into submission. The son is also responsible for the generation of the world. He is a demiurge; he brings about a new order. Skanda's cosmogonic functions are less apparent, but his conquest of the *asuras* is a creative act – it brings about a new order of relative peace. His conquest, we are told, ushered in the Kali Yuga, perpetuating the *dharma* into a new epoch. Similarly, each time he is brought into being ritually it is a creative event. His 'birth' is a new beginning, the symbolic birth of a new cosmos, the initiation of a new mode of being.

Sonship implies primordiality. When Skanda is mythically equated with the sacrifice, the sun, and the *hiraṇyagarbha*, his primordial character is particularly suggested. He was 'in the beginning', both in the sense that his birth took place in the mythical time before the cycle of this era and in the sense that in his person are perpetuated and revalorized the power and function of his divine creator-ancestors, particularly those of Prajāpati, the primordial sacrifice. His primordiality, in turn, gives him immortality, omniscience, and creative power and also associates him with the origin and essence of the cosmos. He was in the beginning, and he was the beginning. Thus, from whatever cosmology one wished to view Skanda, the god could be understood as the world's essence. If one saw the world as taking shape from the primordial sacrifice, Skanda was that primordial sacrifice, born of the fire of the six *ṛṣis,* in the *śara* grass, in the golden mound, etc.; if one saw the world as emerging from the *hiraṇyagarbha,* the golden seed, Skanda was that *hiraṇyagarbha*; if one saw the world as a Cosmic Man, Skanda was that Man. Similarly, other cosmological motifs are linked in Skanda; he is of the primordial lotus born in a thicket of reeds and he is born of the primordial pair personified by Śiva and Pārvatī. Skanda, by virtue of his primordial sonship, serves to integrate many of India's cosmologies into a single view of reality.[2]

Skanda's sonship also connotes wisdom, generated as he is from the sparks of Śiva's third eye and inheriting the omniscience of the cosmic ascetic. His wisdom is akin to his primordiality; because he was from the beginning, he knows the origin of all things. His sonship, therefore, is consistent with the Vedic and post-Vedic notion of sonship which saw the generated one as the 'son of the mind' (*manodbhûta*) (Mahābhārata, Sāntiparva, 12005).

2.1.1 *Youthfulness*

Closely aligned to the notion of sonship, is that of youthfulness. The youthfulness of Skanda–Murukaṉ has been pictured in a number of ways in both Tamil and Sanskrit lore and is celebrated widely today. In relatively early Tamil literature, the term *'Muruku'* itself meant 'youthfulness', among other things. We have argued that in the context of the early Tamil South the god was apprehended as the giver of eternal youth. Those who danced his praise in frenzied worship were afforded a taste of eternal youthfulness, to the extent that their worship was a perpetuation, an affirmation of the joy and verve of life. Moreover, somewhat later in the

Tamil tradition, perhaps by the fourth or fifth century, Murukan̲ is thought of as a child, for children are said to be celebrated as the embodiments of the god (Kali. 81:8–10; 83:14–65).

Similarly, in many references in Sanskrit literature, he is the young god. He is Sanatkumāra, the eternal son. His childhood is but a span of seven days, the *Mahābhārata* myths tell us. His exploits as a child are widely known and loved, particularly by Tamilians. Indeed, the youth of the god is so persistent and so popular a part of his nature, that we do well to ponder its religious implications.

2.1.2 *Eternality*

The one obvious meaning symbolized in the god's youthfulness is that he represents eternality. He is the god who always is, which means, in part, that, for his devotees, he stands above time. This is so not only because he was born and did his youthful deeds 'before time', but also because the measures of time were themselves set into motion by the god's birth and exploits. Time has neither conquered nor aged Murukan̲ in South India. Even though history and culture change, the god conceived by the Epic myth-makers has been ascribed fresh attributes (or had his attributes modified), so that he has been able to survive and persist as an eternally vibrant god.

Murukan̲'s eternality assumes his capacity to purvey eternality to his devotees. Whether it takes the form of perpetual youthfulness and the continuation of joyous life (as in the early Tamil context) or the release from the tyranny of the world (as in the Epic and Śaiva Siddhāntin context), Murukan̲ came to be understood as the author of eternal life for all who sought it.

But eternality is not only a personal possibility. There is even a sense, for some devotees in Tamil Nadu, in which Murukan̲, by virtue of his patronage, has become a symbol of regional eternality. In some circles in Tamil Nadu, Murukan̲ has been implicitly made the patron of regional political aspirations and explicitly seen as the embodiment of the antiquity and persistence of Tamil culture.[3] Murukan̲, in a sense, personifies Tamil Nadu – its hills, fertility, its origin, its destiny. The region is considered eternal and divine insofar as it, like Murukan̲, is understood to have originated in the primordial hills and have persisted with him through several creative periods of cultural change even into a fresh and vibrant present.

Another dimension in Murukaṉ's youthfulness is particularly persistent in rural Tamil Nadu. The early sense of tenderness and freshness caught up in the term *Muruku* seemed to associate the god with the freshly blossomed flowers and vegetation of the hills. His tenderness was akin to the newly opened bud at its aromatic and colorful best. In a very similar vein, Murukaṉ's youthfulness today implies beauty and fragrance. He personifies the unmarred handsome features and the fragrant tenderness to which all persons aspire (or for which they entertain nostalgic memories). But at the same time, Murukaṉ's tenderness and youth embody the fragrance, color and tenderness of the land that is productive. He epitomizes the aspiration of the rural devotee for the eternally fresh crop, and the abundance and prosperity which the devotee seeks from the soil. Murukaṉ's youth is more than the reflection of hope for a human youthfulness. The god's youth embodies the human hope for cosmic youthfulness: that the land be young and still productive, that the region remain young and vigorous and be able to look forward to new measures of greatness; and indeed, that the whole cosmos itself may continue young and able to sustain the life to which it is committed.[4] This hope for cosmic youthfulness, at least on the part of rural and semi-literate folk, expresses itself not so much as a longing for transformation as for affirmation – a hope that life may continue to be near the best that one has known it to be.

2.1.3 *The child as an object of devotion*

One aspect of Murukaṉ's youthfulness which has attained increasing importance in the modern era is his depiction as a divine child worthy of devotion and worship. While there are not yet cultic centers which feature this aspect of the god exclusively, there has sprung up around it a special form of literature in recent generations. This is the poetry known in Tamil as Piḷḷaittamiḻ (literally 'Tamil of childhood'). This poetry expresses in still another way the responses Murukaṉ elicits from his devotees, and is therefore worth some analysis.

Piḷḷaittamiḻ has become an important element in Murukaṉ's devotional literature at least since the seventeenth century, when first Muttu Kumāracāmy and then Kumārakurupara Cuvāmikal used it extensively and skillfully in praise of Murukan̲. This is not a poetry unique to Tamil or to Murukan̲, as it is used in many of the Indian vernaculars to extol the childhood of other gods or goddesses. Hence, while the poetry expresses a certain Tamil spirit and is *apropos* to Murukan̲ it also has a pan-Indian and Hindu character to it. When the poetry is addressed to Murukan̲, as in the case of certain other gods, the poet is said to be under the 'possession of Murukan̲'.

Piḷḷaittamil̲ is generally divided into ten sections. While this division is more a poetic device than a religiously significant one, each section is devoted to one of the ten stages through which all children are believed to pass. The god is made congruent to every human child. Each stage (*paruvam*) becomes the occasion for extolling particular virtues of the god and asking those specific blessings of him that are suggested by that stage. There is also a sense, more apparent in some stages than in others, in which the god is homologized to the life of the cosmos itself and to the rhythm of the poet's own writings. The ten stages make possible prayers for all children, the development of whose life is akin to that of the god; for the life and rhythm of the cosmos; and for the rhythm of the poetry being written. At the same time, the poet and all devotees can also be related to the divine child, not only as a child like him, but also as a parent to him, as if somewhat responsible for his preservation and growth and the extolling of his virtues.[5]

The first stage of the child god's life is *Kāppupparuvam* (the protected stage). In this stage the protection and blessing of important gods and goddesses are invoked for the newborn Murukan̲. The poet prays that their powers may be embodied in the divine child. The infant god is compared to the start of the poet's own work; hence, the god's blessing is invoked for the poetry. More implicitly, the world is seen to be in similar need of the protection of the gods. Equally implicit is the poet's pledge to strive for the preservation of the divine child, of the human children entrusted to him, and of that part of the world for which he is responsible.

The second state (*seṅkīraipparuvam*) is the stage in which the child can nod its head in response to external stimuli. The name is taken from a red (*sem*) plant (*kīrai*) something like spinach greens which sway rhythmically in a breeze. In this stage the head of Murukan̲ is seen as nodding in time with the dancing of the gods. Here again the nodding of the god's head is homologized to the rhythm of the poetry and of the cosmos itself. The dancing of the gods and the nodding of Murukan̲'s head are seen as the rhythm and pulsation of life itself.

The third stage (*talapparuvam*) is the cradle stage roughly approximating the second six months of the infant's life. Here, like all human children, the divine child sleeps, soothed by the singing of gods and goddesses. In a similar way the world and the poet are made to rest by the solace of the divine. The poet asks Murukaṉ for peace and rest, and for cleansing and freedom from the tyranny of guilt.

The fourth stage (*sappāṇipparuvam*) is the crawling stage. It represents a stage in which the child begins to explore and play on all fours. Because it connotes the start of play it is a festive stage, somewhat congruent to the joyousness and festivity found in the orderly pattern of the universe. The poet alludes to the use of festive, colorful and fragrant elements in the worship of the god – the red flowers, sandal paste, and honey sprinkled on Murukaṉ by gods and devotees alike. The poet also prays for the joy of forgiven sin, and the freedom to dance and enjoy life unrestricted in praise of the god.

The fifth stage (*muttapparuvam*) is the stage in which the child can kiss those loved ones who stoop to him. The poet prays the god will 'kiss' him, granting fragrance of his face. The god is described as a thirsty child, who suckled the milk of the six maidens, the four Vedas and the words of *bhaktas*. Made thirsty by the millet and honey fed him by Vaḷḷi, he drinks of the streams and shows the poet where to drink of the fountain of satisfaction. There also appears to be a play on words in this stage. If *muttam* is kiss, *muttu* is pearl, and *mutti* is *moksa*. Thus the poet asks that the child god who is like a pearl and rich in pearls adorn the poet with the pearls of *moksa*.

The sixth stage (*vārāṇaipparuvam*) is the stage in which the child extends his hands to be taken. The poet prays that the god whose arms are all embracing and pervasive will embrace and surround him in times of need. The poet expresses the hope that the cooling breezes from Murukaṉ's hills so abundant with rivers, peacocks, deer, and swans will come and embrace him and the entire world.

The seventh stage (*ampulipparuvam*) is that stage when parents invoke the moon (*ampuli*) to come and play with the child.[6] The moon is asked to come and play with Murukaṉ and can be addressed in any of four ways: *samam* (conciliation or equality) – the moon is equal to the child and is therefore asked to come as a playmate; *petaṉam* (separation) – the child is greater than the moon; therefore, because the moon is different and inferior, it is invited to come as an attendant to the child; *taṉam* (gift) – the child will give gifts to the moon if it comes; and *taṇtam* (punishment) – if the moon doesn't come, it will be punished. Even though this stage is particularly relevant to Murukan̲, because of his mythical association to the moon, it is said by the poet to be a difficult stage about which to sing. Nonetheless, in the stanzas of this stage, the poet implies a variety of relationships Murukan̲ has to the moon. The moon is Murukan̲'s toy; yet the moon is equal to Murukan̲ (for both moon and Murukan̲ are conceived on the same day – the day of the new moon). But the moon has a playful and cordial relationship to the earth even as it has to the child, so Murukan̲ is equated, once again, not only to every child but also to the world as a whole.

The eighth stage[7] (*sir̲r̲ir̲ paruvam*) is the stage when the child around four years of age plays house. The term *sir̲r̲ir̲* means 'small house'. Like all other children, Murukan̲ is said to build houses in play. The poet pleads that the god will protect the former's own home and will refrain from destroying the homes of humanity; in that sense the god is described as more benevolent than mere children, who, once they have built a play house, destroy it.

The ninth stage (*sir̲upar̲aipparuvam*) is the stage, at about four and a half years of age, when the child plays with a small drum (*sir̲upar̲ai*). To the beating of Murukan̲'s drum all the world responds. All the sounds of the world (the trumpeting of the elephants, the murmuring of the ocean, the sighing of wives' longing for their husbands) are in harmony and rhythm with the beating of Murukan̲'s drum. The god provides the basal tone of the world, the constant beat of the rhythm of the cosmos and the bustle of its life.

The tenth stage (*sir̲utērp paruvam*) is the climactic stage of the god's childhood, for like all five year old boys who ride playfully in wagons, the god roams the world in his small chariot (*sir̲utēr*). Riding triumphantly on his elephant, peacock, and chariot, the god grants blessings to the whole world, which is his play yard and pedestal.

The meaning of the god's childhood for the devotee, particularly as the relationship is portrayed in Piḷḷaittamil̲, might be summarized in a few statements. First, while the god is apprehended as a child, the worshipper is as a parent whose worship nurtures the child; the child, in turn, bestows on the 'parent' all the gifts of his own youthfulness, much as Murukan̲ bestowed on his parent Śiva the sacred insight. Second, while the god is apprehended as a child, the devotee may also see himself as a child and is therefore able to benefit from the childlike skills of the god. Third, the god, the devotee, the poet's art, and the cosmos are seen as parallel, with the latter three dependent on the god for their sustenance, rhythm, and spiritual vitality. Fourth, the god, the devotee, the poet's art and the cosmos are parallel – just as Murukaṉ is protected and ministered to by the gods, so too are poetry, the world, and the devotee recipients of all the gods' attention.

The poetry suggests the close relationship between play and worship; both are forms of celebration and re-creation. The child's play reflects and invokes the joy appropriate to certain acts of worship; mythical allusions to the shared mood of play and worship are recalled. Murukaṉ, the child, even in his play is seen as the center of attention and the sustainer of the cosmos. Thus, in the eyes of the poet, he is worthy of devotion.

2.2 *Murukaṉ and the goddesses*

The association of Murukaṉ with goddesses presents a highly complex picture, all the pieces of which do not fit into a tidy whole. There are discrepancies and apparent contradictions even in the myths of Skanda's birth that render it difficult, if not impossible, to ascertain precisely what the association means. In general, however, we can suggest that goddesses are related to Skanda–Murukaṉ in three different capacities: as attendants; as mothers; and as consorts. We shall look at each of these relationships to see what we can infer religiously and historically from them.

2.2.1 *The attendants*

There are frequent allusions in both Sanskrit and Tamil sources to the many female attendants at the service of Murukaṉ. The relationship is not so clear in the early Tamil literature, but we find one or two hints. For example, there is a sense in which the damsels who become possessed of Murukaṉ in the frenzied dance (Tirumuru. 20–60) become the god's attendants, insofar as they are under the influence of the god; yet these women are not 'goddesses'. Another reference to female beings available to Murukaṉ's bidding speaks of the demoness who dances on the battle ground after Murukaṉ has slain his foes (Tirumuru. 73–88). This demoness is apparently a survival of the malevolent goddess who is said to govern the *pālai* (wilderness tract) and who, in the age of chieftainship, is associated with the battlefields. Her dance amongst the slain celebrates the defeat of the enemies of the warrior hero. The implication of her association with Murukan̲ is that the land to which Murukan̲ lays waste becomes a wilderness and that which he subdues is rendered useless and infertile, save as he himself restores its usefulness.

In the Sanskrit literature there are abundant but disparate references to Skanda's female attendants. In the Skanda–Yāga, the god is said to be surrounded by a 'thousand' maidens who are his devotees and assistants. This following, we read in the ninth book of the *Mahābhārata*, was given him by the gods to be his companions and mothers. They were beautiful damsels who lived in trees, open areas, the crossings of four roads, caves, crematoria, mountains, and springs. The attendant damsels of Sanskrit literature seem to have both kindly and malevolent features and seem, therefore, to be roughly analogous to the *cūrarmakaḷir* of the Tamil tradition.

However, the malevolent character of these attendant goddesses is stressed in the third book of the *Mahābhārata* and the second book of the Viṣṇudharmottara Purāṇa. These malevolent goddesses are equated with the female *grahas* and are said to be Skanda's mothers, but also his daughters. They are daughters in the sense that Skanda brings them into being (according to the myth of the third book of the *Mahābhārata*), but they are mothers in the sense that his own character reflects something of the malevolence attributed to them.

The Aṣṭānga Saṃgraha notes that Śiva gave Skanda twelve *grahas*, five male and seven female, to assist him (P. K. Agrawala 1966:150, citing V. S. Agrawala, *Prachim bhāratiya Dokadharma*, p. 51). The Kāsyapa Saṁhitā records that the names of some twenty goddesses were given to the goddess Revatī who is depicted as the chief of Skanda's assistants in that literature. The Revatī–Kalpa in the Kāsyapa Saṁhitā suggests that Revatī had become the most powerful goddess of the Epic age and, having assimilated into her person many other minor goddesses, had attained the status of a Great Mother. The same work says that Revatī was sent by Skanda, in the form of a she-wolf, to devour the demon Dīrghajihvī and assist in the destruction of the demon army. But the *asuras* took shelter in the seed of humans; therefore, Revatī attacks the newly born in search of them. She especially attacks children of those who do not follow *dharma*. At the command of Skanda she stupefies all the impious persons of different castes and kills the wicked ones (P. K. Agrawala 1966:151–52).

But Revatī has many forms, having apparently assimilated the roles of many malevolent goddesses. She was Jātahārinī, for, like many of the goddesses assimilated into her, she attacks the newly born (*jāta*). The Jātahārinī goddesses are classified into three categories, on the basis of the seriousness of illness they cause. *Sādhya* goddesses cause curable illnesses. *Yāpya* goddesses cause lingering illnesses; and *asādhya* goddesses cause incurable illnesses. Interestingly, Mohinī is included in the first category, and in the second are a number of familiar names: Pisāci, Yakṣi, Āsurī, Kālī, Vāruṇī, Ṣaṣṭhī, Yāmyā, and others. The Jātahārinī goddesses were also classified on the basis of the castes or classes they were thought to affect. Some twenty-nine such categories are listed in the Revati–Kalpa. The goddesses are also categorized as to which stage of the child's life they are most known to attack: in the womb, after birth, or while under up-bringing. The goddesses were also categorized by whether they attacked divine beings, humans, or birds (*tirascīṇa*) (pp. 152–53, citing the Revatī–Kalpa).

P. K. Agrawala believes that these various forms of the goddess demonstrate the assimilation of a great variety of malevolent goddesses known in the folk culture (pp. 151–53). It appears that, like Skanda, they represent a new generation of goddesses, propelled into dominance during the changing cultural makeup of the Epic era. This possibility seems confirmed in the myth of the third book of the *Mahābhārata*, in which six of the malevolent mothers, linked, it seems, with the six *ṛṣi* wives and the six Kṛttikas, ask Skanda for the privilege of replacing the older mothers (Brahmī, Maheśvarī, etc.) in worship. This privilege Skanda grants, together with the privilege of possessing his *śakti* and assuming fierce forms for molesting youngsters under sixteen.

It is tempting to conclude that this association of goddesses with Skanda – the rising in eminence and power of the goddess – reflects the adaptation into the Epic myths of a folk, agricultural motif. It is possible that this association derives from an agricultural society, presumably located in the Gangetic plain inasmuch as goddesses and agriculture are often associated – the goddess, fertile or malevolent, often symbolizing the ambivalence of the earth itself. Like the goddess *Kor̲r̲avai* who reigned cruelly in the non-arable wastes of Tamil Nadu and presided over the strewn battlefields, the malevolent goddesses who become linked with Skanda in the Epic mythology may have represented for a relatively primitive people all the forces of nature's destruction and waste which so interfered with the peaceful tilling of the soil and the balance of life.

One hears relatively little discussion today of goddesses serving as the attendants of Murukaṉ. Yet there is considerable awareness on the popular level of the role of goddesses, particularly malevolent ones, in the misfortunes of life – crop failure, disease, death. What appears to be essentially the case is that the goddesses do not so much have the power to control the forces of the world as they personify the forces of the world themselves. That is, they do not change the world; they are the world. All the exigencies of the cosmos are symbolized in the goddesses – its willfulness and unpredictability, its barrenness and fertility, its cyclicality and fluidity, its potential destructiveness and creativity. The goddesses are primarily chthonic forces in and of the world. The contemporary Tamil villager often plays out his attempts to deal with the world in his relationship to the goddess.

2.2.2 *The mothers*

The problem of the mothers of Skanda is as complex as that of his attendants. This is partially because there are so many 'mothers' attributed to Skanda. It is also because, in the case of the malevolent goddesses at least, the women associated with him play the dual role of mother and attendant, and even appear to be the god's consorts and daughters. One strikingly consistent fact is apparent in the Skanda mythology: in no case does Skanda have a *bona fide* mother. His direct filiation is exclusively of the male deities. His mothers are his only by adoption or through some other indirect role in his birth. The six Kṛttikas suckled the babe; Svāhā, impersonating the six *ṛṣis'* wives, received Agni's seed only to deposit it in an appropriate receptacle. Gaṅga, the river, carried the seed to the mountain, but she could not keep it long. The malevolent goddesses were 'adopted' as his mothers by Skanda. Dhārā, the earth, is said in the *Rāmāyaṇa* account to have been able to bear the seed and to have lent her bosom as the birthplace of the god. Even Umā–Pārvatī is denied the privilege of authentic motherhood, and she cursed the *devas* and Dhārā, whom she assumed to be responsible. Yet Pārvatī does adopt as her own the son born of the *tejas* she helped to extract from her consort.

The implications of these various relationships are not altogether clear. We are again reminded of the probability that Skanda was of diverse heritage and that his advent was, as it were, with the cooperation of the entire cosmos – an advent which served to integrate the cosmos into new coherence. We can only suggest here some of the possible meanings inherent in these various motherly relationships.

The role of Svāhā in the birth of Skanda to Agni suggests several things. Minimally, Svāhā serves as Agni's 'messenger', like the *garuḍa*, carrying emanations of the 'sun' to the mountain, where, from these emanations, Skanda is formed. It is also possible Svāhā is intended to represent *soma*. This is suggested by her becoming the *garuḍa*, which in another context – the Suparṇa myth – is equated with *soma*, inasmuch as both are related to the sun, dependent on the sun for energy and serving as messengers to and from the sun. If Svāhā can be understood as *soma*, then the symbolism of her role is even more complex, for *soma* means both moon and the *amṛta* or sacrificial drink which is poured into fire. If Svāhā is *soma*, then her conjunction with Agni, the sun, represents the coming together of sun and moon. The myth in the third book of the Mahābhārata tells us that Skanda was conceived at the time of the 'coming together' of sun and moon. That is, the time was *amavācai*, the new moon. The new moon is the start of a new cycle of time. So Svāhā, if equated with *soma*, may represent the moon's conjoining with the sun to bring Skanda into being, and ushering in a new era or system of reckoning time.

But if Svāhā is *soma*, she may also represent the pouring of the sacrificial drink into the fire (Agni). This ritual act, whenever performed, was intended to bring about immortality and a new mode of being. Skanda, born of the cosmic pouring of *soma* into the fire, is born the immortal one, the new Supreme Being. Hence, every re-enactment of the ritual would be intended to give birth in a fresh sense to Skanda, the integrative and primordial one.

Svāhā's impersonation of the *ṛṣis'* wives appears to serve symbolic purposes. It depicts her 'offspring' Skanda once again as the sacrifice, inasmuch as he is born of the sacrifice-makers. Then too, his relation to the *ṛṣis* conveys to Skanda the attributes of wisdom, whereby he may appropriately be called the son of Brahman. Svāhā's association with the six wives further helps her become an integrating factor through which the six diverse roots of Skanda may be made one. When the fire sacrifice is performed even today in such temples as at Tiruchendur, Subrahmaṇya's birth of and equation with the sacrifice is recalled, and Svāhā's role in the process ritually re-enacted.

The symbolic role of the Kṛttikas seems, in a similar way, to link Skanda both with the oneness of his six forms and with Agni and the sun. In this relationship again is illustrated the six-fold character of the god and his ability to integrate into one the six diversities of the cosmos. We are reminded that Agni is the presiding deity of the constellation Kṛttikas. Skanda is said to have sent the six damsels, who, by then, had been linked with the six *ṛṣi* wives and the six malevolent goddesses, into the sky to become a constellation. This would suggest the role of the stars, together with sun and moon, in making Skanda's birth auspicious. It also links Agni, Svāhā, and the six damsels. The association further suggests Skanda's role as lord of time, for the constellation was used as a reckoner and basis of time, together with other asterisms, sun, and moon. To this day, in Tamil Nadu, the role of the Kṛttikas in the birth of Skanda is remembered. The asterism *Kārttikai* serves as the birthday of the god, and the month *Kārttikai* (October–November) is especially sacred to Murukan̲.

The role of Gaṅga, the river, in bearing the seed of Skanda appears to represent the consciousness of the agricultural community in the Gangetic Valley of the role of the river both in flood and fertility. In later mythology, the river is said more explicitly to descend from heaven, and the vegetation which it waters and fertilizes is recognized as the sustenance of life, given by the gods. Perhaps we are to infer from Gaṅga's role in Skanda's birth that Skanda is like vegetation, born and fertilized by the waters as a prototype of creation. Whether or not that be the case, the cultus of Murukan̲ today ascribes special significance to certain bodies of water – the Gaṅges, the Ṣaṇmukha river at Pal̲ani, the Kāveri at Swamimalai, as well as several temple tanks – as the 'birthplace of Murukan̲'.[8] To dip ritually into these waters is to make Murukan̲ 'come alive' again.

The role of Dhārā, the earth, is even more obscure. It is mentioned, apparently, only in the Rāmāyaṇa account. The reference is probably an allusion to the classical role of the earth as the mother of fertility and one of the agencies of creation. It is interesting that, in this account, before Kumāra is born as himself, his fetus is said to have become Mt. Śveta after Agni and Vāyu had entered it. Skanda is thus equated with a mountain thrust out of the bosom of the earth, which suggests Skanda's role of permeating the cosmos, connecting heaven, atmosphere and earth (as implied in the roles of Agni, Vāyu, and Dhārā). Like the mountains which are his home, he becomes the center or axis of the cosmos.

We should note briefly that in Tamil literature, for example in a reference found in the hymn recorded in the Tirumurukār̲r̲upaṭai, Murukan̲ is said to be the son of Kor̲r̲avai, the early Tamil goddess of the wilderness and battleground. A ferocious goddess, her motherhood of Murukan̲ presumably connotes his inheriting her power, anger, and ferocity. This allusion ties in with his role as a Southern warrior who is thorough in his devastation of foes, and with his association with malevolent goddesses in general through whom he causes or prevents physical suffering. Kor̲r̲avai eventually corresponds to Durgā, who in turn, is equated with Pārvatī. Once again, the integration of Tamil and Sanskrit motifs is apparent.

Skanda's adoption by Umā (as the consort of Rudra) or Pārvatī (as the consort of Śiva) expresses mythically the fullness of meaning implied by Skanda's 'sonship' of mothers. The myth in the third book of the *Mahābhārata* explicitly says that Umā is the same as Svāhā (even as Rudra is equated with Agni). That Pārvatī retains something of the malevolence and terror associated with the earlier malevolent goddesses is implied in the fact that she is said to have given Murukan̲ the powerful lance (*śakti*) with which he could slay his foes. Pārvatī seems to represent the amalgamation of all the goddesses; she is the goddess *par excellence* and, thus, epitomizes the sum of Skanda's relations to his 'mother'. Pārvatī's adopting of Skanda may suggest that Skanda is ascribed the attributes generally associated with the goddess – he is chthonic and comes to represent the character and ambivalence of the world, even as she does. In fact, her adopting of Skanda implies the merging of two or more cultural and religious streams – one representing an amalgam of 'celestial', 'male', pastoral, orthodox traditions through his generation by Agni – Rudra–Śiva the other representing a combination of chthonic, 'feminine', agricultural, folk or unorthodox traditions.

But the reason why the myth-makers avoided ascribing to Pārvatī, or any of the goddesses, an actual part in the generation of Skanda is puzzling. Was it because they wish to depict him as the real and only son of the Divine, born of the self-propagation of the god, with feminine help quite incidental? (Such a 'solo role' of a father-god would not be unique in the history of religions.) Or, is it possible that, by this device, the myth-makers were implicitly saying that the Skanda of the Epics was, after all, more nearly an expression of the orthodox tradition than he was an integration of orthodox and unorthodox? It is true that in the Epic period the integrative character of

Skanda as a wedder of diverse cultures is not as apparent or as complete as it is later in the South when Northern and Southern and pastoral and agricultural (as well as hunting) motifs are caught up in the god (though, even in Tamil literature, he is not depicted as the son of Pārvatī until relatively late, and even then, Pārvatī is not necessarily a mother in any sense other than by adoption).[9] It seems possible that the goddess Pārvatī had not ascended into the place of prominence in the Epic period that she was given in a later period. It is also likely that the goddesses most popular and powerful at the time of Skanda's early emergence were the multitudinous malevolent goddesses who had not yet been clearly assimilated into the orthodox stream. The time of Pārvatī's real dominance, then, would have been after Skanda's ascendancy in the Epic period; this may be part of the reason why her role in the basic mythology of Skanda's birth is secondary.

2.2.3 *The consorts*

As we have seen, there are two persistently important consorts of Murukaṉ. The first, representing the Epic heritage, is Devasenā; the second, representing the Southern Tamil heritage, is Vaḷḷi. Devasenā's name stands for the army of the gods (*deva* – gods; *senā* – army), of which Skanda is made the head. As such, Devasenā assimilates into her person many of the goddesses who make up the army. In the *Mahābhārata* 218:49, for example, Devasenā is identified with eight goddesses, including Ṣaṣṭhī, Lakṣmī, and others. Devasenā was married to Skanda in the traditional orthodox way, according to the Vedic rites.

Vaḷḷi, on the other hand, is a personification of the creeper often described in early Tamil poetry, whose entwining of a tree symbolizes the inseparability of lovers and of devotees from their god. While Devasenā was of the gods, Vaḷḷi was of man, adopted, in fact, by the hunter Nambirājan. Her marriage to Murukaṉ was the result of his long courtship of her and was unorthodox in nature. Their marriage was like that of two hunters; it was based on love resulting from his wooing her, and his use of trickery against her relatives who sought to obstruct that love.[10]

But Devasenā and Vaḷḷi, we are told in the Skanda Purāṇa, were sisters in a former life and daughters of Nārāyaṇa himself, which suggests to devotees a number of symbolic interpretations which are given to the two consorts. The relationship of the consorts to Skanda–Murukaṉ is made to represent the integration of a number of polarities – the Northern, Vedic, orthodox tradition on the one hand; the Southern, Tamil, hunting-agricultural tradition on the other; the celestial realm and the earth; and Vaiṣṇava and Śaiva motifs. This combination of Śaiva and Vaiṣṇava motifs is suggested in the concept of grace said to be portrayed in the god's courtship of each: Devasenā merits the god in a manner more in keeping with Śaiva tradition; Vaḷḷi is pursued by the god in a manner illustrative of the Vaiṣṇava concept of grace in which the divine holds fast even to that soul which does not merit the divine's favor.

The consorts can represent the relationship of souls to the god. But they are also said to represent the relationship of passions to the god – or to the devotee – for the god is often represented as detached from the consorts in a manner consistent with his aspect as brahmacārya. In this case Vaḷḷi symbolizes emotion or passion (*icca*), for love is involved in their relationship; and Devasenā represents the fruit of action (*karma*), for she is given to Skanda as reward for his action. In lieu of the two consorts Murukaṉ often clutches the lance (*vēl*), representing discriminating wisdom (*jnāna*). In a similar way devotees are expected to use discrimination to become detached from emotion and the fruits of action.

In addition to these rather philosophical interpretations of the symbolism of the goddesses, there is a variety of popular nuances identified especially in the role of Vaḷḷi. Vaḷḷi's 'low caste' background makes it easy for low caste peoples, and especially women, to identify with her. The god cares about her; her response to Murukaṉ, like that of Rādhā to Viṣṇu, epitomizes the way in which giving oneself to a god transcends all bonds. Her love, *kalavu*, is unconventional and uninhibited and even supercedes marriage. Further, as younger sister to Devasenā, Vaḷḷi, in a manner consistent with Tamil peasant society, is given more freedom as to who and how she will marry, so long as the older sister has been married in a conventional way (Beck, 1973:17). Not in frequently, in folk Tamil poetry, Vaḷḷi and Murukaṉ argue; he taunts her for her background; she upbraids him for the way in which his background is unconventional,[11] thereby implying, even in the scolding that his divinity transcends human conventions (p. 17). In short, in the relationship between Vaḷḷi and Murukaṉ is played out much of the drama of lower caste peoples in their endeavor to relate to their god: gratitude for his caring; complaint when he is 'absent'; concern for their status in his eyes, and so on. The relationship serves in many ways as an isomorph of the phenomenon of marriage in Tamil peasant society.

The relationship between Murukaṉ and the goddesses is celebrated in significant ways in the contemporary cultus. Paṅuṉi Uttiram, the festival of sacred marriage, remains one of the most popular festivals in Tamil Nadu. Also the *Tirukalyāṇam* or sacred wedding, enacted in the context of virtually every festival in Tamil Nadu, is well attended, especially by the women, even though the ritual is often conducted in the early hours of the morning. The consorts of Murukaṉ continue to stimulate the Tamil imagination.

2.3 *Murukaṉ and the problem of evil*

A theme that recurs often in the mythology and cultus of Murukaṉ is the role that he plays with respect to evil. There are two kinds of malevolence with which the god is generally related. The first includes those forces of evil believed to be at work in the cosmos, usually personified in the *asuras* or demons. The second is physical malaise and personal suffering, which Murukaṉ is at various times seen to both cause and dispel. The implications of his association with these two types of malevolence suggest something of the power his devotees have believed him to have from generation to generation.

2.3.1 *Cosmic malevolence*

In the early Tamil poetry one finds frequent reference to the ubiquitous presence on the mountain passes of the malevolent spirit, *cūr*. The *cūr* of the early poetry either took the form of women or possessed women on the hillsides, and infested mountain springs and waterfalls. The *cūr* caused terror, not only in people but in animals romping on the ridges. Only implicitly is the *cūr* seen as the enemy of Murukaṉ, though the spirit represents the malevolent forces of the hills and the land as a whole. Within the course of a few generations, the later *Caṅkam* and post-*Caṅkam* poetry speaks of *cūr* as a personalized masculine force, which hides in the ocean and is conquered by Murukaṉ.

With the coming of Sanskrit influence, we find the forces of evil personified increasingly in an *asura* or a company of *asuras*. It is not unlikely that the mythology of personified evil proliferates, (and perhaps originates) in the context of the city-state wherein the prince is arrayed against enemies who threaten his domain. It is interesting to note that the name of the main foe of Skanda–Murukaṉ changes in the course of time. In the earlier Northern Epic myths, the *asura* is Mahiṣa, the demon who had been the enemy of Śiva and the goddess. By the time of the later Epic myths, presumably developed in the Gupta era, the major *asura* is Tāraka, and Mahiṣa has either been relegated to the role of a minor assistant or dropped out of the picture altogether. P. K. Agrawala's suggestion seems quite plausible that this change represented an attempt on the part of the myth-makers to develop a new *asura* against whom Skanda could justify his divine strength (1966:137). This would imply that a new and more vigorous enemy of the gods had arisen, perhaps greater than those of the past, and that the strength of Śiva and the Great Goddess, spent in the conquest of earlier demons, was unequal to the new task. There is a need for a fresh young god who could represent the forces of reason and right in battle. By the time of the Skanda Purāṇa, (and persisting today), the main enemy of Murukaṉ in Tamil Nadu is known as Sūrapadma, whose name incorporates the early Tamil term *cūra* with the Sanskrit term *padma*.

The number of *asuras* arrayed against Murukaṉ varies. The cosmic enemy is sometimes represented as one, embodying, as it were, the integration into one being of all malevolent forces. More often in Tamil Nadu, the *asuras* are understood as three in number: Sūrapadma is the chief, the most powerful, and the only *asura* vested with immortality. His two allies or brothers are Sinkamukam (the lion-faced) and Tāraka. In Śaiva thought, these three are thought to represent the three *malas: āṇavas* (ego consciousness), *karma*, and *māyā*. Of the three, Sūrapadma represents *āṇava*, the most powerful and persistent of the *malas*. Amongst non-Śaivites and in a more universal spirit, the three *asuras* are said to represent three *guṇas*, *sattva* (truth or reality); *rajas* (passion or attachment); and *tamas* (inertia or torpor). It is also said that the *asuras* are six in number. These are depicted variously as one *asura* with six faces, or as three brothers with three assistants, or, as six brothers. Most commonly, the six-fold *asura* is said to represent the three *malas* and the three *guṇas*.

An interesting feature of the *asuras* who are Murukaṉ's enemies is their relation to the gods. We have seen that Tāraka, in the *Kumārasambhava*, was granted a boon from Brahmā which gave him his power. Sūrapadma, in the Skanda Purāṇa, was granted immortality by Śiva himself as a reward for the *asura's* great austerities. We notice further that, in the myth found in the third book of the Mahābhārata, Devasenā and Daityasenā are said to be sisters and daughters of Prajāpati; the former is married eventually to Skanda; the latter, on the other hand, loves and is carried off by Keni, the general of the *asuras*. The name of the former means 'army of the gods'; the name of the latter means 'army of the *daityas* or *asuras*'. Both armies, therefore, are generated from the primordial creator, and Skanda is the brother-in-law of his own enemy.

This paradox becomes comprehensible if we recognize the *devas* and *asuras* as representing the duality of the cosmos. The *asuras* who are the *malas* symbolize the world, which, though not ultimate reality, is relatively real insofar as it is generated from the creator. The forces of evil are forged from the same primordial possibilities that shape the entire cosmos. Sūrapadma is not killed, but is transformed into subordinates (the peacock and the cock) which the god uses as his own instruments. In the same way, for the Śaivite, the world is not totally dissolved in the process of liberation. Rather, it is subdued, subjugated, and made to serve the purpose of the god or of the devotee seeking to attain release. The *devas* and *asuras*, then, represent cosmic duality: spirit and flesh; ultimate reality and relative reality; being and non-being. But these two polarities are, after all, generated from the same primordial entity, and are therefore one totality. He who learns to subdue the 'malevolent' aspect of the cosmos is implicitly thought to learn, like the god, to be 'immortal' and to reign supreme above the transcience of life.

2.3.2 *Personal malaise*

A second relationship Skanda-Murukaṉ has to malevolence is that he has been thought able to cause or dispel personal suffering and illness. We can see a definite similarity between the early Tamil sense of Murukaṉ's power over suffering and that of Skanda over infant diseases in the Sanskritic material.

In the early Tamil literature, Murukaṉ was thought to dispel *aṇaṅku*, a term that connoted impersonal inner fear, suffering, or pain, but was also used to identify as semi-personal the force which caused such suffering. The god's priests or priestesses played the role of the diviner; by appropriate use of *kaḻaṅku* nuts or paddy grains, they could allegedly determine the source of the suffering. If Murukaṉ was determined to be the cause, appropriate corrective measures were prescribed: the dancing of the frenzied *veṟiyāṭal*, the offering of rice to the god, or the smearing of a young lamb's blood on the forehead were believed effective in appeasing the god. We argued that this practice persisted in the South from an early hunting society, for we noted among early Veddas a tendency to see the god of the hills as the one who could prevent epidemics and cure illness after appropriate ritual.

The situation is more complex in the Sanskritic literature. We noted that in the Epic myths Kumāra was considered a malevolent god who attacked infants; mythically, he is said to have inherited from Rudra the terrible disposition which could cause disease. Associated with Skanda were hosts of malevolent goddesses and evil spirits (*grahas*) who could inflict the young if they were not appropriately propitiated. An elaborate ritual is described in the Skanda Yāga, by which Skanda, known as Dhūrta, the rogue, could be propitiated lest he cause various forms of physical malaise.

The precise meaning and origin of this role of Skanda in the Epic literature is difficult to ascertain. However, there are a few suggestive clues in Purāṇic and other literature which throws some light on the problem. From these references, P. K. Agrawala has hypothesized a basis for Skanda's association with childhood affliction. Agrawala suggests Skanda was the amalgamation of four folk deities, popularly considered to harass the new-born infant and its mothers or to protect them if properly propritiated (1966:149).[12]

Skanda was seen as the presiding deity of the *grahas* (*grahas* can mean either evil spirits or asterisms of evil influence) causing suffering to infants up to a certain stage of life. The only way to be rid of the ill-effects of these so-called *grahas* was the *bali* offering and the worship (*ārccaṉai*) performed on the *Ṣaṣṭhī* or sixth day (p. 149, citing Viṣṇudharmottara Purāṇa II:22:88). Agrawala notes that the *Viṣṇudharmottara Purāṇa* (II:231–34) reiterates, with modifications, an incident recorded in the third book of the Mahābhārata. Indra produced a host of *grahas* to attack and kill the new-born infant Skanda, but Skanda, assisted by Viśākha, produced a host of *grahas* of his own who subdued Indra's *grahas* and made the latter subservient to Skanda. Skanda allowed these *grahas* to take shelter in the bodies of impure or wrong-doing persons. The same Purāṇa describes a seized person (*grahagṛhita*) and also the measures which can be taken for remedy (p. 149)[13]

One of the implications of this role of Skanda is that Skanda is depicted as a teacher of Āyurveda and the prototype of the practitioner of indigenous Hindu medicine. References to this capacity of Skanda are frequent in the literature (p. 150). Similarly, Āyurvedic literature, in describing the maladies of youth, refers to the numerous diseases and ills caused by the *grahas* and to the cures, offerings, and charms for recovery, including the necessity to propitiate Kumāra (p. 150).[14]

This power of Skanda to avert physical malaise is still reflected in a number of ways in contemporary Tamil Nadu. By the illiterate and semi-literate especially, Murukan̲ is believed to have power to heal diseases and dispel misfortune. Local legends as well as the more universally accepted mythology abound with stories 'attesting' to the god's healing power.[15] The tying of the amulet. duly blessed and purporting to protect the wearer from malevolent influences, can be observed throughout Tamil Nadu; in fact the ritual act of tying the amulet often precedes the start of a festival[16] And, as we have observed, the Skanda-Ṣaṣṭi festival in October–November, is the most dramatic evidence of the current belief in Murukan̲'s power to overcome evil. The festival celebrates the slaying of the *asura*, an event re-enacted on the sixth (*ṣaṣṭi*) day. Even those who do not know the textual descriptions of *grahas* and *aṇanku* understand the misfortunes which befall their own lives. Many of these still turn to Murukan̲ for power.

3. Murukan̲ and his symbols

3.1 *The number six*

One of the most striking and redundant features of Murukan̲'s character is his association with the number six. He is said to have six pilgrimage centers, both in contemporary belief and in early Tamil poetry; his mythology asserts he grew to manhood in six days; he is said to have six different parents; and, most obvious of all, Murukan̲ is frequently depicted with six faces.

This association with six and particularly the six faces appears to have come into the Tamil tradition after the *Caṅkam* period, for there is virtually no reference to six faces in the earlier *Caṅkam* poetry. The first references to the six faces in Tamil literature apparently are those in the Tirumuruk-kār̲r̲upaṭai and the Paripāṭal which are variously dated between the fourth and eighth centuries. Other than those allusions, references to Skanda's six faces are sparse prior to the Cō̲la period, when the iconography of the six-faced Ṣaṇmukan becomes prolific. It is in the Epic mythology that we find abundant reference to Skanda's association with six and some suggestions as to the religious importance of and bases for that association. The least that we can infer from these mythical allusions is that the six faces represent the integration into a single being of a diversity of divine heritages.[17] One of the Epic myths depicts Skanda as generated from six seeds of Agni, the divinization of fire and sacrifice; the seeds were deposited in a receptacle by Svāhā while she was impersonating the wives of the six *ṛṣis* responsible for making the primordial sacrificial fire. Another myth tells us the child Skanda was suckled by the six Kṛttika maidens; then again, he was adopted by six (or by some accounts, seven) malevolent goddesses. By his Epic genealogy, Skanda lays claim to sonship of no less than six parents: Agni, Rudra, Brahman, Svāhā, Gaṅga, and Umā (the last by adoption).[18] Whatever else this mythology suggests it tells us, at the least, that Skanda integrates the authority, attributes and power of each of his parents and heritages.

This integrative character of the number six appears again in the record of Skanda's birth to be found in the Skanda Purāṇa where we find the god generated from six sparks issuing from Śiva's forehead. Some contemporary Tamil interpreters tell us that the meaning of this symbolic event, among other things, is that Skanda is not only of the essence and authority of Śiva, but that he is even superior to his own father. For according to popularly accepted variations of the myth of Skanda's conquest of evil, Śiva is a god with five faces. The *asura* thus represented the totality of evil forces which posed a genuine threat to all the forces of good, and even to Śiva himself, who, in a sense, is depicted as becoming otiose. Only a six-headed warrior of Śiva's generation could be equal to the task (Vijayaraghavachariar 1966; S. Satchidanandam Pillai in conversation).

Sixness, then, expresses for Murukan̲'s devotees the totality of the divine character. Variations of this theme are numberless in Tamil speculation. Swami Sivananda, for example, a popularizing Śaiva apologist, suggests that Skanda's faces encompass the six attributes of the divine: wisdom (*jnāna*); dispassion (*vairāgya*); strength (*bala*); fame (*kīrti*); wealth (*śrī*); and divine power (*aisvarya*) (Sivananda 1963:127). The faces are also said to encompass the five divine functions understood within Śaivism *plus* more.

These five functions are represented as creation (*sṛṣṭi*); preservation (*sthiti*); destruction (*samāhāra*); concealment (*tirobhāva*); and revelation (*anugraha*), In another popular treatise, Sri Kripananda Variar (Variar in Venkatasubramaniam 1961) suggests the six faces of Skanda represent the god's six qualities: felicity, fullness, immortal youth, limitless energy, protection from evil, and spiritual splendor. Even earlier Tamil poets were not adverse to speculating on the divine functions as represented by the six faces. The authors of the Tirumurkāṟṟupaṭai and of the Kanta Kali Veṇpā agree about the symbolic role of Skanda's six faces: One face sheds light in the darkness (this function is related to creation – *sṛṣṭi*); another looks upon and blesses devotees; another witnesses the slaying of the *asura* and all wickedness (that is, destruction – *samāhara*); another enlightens the sage- and teaches the sacred texts to those who listen (revelation – *anugraha*); another guards and preserves such priests as perform appropriate sacrifices (preservation – *sthiti*); the last face gazes affectionately at the consorts (Tirumuru 118ff.; Kanta kali Vēṇpā: 4.).

On the one hand, then, the six faces connote the fullness of divinity and suggest that in Murukaṉ is embodied that divine fullness. But the number six takes on other significance as well, for the number is also used to symbolize the fullness of the cosmos. The god, by virtue of his being six-in-one, is made congruent with the cosmos, also depicted as six-in-one in myth and speculation.[19] Thus, the world's six directions – North, South, East, West, up and down – are said to be encompassed by the god's six faces. The five elements plus the whole are pervaded by the god's presence. This is explicit in references found even in the late Epic and post-Epic myths wherein Skanda's seed is said to have been borne, in turn, by the five elements – ether, wind, fire, water, earth (S. Satchidanandan Pillai 1963:15). Even the author of the Tirumurukkāṟṟupaṭai saw the six functions of the god as occurring in six different places in his domain. The god pervades the world and is homologous to the world.

Popular speculation has taken this homologization even further, for the god is made congruent not only to the world, but to man, who by virtue of his six *cakras* is himself a microcosm. The six faces are equated to the six *cakras* of the yogin's spiritual body: *mūlādhāra* (low navel), *svādhiṣthāna* (mid-navel), *maṇipūta* (high navel), *anāhata* (mid-chest), *viśuddha* (throat) and *ājña* (forehead). Once again, Swami Sivananda takes this even further suggesting the god is the five senses and the mind (1963:127).

Thus, in the interpretations of devotees within the Murukaṉ tradition and in the allusions of myth and literature, the number six is an integrative one, representing totality and homologizing divinity, cosmos, and man. Further, the god's six faces render him in the eyes of at least some imaginative devotees, congruent to any other reality that can be seen in terms of six. For example, Murukaṉ is said to be the way to release because he encompasses the six paths (*adhvās*) Śaiva Siddhānta recognizes as being appropriate for integration: *mantra*, *pada* (words), *varṇa* (letters), *bhuvana* (world), *tattva* (categories), and *kalā* (parts). Or again, the god's six faces are said to be reminders that Skanda is the source of the six orthodox schools of philosophy (p. 127).

This speculation on the number six is also applied to the cultic life. In most Śaiva circles, for example, the temple is considered a microcosm not only because of the ways the central tower or *vimāṉam* is made congruent to the cosmos and human frame, but also because the temple is said to have six *cakras*.[20] The temple's six *cakras* serve to make it in its very design a replica of the universe wherein god, man and world are symbolically conjoined. The speculation on six also gives some clues as to why Murukaṉ's devotees insist there are six centers to Murukaṉ in Tamil Nadu. These six centers serve to sacralize and cosmicize the region. Tamil Nadu thereby becomes the inheritor of meanings associated with older symbols and myths.

The chief catalyst for the wide-spread use of the number six in the Murukaṉ cultus in the South is without doubt the influence of Tantrism. The *Kumāra Tantra*, a manual providing instructions in ritual techniques, was available to Tamil priests at least by the eleventh century though in Grantha script. Within the movement that text reflects is to be found speculation as to the relationships between the symbolism of the Kumāra cultus and Vedic and Epic symbolism. One is reminded, for example, that Agni through six sacrificial sparks generates Skanda. With whatever else this allusion means, it suggests that Agni – the Sacrifice – gives birth to integration and immortality – that is, to Skanda. The intent of the sacrifice was the recreation of the cosmos and the breakthrough from the cosmos to the transcendent. The myth ascribes to the birth of Skanda the same intent. Again, in the later mythical context, Skanda is generated of six sparks from the forehead of the Cosmic Yogi, Śiva. Here Skanda represented the integration and immortality that is born of the yogic discipline, for it is understood by yogins of *Kumāra Tantra* that he who, by yogic discipline attains integration and immortality, becomes Kumāra-Skanda (cf. Danielou 1964: 298–99). That is, the yogin who attains release is one newly born; he has attained a new mode of being; he is Skanda. For such a yogin, as Mircea Eliade has noted, the six *cakras* of the human frame constitute a *maṇḍala* which help him at the same time to create of his body a cosmos and to transcend that cosmos (Eliade 1958:244).

In a very similar way, the six centers of the contemporary cultus of Murukan̲ constitute, for at least some devotees – and particularly those familiar with the Sanskrit heritage of the cultus – a *maṇḍala* by which Tamil Nadu is itself cosmicized and breakthrough from the cosmos to transcendence is believed possible. Skanda, in whom Śiva and Śakti meet, who is the integrative and transcendent one, is embodied in the six pilgrimage centers. These centers thus represent both cosmos and transcendence. In them, the cosmos is constituted and the cosmos is conquered.[21]

3.2 *The red and the gold*

One of the most persistent and striking features of Murukan̲ is his red complexion and his association with gold. His redness encompasses a number of characteristics and motifs, both Tamil and Sanskrit, that shed further light on his comprehensive and integrative nature.

Redness in the early *Caṅkam* literature connoted Murukan̲'s reflection of the whole tenor of the land. The god's complexion embodied the color, vibrancy, and fertility of life. His color seemed to be an affirmation of the fullness and ambivalence of existence. The blood-stained lance and tusks of the elephant with which Murukan̲ was associated served as reminders of the god's fearsomeness and anger, while the god's association with red blossoms like the *kaṭampu* and the blood of the ram or bull suggested his lordship over vegetation and herd. The sun, in this early literature, appears to be of the earth, red in its rising and setting in the hills. The red cock, the awakener, belongs to the god, as does all else that is native to the colorful hills. Thus, on the one hand, Murukan̲'s redness represents his inheritance from *Cēyon̲*, the Red God, of much of the early Tamil character of the land.

In the Epic mythology, the god's redness suggests his association with solar and celestial attributes. The cock, given to the god by Aruṇa, the sun's charioteer, represents more fully the celestial character of the sun. Redness is Skanda's inheritance from Agni, personification of sun and fire, and from Rudra, the angry sky god of the storm. A similar note is struck in Medieval Tamil poetry, for example, in the poem of Aruṇakirinātar, wherein Murukaṉ on his peacock is like the red sun astraddle the blue-green ocean.

Redness suggests, like so many other motifs associated with Murukaṉ, the *coincidentia oppositorium* of which the god is a symbol: cosmic integration – the god representing sky and earth and the wholeness of the cosmos, at the same time. There is more suggested by the red color. Redness seems to connote primordiality in the tradition of Skanda-Murukaṉ. This is particularly implied in the god's identification with the sun and the *hiraṇyagarbha*. As the sun was thought to be a demiurge, generated of the primordial ocean, dispelling darkness and bringing the new creation that was day, so Skanda was associated with cosmogonic power. He was said to be the *hiraṇyagarbha*, the seed and substance of creation.

Primordiality is also implied in Skanda's association with the red lotus, a flower associated with him especially in the post-Epic material. In some mythic variations of his birth he is said to spring out of a lotus in the sacred pool in the Himalayas.[22] In some Somāskanda representations, Pārvatī is holding a lotus, rather than the child Skanda.[23] In several representations (particularly those of Subrahmaṇya. Ṣaṇmukha and Bālasāmi). the god is depicted either holding a lotus in his hand or seated on a lotus. The implication of this association of Murukaṉ with the lotus seems clear, for the lotus is frequently depicted as the primordial flower in Hindu mythology. Thus, Murukaṉ is a lotus, and he emerges from the lotus. The god's redness appears to link a number of the elements which suggest his primordial character.

Redness also represents his fearsome and destructive attributes. The color red was used in the *Caṅkam* poetry to depict anger. Similarly, the early Tamil imagery of Murukaṉ's weaponry dripping with blood is related to his role as destructive warrior. In the Epic mythology, redness suggests a similar function. The red sun dispels darkness and the forces symbolized by darkness. Rudra's redness is consistent with his fearsome role as warrior. We must keep in mind, however, that the destructive connotation of redness is but one side of the picture. We are confronted by the interesting paradox that the Tamil terms associated with redness, *ce* and *ceyyaṉ*, can mean 'good', 'correct', or 'beautiful' and a 'ruddy or virtuous person'. respectively (Tamil Lexicon 1928:1599, 1632). We recall that in the mythology related to Skanda destructiveness is tempered by its function as a creative and preservative necessity. The god destroys that he may preserve the *dharma* or the society. Thus, the ambivalent nature of the god is suggested in his color which itself has ambivalent features.

An obvious connotation of redness has to do with Skanda's relationship with fire and sacrifice. In the Epic mythology, his birth from a golden receptacle, and later in a golden forest, and his emergence from the thicket of *śara* reeds used to make the sacrificial fires, suggest this association. This relationship is intimated in other elements in the mythology: the fact that the *ṛṣis' soma* sacrifice is the occasion for Skanda's conception of Agni; the young god's birth of the wives of the fire-making *ṛṣis*, as impersonated by Svāhā; the generation of Skanda from the sparks in Śiva's forehead which, among other things, seems to imply the relaying from father to son of a predisposition to *tapas*, 'inner heat'; and, most obvious and important of all, the god's inheritance of the character of Agni, personification of the sacrificial fire.

Murukan̲'s association with sacrificial fire implies most importantly that Murukan̲, like the fire and the sacrifice, becomes a microcosm of the world. Fire pervades the cosmos, for in the person of Agni it is found on the earth, in the atmosphere, and in the heavens. The fire is both generated and generator – it is generated from two sticks (*araṇi*), representative of the primordial pair; yet it serves as a 'demiurge' in the sense that it transforms that which is poured into the fire into new substance. The building of the sacrificial fire was intended to be a re-creation of the cosmos, a re-enacting of the primordial sacrifice of Prajapati, and a bringing together of the scattered portions of his person. In a similar manner, Skanda was believed to be the eternal sacrifice, the creative fire by which the world is eternally re-created and time and space are made meaningful in a manner consistent with brāhmaṇic cosmological speculation.

We should note, finally, that there is a relationship between the god's red character and his golden features. The two colors are interchangeable in the iconography of the god, as prescribed in the Āgamas. There seems to be no discernible pattern by which some representations are supposed to be saffron and others red. Both seem to be shades of 'the color of the rising sun' (Gopinath Rao 1916, II:415). In the early Tamil literature bright yellow flowers are sometimes associated with Murukan̲, as well as red flowers. Similarly, the god's dress in the Epic myths is a mixture of golden and red.

It seems fair to say, that the god's golden nature depicts virtually all that his redness does and that gold, the metal of immortality, symbolizes much of what Skanda-Murukaṉ symbolizes. 'Gaṅgeya', the name of Skanda as the one born of the golden seed deposited by the golden river Gaṅga into a forest which instantaneously turned gold, also means 'gold'. Skanda and gold were one. To bring one into being was to bring the other into being. Thus the vocation of the alchemist and the *yogi* were unmistakably equated. The ultimate hope of each was the same.

Murukaṉ is not always represented in red throughout Tamil Nadu today. Wherever he is painted, he is, of course, almost always red. Stone representations of him, however, are seldom painted, so something of the persistent symbolism implied in his redness seems to be missing in the cultus today. Relatively few devotees are aware of the religious significance of the red or gold. Further, not many active priests and swamis are able to offer significant interpretations of what is implied in the god's color.[24] To be sure, some executives of contemporary temples to Murukaṉ, like those of sanctuaries in other wealthy communities, have a penchant for gold. Especially visible are golden domes atop the *vimāṉa* and the golden jewellery which adorns the god at the high point in ritual. Most commonly this gold is said to demonstrate Murukaṉ's greatness – his prosperity and regality.[25] One cannot help but conclude, nevertheless, that the use of gold in many temples has become more nearly a status symbol than a religious one.

3.3 *Teriomorphic images*

Associated with Murukaṉ in various ways is a retinue of animals that bear meaning in the cultus. Chief amongst these animals are the peacock, rooster, and elephant, though more minor roles are ascribed to the ram, goat, horse, and serpent. While each animal has its distinct nuances of meaning, a fundamental theme is operative in Murukaṉ's association with the beasts: the god's relationship to the animal is a mirror of man's coming to grips with the natural forces of the cosmos.

This pastoral theme may be summarized as follows: the animal mythically represents natural forces of the cosmos. It is potentially chaotic or destructive; it threatens the stability of the order. The god subdues the animal; without destroying it, he makes the animal subservient to himself and useful to mankind, The animal becomes a symbol of benevolence or creativity. In Murukan̠'s taming of the animals, he is portrayed as the divine prototype of the pastoralist, even as he was the divine prototype of the hunter, warrior, teacher, ascetic, and king.

In this divine drama, man sees acted out his own relationship with the cosmic forces with which he must deal. Be he hunter or pastoralist, he sees something of his own dilemma and possibility in his relationship to the animal. Eventually, even though the animals themselves may have faded in significance in man's economic and social existence, the meaning of their symbolism remains suggestive. Today, for example, in industrial societies, the machine replaces the animal as symbol of man's cosmic orientation. Like the animal, the machine represents certain biological and physical laws of the universe with which man must come to grips. Like the animal, the machine gives man a vision of himself; through it, man extends his own power and opportunity; he transcends the limits of his time and space. Yet by the animal (or the machine) man is reminded of his own limitations, of the otherness of his context, of its ever-present threat.

This basic theme recurs with varying nuances in the teriomorphic retinue of Murukan̠. At the same time, each symbol bears its own significance in the tradition. It is worth lingering on some of them.

3.3.1 *The peacock*

The most persistent and meaningful of the animals associated with Murukan̠ is the peacock. Even in the early Tamil poetry the symbolism of the peacock was multivalent. The bird's colorfulness and fecundity were consistent with the festive and vibrant life of the hills. The peacock's beauty was often compared to the beauty of women and the beauty of newly foliated vegetation. The peacock was thought to dance in the rain and to be a sure indication of the rain's coming. In this sense the bird was like Murukan̠, for Murukan̠ was also a bringer of rain (Pur̠a. 143). The peacock lodged in the treetops, believed to be the abode of the gods. Its feathers were used to decorate the small pillar (*kantu*) used in worship and the lance victorious in war or used in worship. Thus, the sacral character of the peacock is intimated and its relationship to Murukan̠ established.

We cannot be sure that the peacock was a game bird in the early south, but one or two clues tend to suggest it was. That the fowl was killed seems likely by the fact that its feathers were used for decoration and worship. And, at least among the Veddas, the priest was to refrain from eating the flesh of the peafowl prior to the ritual dance. This implies that, under ordinary circumstances, the flesh of the peafowl was part of the diet of the hunting community. If the peacock were a game bird, then there is a possibility that what occurs in other hunting and agricultural societies may also be true in early South India. We know that in the religion of many hunting societies, game flesh, when eaten, afforded life. There was, therefore, a mutuality – a mystical relationship – between hunter and hunted, the former, in a sense, dependent on the latter for sustenance both in a literal and a religious sense.[26] Suggestive as this possibility is, there is no evidence to suggest so complex a mystical relationship existed between man and peacock in early Tamil society.

The most significant points to be noted about the peacock in the Epic myths of Skanda's birth are the allusions in the ninth and thirteenth books of the *Mahābhārata* which indicate the bird is the favorite son of Garuḍa, named Citrabarhin, and is given to Murukaṉ by Garuḍa to help equip the former for battle. The peacock is linked to the *garuḍa* and is more overtly associated with solar, celestial attributes and with the character of a warrior bird. These attributes of the bird are reflected in its functions described in later Tamil literature. In the Paripāṭal and Tirumurrukāṟṟupaṭai, Murukaṉ is seen as one who, mounting his peacock, can soar into the heavens and, like the sun, 'encircle' the globe.[27] That the peacock, like Murukaṉ, has warrior traits is suggested particularly in the iconography of the South, for example, in the Ṣaṇmukha of the tenth and eleventh centuries in which the peacock on which Murukaṉ is mounted clutches in its claws a serpent. The serpent in that context, appears to be symbolic, at the least, of the primordial, chthonic and malevolent forces of the cosmos which the peacock has subdued.

Precisely when the peacock became Murukaṉ's mount in the South is not clear. In the first three centuries of the Christian era, Murukaṉ was often associated with the peacock in both North and South, but the bird was not necessarily the God's mount.[28] In the fourth and fifth centuries (if my judgment as to the dating of most of the Tirumurrukāṟṟupaṭai and Paripāṭal is admissible) Murukaṉ was recognized as riding the *piṇimukam*, now identified with the peacock (though earlier, apparently, with the elephant) and given the power of flight. And by the tenth century, with the proliferation of the Ṣaṇmukha and other representations, the peacock, rather than the elephant, had become the standard mount of the god.

By the medieval period, the blue-green peacock is also used as a simile for the ocean, both in the poetry of Aruṇakiri and in the myth of the wicked asura who becomes a peacock in the ocean. The god 'tames' it, subdues it, and makes it his vehicle. In this context, the peacock acquires something of the primordiality implicit in the ocean. It is out of the ocean that the sun, identified with the red Murukan̲, arises. The peacock, like the ocean, suggests the primordial chaos and malevolence which Murukan̲ overcomes and makes the instrument of his own purpose. By now also the peacock has come to be associated with all parts of the cosmos – with the colorful, fertile earth; the heavens and the sun; and the ocean. It has become, therefore, a symbol of totality, as Murukan̲ himself represents totality. In this light, it is not surprising that Aruṇakiri writes that the peacock can encompass the entire cosmos and can make it cohere or disintegrate.[29] Murukan̲'s sitting astride the peacock connotes the belief that the god reigns even over totality.

Thus the peacock comes to represent, at least by the medieval period, many of the meanings embodied in Murukan̲ himself – primordiality, integration, cosmic totality. The bird also suggests a certain coalesence of polarities – sky and earth; malevolence and enmity toward the god, together with benevolence and devotion; primordial chaos and the colorful and fertile fullness of the created whole. As Murukan̲ straddles the peacock, the bird represents the cosmos under the mastery of the god who is supracosmic, the earth at the service of him who is transcendant; and the devotee in a posture of usefulness to his god.

3.3.2 *The rooster*

The rooster is another of the symbols that have persisted with Murukan̲ throughout the god's history. The fowl's indirect association with the god is evident in the early Tamil literature. The Tamil term *cēval* could refer to any male fowl and was apparently associated with both Tirumāl and Murukan̲ in the *Caṅkam* poetry. In fact, in Pari. 3, the *cēval* is particularly associated with Tirumāl, for Tirumāl is referred to as *cēvalōn̲* – he of the fowl flag (18) – and *cēvalūrti* – he whose mount is the fowl (60) (Subrahmaniam 1966:376).

Hence, the rooster may have served as another of those links between Tirumāl and Murukaṉ during the era of chieftainship.

The reasons for Murukaṉ's association with the cock in the *Caṅkam* period are not altogether clear. Two functions ascribed to the cock may have been important in this respect. The first, mentioned in Puṟa. 28:8–10, is that of protector of the grain crops, inasmuch as watchers of the millet awaken when the aroused cock crows. The other is that the cock was probably recognized as a virile fecundator (though we have no specific references demonstrating it). Both these functions are also ascribed to the god. It is possible, though we cannot document it, that the cock may have been used in worship (even as it is today), its blood and feathers providing 'atmosphere' for the worship center.

In the Epic mythology we find that the cock is given to Skanda by Ȧruṇa, the celestial charioteer of the sun. The rooster is thereby ascribed solar and celestial connotations. Presumably, its red comb contributed to this linkage. In its solar characteristic, the rooster seems to have assumed some of the symbolism of the *garuḍa* – and N. Subrahmaniam suggests this equation is made in the Pari. 3:60.[30]

Most Northern iconography depicted Skanda carrying the cock in his hand and often tucked into the hip. But, in the South, by the age of chieftainship, as described in the invocation to the Kuṟuntokai, Murukaṉ's cock was inscribed on a banner. This is a significant difference, for the banner was one of the necessary paraphernalia of Tamil kings, as part of the royal insignia of Cōḻas, Pāṇṭiyas and other Southern dynasties. Thus Murukaṉ's kingship is denoted, his bird being a protector, fecundator, and fighter in its own right, and like the peacock, having both solar and terrestial connotations.

3.3.3 *The elephant*

That the elephant is more a Tamil than a Sanskrit element in the heritage of Murukaṉ is a conclusion that is difficult to resist. There are virtually no allusions to elephants in the Epic myths of Murukaṉ, save for one suggestion in the thirteenth book of the Mahābhārata that Varuṇa gave elephants to Skanda for his retinue, together with lions, tigers, and clawed animals.

On the other hand, even in the earliest Tamil literature, the elephant is associated with Murukan̲ in a number of ways. The elephant's ferocity and fighting skill are equated with those of Murukan̲. The elephants are denizens of the hills, the realm of Murukan̲. At one point the elephant is seen as the mount of Murukan̲, as it is probably to the elephant the term *piṇimukam* refers when used in the early poetry to denote the god's mount. Even if the elephant was replaced by the peacock by the Cōl̲a era as the standard mount of Murukan̲ in Tamil Nadu, the elephant has persisted in association with Murukan̲. Even today, at appropriate times during festivals to Murukan̲, the god is brought in procession, mounted on an elephant.

One of the most obvious roles given to the elephant is its association with Southern kingship. The elephant is one of the ten insignia of royalty, as it is the king's mount and ally in battle. One thing that the elephant's association with Murukan̲ affirms is the god's right to be termed a divine king in the Tamil tradition. That the elephant also represented malevolent force, subdued by the god is suggested by the fact that one of the *asuras* which Murukan̲ overcomes (one of the heads, in fact, of the six-headed Sūrapadma whom Murukan̲ destroys on Skanda-Ṣaṣṭi) has an elephant's head.

But there is ambivalence in the character of the elephant. Unsubdued, the elephant is malevolent; subdued, he is a benevolent ally of man and god. This ambivalent nature and pattern of development may be reflected in the rise of Gaṇapati. H. Heras and Venkatakrishna Rao note that many of the Purāṇas are full of myths denoting the rivalry of Skanda and Gaṇapati jostling for position. Battles are said to have occurred in which each could claim victory, but Skanda devotees find special significance in the fact that Ganeṣa frequently loses a tusk after a scrap with his powerful brother (Heras 1956: 194). One of the implications is that Skanda saps the elephant of some of his ferocity and 'harnesses' his power in such a way as to make him fit for the service of man and god.

Yet the elephant does not seem to attain the comprehensive and cosmic symbolic character in the Murukan̲ myths that the peacock does. There is, for example, no certainty that Murukan̲'s elephant ever attains a celestial character. To be sure, there is a hint of it when we find Devasenā called in Tamil, *Devayān̲ai* (elephant of the gods).[31] But, by and large, Murukan̲'s elephant seems to be of the earth. This chthonic and rather pragmatic role of the elephant is consistent with the functions it performs in behalf of some temples of Murukan̲. The elephant pushes the temple cart in procession and brings sacred water for *apiṣekam*. The live elephant seems to symbolize little more than the docility and passivity of those devoted to serving Murukaṉ; it is the cosmos subdued. Also suggestive is the use of the elephant – whether live or dummy – in festival processions. Murukaṉ rides the elephant, almost invariably, *before* or *into* the re-enacted battle. But Murukaṉ rides the peacock *after* the battle. I take the significance of this distinction to be that the triumphant Murukaṉ is a cosmic Murukaṉ, who has ritually attained supremacy of all space. The Murukaṉ of the elephant, on the other hand, is an 'incarnate' Murukaṉ, humanized, as it were, on his way to the cosmic battle. Be that as it may, the peacock has superceded the elephant in Murukaṉ's symbolism, though the latter continues its association with the god.

3.3.4 *The ram*

The ram (*āṭu* or *katā*) is used infrequently today as a vehicle for Murukaṉ and even more rarely is depicted in one of the hands of the sculptured Subrahmaṇya, Senāpati, or Ṣaṇmukha (Gopinath Rao 1916, II:427, 434, 437). The most important myth suggesting the significance of the ram is that which speaks of the ram's running wild on the mountainside when Murukaṉ was but a child. Created of the *ṛṣis'* sacrifice, the ram waxed out of control and terrorized the realm of the gods. But Murukaṉ, still only a few days old, had the ram brought to him and playfully rode it, thereby subduing it and making it his permanent instrument. This recurrent theme, intimated here, of the god's conquest of malevolence is also illustrated by the fact that one of the heads of the six-headed Sūrapadma in contemporary festival enactments is that of a ram.

That the ram was created by the *ṛṣis'* sacrifice may be suggestive. Like the god, the ram may have been intended to serve as the cosmic sacrifice, the 'scapegoat', as it were of the world. The ram's association with sacrifice may also help link this Epic allusion to the early Tamil practice of using the blood of the ram (or lamb) in sacrifice. A not uncommon practice especially in pastoral worship, the sacrifice effects a mystic relationship between the sacrificed victim, the worshipper, and the god; the worshipper and his god meet in the sacrificial animal. Moreover, the ram helps to further link Skanda with Agni (both of whom were associated with sacrifice), inasmuch as Agni is also given a ram as his mount.

3.3.5 *The serpent*

The serpent's association with Subrahmaṇya is a strange one. It is virtually ubiquitous; for at most shrines and temples of Murukan̲ serpent icons can be found at some point. The snake is also commonly depicted clutched in the talons of the peacock. Yet seldom is the snake shown on or near the person of the god as is so common with both Śiva and Viṣṇu. And even more striking, there is a remarkable paucity of myths and even references to the snake in the officially recognized mythology of the god. The snake's significance seems to be more implicit than explicit.

One meaning ascribed the snake is its malevolence. Implied in its very nature, the snake's destructiveness and dangerous aspect is expressed explicitely when we are told that it represents one of the *malas*, which together with the peacock and cock, was 'leftover' after Murukan̲'s conquest of the *asura*.[32] On the other hand, the snake is also vested with a beneficial power, especially that of fertility. Women circumambulate the *nākakkals* (snake stones) primarily in the hope they will bear a child.

These two functions – malevolence and fertility – are fairly clear in the Subrahmaṇya context, even though there are few myths or explicit statements of support. Yet there are implicit connotations to the serpent. Some of these are especially suggested by the classic portrayal of the serpent in the clutches of the peacock. In this pair of creatures is depicted an integration of polarities; sun and water; chaos and cosmos; heaven and earth; good and evil; the warrior and his foe; the hunter and his game; the bird and its prey. Various other dualities are suggested as well: the divine clutching the soul: the god (or the soul) mastering the world and its passions; being demonstrating its superiority over non-being; and others.

One interesting myth relative to the serpent's character occurs in a Malayali folk variation to the general Tamil tradition.[33] It seems when Murukan̲ imprisoned Brahmā for the older god's ignorance of spiritual truth, Brahmā cursed the playful child to become a snake. Unable to find their child anywhere Śiva and Pārvatī, as they continued their search, prayed and fasted that he be returned to them. Years passed; the world became darker and darker, and the gods more terrified. At last Śiva learned from Brahmā that Subrahmaṇya was a snake. Therewith Śiva touched the head of the snake and Subrahmaṇya emerged from within its skin. Immediately, the world became light again and order was restored.

The implications of this myth are several. Subrahmaṇya is the same as the snake and both appear to be associated with primordiality. The snake is malevolent; its reign is chaotic and dark. And yet, the snake is the primordial substance from which Subrahmaṇya, now personifying the new order, emerges. The snake's fertility or parenthood is thus implied, and Subrahmaṇya's rebirth represents the coming of a 'new creation'; he is to reign supreme in the new age.

Perhaps this myth tells us as well as anything else why women continue to circumambulate the serpent icons. There is a hope that they like the snake, will 'give birth'. Every birth, it seems, is a re-enactment of the coming into being of Skanda, the divine infant, and of the cosmos itself.

3.4 *Weaponry*

One of the features of Murukaṉ which best reflects the historical continuity and discontinuity of religious symbolism is his function as a warrior-king. It is apparent that this role is the most dominant theme in the Skanda who is patronized by Śakas, Kuṣāṇas, and Guptas. He had become the prototype for some of the Northern kings of the post-Mauryan period who, influenced by Middle Eastern notions of divine kingship and inheriting the Indian vision of the universal emperor (*cakravartin*), began to assume the role of 'king of kings' and 'supreme lord' (Basham 1963:84). The king and his palace became one of the foci in the city-state, surrounded by the court, the artisans, and much of the cultural life of the city. The king's authority was divinely bestowed even though he was still responsible to his priests, his ministers, and in theory, at least, to his subjects. Following in the mythological train of Rudra and Indra, Skanda was given Indra's role as general of the divine army (*senāpati*) and inherited the armies of Rudra-Śiva. He was duly anointed with the water denoting sovereignty in the tradition of Varuṇa. With Śiva's bow and Pārvatī's *śakti* he was empowered to defeat the *asuras*,

Even in the late *Caṅkam* period in Tamil Nadu where the chieftain did not have the power of the northern *kṣatriyas*, and where much is yet to be learned about the character of urbanization, there is literary and archeological evidence that towns did exist, that significant buildings had been erected, that extensive trade was carried on and that urbanization did influence the religious life. In particular, festivals were urbanized and poets associated gods like Murukaṉ with urban chieftains and ascribed to the deities military and regal attributes. By the fifth century A.D., Murukaṉ had been ascribed most of the ten insignia of Tamil kingship: a weapon, a banner, umbrella, war-drum, mount, elephant, chariot, garlands, crown, and capital city. For several centuries, he was depicted as a regal god, consistent with the spirit of Southern kingship, fearsome, virulent and benevolent protector of the capital city. Yet, in the South, Murukaṉ never attained the military prowess ascribed to Skanda by Epic mythmakers.

Some of the symbolic paraphernalia associated with Skanda-Murukaṉ are directly related to his military character and tended to decline in significance or change in manner when his military character itself came to be de-emphasized. It is interesting that many of these symbols are only derivately Skanda's and are more commonly associated with other deities. For example, in some of his aspects, Skanda bears a trident (*tirucūlam*; Sanskrit *triśula*), the three-pronged weapon most commonly associated with his father Śiva. Apart from its obvious military use, the trident undoubtedly connotes the unitary quality of reality as perceived in threes. Its use in the possession of Murukaṉ implies in another way his inheriting his father's military and integrative features. The bow (*taṉu*) is another weapon said to have been given him by Śiva, though it also is associated with Murukaṉ's role as a hunter – or hero. Similarly, the dart (*pāṇa* or Sanskrit *bāṇa*) is a gift of Indra and connotes Skanda's receiving military prowess from the older general of the divine army. The dart was used to pierce the Krauñca mountain where Bāṇa, the last of the escaping demons was slain. We cannot be sure what is intended by that play on words more than to connote the superiority of Skanda's weapon and skill over those of the *asuras*. The shield (*kēṭaka*) is also a part of Murukaṉ's armor, apparently given by Agni according to the Paripāṭal.[35] The conch (*caṅku*) is used, we are told in Tirumuru. 184, to signal the battle charge and also is used with trumpets to herald the god's triumphal coming. In fact, the conch's use in the measuring of time suggest Murukaṉ's role as harbinger and measurer of time. The *vajra* (thunderbolt) is another weapon sometimes ascribed to Skanda. Far more commonly associated with Indra, the *vajra* served not only as a weapon of war, but also as the cosmic thunderbolt which rent the primordial dragon Vṛtra in twain that rains could be leashed on the earth. But Skanda has very little relationship to a storm god except in the most indirect sense by which he is said to cause rain and to subdue chaotic forces. Hence, in his hands, the *vajra* serves a primarily military function and secondarily suggests an association with the elements of the storm and fecundity.

Some of the god's symbols suggest not only the military role of Murukan̲, but also suggest the god's relationship to kingship. One of these is the bill-hook or elephant goad (*aṅkucam*), used to goad the elephant by Southern chieftains who used elephants in their military retinue. The instrument in Murukan̲'s hands connotes not only his military prowess but his divine kingship in the Tamil sense (cf. Tirumuru. 162). The bill-hook was also carried by the Vedda priest dancing the prehunt ritual. The function of the instrument in that context is not clear, but perhaps it was to symbolize the priest's capacity to slay game ritually or to ward off epidemic. At any rate, the instrument seems to help link the work of the priest and the chieftain-king with that of the god. Another instrument with particularly Southern roots, at least when associated with Murukan̲, is the *pāca* (Sanskrit *pāśa* – noose or fetter). The *pāca* was used to capture wild animals, especially elephants, and it is used by a number of the gods to subdue *asuras*. But *pāca* also refers to the worldly bonds of Saiva Siddhanta. The *pāca* in the hands of Murukan̲ seems to connote his capacity to subjugate evil and reign as king over the bonds of the world. The *cakra* (wheel) appears to be more Northern but it was adopted fairly early in Southern imagery, as attested by the Tirumurukār̲r̲upaṭai. Therein Murukan̲ is depicted as holding a wheel in one of his hands (164). The wheel was not necessarily associated with kingship in the South but was a common symbol of Northern kingship, tying together the king's military and regal roles, particularly after the time of Aśoka. The circle also had connotations of perfection, totality, and universality, all roles which the sacral king was supposed to fill. That Murukan̲ was thought to embody the vision of the universal emperor (*cakravartin*) is implied in his association with the *cakra*. And the garland (*malai*) which adorns the god's neck, often in the shape of a wheel, is itself one of the insignia of Southern kingship.

Thus, the military character of the god becomes particularly prominent in the context of urbanization and the rise to power of the warrior-kings, and some of Murukan̲'s symbolism is associated with that stage of his history. But, on the other hand, Murukaṇ's militaristic stage is part of an ongoing continuum in his history. His militarism, for example, is not inconsistent with his role as paradigmatic hunter in the early Tamil context. Indeed, it appears that warrior motifs were 'grafted' onto hunter motifs in the South in the later *Caṅkam* literature. Nor is Skanda's militarism that far removed from his role as teacher-philosopher. This latter role is already implicit in his capacity as Divine prototype of the *kṣatriya* princes. In that capacity he is said to have taught *brāhmaṇs*. For example, the *Kathāsaritsāgara* mentions that a brāhmaṇ named Vyādi worshipped Kumāra to obtain knowledge, and another brāhmaṇ named Varṣa learned all branches of knowledge from Skanda after performing penance. The same work says that the Katancra system of Sanskrit grammar originated from the six mouths of Kārttikeya, who in the form of Skanda was reported to have taught this simpler system to the minister of a Sātavāhana king. These references illustrate the dual character of Skanda – warrior and teacher-philosopher; as such, he was, for the Epic kings and myth-makers, the divine king par excellence. In the later stages of the god's history, the capacity of Skanda as teacher-philosopher has become dominant and that of warrior king has receded into relative insignificance. As a result, the military imagery either becomes less common or is transferred in meaning and intent onto other forms. Nowhere is this transitional process better illustrated than in the symbolism ascribed to the lance.

3.4.1 *The lance*

There are two basic types of lance associated with Murukaṉ: the *vēl*, a Tamil term denoting a leaf-shaped lance; and the *śakti*, a Sanskrit term denoting the double – or triple-headed lance, commonly associated with the goddess.

The *vēl* as an instrument of war apparently came into prominence during the period of chieftainship in the South. But this *vēl* of the second or third century seemed to bring together several earlier sources. Its predecessor in the hunting community had been the arrow or spear of the hunter-chieftain. The blood-soaked tusk of the elephant was also equated with the lance, a relationship which apparently helped link Murukaṉ and the elephant. Also linked to the lance was the leaf of the *vēṅkai* tree, a factor which helps associate Murukaṉ and the *vēṅkai*. The *vēl* is also known as the instrument of the priest of Murukaṉ, the *Vēlaṉ* (literally, a bearer of the lance) who carried a ritual staff, arrow, or bill hook. Murukaṉ himself becomes known as *Vēlan*, partially because he is the bearer of the lance *par excellence* and partially because the priest in raiment and function personified the god. Thus the lance seemed to coalesce around the person of Murukaṉ the role of the hunter, the elephant, the *vēṅkai* tree, and the priest.

By the age of chieftainship, the lance is an instrument of war and a symbol of the warrior. It was apparently used in worship by this time, as it was often bedecked with peacock feathers and adorned with a neck plate with small bells attached. It was used, so it seems, to represent the fallen warrior. That the lance (or at least, a weapon) was a symbol of Southern kingship is clear from the fact that a weapon is listed as one of the ten required insignia of a king.

Of the *śakti* less is written in the Epic myths. The origin of the *śakti* is described in the myth of the third book of the Mahābhārata: when Indra split Kumāra's side with his *vajra*, from the split portion, Viśākha sprang into being, bearing a *śakti*. From that same blow the *grahas* and malevolent goddesses are said to have come into being. The *śakti*, together with the *grahas*, overcome Indra, his *vajra*, and the deities. This allusion may mean two things. First, the *śakti*, in the hands of Skanda, proves to be more powerful than the *vajra* of Indra and enables the youth to subdue the older god, suggesting that Murukaṉ is born to succeed Indra as the celestial warrior, and to be greater than the latter. Second, the *śakti* may be an analog for the malevolent *grahas* and goddesses, for both the lance and the goddesses are called upon to do the same task, namely, to subdue the immediate oppressors. This possibility is enhanced by the allusion in Skanda–Purāṇa that Pārvatī, by this point embodying all the goddesses, gives to Murukaṉ the *śakti* with which to battle. This equation of *śakti* and goddesses opens up several possible lines of interpretation. Most importantly, the *śakti* comes to represent all that the goddess does – her energy, malevolence, and cosmic ambivalence.

The lance in association with Murukaṉ could be either a Tamil *vēl* or a Sanskrit *śakti*. Since the medieval period, however, the lance in Tamil Nadu has been more frequently depicted in iconography as a *vēl*. Indeed, some Tamil devotees of the god stress the importance of the lance's being a *vēl*, presumably to stress the uniqueness and Tamilness of the god.[36]

The most consistent interpretation given to the lance is that it is the instrumentality by which the god – or the devotee for whom the god exercises his prowess – can perform his tasks. In the case of the god who is a warrior and military hero, the lance represents his destructive power. In the case of the god by whose destruction of the enemy a new order is created, the lance represents the god's energy, force and creative power. When in the medieval period the entire cosmic battle is understood metaphorically and the *asura* comes to represent the spiritually malevolent *malas*, the lance comes to symbolize that discrimination or wisdom by which evil is mastered. In this context, the lance connotes the god's omniscience and his capacity as the purveyor of intelligence.

Today Murukaṉ is not the prototype of potentates and kings doing their *dharma* by preserving the state as a sacred world. True, for his most chauvinistic of devotees there is a sense in which Murukaṉ remains patron god of a region, preserving its alleged 'purity' and integrity over and against all cultural incursions. But more significantly, life's battlefield has been internalized. Murukaṉ has become the prototype of the individual devotee fulfilling his *dharma* by the conquest of the passions and bonds of existence. The lance now becomes the instrument of spiritual victory, the means to the conquest of all misfortune. The lance reminds devotees, that of all the forces of the cosmos, Murukaṉ is the most powerful and that his power is paradigmatic of the power available to all who bring wisdom and will to bear on life's obstacles.

But the lance represents more than the power of god or man. In contemporary ritual the lance often represents the god himself, in his totality, for the lance is often used as the representation of the god.[37] Moreover, when the lance as *śakti* is in the clasp of Murukaṉ, the two together represent the integrating of dualities in a manner consistent with Śaiva thought: Murukaṉ and his lance are Śiva-Śakti, the cosmic pair. In the two are embodied a spectrum of Śaiva dualities: god and soul; heaven and earth; god and world; and a number of others.

There is also a more specific interpretation commonly given to the lance and related paraphernalia in the context of Śaiva thought. Iconographically, the lance is usually depicted resting against the right shoulder of the deity; its base is slanted diagonally toward the peacock mount and its point is directed toward the banner on which the cock is inscribed. Some Śaiva interpreters suggest the peacock here represents *vinṭu* or the world with all its variety, earthiness and sensuousness. The rooster is said to represent *nāta*, 'ether' or primordial sound, because of the numinous character of its crowing. Thus the two extremes of the cosmos are represented by cock and peacock. In this context, the lance becomes the connecting entity, which penetrates the two extremities of the cosmos and holds the cosmos together.[38]

4. Some concluding questions

4.1 *Cultural coalescence and agencies of acculturation*

The history of Murukaṉ illustrates a process in the history of religion and culture that has been variously interpreted. In its simplest terms, Murukaṉ's history reflects the convergence of two cultural streams – one which has been called 'Sanskrit' and the other 'Tamil'. In using these terms one does not mean that either of these cultural streams is monolithic or unidimensional but rather that each is a cultural complex fed by a number of tributaries which coalesce and flow, in the literature and lore of the two continuing traditions, and which, as they meet, coalesce into a creative new cultural amalgam. Robert Redfield's terms the 'great tradition's' merging with the 'little tradition' are *à-propos* for this process only so long as we remember that the terms 'great' and 'little' are not value judgments by which either cultural stream is to be evaluated, and that the term 'tradition' in either case is not to be understood as single, undiversified units. McKim Marriott has called this process 'universalization' (1955:211–18) to suggest that all the constituent units of a cultural amalgam are catalysed and influenced by the universalizing agency of a continuing cultural stream. This does not mean that the cult of Subrahmaṇya today is precisely the same all over India but rather that the peculiarly Tamil heritage to which the deity has been adapted gives it a somewhat different character in Tamil Nadu than it would have in West Bengal, for example. Indeed, its peculiarly Tamil heritage has afforded the Skanda cult a popularity and cultural identity in Tamil Nadu that it apparently does not enjoy in West Bengal.

Other terms have been employed to characterize these two cultural streams. Mandelbaum speaks of a dichotomy between 'transcendental' and 'pragmatic' religion. Yet we cannot believe that religion in Tamil Nadu is never 'transcendental' and that religion as expressed in early Sanskritic literature is never pragmatic. The terms become more appropriate if they remind us that the religious imagery of the Epic Skanda is of a different tenor than that of the early Caṅkam Murukaṉ. We observed in earlier chapters, for example, how the mountains of the Epic Skanda are invariably the domain of the gods. In Purāṇic cosmology they constitute the center of the cosmos; they are celestial. In contrast, the hills – and indeed the poetry itself of early Tamil literature – are relatively secular and earthy. The hills are the abode of the *kuriñci*, who are given to dance, to love play, and to other very human endeavors. These hills are fertile and colorful, replete with fauna and flora. Even the sun in this poetry seems to be of the earth, as it rises out of the hills and is apprehended in the redness of the foliage. In sum, the hills associated with Murukaṉ, like the poetry itself, suggest the verdancy, verve, and vibrancy of the earth.

Pursuing this characterization further, one may argue that the gods of the Epic sources are gods of the sky – or at least of the higher reaches of the cosmos – and that the gods of the *Caṅkam* period are gods of the earth. Other distinctions in the religious imagery of these two bodies of literature can be noted. In the Epics, one finds the imagery of sacrifice, celestial cosmic battles, discourse with the gods, primordial forests and lakes, and many other suggestions of a transcendent religious perception in which the gods live in a world separated from man. In the *Caṅkam* poetry, the imagery is more frequently that of the hunt, epidemic, vegetation, a world in which man and god share a still undifferentiated cosmos.[39] Whatever terms one uses, this difference of perception is not that of a 'literate' versus a 'popular' one, for there is nothing illiterate about the *Caṅkam* perception, and there had been considerable interaction between literate and popular imageries throughout the history of Murukaṉ. Nor is it the difference between 'orthodox' and unorthodox religion, for there are 'unorthodox' components that have gone into the Epic imagery. Rather, the difference of perception is a cultural one, the product of the vision of a creative human spirit addressing differing cultural contexts.

But it is too simple to view the process of acculturation merely as two streams becoming one. It is important to stress that there were several cultural components that have influenced the Murukaṉ tradition and South Indian history. In the present study, we have drawn attention to some of the influences. Further research is needed to define more clearly the role these identifiable sources had in the development of the Skanda–Murukaṉ cult and in the history of religion in South India. For now we shall summarize some of the probable sources of influence on the cultus and raise questions for further research:

In the emergence of Skanda to prominence in the Epic period, at least three, and possibly four or five communities or cultural impeti have been noted. The most important seems to have been the city-state and the rise of the princes to power, particularly in the Śaka, Kuṣāṇa, and Gupta dynasties.

There is, however, much more to be learned about the cult of Skanda in these kingdoms, particularly about its ritual life, about how and why the god came to be associated with these princes, and about the relationship between the official 'state' cult of Skanda (if indeed there was one) and popular worship of the god.

Then, too, there is the probable influence of a brāhmaṇic community in the Epic mythology which was particularly interested in the sacrificial elements of the cult and who seemed to be most concerned for linking the new god Skanda to an authenticating Vedic tradition. We still know rather little about who these myth-makers were, what their relationship to the princes and the cities was, how the ritual elements of their cult differed, if at all, from the princely cult.

There is also reason to believe that the civilization of the Gangetic valley served as a contributor or catalyst to the Skanda mythology. It is at least possible, if not probable, that the mythology of the river's role in Skanda's birth, the god's association with malevolent mother goddesses, and certain agricultural motifs may have been derived from peoples of the Gaṅges valley. Far too little is yet known about this civilization or complex of civilizations, its origins, and its religious life to be certain of its influence on the Skanda cult. There is considerable room for further research to be done in that context.

Apart from the peoples of the Gangetic valley, it is not unlikely that folk of other tribes or communities were influencing the mythical and cultic life of the Epic period. Precisely what their influences were on the Skanda cult is still only fragmentarily known. As to what extent the Gangetic cultures and other folk were themselves influenced by early Southern sources even before the Epic literature became known in the South is a still largely unexplored question which may yield some interesting answers.

Then again, what role, if any, did the Alexandrian incursion and the resulting Hellenization play in the emergence of the Skanda cult in North India? N. Gopala Pillai argued in 1937 that the Dionysian cult came into North India with Alexander and gave birth to the cult of Skanda (pp. 958ff.). He based his case on Skanda's similarity to Dionysos and on evidences that Alexander was known as Iskander in Asia and was associated with Dionysos in an Arabian myth. Interesting as this suggestion is, it does not take into account several factors, not the least of which is that those elements about Skanda–Murukaṉ which sound most 'Dionysian' are found in the early Tamil literature and not for the most part in the Epic accounts of Skanda. Pillai also fails to recognize the agricultural or 'pre-Āryanized' stage of either Dionysos or Murukan̲.[40] Nonetheless, it may not be impossible that the name of Skanda was associated with Alexander, in a way still not precisely understood[41] and that elements of Skanda's Northern iconography were derived or influenced by the impact of post-Alexandrian Hellenization. Should that be the case, precisely who were the agents of such influence, the *kuṣāṇas* or others? These are questions which might still be explored with some profit.

The early civilization and religion of the Tamils presents a similar complexity. We still can not be certain of all the precise factors comprising early Tamil culture. The contributing elements in the cult of Murukan̲ are even less precisely understood. But at least some questions can be posed!

Who were the *kur̲iñcis* after all? Were they a premegalithic people? Were they Dravidian or pre-Dravidian? To what extent were they influenced by cultures outside of South India? What is the historical relationship, if any, between the *kur̲iñcis* and the Veddas of Ceylon or other tribal groups still existent in South or Central India? What more can archeology tell us about them and the cult of Murukan̲ in the days of early Tamil civilization?

What relationship was there between the megalithic peoples and the Murukan̲ cult in South India, if any? Did this cultural migration bring in any religious imagery or cultic elements from the upper Middle East that became a part of Murukan̲ cult in the South or did the megalithic culture provide an impetus in the South which led to independent creativity in Tamil religion?

What was the role, if any, of Roman and Mediterranean merchants in the religious life of South India in general and in the development of the Murukan̲ cult, in particular? Is there any historical connection between Murukan̲ and Dionysos?

To what extent was the Murukan̲ cultus influenced by Ceylonese civilization and religion? If it was Ceylonese civilization that catalyzed the 'urbanization' process in early Tamil civilization, as Clarence Maloney argues (1970:602ff.), was its influence on Murukan̲ any more than that of providing the impetus for urbanization during which the cult of Murukan̲ was brought into the cities, and the god assumes more of the character of warrior and military hero?

What more can archeology and linguistic analysis tell us of the Pāṇṭiyaṉ patronage of Murukaṉ? For example, were there temples and pilgrimage centers for Murukaṉ even in the early days of the *Caṅkam* period in the territory of the Pāṇṭiyas, and, if so, what relationship do those older centers have to the later ones? Evidence, both literary and archeological, is still meager.

Then too, precisely who were the agents of Āryanization in the South? It is commonly held that there were at least two agencies of Āryanization in the South from North India: Jain, Buddhist, brāhmaṇ, and other 'Āryans' in migrations from the north; and the influence of certain dynasties, chieftainships, particularly that of the Kadambas, the Pallavas, and Sātavāhanas. Yet we still know very little, save in general terms, about the way this process occurred in the Skanda–Murukaṉ tradition. What was the extent and nature, for example, of the Kadambas' devotion to Skanda? Under the aegis of which communities does Murukaṉ become associated with Śaivism? What more can we know not only of the process of Āryanization but of the Dravidianization of these migrants of chieftains with ties to northern India? And what role, even if an indirect one, did Jains and Buddhists from North India have in the eventual merging of religious perspectives outlined in this study of Murukaṉ?

Medieval Tamil Nadu leaves us with still more questions relative to the precise agencies of acculturation as they are at work in the Murukaṉ tradition. Is there, in fact, an identifiable relationship between the *brahmadeya* and Murukaṉ? What are the specifics of this relationship and in what ways does such a relationship connote change and innovation in the cultic life of Murukaṉ? Similarly, is there a discernible relationship between the proliferation and growth of the cult of Murukaṉ during and after the Cōḻa period and the emergence of the Vēḷāḷars as a socially significant community?[42]

Then again, there is considerably more to be learned about the ways folk elements in various locales have merged with generic symbol-systems and mythologies around various temples and pilgrim centers of the Murukaṉ cultus from medieval times to the present. Each temple has its own mythic history and is often linked not only to the Murukaṉ mythology as a whole but to the cultic and mythic traditions of specific locales. The detailed study of particular temples should yield more insight into the ways local imageries and myths inform the generic stream and vice versa.

In sum, there have been many agencies which have contributed to the development of Tamil religion in general and the Murukaṉ cult in particular. The present study serves only as an introduction to the history of Murukaṉ, for it has dealt with this complex process in outline form. The directions and need for further research are abundant.

4.2 *Whither Murukaṉ?*

Gods and religious symbols do indeed serve as commentary on man's imaginative use of the givens of each historical context. We should expect, therefore, that the contemporary forms of the cultus – the symbols and imageries of the present – can tell us something of the contemporary mood of Tamil India and of the cultural realities by which religious man lives. The experience of the past encourages us to assume that there will be a continuing relationship between culture and symbols, history and myth, god and man. Thus a reflective reading of the cultic symbols of a god like Murukaṉ enables us to discern something of the character of 'modernity' and should provide a few indications of the cultural trends of the future.

This study has affirmed the undeniable popularity of Murukaṉ in Tamil India today. In the introductory chapter some reasons for this popularity and some of the ways in which the cultus reflects the contemporary Tamil moment were noted. But questions remain: How long can the cultus of Murukaṉ be popular in Tamil Nadu? To what extent does it now and will it address itself to the character of 'modernity'? and to what degree does the cultus help to shape the Tamil moment?

We have argued that the cultus reflects Tamil Nadu's modern mood in several respects – the regional pride; the need for self and regional identity, characterized in part by the evoking of archaic symbolisms; the concern for democratization; etc. Yet, one can not help but wonder whether Murukaṉ will survive the encroachment of technology and demythologization and the increased 'secularization' of Tamil life.

In a superficial sense, Murukaṉ's temple authorities are incorporating technology into the cultus. Improved technology has meant the renovation of temples, the installation of public address and lighting systems. Modernity is a new winch train on which pilgrims may ride up the hill to the temple at Paḻani. It is a neon lance emblazoned on the *Kōpuram* at Tiruchendur, and a neon *ōm* blinking on a *Kōpuram* at Swamimalai. Modernity is gaudy paint on temple *Kōpurams* and walls. Modernity is the installation of air conditioners in the inner sanctum; the construction of hotels and choultries for pilgrims; it is traveling to a pilgrim center by bus or train.

But in a more substantive sense, the jury is still out on the cultus' coming to grips with the demythologizing age. To be sure, the cultus has not yet been significantly threatened by it. Yet who knows what the next generation or two will demand? Temple priests, by and large, are not in a position to provide a post-technological apologetic, as they are usually ritual technicians, steeped in their own traditions, but hardly cognizant of the larger world of scholarship. Similarly, *devasthanam* and temple administrators are busy in the housekeeping chores of presiding over a temple's financial affairs and stage managing its programs. There are still few executive officers who are theologically or aesthetically articulate.

The ability of the cultus to adapt to the future will depend, to some degree, on the success of such experiments as have been tried in recent years. For example, the Pal̲ani temple complex supports four colleges and benevolent institutions, including an institute for oriental studies, where a master's degree is now available in the religious and cultural traditions of India. It is the explicit hope of the institute that graduates will be placed as executive officiers. Other temples have occasionally sponsored sessions to train lay Hindus to educate the public about the tradition, while a larger number of temples sponsor professional recitals of music, dance, and drama. Pressure from the state government and groups within the tradition have led to revisions or modifications of the ritual pattern, including the increased use of Tamil in worship and of non-brāhmaṇ persons in at least subsidiary roles in the ritual. However, to what extent these modifications are theologically substantive rather than political is still a moot question.

There is an occasional swami committed to social change and religious reform or who has shown unusual insight or oratorical skill in addressing the young. A case in point is the Kun̲r̲akkuṭi Aṭikal, who has helped to found and has been the chairman of an association of Śaiva *maṭams*. Since 1952 the Kun̲r̲akkuṭi Aṭikal has been in the forefront of the movement to increase the use of Tamil in ritual and to train non-brāhmaṇs in the Śivāgamas and ritual traditions preparatory to their serving as priests. He has also sponsored programs in social service, including the establishment of schools, orphanages and a hospital. Influenced by Marxist principles, he is an advocate of a classless society and of a Śaiva religion responsible to the times.

Experiments in the modification of religion are effecting the Murukaṉ cultus, but to what extent will Murukaṉ himself be influenced by a technological and post-traditional imagery? Will the god be ascribed still newer meanings and embody a mythology more fully reflecting the technological age? To answer the questions affirmatively, the cultus will undoubtedly have to engage in the raising of important related questions: What are the religious dimensions of the 'secular' technical age? What are the symbols now beginning to make sense to such an age? What are the aspirations of modern man in South India and what will they be? Are the aspirations and religious intentions of a given tradition still valid? How new is 'modernity'? How can 'modern' man discover himself by rediscovering the religious heritage of his present? Is 'Westernization' an inevitable part of the South Indian scene that must be integrated into traditional religious patterns?

It may be that Murukaṉ will survive the pending cultural upheaval and go on to a new levels of popularity. On the other hand, the history of religions is strewn with the remains of gods and symbols that have become otiose or have had their meanings transferred onto fresher symbols when historical change demanded it. Will Murukaṉ have a similar fate?

If Murukaṉ does not survive, what god or symbol could take his place? This is, of course, difficult to predict. It is quite possible that some overtly religious symbol or god from within the Hindu tradition itself will emerge to a new place of prominence. For example, already rising in popularity in the western portions of Tamil Nadu, especially since the early 1950's, is the god Aiyaṉār or Aiyappaṉ. This deity or combination of deities is associated with a heritage dating back into the medieval period when a cult of Harihara-putra (son of Viṣṇu and Śiva) spread in South India. But since the 1930's the god has become increasingly popular in Kerala, and particularly in the aspect of Śāstā as enshrined in the forested prototypal temple at Sabarimalai. In the early 1950's P. T. Rajan, active in the non-brāhmaṇ movement in Tamil Nadu, had the icon of the deity paraded throughout Tamil country. Since then, Aiyaṉār shrines have sprung up in such places as Coimbatore and Ootacamund and the number of Tamil pilgrims to Sabarimalai has increased manifold. Aiyaṉār *bhaktas* suggest, explicitly or implicitly, that the god's attraction is based on several factors: One is the classlessness of the community of the god's worshippers (though women of childbearing age have heretofore been excluded from Sabarimalai); yet all males are said to be equal in the presence of the god; in pilgrimage, master and servant call each other 'Aiyappa' and share their common humanity in the wilderness surrounding Sabarimalai. Another attractive feature of the deity is that mythically he integrates Śaiva and Vaiṣṇava motifs more fully even than Murukaṉ, though in ritual the cultus is more nearly Vaiṣṇava than Śaiva. Also, there is a sense among the devotees of Aiyappaṉ that his power is real and indeed supercedes that of the 'older' gods. Stories of miracles occurring at Sabarimalai (including preservation from wild beasts) make the rounds of Tamil Nadu and enhance the god's reputation. More esoterically, the popularity of the god and particularly the wilderness character of the cultus at Sabarimalai bespeaks a kind of urban nostalgia. There is the sense of longing to return to the 'open spaces', the natural beginnings, so apparent among city-dwellers in many societies. And not least of all, Aiyappaṉ has a supra-Tamil aura about him. He is not a mere provincial or parochial god, caught up in the political concerns of contemporary Tamil Nadu. Persons weary of or uninterested in such concerns find Aiyappaṉ refreshingly 'universal'.

Together with the possible rise of a 'new' god, there is the possibility that certain 'secular' or crypto-religious phenomena will come to have religious connotations and functions. Two such developments will illustrate this phenomenon. In the earliest years of the *Ṭirāvita Muṉṉeṟṟa Kaḻakam*'s rise to power, that political party served as the vehicle for religious or quasi-religious aspirations in Tamil Nadu. The pictures of political leaders in general, for example, have taken their places on South Indian walls alongside of or in place of those of the gods. The picture of C. N. Annadurai, founder of the DMK, now is sported prominently with those of others. Statues of Annadurai and other early Tamil 'heroes' have sprouted up throughout the state, much like icons of a religious yesteryear. A memorial to Annadurai erected along the Marina in Madras is popularly considered Anna's *samādhi* and is visited by thousands of pilgrims each month. Ramaswamy Naicker, leader of the DMK's parent *Ṭirāviṭa Kaḻakam*, for all his rationalism and indebtedness to Thomas Paine, Robert Ingersoll and others of similar bent, dressed in black robes and was given the respect by his followers that is usually associated with saffron-clad swamis.[43] The DMK, whether consciously or not, adapted symbols that are highly pregnant in the religious heritage of the Tamilian: the rising sun, symbolic of the coming of the new creation and the new mode of being to which religious man aspires; the banner, associated with Tamil kingship and the gods; the colors red and black, colors which in Tamil Nadu symbolized a variety of things, including various aspects of divinity; the procession; and the use of foliation and peacock feathers. In short, the political party has been a vehicle through which a younger generation has at some times hoped to fulfill their aspirations for a new world.

A second 'secular' development with a religious aura is the growing popularity of the theater. The theater has inherited something of the intent of the temple. Once again, the pictures of the movie stars are ubiquitous; the stars have become idols living in that mythical land to which so many Tamilians seem to want to be carried away. The theater constitutes another world, where the viewer can be something he cannot be in his ordinary 'profane' sphere of existence. He is transported to another world where he can, however momentarily, transcend the limitation of his own time and space. Not coincidentally, the cinema has continued the use of sung poetry, so much a part of the Tamil cultural and religious heritage. The film, like the ritual of the temple, creates a new world into which the viewer can be taken. Like ritual at its best, cinema at its best sends the participant out of the arena, a transformed person. Conversely, as with too many rituals, so with too many cinemas: the transformation is only temporary and more apparent than real.

But can these symbols of a secular age be permanent or endlessly satisfying? Many already think not. Indeed, if anything, recent years have witnessed a resurgence of 'faith' as a continuing stream of Tamil peoples visit the temples. Nevertheless, any cultus which seeks to make sense in this emerging era must presumably be aware of at least two complimentary concerns. First of all, the religious community seeking to offer viable religious symbols in the South Indian context has to be aware of the human aspirations and concerns which have not been adequately or explicitly addressed by the traditional religious heritage of South India; the need for community in equality; the hope for full human dignity; the aspiration for the building of a new nation; the longing for social justice, etc. This encompasses the need to build a new world in which there will be a birth of new intentions and hopes. A new world rightly requires the death or otiosity of symbols that have lost their meaning and a sensitivity to the restlessness, doubt, and searching of a people disenchanted with old formulae. Any 'new' god would thus serve as a judgment on old gods; it requires a death or at least a modification and reformulation of old meanings. Such is the history of symbols and gods.

Conversely, any new religious symbolism can not afford the luxury of being deceived into shallowness by apparent 'newness'. For a 'new' religious symbol to make sense in South India requires that the heritage of both the symbol and South India are understood in such a way that the two are brought together in a manner consistent with the history of both as well as with the mood of the moment. The profoundly persistent intentions of religious man in South India, as elsewhere, cannot be ignored, for these intentions have informed the present even in the context of cultural change. A 'new symbolism' may make particular sense in Tamil India insofar as it addresses itself to the persistant religious intentions of man who has found meaning in such motifs as the divine son, the primordial demiurge, the cosmic light, the integration of polarities, 'water' of life, the lord of the city, the lord of hills, the cosmic man, and others. The positing of 'new' symbolisms requires seeing meaning for man in history and re-expressing the meaning of the symbol in terms that make sense to the cultural context of the age in which it is expressed.

Some may argue that such a conscious structuring and interpretation of symbols is inconsistent with the way symbols so often come to reflect only implicitly and unconsiously the meanings of an era. Such persons might remember that almost every age has had its myth-makers who help make explicit the religious intentions of the age. Perhaps the relationship between explicit and implicit understandings of religious meaning are not unlike the relationship between literate and 'popular' religion in the sense that there is an interplay between both poles. One pole informs the other, and each is dependent on the other for its existence and persistence. What I am suggesting is that Tamil Nadu will need a new generation of myth-makers, sensitive to the implicit intentions of religious man in the present and to how these intentions are related to the explicit mythological heritage of the past. Who these myth-makers are may well determine what the religious future of the Tamil people will be.

Notes

Notes to Chapter 1: 'Introduction: Murukaṉ as an expression of Tamil religion'

1. These figures are the result of research done by Mr. Sankaranarayanan, former executive officer of the Śrī Subrahmaṇyan Temple at Tiruchendur and formerly assistant deputy commissioner of Tamil Nadu's office of Hindu Religious and Charitable Endowments. The three largest temples of Murukaṉ are those at Paḻani, Tiruchendur, and Tiruttani.
2. For more extensive presentations of the history of discussions about the development of gods, see for example, Mircea Eliade (1966:108–34); Andrew Lang (1900: Chapter 1); Whilhelm Schmidt (1931: Parts II and III).
3. The hill god embodies *teyvam* in *Kali.* 39:26; the sea god in *Kali.* 7; Tirumāl in *Cila.* 11:160; and Agni in *Cila.* 15:143, 144; 22:1,2,148; and elsewhere (Subrahmaniam, *Pre-Pallavan Tamil Index*, p. 452).
4. *Aka.* 372:1 (hillside): *Narr.* 343:4 (banyan tree); *Narr.* 216:6 (*vēṅkai* tree).
5. Murukaṉ: *Aka.* 152:17; *Kuṟun.* 208, 209; *Cila.* 24:85; 26:64; Śiva: *Aka.* 9; *Kali.* 1; *Pari.* 5:13; *Cila.* 30:2; *Tirumāl*: *Pari.* 3:43; goddess: *Patiṟṟu* 66:15; and elsewhere.
6. It seems likely that, with the increased Sanskritization of the Tamil language the term *tēvaṉ* is used to connote the concrete, masculine form of god and *Teyvam* is used more for the abstract form.

Notes to Chapter 2: 'Murukaṉ in the early South'

1. For dating and much of the description of Paleolithic man in India, I rely largely on H. D. Sankalia (1962:37–123).
2. Sankalia (1962:151) dates the Mesolithic stage at 10,000 to 4000 B.C. Sankalia is less convinced that the microlith-users developed Neolithic skills. But Gordon (1950:73) notes that microliths have been found in the same strata as black, red, and brown pottery sherds and pestles for pounding grain.
3. While Wheeler and Gordon suspected that there was some cultural influence from Northeast India into the South because of an assumed relationship between the stone-axes of the South and those of the Northeast (Gordon 1950:82), H. D. Sankalia thinks the use of

polished stone may have radiated south and west from the Raichur and Bellary areas in Andhra and notes that polished stone is common to the Neolithic cultures of the East Coast (Sankalia 1962:153ff.). In fact, South Indian stone axes are quite different from those of the Northeastern Neolithic complexes. The latter, known as the shouldered axe belong to the wider Southeast Asian family, while the Neolithic axes of South India and the Deccan belong to the West Asian prototypes (K. V. Raman in a conversation February 2, 1972). Further, the South Indian neolithic culture includes the making of pottery, either by hand or turn table, while no pottery has yet been recovered from Northeastern Neolithic sites (Sankalia 1962:153ff.)

4. While the iron culture of the Indus Valley is comprised largely of a racial stock known as Mediterranean – a people slender of build, of short to medium height, long headed and oval faced (Sastri 1966:59), the racial composition of the Neolithic people in the South is not clear. However, there has been observed in the South a proto-Australoid stock with long heads, protruding faces, broad flat noses, and pronounced brow-ridges. This Austric people, who such scholars as S. K. Chatterji believe came into India through the Northeast, also may have influenced Indonesia and Southeast Asia. Piggott notes that three skulls of this type have been found at the Indus Valley site, attesting that this cultural layer helped comprise the peoples of Harappa and Mohenjo-daro (Piggott 1962:148–50). Piggott thinks the Proto–Australoids are the same as the Veddoid or Negrito culture in the South (p. 147). It is also possible that this 'element entered into the composition of the so-called exterior castes and forms the basis of jungle-folk like the Chenchus, Malayans, Kadars, Karumbas, and Yeruvas' in Central and Southern India (Sastri 1966:59). Chatterji believes this Austric people brought a rice culture into India and that they contributed the cultivation of the banana, cocoanut, betel, brinjal, pumpkin, lime, and cotton; the development of the arrow and digging stick; the manufacture of sugar from cane; the use of turmeric and vermillion; the domestication of the horse or pony, the fowl and the peacock; familiarity with the elephant; the weaving of cotton cloth; and certain cosmogonic myths (Chatterji 1954:148ff.). At least one archeologist, Mr. Gururajarao of the Department of Archeology, University of Madras, in a conversation with me on February 4, 1967, termed Chatterji's thesis 'unassailable', but noted it could refer only to developments in the first millenium B.C., and not earlier.
5. Both Zeuner and F. R. Allchin have concluded that ashmounds found in the Southern Deccan were of cattle pens (cf. F. R. Allchin 1953). There is little doubt that a form of sedentary pastoralism had developed at least by this time.
6. This is H. D. Sankalia's estimate (1950:7); F. R. Allchin, dating the cattle pens of Utnur and other Deccan sites by the radiocarbon technique suggests the pastoral skills (and possibly the chalcolithic industry) may have developed as early as 2160 B.C. and lasted until 750 B.C.
7. There are at least two main theories as to how elements of the megalithic culture migrated into South India. The more traditional view, accepted by N. R. Banerjee and most archeologists, is that the culture moved from Iran southward along the Indian coast leaving megalithic remains in the area of B̲aluchistan around 1200–1100 B.C., and, driven South after the coming of the Aryans, arrived in the Deccan about 800 B.C., and at the southern tip of India by 700 B.C. (Banerjee 1965:55ff.). This argument for the Northwest

migration of the megalithic culture and its basic identity with a proto-Dravidian peoples may be enhanced by the recent conclusions of a group of Soviet linguists, headed by Professor Knorozov, who, after comparing the structure of the language found on inscriptions in Indus Valley seals with the structure of several common language families, concluded that the structure of the language of the Indus Valley was most nearly akin to that of the Dravidian and hence may have to be termed 'proto-Dravidian'. This would imply, as far as archeologists are concerned, only that there was some relationship between the language of the megalith-builders and that of the Indus Valley culture, and not that the peoples of the two cultures were the same.

Another theory, posited primarily by Fürer–Haimendorf, suggests that the megalith-builders came from the West by a maritime route and settled mainly in the South. While most archeologists think the one or two megalithic sites found in northwest India are remains of the culture as it moved southward along the coast (Srinivasan and Banerjee, 1953:114, citing the presidential lecture delivered by Fürer–Haimendorf to the Archeological Society of India in 1950), Fürer-Haimendorf considers these northern outposts and Dravidian pockets of Brahui speakers the result of colonization by a maritime people, who were by then firmly settled in the South (Ghosh 1952:3).

8. It is unlikely that urn burials lingered into the medieval period as anything more than a misunderstood memory. Naccinarkiniyar, a commentator of the fourteenth century mistook urn burials for Jain burials, evidencing a lack of familiarity with ancient custom and its significance (K. V. Raman in a conversation citing K. R. Srinvasan's article [1953]).
9. For this discussion of the history of Āryanization in the South, I depend largely on Sastri, 1966, pp. 82ff.
10. Nilakanta Sastri notes that the Sutta Nipata of the Buddhist canon mentions that a teacher named Bavari, who was learned in the Vedas and performed Vedic sacrifices settled in a village along the Godavari river in the Central Deccan (1966:69). The legend of Agastya, formulated and elaborated by the Āryanizers, is an attempt to show that civilization was brought to the South by the migrating 'missionaries'. Sastri thinks there may have been some historical person or basis for the legend that developed. Similarly, attempts to isolate a 'Dravidian script', irrefutably uninfluenced by Sanskrit language have heretofore been unsuccessful; nonetheless, there is evidence enough that there was culture and some degree of civilization in the South prior to the Sanskritic impact.
11. One hypothesis has it that the Pāṇṭiyas were chieftains who settled in the Indo-Ceylon straits by the fourth century, B.C., having descended from noble lineage in Gujerat (Maloney 1970:603ff.). This is still a speculative hypothesis at best; nonetheless, there are occasional literary and inscriptional hints•that some intercourse existed between the Pāṇṭiyan chieftains of South India and Ceylon. An inscription at Tirupparaṅkuṉṟam attributed to the second century B.C., outside of Madurai, for example, refers to a Ceylonese householder (Īla kuṭambikaṉ), who apparently made a grant to a cave-resort at that spot (p. 612).
12. The *Iṟaiyaṉār Kaḷaviyal Uṟai*, an eighth century work mentions most of the anthologies and some others that have since been lost. In the last century V. V. Swaminathar Aiyer collected most of the anthologies, including several which had already been printed and others available only on palmyrah leaf, and published them in the two collections.

13. Pillai tends to date the poetry between 150 A.D. and late in the third century. Kamil Zvelebil tends to place it earlier, perhaps by as much as a century.
14. K. A. Nilakanta Sastri and K. V. Soundarya Rajan incline toward a later period – around the eighth or ninth century; Kamil Zvelebil favors a period prior to the sixth century, but not prior to the fourth century. For reasons that will become apparent, I am inclined to place the major portion of the Tirumurukāṟṟupatai and the Paṟipāṭal somewhere in the late fourth or fifth century, with some portions of the Tirumurukāṟṟupatai possibly being even later.
15. Such commentators on the early *Caṅkam* literature as Kamil Zvelebil, Vaiyapuri Pillai, and J. V. Chelliah note this 'terrestrial' character of the early Tamil spirit.
16. There is a basic reservoir of poetic moods and anecdotes. For example, there are particular times when a girl in love is supposed to speak, when her maid is supposed to speak, etc. These attitudes and moods of clandestine love are described in Tol. Poruḷatikāram, 92–141.
17. This description is taken from M. K. Thangavelu, (1963:70–73), citing Aka. 282:17–18; 353:3–7; Kuṟun. 264:1–6; Naṟṟ. 268:7–10; Aiṅkuru. 245, 248, 249.
18. This account of counting paddy grains is recited by Thangavelu as reconstructed by an unnamed commentator from contemporary village practices.
19. Note that all citations of anthologies in the Pattupāṭṭu are to the translated edition found in J. V. Chelliah (1962).
20. This attitude is explicit in Aiṅkuru. 250, which I have roughly translated to read as follows: 'O dice which never lie, this one who makes her suffer is not he who has masculinity and attains victory (Murukaṉ). It is not he who possesses the forest in which the creepers blossom and where there are beautiful peacocks like blue pearls dancing in the mountains.'
21. This may be a Jain term; probably it represents a later motif, nonetheless.
22. I have found no direct evidence definitely linking the sun and the divine in a pre-Āryan period in the South. Nonetheless, the tenor of the literature suggests that the sun is of the earth, born of the hills and apprehended in the redness of the foliage. At the same time, an impressive number of the 'aboriginal' tribes of North Central and Eastern India, in which hunting was the initial mode of living, had 'supreme deities' with celestial, solar attributes. Tarak Chandra Das (1954:421–32) notes that the following tribes have a deity associated with the sun: Oraons, Mundas, Hos, Asurs, Korwas, Kharias, Birhors, Malors, Malpaharias, Bhuiyas, Inangs, Khonds, Gonds, Santals, and in the South, the Chenchus, Uralis, and Kanikkers. He adds that tribes in Chota Nagpur in the hinterland of Orissa have a particularly well-developed celestial god, who is creator of man, animals, plants, gods, and spirits and is omnipotent and omniscient. W. Koppers (1940–1941:325) notes that worship of the sun in central India has two roots – one Āryan and the other from such primitive Dravidian tribes as the Gonds. Mircea Eliade, from his discussion of sun gods in *Patterns in Comparative Religion*, encourages us to believe that early hunting societies in general believed in the relatedness of heaven and earth and were aware of the sun as hierophanous. Hence, we are inclined to believe there was a veneration of the sun in some form in the early South.
23. Note also that *ceyyavaṉ* means the 'sun' or 'Mars' (*Tamil Lexicon* 1928:1632).
24. Aka. 266:21; Kuṟiñci. 51; Kuṟun. 1:3; 209:19; Puṟa. 125:20; 14:9; Aiṅkuru. 242; cf. Tirumuru. 61, 271; Paṟi. 5:213, 54; 6:69, 21:53.

25. Srinivasan notes that the term *kōyil* (from the root *kō*) is used to denote a temple only once in the Cilappatikāram and on three inscriptions prior to the tenth century. Prior to the tenth century the term usually connoted a palace or chieftain-king's residence.
26. There is no reason to assume that the Tamil *cūr* and the Sanskrit *asura* are etymologically related. The Sanskrit term *asura* appears to come from the root *as* which connotes 'breath', 'life', of a 'spiritual, incorporeal, or divine' nature. While *asura* is used in the Ṛk Veda to mean a 'good' or 'supreme spirit' as with Varuṇa, it can also mean 'chief of the evil spirits' (RV II; 30, 4 and VII:00,5) or an 'evil spirit', 'demon', 'ghost', or 'opponent of the gods' (e.g., RV. VIII:96,9). (Monier-Williams 1951:121). The Tamil term *cūr*, on the other appears to have a fundamentally different root. Its possible meanings are: 'fear'; 'suffering, affliction, sorrow'; 'disease'; 'pungency'; 'deceit, guilt'; 'cruelty'; 'malignant diety', or, in a different context, 'valour, fearlessness' (*Tamil Lexicon* II:1564, 1565).
27. Twice in the Akananuru; once in the Aiṅkurunuru; once in the Kuṟiñcipāṭṭu; twice in the Peṟumpāṉāṟṟupaṭai; once in the Ciṟuppāṉāṟṟupaṭai; and six times in the later Paṟipāṭal. N. Subrahmaniam (197) notes these allusions.
28. N. Subrahmanian (1966:197) notes such allusions twice in the Akananuru; four times in the Pattiṉappalai; and once in the Cilappatikāram.
29. For example, the girl possessed of Murukaṉ is like a creeper swaying in the breeze. It should be noted that there is a difference between the Tamil words, *valli* and *vaḷḷi* with the retroflexibility. The first means primarily 'creeper' but can also mean a young lady; the second is used to refer to Murukaṉ's consort, but can also refer to a creeping plant. It seems likely the two became interchangeable.
30. The term *piṇimukam* is ambiguous in meaning as it can connote either the elephant or the peacock. It refers primarily to Murukaṉ's mount, perhaps first to the elephant mount, then derivatively to the peacock mount.
31. The 'large troops' may be a Northern contribution.
32. Dr. Nagaswami, of the Tamil Nadu Archeology Department, in a lecture delivered at the University of Madurai, February 14, 1972.
33. Harkness, *Aboriginal Race of the Neighboring Hills* (1832), cited without publication data by Thurston (1909:Vol. IV, p. 168).
34. Even the Chenchus, who apparently have some relationships to the Iralus and Yanadis, and who may have migrated into Andhra Pradesh from the Anamalaya forest of North Arcot district and from the Mysore plateau, continue some vestiges of the early culture and religion we have been discussing. To a tribal god, Chenchu Devata, honey and fruit are offered and a semi-demonic being known as Narasimha, is said to have carried off beautiful Chenchu damsels. Their diet is that of the forest: fruits, peacocks, crows, lizards, black monkeys, tamarinds and bears, together with cereals and yams. Like the Kadars who espouse the bill hook, the Chenchus use a weaponry of the forest (Thurston 1909:27–42).
35. For this description I rely on H. Parker (1909) and on C. G. and Brenda Z. Seligmann (1911). The Seligmanns observe there are three types of Veddas: the 'wild' Veddas of the inner forests; the village Veddas who have undergone Sinhalization, and the coastal Veddas who have experienced to a greater degree the influences of Tamil culture (1911: 29ff.).
36. Parker notes that the Pali literature of Ceylon refers to the Veddas as 'Yakkhas', a term

which appears to connote, citing H. Nevell, 'users of the arrow' and unfriendly hunters, who settled Ceylon before the Buddhist civilization was established. The Seligmanns concur that the Veddas are historically associated with the aborigines of the island, that is the Yakkhas, and that they were on the island prior to the sixth century B.C. when a prince Vijaya was said to have married a Yakkini princess (Seligmanns 1911:4).

37. Might this imply that the peafowl is eaten by the hunters regularly? Parker also notes that the peafowl's feathers are used for feathering the arrows of the hunters.

38. Parker notes that priests (*pucāris*) in South India must refrain from eating fowls, pigs, peafowl and turtle (Parker 1909:192).

39 Aiyanar is thought to have emerged from the right hand of Śiva after Śiva is mated with Mohinī, a feminine incarnation of Viṣṇu (Parker 1909:147). There are a variety of myths about the birth of Aiyanar, all of them reflecting Sanskritic influences. The one alluded to here in which the god emerges from Śiva's right hand depicts him as dark blue or black and riding the elephant or horse. He is also known as Nayanar or Hari-Hara-Putra (son of Śiva and Viṣṇu) (Parker 1909:147). Another myth, undoubtedly much later, shows how both Skanda and Ganeṣa are brothers and is adapted from Purāṇic myths: Mohinī (the incarnation of Viṣṇu) was bathing in a river while her husband Iśvara was away. She created from reeds a prince to stand watch. Iśvara was told that the wicked demon Shasmasura was peeking at his wife. Iśvara came and decapitated the prince believing him to be the demon only to have Mohinī scold him. Iśvara brought the prince back to life by putting on the head of his own elephant and called him Gaṇa Deviya. Meanwhile, Mohinī created seven other princes from elements nearby: a plant, grass, cloth, leaves, sand, creepers, and fruit. Iśvara embraced the princes as his own – one escaped, but the other six were squeezed together and became the god Kanda–Swami with six faces and twelve hands, who rides on a peacock (pp. 156–57). Parker believes Aiyanar of the earlier myth to be Ganeṣa, but at that stage it could represent either Skanda or Ganeṣa, as both are sons of Śiva and share a similar prehistory.

40. Gordon Childe, D. H. Gordon, and Fürer–Haimendorf from the standpoint of archeology, and N. Subrahmaniam as a historian of language, are inclined to see Middle Eastern roots in the Megalithic peoples. Those who believe the Megalithic culture came overland from the Iranian-Anatolian plateau also concede the possibility of some Middle Eastern influences, either after the people arrived in India (as Kamil Zvelebil does) or before they migrated. Interestingly, quite independently, W. K. C. Guthrie (1950:157), notes that Anatolia is a region where the cult of ecstasy is particularly deep-rooted and may have been the home of the Dionysiac spirit which spread from Thrace and Phrygia into Greece. We cannot be sure, however, that this 'cult' was present in Anatolia in 1500 B.C. when the Megalithic culture was believed to have been there.

41. References to merchants and traders from the West are abundant in the early *Caṅkam* literature. L. D. Barnett posits the earlier date for this trade catching up the opinions of several Tamil scholars who feel certain Greek words stem directly from items brought by merchants from South India. In this category are pepper (Greek: *peperi*; Tamil: *pippali*); rice (Greek: *orutsa*; Tamil: *arici*); ginger (Greek: *tsiggiberis*; Tamil: *inciver*) and cinnamon (Greek: *karpion*; Tamil: *karappu*). It is also suggested that such goods as pearls, muslin, silk and tortoise-shells came from South India (Barnett 1922:593ff.; cf. T.

Balakrishnan Nayar 1963:121–34). However, K. V. Raman noted in a conversation, that this trade with the Mediterranean world must have post-dated the discovery of the Hippalus winds, and that therefore contacts between Greece and South India were 'extremely unlikely'. He concedes that contacts with Rome were numerous, but that these contacts were almost exclusively of traders coming to South India for such goods as spices and cotton.

42. K. V. Raman expressed the certainty of this relationship with the Mediterranean world in a conversation with me, but did add that there is a time lag between the finds of the Mediterranean world and those of South India. For example, many of the artifacts of South India thought to be similar to Mediterranean ones are found in the megalithic context, whereas their Northwest Asian counterparts are found in a Neolithic or pre-Iron context.

43. Guthrie makes a clear distinction between the vibrant agricultural Dionysos of Thrace and the more restrained Greek Dionysos. The former is responsible for hunt, vegetation and herd; the hills associated with him, Guthrie insists (1950:211) are clearly terrestrial and fertile, quite different from Mt. Olympus which pierces the heavens and where Dionysos is later believed to have found a home. Guthrie attributes this later development to a fusion of pastoral Āryan motifs with agricultural Mediterranean ones, a process, which, as we shall see, occurs in the Murukaṉ tradition in South India. For other descriptions of the agricultural deities of the Mediterranean, see W. F. Otto (1965) and Ronald Frederick Willets (1962).

44. I consider the dance of the damsels to be an agricultural motif not only because it is so in the Middle East and because agricultural societies are often matriarchal, but primarily because the earlier forms of this dance, both in the early *Caṅkam* poetry and in the primitive Vedda tradition, was by priest (or by a person seeking to be relieved of suffering), and apparently not by a company of women. I would guess this dance of women was grafted on to the earlier dance of the *vēlaṉ*.

45. K. A. Nilakanta Sastri in an unpublished paper entitled 'Murugan' delivered to the Archeological Society of South India at Madras on September 22, 1964, suggested that the term may be rooted in the Persian *murugh* which originally meant 'bird' and derivatively means 'cock' or 'sun' and which in Zend develops to *muruk*. While this is consistent with Sastri's thesis that the megalithic people came from Iran (and, hence, could have some plausibility), Sastri, surprisingly and undocumentably, tends to believe the term came into India through the Indo-Āryan, Sanskrit stream. It is true that archeological finds at Adichanallur, a megalithic site in Tinnevelly District, includes a 6 inch bronze cock, which Sastri assumes is associated with the Murukaṉ cult. However, we have no evidence that the Adichanallur cock was, in fact, associated with Murukaṉ. (It may only mean that the cock was domesticated around that time – that is probably no earlier than 700 B.C.) Nor is the Tamil word *muruka* ever associated with the meaning 'cock' – even though in the development of the Murukaṉ tradition, the god is associated with the cock in several respects.

N. Gopala Pillai (1937:980ff.) suggests the term has affinity to a Babylonian and Cushite god of hunting and of war named Murik, Mirukh or Mirihk and from which term he believed the name *Mars* to have derived. Again, however, the Tamil term *muruku* never means 'warrior' or 'hunter'.

46. One is also reminded of the flower stalk (*mugura*) used in the Vedda priest's dance.

Notes to Chapter 3: 'The early Sanskritic tradition and the Southern sequel'

1. Even to summarize the variety of positions taken on this question would require a book. Generally, the positions range from that of Heinrich Zimmer and Joseph Campbell (cf. Zimmer 1951, and Campbell 1962) who tend to think most of the later development of Hinduism was 'Pre-Āryan' to that of J. A. B. van Buitenen who concedes only that some non-Āryan influences may have been adapted into the tradition, but whether and what they were are difficult, if not impossible, to document, because of the lack of literary evidence. Somewhere between these two positions are those of such scholars as Jan Gonda (e.g., 1954) who cautions against the careless use of such terms as 'pre-Āryan,' but concedes some non-Āryan influence in the orthodox development; Charles Eliott (1921:I, 15) thought that though no significant literary documents are yet at our disposal, much of Indian religion is essentially different from the purely Āryan motifs found in its early stages. To native India he attributes such deities as Śiva, Kṛṣṇa, Rāma, Durgā, and such ideas as metampsychosis and divine incarnations; he terms these the contributions of 'Dravidian religion', a misleading term, in my judgment, based on the assumption of the pan-Indian character of the Dravidian culture. Mircea Eliade (cf. 1964) sees Indian religion as a fusion of pastoral, Āryan motifs and native agricultural motifs. In general, my own position assumes that the 'Northern' tradition is an amalgamation of both Āryan and non-Āryan, pastoral and agricultural roots with emphases and characteristics that change as cultural settings change.
2. Jan Gonda notes that in Semitic phrases the term 'son' and the genitive of a word can connote, in a similar way, a person characterized by a quality. For example, Prov. 31:15 speaks of a 'son of misery'; I Sam. 20:31 a 'son of death'. Sonship can similarly connote a generic category of belonging, for example, in Arabic, a traveler is a 'son of the way'. A weaver can be a 'son of a weaver', an inhabitant the 'son of a town'. Gonda writes: 'An individual representing an idea – whether it be the idea of a nationality, a family, a trade, technical skill, or religious conviction – can be indicated as its manifestation in flesh and blood, and conceived as having sprung from it' (pp. 104–5).
3. For example, both Rudra and Agni are demiurges; both are warriors; both are associated with the sun; cf. RV. II:1; Śatapatha Brāhmaṇa VI:1:3, 18; AV. VIII:8:17, 18; Mbh. II:31:44 and Mbh. III:225:26.
4. Aiyangar notes that in Śvetasvara Upaniṣad IV:12 Rudra is Hiraṇyagarbha, whereas in the Śvetesvara Upaniṣad III:4 and in the Mahānarāyana-Upaniṣad X:3 Rudra begets Hiraṇyagarbha.
5. To attempt an historical reconstruction of the factors behind the development of these early motifs would be hazardous and purely speculative. Father H. Heras, for example, has suggested that the notion of personalized sonship, appearing late in the Ṛk Veda is rooted in the Indus Valley religion, wherein he finds a clearly developed notion of a god with a son complete with names! He thinks he can find in the Indus Valley inscriptions the names Murukaṉ, Vēlan, and Anil (son of An) all used to refer to the son of the high god, An. I find the suggestion close to preposterous, and at best, undocumentable. My own feeling is that the development of the notion of sonship in Vedic and post-Vedic

speculation and mythology is rooted in two concerns: (1) cosmogonic speculation, for in virtually every cosmogony, a demiurge must be posited to assume the role of creator for that primordial entity which is either otiose or inactive. (2) Cultural change, which brought about the emerging popularity of a different deity over a period of generations, who, nonetheless, had to be understood as following in the tradition and receiving the power and benediction of a 'father' accepted in the orthodox tradition.

6. These references are noted by K. A. Nilakanta Sastri (1964:7–8). Sastri doesn't specify the precise location of the reference in the Baudhāyana Dharmasūtra. He is inclined to date these references in a pre-Buddhist era, but concedes the Dharmasūtra passage at least may be somewhat later. I am inclined to believe that neither Ṣaṇmukha nor Gaṇapati can be dated as early as a pre-Buddhist period, at least in any official ritually orthodox level, for reasons that should become apparent.
7. 'Dhūrta' is a term apparently derived from the verb *dhurv* (to give trouble, injure, kill). In this ritual, Skanda is thought to be a 'rogue', for reasons that become clearer in one of the Mahābhārata myths. Here it is enough to note that it is not surprising that Skanda is ascribed certain malevolent attributes, for Rudra, his father, also had a terrible nature at a certain point in his development.
8. The text appears to be corrupt and should read *suta* (son) rather than *subha*, according to V. Raghavan who translated this passage orally to me on January 25, 1967.
9 The use of flowers, fruit and food stuffs in worship by this time is striking. This is not, as far as I am aware, a phenomenon reflected in Vedic worship, though not enough research has been done yet on the problem.
10. This text was translated orally to me by V. Raghavan on January 25, 1967, and by Charles J. Goodwin (1893:v–xiii). While the translators decline to date this text, I am not convinced that the passage reflects any substantive factors which would demand it be dated prior to the Epic period. In fact, I am inclined to assume the passage is roughly contemporaneous with (or possibly even later than) the myth of Kumāra's birth to Agni recorded in the third book of the Mahābhārata. The two texts reflect many similar motifs.
11. K. A. Nilakanta Sastri (1964:12, 20) suggests that the movement of son and moon together is significant. It constitutes a kind of 'mating' of Soma and Agni, for the sun (Sūrya) can also be Agni; and Soma can also mean the sacrificial drink sometimes equated with *amṛta* which is poured into the fire (Agni). From such a ritual act is Skanda born. Soma is also equated with the Garuḍa bird in the Suparṇa myth; therefore, Sastri thinks it all the more significant that Agni's wife, Svāhā, became a garuḍa bird to escape from Agni's presence. The suggestion is that this coming of the sun and moon together represents the birth of Skanda from Soma and is the early basis for Skanda's eventual name, Somā-skanda.
12 The relation of Skanda's birth to the wives of *ṛṣis* or austere brāhmaṇs may link the notion of 'wisdom' discussed earlier with the Skanda tradition, and serve as part of the basis for the emergence of Skanda's name Subrahmaṇya (having the quality of Brāhman). Vāc (and Sanatkumāra) was similarly thought to be the son of Brāhmaṇ (Kaṭha Upaniṣad IV:6). Narayaṇa Aiyangar (1901:40ff.) makes a similar assumption, but with mental leger-demain more speculative than sound.
13. The golden receptable (or pond) and the *śara* reeds serve to link Skanda further with Agni and the sacrifice. Dr. V. Raghavan, in a conversation on January 11, 1967, noted

that *śara* refers to kindling wood which serves as the basis for fire. N. Venkataramanayya (1930:74) sees a relationship between Skanda's birthplace and the pond of reeds where Agni is said to have hidden from the gods. (Taittirīya Saṃhitā II:6:6; RV. X:52; Śatapatha Brāhmaṇa VI:3:1 and VI:31–32).

14. Narayana Aiyangar (1901:48ff.) thinks the springing out of Viśākha and the Kumārikas and Kumāris (boys and girls) from Skanda's side is intended to signify the creation of the moon and the stars from the sun. These offspring (Skanda graha) Nilakanta Sastri points out ('Murugan̲', p. 21) are malevolent spirits which possess and vex juveniles under sixteen years of age. Worshipping Skanda thus is supposed to cure children of ailments. Sastri thinks this links up with the Vēlan̲'s diagnosis in early Tamil literature of Murukan̲'s causing ailments in young girls. It should be noted that Kumāra (and earlier Rudra) was linked to illness in children. The Skanda–Yāga ceremony is an example; also, in connection with the Medhājana and Āyusya ceremonies, it is said that 'Kumāra attacks the boy newly born' (Pārāsargṛhya–Sūtra I:16:24). Elsewhere, Skanda (alias Mahāsena) is one of those who can remove evil spirits (Mānavgṛhya Sūtra I:14). Earlier, Rudra was believed to have been the cause of diseases: he is invoked to keep all free from disease (ṚV. I:114,31) and he is beseeched not to affect children with diseases (ṚV. VIII:462). For these references and the translation I am indebted to Manmatha Mukhodhyay ('Some Notes on Skanda–Kārttikeya' p. 313).

15. These goddesses are similar to the seven malevolent goddesses found amongst primitive peoples in India and who exist even today in popular Tamil imagination. The Sanskrit names of these goddesses are Kaki, Hāhīna, Malinī, Brmhila, Aryā, Pālita, and Vaṭimitra. The apparent repetition of malevolent 'goddesses' becoming Skanda's mothers within this myth is striking. One of these terrifying goddesses who is both daughter and mother of Skanda is identified in this section as Krūra, 'daughter of a sea of blood' (Aiyangar 1901:54). This same episode names her as one of the 'original' mothers, indeed the one who served as Skanda's wet nurse. Interestingly, Krūra's seat is said to be the Kadamba tree. This aspect of the myth seems to stress again the terrible and destructive character of Skanda. One is also tempted to see it as one of the ways in which the Mahābhārata, in particular, and the Sanskritic tradition in general, picks up material and motifs from 'non-Āryan' sources.

16. The significance of the goat head is obscure. Clearly both Agni and Skanda have goats' heads; according to Aiyangar (*ibid.*) it was from the goat's head that Viśākha made the śakti – the energy and weapon with which Skanda does battle. It might, therefore, represent fecundity and power (the horned goat is virile and powerful). Manmatha Mukhodhyay 1931:313) mentions a seal, dated in the Śaka-Kuṣāṇa period (around the start of the Christian era) on which is inscribed a goat-headed deity, with three female attendants and a male child standing to the right. The deity appears to be Agni, known as Harinegameśī in the Nemināthacarita and Negameśa in Brāhmanical Sūtra literature. Harinegameśī is known both as the divine general and the transferer of the divine fetus in a Kalpasūtra story. Skanda is known as Naigameya (son of Negamesa). Mukhodhyay mentions these references but fails to give the specific passages. He also cites Bühler, Epigraphical Indica, II:314, and Smith, *Antiquities of Mathura*, Plate XVIII, p. 25.

17. The name 'devasenā' means 'army of the gods'; hence, Skanda is known as Devasenāpati,

lord of Devasenā and of the divine army. Earlier (Aitreya Brāhmaṇa III:22:7) Senā (army) is the wife of Indra. Indra's giving Devasenā appears to be another way of saying Skanda replaces Indra as general of the gods' army (Mukhodhyay 1931:316). Mukhodhyay thinks the Kṣatriyas in the Epic period were appointing generals for their armies and that this mythological occurrence reflects what was actually happening historically. A general assumes the warrior role of the king, while the king is left for more passive roles. It is suggestive that Indra becomes known as Devarāja (king of the gods) and is virtually impotent and otiose in these Epic myths.

18. This is an apparent allusion to the account of Skanda's birth to be found in the Rāmāyaṇa.
19. This account is condensed and reconstructed from Pratap Chandra Roy's translation (1966); from paraphrases and accounts given by Aiyangar (1901:37–69); Sastri (1964:9–19); Sörenson (1904:640–42); and from oral translation given me by V. Raghavan on January 25 1967.
20. This six-day 'career' of Skanda is summarized by V. Raghavan in an unpublished, untitled English translation of an article first published in Tamil, p. 2 and also by Sastri 1964, p. 12.
21. It should be noted that in the Taittirīya Brāhmaṇa I:5, 5 and 25 Agni is said to be the presiding deity of the Kṛttikas. The repetition of the motherhood of six (or seven) mothers is striking. In these is linked the malevolent goddesses, the constellation Kṛttikas (Pleides) and the ṛṣis' wives. The Kumāra Tantra later prescribes that in *svayampradhāna* (self-existent) temples of Subrahmaṇya, icons to the seven mothers are to be set up (Mukhodhyay 1931:316, citing Gopinath Rao 1916:II, 423).
22. One is reminded of the image of Skanda surrounded by females, animals, and followers of various kinds which is depicted in the Skanda-Yāga.
23 The gifts of the gods convey significant symbolic connotations. The gifts of Indra and Śiva connote their entrusting to Skanda the role of general and warrior once theirs. The peacock is here linked to the Garuda and has solar, celestial attributes. The snake, linked to the deep, Varuna's domain, has connotations of primordiality and fertility in the Skanda mythology. The waterpot and receptacle are linked as the container of immortality, by virtue of its being given by the life-giving river and as it holds the sacrificial *soma* (cf. *supra*, p. 82, n.1). The deer skin, the garb of all ascetics, is Skanda's dress in his capacity of *brāhmacarya*, and is appropriately given by Brahmā, the personification of primordial wisdom. The cock is here associated with the sun and the dawn, for Aruṇa is the charioteer and forerunner of Sūrya, the sun.
24 Summarized from P. C. Roy, (1966); from Sorenson, (1904:640–62), and from an oral translation afforded by V. Raghavan on January 25, 1967.
25 Here the goat is related to the moon, tending to confirm Aiyangar's suggestion that Viśākha symbolizes the moon, for in an earlier myth Viśākha and the goat-headed child are related.
26. This summary is based on P. C. Roy, (1966) and on an oral translation provided by V. Raghavan on January 25, 1967. Note that gold and Skanda (both Gaṅgeya) are equated. This implies the sacral character of gold and the sacred role of the alchemist.
27 Some scholars think the poem is based on the account of the myth as found in the Śiva Purāṇa, while that found in the Skanda Purāṇa, though elaborating on it, is nonetheless, generally consistent with it.

28 There is still no certainty as to the precise date of Kālidāsa's life. He is mentioned by name in the Aihoḷe inscription dated 634 A.D. That he lived before Vatsabhūta, author of the Mandasa inscription dated around 472 A.D. seems likely as the inscription apparently copied ideas from Kālidāsa. Some scholars, including M. R. Kale and V. Raghavan, date Kālidāsa earlier than Asvaghoṣa of 78 A.D., largely on the grounds that some of Asvaghosa's ideas similar to those of Kālidāsa may be copied from the latter. But most Western Scholars tend to place Kālidāsa somewhere during the reign of the first three Gupta kings: Chandragupta (c. 357–413 A.D.); Kumāragupta (413–455); and Skandagupta 455–480). As for the last eight cantos, V. Raghavan in a conversation with me on January 11, 1967, said he thought they could not have been written prior to the sixth century (Kale 1913:x-xiv).

29. In the Skanda Purāṇa, Tāraka, because of great austerities is granted the boon of immortality by Śiva himself. Also, Tāraka by now has replaced Mahiṣa as the chief opponent. Further, the *asuras* were really 'good guys' gone bad. In later mythology, Tāraka or Sūrapadma, as he is known in the South, is not destroyed because he is immortal; rather he is changed into a tree, then a cock and peacock which Skanda proceeds to use as his own assistants. Prithri Kumar Agrawala (1966:137), suggests that Tāraka replaces Mahiṣa in the Gupta period, for no reference to Tāraka seems datable prior to that time. Agrawala thinks Mahiṣa was known as the enemy of Siva and the goddess, and Tāraka's replacing Mahiṣa represents the positing of a 'new' enemy for the new god.

30. In the Skanda Purāṇa, it is not Śiva's semen but sparks from his forehead which give birth to Kumāra – a significant symbolic difference. In the first Mahābhārata account it is Agni's *retas* from which Kumāra is born; *retas* definitely means 'semen'. In the Rāmāyaṇa account and in the Kumārasambhava the term used is *tejas* which can mean 'semen', but more commonly means 'splendor', 'energy', 'majesty' or even 'fire' (McDonnell 1969:112). (These definitions were confirmed by V. Raghavan in a conversation held on January 11, 1967.) Also worth noting is the fact that throughout the Skanda mythology, Skanda has a mother or mothers only by adoption.

31. Condensed and reconstructed from a summary by Aiyangar (1901:76–77), and from a translation of the first eight cantos of the Kumārasambhava by Kale.

32. This comment is also noted by Nilakanta Sastri (1964:21) and by Raghavan (1961:2). It should be added that Patañjali also mentions images to Śiva in the same context.

33 Raghavan does not cite specific references.

34. Raghavan suggests that this progression toward identification started with six separate deities, became four deities, then two – the dual deity Skanda–Viśākha and, finally, all were merged in the six-headed Skanda. D. R. Bhandarkar (1921:22–23) similarly thinks Skanda was originally four distinct deities. He bases his argument on three points: (1) Patañjali's reference; (2) four names – Kumāra, Skanda, Viśākha, and Mahāsena – are listed on Huviṣka coins together with four figures; (3) Amarakosa (fourth century A.D.) mentions only one of these names in each of the four lines of his two verses concerning Kārttikeya. On the other hand, Mukhodhyay (1931:313) noting Plate XVIII in Gardner's *Catalogue of Coins in the British Museum*, pp. 149–151, argues convincingly that only Skanda and Viśākha were distinct at one time. The other names, he says, are merely names of Skanda. He points out that of the Huviṣka coins in question, one of them has

two figures and three names, another has three figures and four names, and in each case only one figure appears to have a halo, while the other figures could well be attendants. He further cites passages in which Mahāsena (Mānavgrhya Sūtra II:14) and Kumāra (Suśruts Uttara Tantra XXXVII:1) are identified with Skanda.

35. This is a difficult problem. Nilakanta Sastri (1964:8), N. Mukhodhyay (1931:316) and Adolf Friedrich Stenzler (1894) think the Mahābhārata III account precedes the Rāmāyaṇa account. But Narayana Aiyangar (1901:561) and V. Raghavan (1964:1) tend to believe the Rāmāyaṇa account precedes that of the Mahābhārata, assuming the writer of the latter was familiar with the former. However, it should also be remembered that the Mahābhārata is hardly a monolithic book, written by a single author, but a compendium of varied stories, many of them preserved by different families and onto which later generations added (J. A. B. van Buitenen in a lecture delivered in Foster Hall, University of Chicago, February 21, 1966). This suggests the possibility that the variations in the Agni and Rudra myths may reflect not merely the progression of time, but the fact that each myth was preserved by different communities and reconciled only at a later time when both traditions became known.
36. Similarly, in Basarh, Spooner discovered an oblong seal bearing a fan-tail peacock said to date from the reign of Kumāragupta I. In Rajghat, another seal was found on which is inscribed a fan-tail peacock with the legend 'suragupta' in Gupta script. The assumption is that the peacock emblem is an image of Kumāra's vehicle. (Banerjea 1956:199–200).
37. Elsewhere, in Bhita, on a seal dating from the third or fourth century reads the inscription: 'Of the illustrious Maharājah Gautamīputra Ursadhaja, the penetrator of the Vindhyas, who had made over his kingdom to the great lord Kārttikeya' (Banerjea 1956:143).
38. Sastri suggests, citing Soundarya Rajan, that the Kārttikeya figures of the Nagurjunakonda shrines are similar to some attributed to the Kṣatrapas, to whom the Ikṣvākus were related by marriage, and that the Ikṣvākus may indeed have borrowed these forms from the latter (Sastri 1964:22–24, citing K. V. Soundarya Rajan 1961:21–25; cf. Sastri 1966:100).
39. Mortimer Wheeler in 1948 (*Ancient India*, No. 5:10ff.) urged that archeology explore the Gaṅges Valley for further insights into the development of Indian religion. He suggested that even as the Indus gave India its name, the Gaṅges gave it its religion. Unfortunately, archeology has not yet been able to clarify the role of the Gaṅges Valley in the development of the Epic tradition other than to note that at such sites as Hastinapurna, Tiplat, and Ahichchhatra, traditionally associated with the Mahābhārata, there was a rather well developed Neolithic culture during the first half of the first millenium B.C., in which sophisticated painted grey pottery was made; iron, copper, and the horse were used; and rice, beef, pork, and venison were eaten and that this culture was followed, approximately 600–200 B.C. by a more advanced culture (Banerjee 1965:13–14; Sankalia 1962:183–85). S. K. Chatterji's linguistic argument for the contribution of 'proto-Australoid' Neolithic people to the culture and religion of northeast India during the first millenium B.C., may be recalled in this context, though it is not certain archeologically, what influence, if any, these people had in the Gaṅges Valley.
40. N. Gopala Pillai (1937:980ff.) argued that the Skanda cult was borrowed from Greek influences, but his argument is based less on demonstrable historical evidence, as on structural similarities.

41. Mukhodhyay (1931:310) notes that there are several references in Sanskritic literature written during or immediately preceding the Epic period in which *kṣatriyas* are depicted as teaching brāhmaṇs. In the Bṛhadāraṇyaka Upaniṣad, Jaṅaka–Vardhama, a *kṣatriya*, teaches Aśvartaśvi Baida and Ajātasatru destroys the pride of Bālākim. In the Chāndogya Upaniṣad a king, Pravāhana Jaivali, is depicted as teaching some brāhmaṇs the doctrine of transmigration and rebirth. In the same Upaniṣad Aśvapati Kaikeya teaches the doctrine of the universal soul to five brāhmaṇs. In the Kauṣītaki, Citra teaches the brāhmaṇ Śvetaketu, the son of Guatama. The account of Sanaṭkumāra's teaching Nārada the essence of Ātman in the seventh chapter of the Chāndogya Upaniṣad may reflect a similar motif. These stories seem to denote either that the brāhmaṇs sought to flatter and religiously legitimize the *kṣatriyas*, presumably in order to gain their patronage and influence, or that the *kṣatriyas* did indeed influence the development of philosophical mythical thought. This latter possibility seems likely enough in a post-Buddhist period.
42. Helpful in this discussion is a paper first read at the fifteenth session of the All-India Oriental Conference and later published independently by P. S. Subramania Sastri (n.d.)
43. The term *pārppān* literally means 'seer' or learned man (from the root, *pār* – to see). Hence the word may be used to connote persons who are wise in knowing the meaning of life. They are part of the structure of early Tamil society even in the time of Tolkāppiyar (Tol. Puṟattiṇai 20) and could presumably refer to seers apart from the brāhmaṇic community. Nonetheless, the term is usually understood to refer to brāhmaṇs (*A Dictionary Tamil and English* 1933:688; cf. Subrahmaniam (1966:555). Incidentally, the four strata of early Tamil society, according to Tolkāppiyar are similar and easily adapted to the caste system: the *arivar* (those who know), *aracar* (kings or chieftains), *vaṇikar* (merchants), and *vēḷāḷar* (farmers).
44. This apparently combines the routing of the southern *cūr* with the Northern *asura*.
45. This word can be translated in a number of ways: the most likely in this context include a shield or coat of armor; an elephant; or a cock.
46. By the time of the *Skanda Purāṇa*, Murukaṉ is also thought to be the son-in-law of Viṣṇu, for his two wives are understood to be sisters and the daughters of Viṣṇu in a previous birth.
47. The author of the Tirumurukāṟṟupaṭai is said to be Nakkirar. The poem is included in the Eleventh Book of Śaivism, constituted preponderately of pre-*Tevāram* poems and possibly collected under the patronage of the Cōḻas. The basic tenor and style of the book seems quite consistent with the Tamil period around the fourth or fifth century; however, I believe it is possible that at least portions of it, particularly the description of the six-headed, twelve-armed Skanda may have been inserted later, possibly at the time of collection, for it was during the Cōḻa era that the iconography of Ṣaṇmukha blossomed in the South. The poem is one of the sacred hymns of the Muruka tradition. Its title can be translated 'A Guide to Murukaṉ' and refers to a kind of poetry used earlier to direct fellow-bards to patrons who were known for their generosity. This is apparently the first Tamil poem devoted entirely to a deity and qualifies the poet to be termed, as he is by T. P. Meenakshisundarum, the 'earliest of Tamil mystics', though he doesn't yet fit into the bhakti tradition (T. P. Meenakshisundaram 1957:309–19).
48. Line references are to the English translation found in J. V. Chelliah (1962).

49. This appears to be one of the earliest references in Indian literature to the myth of Murukan̠'s slaying the *asura* in the form of a mango tree in the ocean, though the Cilappatikāram (canto 6) alludes to it, and Aka. 59 and Perumpān. 11. 457–9 refer to the god's battle with the *asura*. The basis of this tradition of the *asura's* assuming the form of a mango tree and hiding in the ocean is not clear. It may have been an oral tradition; or it may have been adapted from the myth of Tirumāl's destroying the *kaṭampu* tree in the ocean. We are also reminded that, in the Tamil tradition, tutelary trees of chieftains were often destroyed by enemies in battle (Subrahmaniam 1966:377). The myth is greatly elaborated and described later – for example, in the Kallāṭam 1–65 (eleventh or twelfth century).
50. In earlier Tamil poetry, the malevolent goddesses are often associated with the desolate wilderness (*pālai*) tracts of land which, in time, come to be associated with the battlefields strewn with the dead after kings triumph over their foes in battle. Later philosophizing over these dancing demonesses make them representative of the victory of the deity over the soul's foes.
51. This entire description suggests the possibility of a later date for this passage. Iconographically, Murukan̠ does not seem to be depicted as having six heads and twelve arms and astride a peacock until about the tenth century. Nor have I found any earlier evidence in literature that each arm or each face is given a specific function. This too seems more appropriate to a later period when philosophizing about symbols blossoms.
52. Each of Murukan̠'s six traditional shrines are mentioned in this poem. Once again, the mythology surrounding these traditional places of worship is elaborated by the time of the Skanda Purāṇa. Inasmuch as there were no permanent stone temples in the South prior to the Pallava period, in the late sixth century (cf. Srinivasan 1960:136), these shrines must have either been built of temporary materials – or the references in the poem must be later interpolations, or the entire poem must be later.
53. This is an allusion to the myth of Murukan̠'s imprisoning Brahmā in childish sport for Brahmā's ignorance of the meaning of the sacred syllable and for his 'arrogant' declaration that Murukan̠'s power was vested to Murukan̠ by Brahmā. The myth is elaborated in the Skanda Purāṇa, but, to my knowledge, does not appear in the Epic accounts, nor in earlier Tamil literature.
54. One of the sacrifices performed is the *vēḷvi* which can be translated simply as 'sacrifice' or 'worship'. *Vēḷvi* was associated with Murukan̠ worship even in the early poetry (e.g., Aka. 13:11; 220:6). In fact, in at least one passage (Maturaik. 1:38), Murukan̠ is *vēḷvi*. The implication is that by performing the sacrifice (and eventually, yoga) Kumāra is brought into being. This makes possible the observation made by Alain Danielou (1964: 298–99) based on what happened later in the Skanda tradition, that the yogin who controls his passionate desires gives birth to Kumāra. Similarly, as the human body replaced the fire as a microcosm of the universe, the six Kṛttikas are thought to be divinities of the fire and then the six subtle centers of the yogin.
55. Kor̠r̠avai was the Tamil goddess of war often associated with the desolate area (*pālai*) and the battlefield. Murukan̠'s sonship of her is apparently mentioned here for the first time in Tamil literature. Presumably, the association suggests Murukan̠ has 'inherited' her fiercesomeness and destructive capacities in battle. It may also serve to link the varied traditions which depict the god as having malevolent mothers.

56. The references in this benediction to Muruka's wisdom are significant. The Tamil term is *solmalai* (literally, 'mountain of words'), which links Murukaṉ to earlier Sanskritic motifs of wisdom and source of truth. It is also related to the developing Tamil tradition that Murukaṉ is the source of the Tamil language and literature. He becomes known as the giver of words and inspiration to the Tamil poets.
57. While virtually all of the motifs reflected in this benediction could have been known to the poet by late in the fourth century, it would not be surprising, because the tenor of this poem is somewhat different from that of the rest of the poem and some of the motifs seem more consistent with a later period, if this benediction was inserted at the time the poem was edited.
58. This famous Tamil epic is said (principally by Kamil Zvelebil in a lecture delivered at the University of Chicago, May 2, 1966) to have been written, at least in part by a *Cōḻan* prince, Ilanko Akikal, at some point in the fifth century. The references to Murukaṉ in the epic are certainly no more 'advanced' than those of the Paripāṭal or the Tirumuru-kāṟṟupaṭai; in fact, if the date of the epic were determined from such references alone, the epic could have preceded these other works. The epic portrays a number of Jain influences, however, and other characteristics which lead some scholars to date it during the fifth century.
59. The words are from Alain Danielou's translation (1964:7).
60. There is striking resemblance between the dance of the cowherd girls with Kṛṣna, recorded centuries later in the Bhāgavata Purāna, and that of the damsels 'with' Murukaṉ. In fact, T. P. Meenakshisundaram (1957:316) thinks the god is believed to be dancing between every pair of girls and that the style of the dance is therefore very similar to the *rāsalila* of Kṛṣna and the *gopīs*. However, the evidence from the literature seems to be ambiguous: on some occasions there is but one person impersonating the god (apparently the priest); on other occasions, the hunter men folk may be impersonating the god as they dance, duly lubricated by toddy.

Notes to Chapter 4: 'The Medieval period'

1. This is a position consistent with that of Kamil Zvelebil, expressed in a lecture at the University of Chicago on April 18, 1966.
2. Nilakanta Sastri thinks that the Kalabhras may have patronized Buddhism. He suggests this because in the contemporary Buddhist Pāli works of Bhuddhadatta mention is made of an Accutavikkanta of the Kalabhrakula, during whose reign Buddhist monasteries and authors enjoyed much patronage in South Tamil Nad. In any event, this era in which orthodox Hinduism was disrupted is described, whether literally or mythically, by later Hindu apologists as a tragic era. The *Periya Purāṇam* of Sekkilar, attributed to the twelfth century and purporting to be an extolling of the historical and religious significance of the Śaiva bhakti poets, is particularly full of such sentiment. In at least one passage of the *Periya Purāṇam*, the Mūrtti Nāyaṉār Purāṇam, stanzas 12 and 13, one of the Kalabhras is referred to not as a Buddhist, but as a Jain.

3. Srinivasan believes the *kantu*, mentioned in an earlier chapter as being a worship center amongst the hill peoples, was a wooden, not a stone, pillar (1960:131). If the *kantu* was stone, it was apparently of a different structure and function than the stones (*naṭukal*) used as memorials. Nonetheless, Srinivasan's point would be negated.
4. Two examples from Tirumular's *Tirumantiram* will illustrate Skanda's place in the *bhakti* literature of this period. Stanza 520 reads: 'When the devas praised Śiva as the "Lord, Our Master', and appealed to Him against the might of the Asura, Arumugan of the coral complexion was ordered by Him to go and kill their enemy.'

   Stanza 1026 reads: 'Take it that Kandan is the Son of "My Father, the Lord", because the six circles [balls of fire] appeared as the six faces before the Father and because Kandan the god became integrated [as one Deva].' These unpublished translations are by N. Subrahmaniam.
5. The term Somāskanda by this time, according to K. A. Nilakanta Sastri, appears to be a Sanskritic compound combining the words *Sa* (with) and *Umā* and *Skanda* and refers to Śiva as the dominant figure (Sastri 1963:59).
6. These datings are provided at the sites by the Archeological Department of the Government of Tamil Nadu and cited by Sastri 1966:171.
7. K. A. Nilakanta Sastri (1963:57–58) thinks the Pallavas adopted the Ganeṣa motif by the eighth century from the Cālukyas, where Ganeṣa was apparently a part of Śiva's family in sculpturing since the fifth or sixth century; Ganeṣa is included, for example, in a panelling found in Guntur District, Andhra, in Cālukya territory which C. Sivaramamurti dates no later than the sixth century (cf. C. Sivaramamurti (1962:12–13 and Plate 1b). The Pāṇṭiyas similarly depicted the Gaṇapati motif earlier than the Pallavas, perhaps because the Pāṇṭiyas were often politically aligned with the Calukyas (Sastri 1963:60). H. Heras (1956:179) citing Miss Betty Getty (1936), thinks that Gaṇapati seems only to have been known to the uneducated classes before the sixth century.
8. Tirupparaṅkuṉṟam, it should be noted, is now a major pilgrim center for Murukaṉ and is associated with one of the six traditional sites believed to have been mentioned in the Tirumurukāṟṟupaṭai, but, in fact, possibly listed by the editors at a later date. However, K. V. SoundaryaRajan of the Government of India's Archeological Survey, Southern Circle, believes, because of this carving at Tirupparaṅkuṉṟam and others in Pāṇṭiyan country, the poem should be dated about the eighth century at a time when the rock-cut cave temples were appearing in Pāṇṭiya country. Mr. SoundaryaRajan has noted a few other representations of Skanda in rock-cut caves which unfortunately have not yet been adequately described in literature.
9. Similarly, in Pallava cuttings there are at least some scholars who believe Skanda as a guru can be found even in the earliest sculpturing. K. R. Srinivasan and Jouveau-Dubreuil identified at least two controversial figures at Mahabalipuram – one in the Trimurti shrine and the other on the ground floor of the Dharmarayaratha – as a Brahmaśāstā (teacher of Brahmā) rather than as a Brahmā, as the figures had been traditionally identified. The figures are indeed consistent with Gopinath Rao's description of the Brahmaśāstā as one representation of Skanda: one face (not four, as a Brahmā figure might be expected to have), two eyes, and four arms – one bearing the *akṣamālā* (beads), one the *kamaṇḍalu* (waterpot), one in the *abhaya* pose, and the other in the *varada* pose. A similar figure can

be found in a lower rock-cut cave at Tiruchirapalli, K. R. Srinivasan, (1964:159), citing Jouveau–Dubreuil, *Archéologie du Sud de l'Inde* II, 49; and Gopinath Rao (1916, I:251–56 and II:439).

10. This is not the place to reconstruct the history of Ganeṣa. Nonetheless, it may be useful to note that H. Heras (1956:178), Getty (1936:25) and R. G. Bhandarkar (1913:147–48) recognize that Ganeṣa is propelled into official prominence by this time. They tend to see him as having been associated with four demons named Vinayaka (Aitareya Brāhmaṇa I:21) whom Rudra combined and made the leader of the Gaṇas, "Gaṇapati". By his becoming Gaṇapati he assumed the title earlier given to Brāhmaṇaspati (ṚV II:231), to Indra (ṚV X:112:8), and eventually to Śiva. Thus Gaṇapati appears to have a history of development from an enemy of the gods and a deity of the Śudras (Edward W. Hopkins 1895:487), to an attendant of the gods, particularly of Śiva; to a leader of the divine forces, and, eventually, to a place of supremacy of his own. During the period under discussion, Gaṇapati was adapted as part of Śiva's official family in the South; there are myths in the Gaṇapatya cult, attempting to depict his superiority over Skanda. One claimed by both traditions and found in Paḻani, is that in which Gaṇapati and Skanda are asked to compete to see which is rightfully to be Śiva's heir. To him who circled the world first was to be given the fruit symbolic of supremacy. Skanda mounted his peacock and soared around the world. The portly Ganeṣa merely walked around his parents, saying in effect, 'You are the world'. To Gaṇapati was given the fruit; but when Skanda protested, as consolation, Śiva said to Skanda: *Paḻamnī* ('You are the fruit'). It is interesting in this context to reiterate that, hereafter, though Skanda retains his militaristic imagery, it is given non-militaristic interpretation; nor does he ever again seem to be the patron war god for chieftains of kings. There are other factors involved in this development, as we shall see, but part of the reason for this may be Ganeṣa's arrival on the scene and his edging out Skanda's supremacy as heir in Śiva's family.

11. It is striking to note in this connection that, to some degree after 800 A.D. and more abundantly after the ninth and tenth centuries, Śiva is depicted less in anthropomorphic and iconic form as in aniconic form, and particularly in the form of the lingam (Srinivasan 1960:192ff.). K. R. Srinivasan suggests several reasons why the lingam may have become an important representation of Śiva in this period, including the extending Southward from Andhra and Cālukya country of phallic and fertility cults; references by Sambandar and later *bhakti* poets to Śiva as a pillar; association of the lingam with the *kantu*, the *tari* (a crudely dressed stone), and the *kampaṉ* or pillar used earlier in worship; and a Śaivite attempt to provide an answer to the Vaiṣṇava myth of Viṣṇu's emergence from a pillar. This development could also be related to the growing emphasis on philosophizing of the Cōḻa era, particularly the effort of Śaiva Siddhānta to view the divine as an abstraction. Whatever the factors comprising the emergence of the lingam as a representation of Śiva, it implies that Śiva was becoming more abstract and less concrete; hence, the emergence of the concrete and, possibly, more readily available, sons of Śiva may have represented their coming to greater eminence in the devotional life of the Śaivite.

12. Srinivasan also notes that other representations of Bālasubrahmaṇya constructed in this area and in this early Cōḻa period show the god's hands holding the *akṣamālā* and the *śakti*, both of which symbolize in part the deity's attribute of wisdom and creativity. The *ciṉ-*

mudra is a gesture in which the forefinger touches the base of the thumb as in a circle, and are separated from the remaining three fingers which remain erect. The gesture is interpreted in terms of Siddhāntin philosophy, as representing the god (thumb) and the devotee (forefinger) being joined, though remaining distinct from each other. The devotee is detached from the three *malas* or *pācas* (fingers) which are ego-consciousness (*āṇava*), involvement in desire (*karma*) and worldliness (*māyā*).

13. This point was also noted by K. Soundaryarajan in a conversation with me February 9, 1967.
14. This description of the temple is taken from Gopinath Rao, 1916, p. 421, citing instructions for building temples outlined in the Āgamas. Of course the instructions scrupulously outlined in the Āgamas were not necessarily followed meticulously. Even today, variations in architecture and ritual from that prescribed in the literature have been introduced because of expediency and mitigating circumstances.
15. One is struck by the similarity between these medieval sacred sites, particularly the 'outdoor' settings, and those listed in the early Caṅkam poetry as being sacred to Murukaṉ.
16. It should be noted that the dominant *vimāṉam* or central tower is peculiar to the early Southern temple, and is particularly large in the early Cōḻa period (800–1100 A.D.). By the 'late Cōḻa' era (1100–1300), the *vimāṉam* was smaller and the *kōpuram* (tower entrance) had been adapted from northern temple architecture and assumed architectural, if not symbolic, dominance. The origin of the *vimāṉam* in the Southern Temple is an interesting problem. Most scholars generally concede it is an adaptation of the Buddhist stupa, but N. Venkata Ramanayya (1930) argues an interesting if inconclusive, case for the possibility that both *vimāṉam* and stupa have roots in the megalithic rock monuments and hut urns used to memorialize the dead.
17. When we seek to interpret the profuse symbolism associated with Skanda–Murukaṉ, and his relationship to the goddess, we shall note that Vaḷḷi is a primarily Southern consort, and that his attachment to the consorts is, at least from one point of view, minimal! This clutching of the lance is intended, among other things, to symbolize the god's freedom and his power to free (with the instrumentality of the lance) from all that binds.
18. We notice two types of lance used in the iconography of Skanda–Murukaṉ. The *Śakti* is a double- or triple-pointed lance, generally rooted in the Epic tradition and believed to have been Skanda's by virtue of the goddess' giving him of her energy. The *vēl*, rooted in the early Tamil tradition, is leaf-shaped and by about the fifteenth century is generally interchangeable with the *śakti* in the Southern iconography of the god.
19. A few examples of a Brahmaśāstā dating to the medieval period still exist in the South. C. Sivaramamurti and T. G. Aravamutham, formerly co-curators of the Madras museum, found an isolated sculpture in the fields at Valasaravakkam, eight miles from Madras; this image was assigned to the thirteenth century. V. Raghavan noted that the image still worshipped in the *garbhagṛha* in the Tirupporur Temple thirty miles from Madras is a Brahmaśāstā, probably assignable to a date considerably later than the thirteenth century. A similar image also exists in the Kudakarkōil in Tanjore District and another lies in the ruins of a dilapitated temple at Tirūr near Tiruvellore (Raghavan 1939:112).
20. A variation of this may be represented in the portrayal of Śiva's family found in the panellings added early in the ninth century to the Pallava Kailāsanatha Temple in Kanche-

epuram. Śiva and Parvatī are with two children; the one child standing directly behind Śiva's ear may be Subrahmaṇya.

21. The phrase is Gopinath Rao's used frequently in his description of Subrahmaṇya's iconography (1916, II:415ff.).
22. For example, the birth of Kārttikeya is described in varying detail in at least the following Purāṇic passages: Linga Purāṇa I:104, 105; Vāyu Purāṇa 72:24ff; Mātsya Purāṇa 5:26ff and chapters 146–160; Śiva Purāṇa, chapters 9–19; Brahmānda Purāṇa (II:65; III:11); Vāmana Purāṇ, chapters 57 and 58; Śiva Mahāpurāṇa 2:4 and 1–12; Padma Purāṇa 6:28 and Skanda Purāṇa 1 (i), 20–30 and 1 (ii), 20–32. (P. K. Agrawala 1966:136). Agrawala argues that some, if not most, Purāṇic accounts were reduced to writing in the Epic period. Citing Hasra, *Purāṇic Records on the Hindu Rites and Customs*, pp. 93–96, he suggests the Linga Purāṇa, though it was a relatively early Purāṇa, attained its present form by 600 A.D. References made to the birth of Kārttikeya in the Viṣṇu, Markaṇḍeya, and Viṣṇu Dharmottira Purāṇas he dates as Pre-Gupta inasmuch as they fail to mention the demon Tāraka, which he believes was developed during the Gupta period. The Vāyu Purāṇa account may be slightly later, in his terms, because it does make passing reference to Tāraka. The Śiva Purāṇa, as we noted in an earlier chapter, may have been available to Kālidāsa. The same may be true of the extensive account in the Mātsya Purāṇa. The most extensive of the early Purāṇic accounts is that found in the Mātsya Purāṇa, where Skanda is a member of Śiva's family and is born in a manner very similar to that described in Kālidāsa's *Kumārasambhava* (P. K. Agrawala 1966:138), citing V. S. Agrawala, *Mātsya Purāṇa – A Study*, p. 237.
23. There are few clues as to the date of the Skanda Purāṇa. Several scholars note that Haraprasad Sastri discovered in Nepal a portion of an old manuscript of the Skanda Purāṇa written in the Gupta script. He and C. Bendall, on paleographic grounds, assigned the manuscript to the seventh century. This would suggest there was a body of literature prior to that time which could be termed 'Skanda Purāṇa' but, presumably, elaborations were added throughout later centuries. Some of the mythology of the Skanda Purāṇa is undoubtedly post-Gupta and consistent in spirit with the medieval South. Hence, I include discussion of the collection in the present context. Cf. Moriz Winternitz. 1959:57; Heras 1956: 176.
24. The ram is still used, but only occasionally on festive occasions, as a vehicle for Murukaṉ. The ram is undoubtedly related structurally to the goat which appeared in the Epic accounts. This myth is reported by V. S. Chengalvaraya Pillai, 1954, p. 3, and was narrated in contemporary terms by Embar Vijayaraghavachariar (1966).
25. Reconstructed from V. S. Chengalvaraya Pillai 1954, pp. 3–4; from Embar Vijayaraghavachariar's Hārikathā (1966), and from a film entitled 'Kantan Karuṇai' (The Grace of Skanda) (1967).
26. Summarized and abbreviated from V. S. Chengalvaraya Pillai 1954, p. 4 and 'Kantaṉ Karuṇai. This myth is poetically embellished in a *bhakti* hymn appearing in the *Kallāṭam* (lines 1–65), a Tamil work attributable to a period between the eleventh and thirteenth centuries according to Prof. A. S. Gnanasambandan, partially on the basis of its dependence on *Iṟaiyanar kaḷaviyal-Nakkirar uṟai*, an earlier treatise commenting on the mythology found in the late *Caṅkam* materials. The *Kallāṭam* hymn likens the subdued *asura* to

fire, the ocean, a tree and a mountain; he is like a great coral reef under the ocean. The hymn includes a suggestive analogy that the peacock rising out of the ocean presses the head of the primordial snake causing the snake to spew out red 'jewels' like suns, illuminating the world. This imagery is suggestive and seems to imply that Murukaṉ's overcoming the *asuras* is an act analogous to the creation of the world and represents his mastering the elements of the world – the ocean, the mountain, etc.

27. In the original text, called the *Sthāṇava Vaibhava Kāṇda, Jayantipura Māhātmya*, Chapters VI–VIII of the latter part of the Skanda Purāṇa the story differs from the way it is popularly told. In that context, Vaḷḷi and Devasenā were married to Ṣaṇmukha in primordial time, but Vaḷḷi, somewhat vain, derided her co-wife Devasenā. Ṣaṇmukha himself told her she must be born of an animal and brought up by hunters. She is therewith born of a doe, the celestial damsel Kanchara. She is brought up by the Pulkaśas, celestial damsels cursed by the saga Hema to be children of the hunt. The locale of the event is the Himalayas, rather than in Tamil country.
28. Here again, the Jayantipura version of the Skanda–Purāṇa accounts differs from the popular variation in which it is the girl who is willing to marry Kumāra, but her father who resists, insisting she is intended only for Ṣaṇmukha. Kumāra decides to have some fun, thus changing himself into the form of a tree. No mention is made of his becoming an old ascetic, however. Nor is Tiruttani mentioned.
29. Reconstructed from V. S. Chengalvaraya Pillai 1954, pp. 3–5; an unpublished translation of the appropriate portion of the Skanda Purāṇa text rendered by V. Raghavan; Embar Vijayaragavachariar's Hārikathā (1966) and the film 'Kantaṉ Karuṇai (1967). It should be noted that the basic story is told with variations and embellishments by each individual story-teller.
30. This is the suggestion of N. Murugesa Mudaliar, editor of the *Śaiva Siddhānta*, proffered in a conversation with me on December 15, 1966.
31. A notable exception is the representation of Murukaṉ and Devasenā found in Tirupparaṅkuṉṟam and noted earlier.
32. This is explicitly suggested by S. Satchidanandan Pillai (1963:17), and by A. S. Gnanasambandan in a conversation.
33. Noted by V. S. Chengalavaraya Pillai 1954, p. 7, citing the Tanakai Purāṇam, the *stālapurāṇa* purporting to give the mythological history of the Tiruttani Temple. The *Stālapurāṇas* may, in fact, be the product of the modern era rather than of the Medieval period, but I refer to them in this context because they illustrate the spirit of what was already occurring in the Medieval period.
34. V. S. C. Pillai notes that poets Ottakutai and Aruṇakirinātar subscribe to this view and that it is explicitly recorded in the Cīrkaḻi Purāṇa, of the twelfth century.
35. Noted by M. Arunasalam in his introduction of Kumāragurupara Swamigals Kanta Kali Veṇpā (1949).
36. This is a comment often made to me by various non-professional devotees who have talked to me about the Murukaṉ tradition.
37. This description of the nature and role of the *brāhmadeya* has been made by Burton Stein, historian of medieval South India. Dr. Stein's position was communicated to me in a conversation on February 10, 1967, and in a verbal report of his research findings given at

Poona on January 14, 1967. His history of medieval South India will be published shortly.

38. One or two examples of inscriptions will suffice which illustrate the king's sacral functions and 'greatness'. In the Visvanathaswami Temple in Tenkasi, Pāṇṭiyaṉ king Parakrama is extolled in 1451: he is the embodiment of the virtue of all his ancestors; he understood Tamil and Sanskrit sciences; he was crowned to protect humanity; he wore the lotus feet of Śaṅkara and wielded a just sceptor; his white umbrella sheltered the world; he gave his people rain; he rooted out the weeds of sin and raised the crop of virtue; he routed the enemy kings (Dikshitar 1952:151). Earlier (1186 A.D.) in Pithapuram in Godavari District in Cālukya country, Vēlānanda is glorified: even as Kumāra was born of Śiva to protect the world, so was born Prince Goṅka, skilled in royal sciences (*ibid.*, p. 244). Burton Stein is inclined to regard this sort of language as 'rhetoric' designed to legitimize the kings in face of the *brāhmaṇ* power.
39. This is Burton Stein's observation, made to me in the conversation of February 10, 1967.
40. This point that the *brāhmaṇs* exceeded the warrior chieftains in actual power and as purveyors of the cultural heritage is the result of Burton Stein's research and is not yet accepted by most South Indian historians. I do not wish to push the point except that it may help explain why there is so strong an emphasis on the philosophical character of the god in question and a minimizing of his military attributes. To be sure, the 'warrior' character of the god doesn't disappear entirely as witnessed by such inscriptions as the one from the Cālukya country noted above.
41. I am inclined to believe that, in general, 'Sanskritization' is particularly intense during the Cōḻa era, and 'Tamilization', while it may have been occurring more subtly at the same time undergoes a resurgence during the Vijayanagar era (mid-fourteenth to mid-sixteenth centuries).
42. Cited from Tirumular's Tirumantiram VIII:28 and translated by S. Satchidanandan Pillai (1952:7).
43. A few commentaries may be mentioned: In the sixteenth century Marai Gnana Sambandar wrote *Par Mata Timara Bhanu*: Sivagna Yogi of Cōḻaṭēca wrote some twelve books, including commentaries on the Śivañāṉam Pōtam and Śivañāṉa Siddhiyar; Gnanaprakasar of Jaffna wrote in Sanskrit such books as *Śiva Yoga Saram* and *Śiva Sannadhi Mahātriya Sangraham.* In the eighteenth century Śivagnana Yogi wrote Tamil commentaries on the Śivañāṉa Pōtam; and in the nineteenth century Subramanya Desikar added to the already vast literature (S. Satchidananandam Pillai 1952:8–9).
44. For most of this and the following discussion of the *pati, pacu,* and *pāca* of Śaiva Siddhānta I am indebted to S. Satchidaṇandam Pillai (1952) and V. A. Devasenapati (1963). Both publications are based primarily on lectures delivered under the Sri-la-Sri Arulnandi Sivacharya Swamigal Sivajnana Siddhiyar Endowment, Mr. Satchidanandan's in 1952 and Mr. Devasenapati's in 1959.
45. S. Satchidanandam Pillai 1952, p. 20, citing stanza number 52 of the Śivaprakāśam as translated by K. Subramanya Pillai, on p. 19 of an unspecified edition, published by the Dharmapuram *maṭam*.
46. The five forms, mentioned earlier, are Brahmā, Viṣṇu, Rudra, and Māheśvara (*rūpa*) and Sadaśiva or Śiva linga (*rūpa-arūpa*).
47. The six Adhvas or paths of Śaiva Siddhānta are: *mantra*; *pada* (words); *varṇa* (letters);

bhuvana (world); *tattva* (categories); and *kalā* (art). The four classes of birth are: from eggs, from dirt, from seeds, and from the womb. The seven kinds of existence are: plants, marine creatures, reptiles, birds, beasts, human beings, and celestial beings.

48. There are four means to salvation in Śaivism: *Carya* (bodily service); *Kriyā* (ceremonial worship); *Yoga* (inward worship); *Jnāna* (realization of the supreme wisdom).
49. The bestowal of grace (*Śakti Nipāta*) is of four types as given to four different types of soul: the very dull; the dull; the keen; and the very keen.
50. At a particular stage in the Siddhāntin's attainment of salvation, the Lord is said to appear before him and 'initiate' him with a look (*Cakṣu Dīkṣā*).
51. There are sixty-eight instruments said to be a part of *pāca* (the bonds), sixty of these instruments belong to the physical body, and eight to the subtle body.
52. The sacred ash (*vipūti*; Sanskrit: *vibhūti*) is highly symbolic in Śaivism. It is the ash of cow-dung burned with appropriate Śaiva mantras and represents the *malas* or three impurities, which have been burned and thus purified. When smeared on the forehead, usually in three streaks, they symbolize the purification of the three *malas* which beset the worshipper. It should be noted that in Tamil the cow is known as a *pacu* and its dung as *mala* (S. Satchidaṇandan Pillai 1952:39).
53. The *Rudrākṣa* (literally *akṣa* – tears of Rudra) are beads draped around the neck, whose meaning is suggested by the Upaniṣadic myth that Mahādeva wept at hearing of the suffering of the *devas* at the hands of the *asuras.* Wearing the beads is intended to be a re-enactment of that divine compassion (*ibid.*). The beads are fashioned from the fruit of a tree said to grow high in the Himalayas and believed to have 'medicinal' attributes.
54. The ten insignia of royalty (*tacāṅkam*) common to Tamil kings, listed in this paragraph are: hill, river, land, city, steed, elephant, floral wreath, banner, drum, and authority or sceptor.
55. Kumārakurapara Cuvāmikal, *Kanta Kali Veṇpā.* I have underlined non-English words, but have added no diacritical marks.
56. This estimate is S. Satchidanandan Pillai's (1962–63:3). Others are more skeptical of the precise backgrounds – indeed, the precise identity of a number of the poets. Yet, it is generally agreed that a substantial number of poets were, in fact, non-*Brāhmaṇ*.
57. Note that in the Bhagavad-gita, at least four cosmologies are implicitly coalesced. The world is seen in turn as the result of primordial sacrifice; as the result of a cosmic tree; as springing from a golden reed; and as the product of *puruṣa* and *prakṛti*, the primordial pair. *Bhakti*, in the context of these cosmologies, is re-creation or return to the Ultimate Reality which is the source of immortality. This is so because *bhakti* is the ritual sacrifice; it is becoming disattached from the sense world and returning to the roots of the cosmos; it is being reborn through the navel of the cosmos and finding passage to the realm of immortality.
58. We suggested earlier that this concept of grace seems expressed in the myth of Murukaṉ's wooing of Vaḷḷi. It might be noted that the Vijayanagar era witnessed a resurgence of Vaiṣṇavism, and, at least in the view of historian Burton Stein, a renewal of democratization. We should also note that the School of Maṇikavācakar within Śaivism is also committed to this concept of grace.
59. The three branches of Tamil learning are literature, music and dance.

60. While Pillay does not document his sources, much of his discussion on this point is taken from N. Subrahmaniam's *Sangam Polity* or K.A.N. Sastri's *History of South India.*
61. Pillay doesn't cite his source for this information. It should also be noted that 'Āryans' could also include non-brāhmaṇ castes.
62. Once again, Mr. Pillay does not document why he concludes these particular customs had Tamil origin. Nonetheless, there can be little doubt that in several centuries of living in the South, the brāhmaṇ community adapted some Tamil customs. Indeed it may have been this very flexibility which contributed to the Hinduization of the South.
63. Burton Stein's thesis is not yet popular amongst South Indian historians, but he insists it is documentably tenable. Nonetheless, both Vaiṣṇavas and Śaivas concede that the Cōḻa era was predominantly Śaiva and that the Vijayanagar era brought about a Vaiṣṇava resurgence and a degree of democratization.
67. This is the suggestion of K. V. Soundarya Rajan, made to me in a conversation on February 9, 1967.
65. As translated by Prof. A. S. Gnanasambandan and me for a forthcoming volume of translations of some of Arunakiri's works.

Notes to Chapter 5: 'Lord of space and time – Expressions of Murukaṉ in the contemporary cultus'

1. Periāḻvar addressed some lines to Kaṇṇaṉ as a child deity in the eighth century, but it is Ottakkūttaṉ who wrote the first full-fledged piḷḷaitamiḻ when in his Koluttuṅkaṉ Piḷḷaittamiḻ he sings in praise of Koluttuṅkaṉ II, a Cōḻa emperor. The first fully formed piḷḷaittamiḻ addressed to Murukaṉ is probably that of Muttu Kumāraswamy, a contemporary of Tirumalai Nayak, though there are intimations of the form in Aruṇakiri's work. (For these historical notes I am indebted to Prof. A. S. Gnanasambandan of Madurai University and to V. S. Chengalvaraya Pillai, in an introduction to E. V. Venkatasubrahmaniam's volume of piḷḷaittamiḻ entitled Tiruttaṇikai Murukaṉ Piḷḷaittamiḻ [1964], and to the author of that verse himself [pp. VIII–XI].)
2. I am indebted to Prof. A. S. Gnansambandan of Madurai University for his comments on the impact of these men.
3. From conversations with Prof. A. S. Gnanasambandan and with 'Madurai Somu'.
4. The budget of the Sri Taṇṭāyutapāṇicuvami Devasthanam in Paḻani, for example, jumped from two million to four million rupees between 1967 and 1972.
5. One tradition suggests this temple takes its name from *Āvi*, one of a family of Veḷīr chiefs (*Kaṭaiyelu vaḷḷal*) who were said to be patrons of Tamil letters. The local myth has it that the name also represents several of the cosmic worshippers believed to have worshipped Murukaṉ in this place: *Tiru* (Lakṣmī); *Ā* (*Kāmadhenu*, the cosmic cow); *Iṉaṉ* (the sun); *Ku* (the earth); and *Tī* (the fire). Figures of these divinities installed within the temple perpetuate the myth.
6. For much of the data on the Paḻani myths I am indebted to J. M. Somasundaram Pillai (1963; 1970).
7. Legend has it that the principal icon was consecrated by one Siddha Bhogar, who was said

to have used the hill as an ashram and to have devised the amalgam of which the icon is alleged to be made. The *bhogar*, the myth says, was an alchemist who learned the secret of immortality. He was supposed to have been a contemporary of Agastya, the mythic bringer of culture to Tamil Nadu, and to have lived for centuries engaged in missions of mercy in South India to which he was believed to have come from the Himalayas. The *bhogar* was believed to have combined nine medicinal – poisonous compounds into an immortal amalgam from which the principal icon at Paḻani was made. Pouring sandal paste, milk, and other elements on the icon in worship is said to have a 'chemical' effect which is believed to perpetuate the icon's immortality and to enhance its power to work creative miracles on behalf of devotees. Legend further maintains that descendants of Pulippāṇi, a disciple of the Siddha Bhogar, served as priests at the main shrine at least until the sixteenth century when the general of Tirumalai Nayak of Madurai (1623–59), one Ramayappan, introduced Aṭi-Śaiva Śivacaryas to officiate in *pūjā*. This tradition, in fact, suggests the possibility that the temple became Śaiva and associated with Murukaṉ relatively late (J. M. Somasundaram Pillai 1970:8).

8. However, few remnants that can be identified as survival of an aboriginal hunting culture have been found in the Paḻnis as yet. But the presence of dolmens attests to the influence of the megalithic culture. And the tree-dwelling people now known as Paliyans may have preceded the megalith-builders inasmuch as their food is of the gathered variety: honey, roots, and leaves.
9. Paḻani is said to be the second largest supplier of human hair in India for the making of wigs.
10. The *kāvaṭi* is of two types. One type is that of a pole, from which is hung two burdens, usually baskets containing offerings for the god. The other, more commonly used in the *kāvaṭi* dance, is a pole from which an arch rises, decorated at each end with peacock feathers. Carrying either type of *kāvaṭi* is 'carrying the mountain' as Iṭampaṉ did. A dance with the second type of *kāvaṭi* is said to resemble the peacocks dancing in praise of Murukaṉ. The dance may be done solo or in concert with other *kāvaṭi* bearers, who often appear to be in a semi-frenzy and may accompany themselves with singing or chanting. The dancing includes twisting, spinning and transferring the *kāvaṭi* from shoulder to shoulder.
11. H. R. Pate, *Gazeteer of the Tirunelveli District* (Vol. I:1917), pp. 506ff. Also recorded by J. M. Somasundaram Pillai, 1948, p. 17. It is said one Vatamalayappa Pillai led the excursion to recover the icon, either by negotiation with the Dutch who had withdrawn to Ceylon, or, as tradition insists, by 'miraculously' recovering it from the sea. This incident was originally recorded by M. Rennel (*Description, Historical and Geographical of India*, Berlin, 1785), from a story told him by a Dutch sailor. Rennel wrongly identified the site as Tuticorin.
12. The precise intent of the *cūra*'s becoming a red underwater mango tree is not clear. It may be an allusion to coral reefs thought to have been visible in this area at some time. Or it may have been an attempt by the myth makers to equate Murukaṉ's foe with all the hostility, force and chaotic malevolence embodied in the ocean.
13. Aruṇakiri speaks of the vividly red Murukaṉ, subduing and riding through the cosmos on his blue-green peacock, likening the pair to the sun's rising over the ocean. Similarly, the author of the Kallātam speaks of the ocean as a primordial serpent, whose head, when

pressed, gives birth to many sons, each sun signalling the start of a new day (cf. Zvelebil 1965:157).

14. This delightful tale was told me by one of the temple priests who ushered me through the cave during a tour of the temple.
15. Vaiṣṇava Madhvan priests who were Tulu brāhmaṇs from Mangalore were intalled to preside at the central shrine of the temple, either by Maharajah Marthanda Varma (1729–1758) or by Dalavai Ramappayyan, prime minister of Tirumalai Nayak (1623–1659). At least this is the suggestion of J. M. Somasundaram Pillai (1948:17). A century or so later some Śaiva Tulu brāhmaṇs known as Mukhāṇiars, who like the Madhvans before them were from Mangalore and were steeped in Tantric traditions, were installed to preside over special rituals in the temple.
16. It is interesting that, in many ways the present hill known as Tirupparaṅkuṉṟam does not match the description given in the Tirumurukāṟṟupaṭai. The original rock-cut shrines, which cannot be dated prior to the eighth century, were apparently not even initially Subrahmaṇya shrines, as the sculpting is both subsidiary and later (Durgā is the central figure of the rock cut shrine in the lower caves), nor is there any original carving of Subrahmaṇya in affectionate embrace of Devasenā, as the Tirumurukāṟṟupaṭai suggests. The hill is neither verdant nor infused with springs as originally described. Incidentally, in contrast, the shrine known as *Lāṭaṅkōvil* sculpted at the foot of Āṉamalai, just northeast of Madurai, fits the description more accurately. That hill 'weeps' when it rains; there is a pool of rain water at its top; peacocks gather there when it is wet. More significantly, perhaps, the rock cut shrine depicts Subrahmaṇya seated affectionately beside Devasenā, and a figure, probably a Pāṇṭiyaṉ king doing obeisance at the right. However, that shrine has been officially dated in the late eighth or early ninth century, though that dating has been debated. At any rate, it seems not impossible that the original Tirupparaṅkuṉṟam was other than the present one.
17. That 'Sekunder' is thought to be one and the same as Murukaṉ was intimated to me by Muslim pilgrims, who, however, could only explain that 'Sekunder was a king in the time of Murukaṉ' who was related to Murukaṉ in some obscure way. N. Gopala Pillāi (1937: 986ff.) based his hypothesis that the Skanda cult derived from the influence of Alexander on Northwest India largely on the belief that the name 'Skanda' was a corruption of Alexander's Asian name 'Iskandar'. Few responsible scholars take this possibility seriously.
18. This is the popular belief of the local community shared with me by my illiterate guide.
19. In actuality, this celestial conference is said to have taken place where Murukaṉ rests with *Devayāṉai* at *Āvinaṅkuṭi*, a place which temple authorities at Paḻani also claim as referring to Paḻani.
20. Like virtually all heads of Śaiva *maṭams* (monasteries) Kuṉṟakkuṭi Aṭikal claims ordination to the priesthood by apostolic succession from Meikanta Tevar, author of the Sivañāṉa Pōtam. The Kuṉṟakkuṭi Aṭikal is also one of the most controversial of Śaiva swamis. He is committed to social change, ritual reform, land and wealth redistribution, and Tamil resurgence. He has been influenced by Marxism.
21. This temple is not a carbon copy of the Paḻani Temple, either in architectural style or pattern of worship. One of the more important festivals of this temple, for example, is the Skanda–Saṣṭi, commemorating a mythical event that is less important at Paḻani

than at Tiruchendur and other places. In a similar way, virtually every temple embodies and re-enacts much of the total cultus, though often each stresses particular aspects that relate to its own peculiar sacrality.

22. For more extensive description of ritual chronometry in the Murukan̲ cultus, the reader is referred to my essay: 'Chronometry, Cosmology, and the Festival Calendar in the Cultus of Murukan̲', in *Interludes: Aspects of Festival Life in South India and Ceylon*, edited by Guy B. Welbon, to be published shortly.
23. These twelve sacred moments (*tirukālaṅkaḷ*) include three that occur between midnight and pre-dawn, which virtually no Śaiva temples observe; six that fall between pre-dawn and noon, by far the busiest period in Śaiva temple life; and three that occur between dusk and late evening. None of these hours are unique to the Murukan̲ cultus, but all Murukan̲ temples will observe anywhere from four to nine of these.
24. So close is the relationship between moon and Murukan̲ it has moved N. Subrahmaniam to suggest the cultus of Murukan̲ originated as a cult of the moon in the Middle East. While we cannot rule out the possibility of Epic India's being influenced by Middle Eastern sources, it seems more likely to this writer that the emergence of Skanda as a prominent deity for such Epic dynasties as the Śakas and Guptas, and the growing significance of lunar calculations in chronometry were happening conjointly and perhaps, at first, even coincidentally in the period between the Mauryan and Śakan dynasties.
25. Cf. Pur̲anān̲ūr̲u canto 400, lines 1 and 2 where the 15th *titi* is mentioned.
26. For records of most of the following schedules, I am indebted to the festival calendars of the Śrī Taṇṭāyutapāṇi Cuvami temple in Paḻani (Urcavaṅkaḷin̲ Vivaram (1966–1967ff.) and to conversations with priests at the Srī Subrahmaṇyaswamy temple in Tiruchendur.
27. Sāstri cites a phrase from an unspecified text: '*ulkā hastā narāh kunyuh pitṛṇām mārga-darśanam*'.
28. T. S. Kuppanna Sastri insists that this system is known and used in the ṚK Vedic period, on the basis of a passage in ṚK Veda X 85–13, which, he suggests, shows that individual days derived their names from the asterism with which the moon is found on that particular day, (T. S. Kuppanna Sastri 1968:52). Similarly, passages in the *Kauṣītaki Brāhmaṇa* XIX 2–1–4 and V–1) suggest that the lunar months were named on the basis of the asterisms near which the respective full moons occurred (p. 53). Further, inscriptions of the Aśokan reign do include an occasional reference to *nakṣatra* days (T. V. Mahalingam 1968:63). On the other hand, Y. Subbaralu states that of the *pañcāṅka* elements only the *titi* had come into regular use prior to 500 A.D. Indeed, references to the *nakṣatra* system are very few, if not absent, on Sātavāhana, early Śaka and Gupta inscriptions.
29. This was the observation of chief priests at the temples at Tiruchendur, Kun̲r̲akkuṭi, and Vaṭapaḻani. There is a certain inconsistency about this claim inasmuch as both *Kārttikkai* and *Vicākam* are said to be the god's 'birthday', but are situated at the opposite 'ends' of the cycle of asterisms, some thirteen days apart. Yet the myths of Skanda's birth tell us the god grew up in six days. How then could Skanda have been 'nurtured' on *Kārttikai* and then 'integrated' on *Vicākam*, some thirteen days later, and, at the same time, 'born' on both days. Is it possible the two asterisms are intended to represent 'poles' in the cycle – something like the new and full moon or the winter and summer solstices – thereby suggesting the concept of fullness or completion?

30. This myth was narrated by the former chief priest at the Śrī Subrahmaṇyacuvāmi temple at Tiruchendur.
31. It is apparently not until the Epic period that the solar year is divided into twelve lunar units which are used regularly in chronometry. Prior to that the Vedic year had been divided into three seasons: summer (*grīṣma*); rains (*varṣa*); and winter (*hemanta*), which were, in turn, divided into six tropical periods: *vasanta* (spring); *grīsma* (summer); *varṣā* (rains); *śarad* (autumn); *hemanta* (dewy) and *śiśira* (cold). Eventually, these were again subdivided into twelve tropical months: Madhu, Mādhava, Śukra, Śuci, Nabha, Nabhasya, Isa, Ūrja, Saha, Sahasya, Tapa, and Tapasya (T. S. Kuppanna Sastri 1968:55, citing *Taittsam.* Bṛ. VII, 5–1).
32. There are two schools of chronometry extant in South India. The first, known as *cauramāṉam*, measures the year by solar means, determining the start of each month by the day on which earth, in its orbit around the sun, sees the sun in the eastern horizon for the first time in juxta-position with one of the twelve constellations – that is, on the day the sun 'enters' the house of the constellation. This system is used in Tamil chronometry. The alternate system, known as *cāntiramāṉam*, is based on lunar calculation by which the month starts with the new moon. This system has been used in Andhra for some centuries.
33. This was expressed in conversations, by such priests as the former chief Mukhāṇiar priest at Tiruchendur and by such scholars as Prof. A. S. Gnanasambandan of the University of Madurai.
34. Note that neither the Tamil nor the Telegu year actually observes the solstices and equinoces, but rather marks these four junctures by the start of either the month or the lunar cycle respectively *after* these junctures.
35. This is consistent with the pattern suggested by the former chief Mukhāṇiar priest at Tiruchendur. If one were to label the Tamil seasons on the basis of the cycle of heat and cold they would roughly be as follows: 'Winter': September 21–December 21 (these are the coldest, rainiest months); 'Summer': March 21–June 21 (these are the hottest months); 'Spring'; December 21–March 21 (this period marks the increase of heat, the planting of the semi-annual crop and the budding of the annual blossoms); 'Autumn' is June 21–September 21 (this is a period of cooling, marked by Southwest monsoon, the planting of semi-annual crops, and the harvesting of some crops.
36. Such temples, as at Tiruchendur, do celebrate a festival to Murukaṉ in the month of Āvaṇi (August–September), but this is not celebrated throughout Tamil Nadu. This exception will be discussed later.
37. This was made explicit by the former chief Mukhāṇiar priest at Tiruchendur.
38. It is worth noting that this phenomenon of spirits' returning from the dead marks in several religious communities the time immediately preceding the new year.
39. Tiruchendur, for example, observes this, but Paḻani does not. This festival clearly does not fit neatly into the pattern outlined!
40. It may not be coincidental that the Tiruchendur temple, but not many others celebrate the *māci* festival, inasmuch as the Tiruchendur temple is virtually alone in celebrating the homologous pūjās: the *Kālamattyacanti* (7:30–9:00) and *Vittyakalacanti* (9:00–9:30).
41. It is striking that the festival celebrating Murukaṉ's marriage comes *after* those festivals

celebrating his triumph over evil and *before* the festival celebrating his final reigning in triumph, as, consistently, in the Tamil festivals associated with Murukaṉ, the god's marriage *follows* his conquest of the *asura* and *precedes* his reigning in final triumph. Should we conclude that the series of festivals is intended to re-enact the career of the god in a manner consistent with the intent of each festival?

42. For further discussion of the significance of this festival and of ritual marriage within Śaivism, see Brenda Beck's commentary on 'A Praise Poem for Murugan' (1973); Wendy O'Flaherty (1969); and my own discussion of *Paṅkuṉi Uttiram* in a forthcoming volume on the ritual life of the Murukaṉ cultus.
43. Note that while Tamil months start with the entrance of the sun into a new sign of the zodiac and the Telegu month starts with the new moon the distinctions are often blurred in the minds of devotees and priests. Hence, Tamil priests and devotees can think of new moon days starting important solar periods and such full moons as that of *Vaikāci* as climaxing or terminating the 'daytime' months.
44. For some Śaiva temples, more generally, the *nakṣatra pūram* sometimes is associated with a mythical event in the life of Śiva, so the festival of this occasion may be theological in nature for such temples. At Tiruchuḻi, for example, a village some seventy miles south of Madurai, the *Āṭippūram* is a festival in which the betrothal of Mīnakṣi to Sundareśwaran occurs. The theme of *Āṭippūram* nonetheless, is usually associated with fertility.
45. Bathers are described as gamboling in the waters, garlanded and smeared with sandal; often astride elephants or horses. One crop of rice has been harvested and gathered in sheaves, while new paddy has been planted. There is the drinking of intoxicating beverages. The waters cause the *vēṅkai* and the mango to blossom. The rivers are described as like human passions or like militia in motion. One might add that a hint or two in those passages suggest that winter rains as well as summer rains are being referred to. The *Vēṅkai* and the mango, for example, blossom in April–May not August–September. And the Vaikai today is more nearly flooded by Northeast monsoon rains than from Southwest monsoon rains, though, to be sure, reference is made to waters flowing from the hills where the Southwest monsoons are severe; further, dams today impede the flow of water in July–August. However, if winter rains are indeed referred to, the festival may have been incorporated into the Skanda–Sasti festival which occurs at the height of the Northeast monsoon.
46. The former chief Mukhāṇiar priest at Tiruchendur made this claim. Kerala's new year does start in *Āvaṇi*, when the sun enters the new sign of the zodiac after the autumnal equinox rather than after the vernal equinox, when the Tamil new year starts. It may not be coincidental that, in Kerala, the southwest monsoon from June to August tends to be particularly severe (as compared with the Northeast monsoon in Tamil Nadu) and that Kerala still celebrates a significant festival at the same time that the *Āvaṇi* festival is celebrated in Tiruchendur.
47. The first inscription referring to the weekday is apparently that on an Eran Stone Pillar of Buddha Gupta, ascribed to the year 484 A.D. (Mani 1968:95). Nor are there many references to the weekday in literature prior to the Christian era if one can assume that the Purāṇas, the Dharmaśāstras, and Siddhāntas were written later. Nor is the number seven consistent with the general numerology of brāhmaṇic chronometry in which the

number one, three, nine, and twenty-seven are prominent. The myth of the origin of the astronomic calculations in the brāhmaṇic tradition is on this wise: In the beginning was primordial light. Light evolved into three components called Brahmā, Viṣṇu and Rudra; these three gave birth to the nine planets, which, in turn, gave birth to the twenty-seven *nakṣatras* (recited in a conversation by an anonymous astrologer in Madurai).

48. The Kuṉṟakkuṭi Aṭikal, for example, was inclined to 'demythologize' the festivals held at Kuṉṟakkuṭi in Ramnad District. Such demythologizing may imply a dismissal of much of the significance of brāhmaṇic chronometry and of brāhmaṇic influence generally in the cultic life of the temple. But, at the same time, an anonymous swami, resident at Paḻani, remarked in a conversation during one festival that of the three major festivals at Paḻani, each was generally attended by a different set of peasants relatively free from their agricultural chores. For instance, *Tai Pūcam* in January was attended largely by peasants from Kerala. *Pañkuṉi Uttiram* in March was attended largely by peasants from Coimbatore District, and *vaikāci vicākam* in May was attended largely by peasants from Salem District.
49. This was a comment made to me by a number of priests and devotees in Madras City.

Notes to Chapter 6: 'The many facets of Murukaṉ'

1. Other theological devices for integration include myths of androgyny and of sacred marriage. Indeed, virtually all religious symbols serve as *coincidentia oppositorum*. See Eliade 1959:86–107.
2. We are reminded that, in the Bhagavad–Gita, Kṛṣṇa plays a similar role, integrating in his person at least four major cosmological viewpoints implicit in the Gita: the primordial sacrifice, the Cosmic Man, the Cosmic Tree, and the *Hiraṇyagarbha*.
3. As we have seen, there is no 'pure' Tamil culture extant. However, there is no doubt that a mass of Tamilians imagine Murukaṉ to be more Tamil than Sanskrit.
4. I am referring here to a feeling – a feeling which I think was confirmed by conversations with worshippers, but which I must confess was basically subjective – that came to me after observing more than one colorful rural festival. It was a feeling that illiterate and semi-literate worshippers of Murukaṉ were, after all, seeking of him not any great change in their circumstances. In that sense, the god's youthfulness seemed to represent for them a certain changelessness, a constancy in their lot. I could not be sure that what they sought was really a breakthrough from their lot so much as some assurance that their lot was, after all, within the purpose of the god.
5. For much of this interpretation of Piḷḷaittamiḻ I am indebted to Mr. Ebenezer from Nagercoil, Kanyakumāri, and now a public school teacher in Kodaikanal, who has spent a number of years in the study of Tamil poetry. One sampling of this poetry used in this analysis is that written by E. V. Venkātasubrahmanyan, a *guru* in the *maṭam* (cloister) at Tiruttaṇi. The poem is entitled Tiruttaṇikai Murukaṉ Piḷḷaitamiḻ.
6. Many Indian parents invite their children to look upon the moon and to think of it as an ornament or toy placed in the sky for the pleasure of the child.
7. The last three stages are different for male and female children and deities, according to

Mr. Ebenezer. The last three stages for females are *ammāṉai* (a kind of play, particularly juggling); *nīrāṭal* (water ballet often accompanied by singing); and *uñcal* (swinging and singing, especially in praise to the god, while swinging).

8. Note that Skanda's birth of such agencies as water, earth and fire makes him a paradigm of the cosmos itself, for these agencies were also operative in the cosmogonic process (cf. Chandogya Upaniṣad VI).
9. It is interesting that when Ganeṣa is accepted as a member of Śiva's family somewhat later in the history of Hinduism, he is often (but not always) depicted as the son primarily of Pārvatī and only secondarily of Śiva. But even then Ganeṣa is usually 'produced' by Pārvatī and never born of Pārvatī's womb. One such myth, recorded by H. Heras (1956: 200), is found in an undesignated passage of the Brahmavaivarta Purāṇa: Pārvatī, desperate that she had no son from Śiva, offered many prayers and sacrifices. She heard a heavenly voice telling her to return to her home to find her son. Upon returning she found a beautiful youth whom she and Śiva accepted as their own son. To commemorate this event they held a great feast to which all the gods were invited. All admired the youth save Śaṇi (Saturn) whose eyes remained fixed to the ground. Pārvatī, angered, commanded Śaṇi to look upon her son. As soon as Saturn's eyes were raised, the head of the youth turned to ash; the gods were dismayed. But Viṣṇu, mounting his *garuḍa* flew to the banks of the Puṣpabhadra where he found a sleeping elephant. Returning with the elephant's head he put it on the youth's shoulders thereby restoring him to life.
10. Swami Sivananda, popularizing imaginatively (1963:128), suggests Murukaṉ's marriage to Vaḷḷi combined both the Paisāca and Gandharva modes of marriage, the first based on love, the latter as the result of forceful abduction of the girl.
11. For example, in one folk hymn, 'A Praise Poem for Murugaṉ', translated by Brenda Beck and R. Balaji Rao, Vaḷḷi complains that Murukaṉ's father, Śiva, had haunted graveyards, his mother had once danced like a prostitute, his uncle (Viṣṇu) had made a mad attempt to measure the world in three steps, etc.
12. Agrawala bases his argument for the four original deities largely on two or three scattered references: the Liṅga Purāṇa I:82:16 describes Śiva as surrounded by his four sons. The Viṣṇu Purāṇa I:15:115–16 tells the myth of the origin of Śākha, Viśākha and Naigameya – as brothers. These references might tend to bolster the argument that there was an amalgamation of six gods, to four, and eventually, to one. On the other hand, they are not conclusive, and could simply be a reference to the various forms of Skanda.
13. Extensive descriptions of the *grahas* and of the remedy for them is included in the literature of Āyurveda. The Bhūtavidya or Grahavidya of the Āyurveda Saṁhitās describes a ritual of remedy that is similar to that found in the Skanda Yāga. Agrawala suggests that aspects of this domestic ritual have survived in the present *Ṣaṣṭhipūjana* performed after the birth of a child.
14. Agrawala cites the fifth division of the Astāṅga Āyurveda, called Kumārabhṛtya or Bālah.
15. Virtually every temple site sacred to Murukaṉ in Tamil Nadu has its collection of 'incidents' of healing purported to have taken place. At Paḻani, for example, I was told that the reason the lepers gather near the temple is that they hope Murukaṉ will heal them as he healed some 'in the past'. Particularly at Paḻani where local tradition insists some medieval *bhogars* or medically-proficient Siddhas lived is the healing character of the resident

deity stressed. None the less Tiruchendur also has its traditions of healing in the waters of the Bay of Bengal. And more than one pilgrim has told me of a personal experience in which Murukaṉ 'healed' an illness.

16. In the Paḻani temple, for example, the following festivals are preceded by the tying of the amulet to the arms of deities and priests: Skanda–Ṣaṣṭi (November), Tiruvāturai (December), and Paṅkuṉi Uttiram (March). Cf. *Uṟcavaṅkaḷiṉ vivaram.* [Details of Festivals] (1966–1972).
17. We are reminded that scholars like V. Raghavan and D. R. Bhandarkar have suggested that Skanda represents the eventual integration of six distinct but related deities which were worshipped in the early Epic period. Unfortunately, we do not have enough historical evidence to make us certain this actually occurred.
18. cf. The account in the ninth book of the Mahābhārata in which four of these parents – Rudra, Pārvatī, Agni, and Gaṅga – appear before Skanda to claim him. To satisfy each he divides into four forms: Skanda, Viśākha, Naigameya, and Śākha – two other forms were also ascribed to Skanda: (Sanat) Kumāra, son of Brahman, and Mahāsena.
19. Note that in varying circumstances, the world is said to have five directions – the four plus center; eight directions – the four plus the four between; or sixteen directions – the eight plus the eight between.
20. The Mīnatṣi temple museum in Madurai lists the following equations: the flagstaff is the *mūlādhāra*, the *cakra* situated between the anus and genitals; the *svādiṣṭhāna*, at the root of the genitals is the sacrificial altar or *liṅkam* where oblations are poured; the subsidiary *vāhana*, a vehicle of the presiding deity is the *maṇipūta*, at mid-navel; the main icon is the *anāhata*; the main *vāhana* is the *viśuddha*; located at the base of the throat; and the inner sanctuary, *garbhagṛha*, is the *ājñā*, located between the eyebrows. There is no unanimity amongst temples as to these equations, however.
21. This basic relationship of the six centers to the yogic *cākras* and the sacrificial sparks has not been made explicit in myth, but have been indicated to me in conversations with a few anonymous though thoughtful devotees. A similar phenomenon is to be observed in forms of North Indian tantric pilgrimage where four pilgrimage centers are associated with the goddess Satī by means of a myth to be found in several places including the *Brahmavaivarta Purāṇa* I, 10, 12, and IV, 43, 25. The myth notes that the mother goddess Satī immolates herself after being insulted by Dakṣa at the latter's sacrifice. Śiva, inconsolable at his consort's death, wanders about earth with the dead Satī on his shoulder. The gods Brahmā, Viṣṇu and Śaṇi, trying to console Śiva by disposing of Satī's body, enter the goddess' body by means of *yoga* and disperse it. Where the pieces of the body fell became the *pithas* or holy seats of the goddess where she is to be seen living with her husband (cited by Bharati 1963: 148–49).
22. The Pari. 8:10–13 alludes to Murukaṉ's birth of a lotus in an Himalayan pool.
23. A representation of a Cōḻa Somāskanda in which Pārvatī holds the lotus is on display in the Government of Madras museum. To be sure this phenomenon is not unique to Skanda, as goddesses are frequently depicted with lotus in hand. Yet the structural relationship of Skanda, lotus and goddess to primordiality is nonetheless illustrated.
24. One swami, the Kuṉṟakkuṭi Aṭikal, did suggest that Murukaṉ's redness represented his generation of *Cēyoṉ* and Agni. However, most of the priests and other swamis of whom

I have asked the meaning of redness have had to confess they would have to 'think about it a while'.

25. Often this rationale for the use of gold is followed by a rhetorical question: Is anything too much for the Lord?
26. Claude Levi Strauss makes this observation and goes even further, suggesting that the sustenance afforded by the animal (or, later, by the plant) constitutes a kind of 'immortality', for the species of animal (or bird) continues despite the death of a single animal, and the hunter acquires certain attributes of the hunted by eating its flesh (Lēvi–Strauss 1963:92ff.).
27. The Paripāṭal 9:1–5 refers to Indra's giving the peacock to Murukan̲ in another allusion to the peacock's warrior character.
28. On display in the Government of Madras Museum is a crude stone carving attributed by the Archeological Department to the first three centuries A.D. It depicts Skanda standing beside the peacock. The carving is a Northern one found in Mathura. To be sure, gods are often depicted as standing beside their mounts; yet we have little cause to believe the peacock was Murukan̲'s standard mount in the early centuries of the Christian era, especially in the Tamil context.
29. Aruṇakiri's Kantaralaṅkāram 65 reads, as translated by A. S. Gnanasambandan and me for a forthcoming volume:
    O Lord on the peacock,
    Which spreads its tail across the sky
    And drives away the elephants
    Of the eight directions
    And moves the eight mountains, . . .
30. N. Subrahmaniam suggests this equation is made in Pari. 3:60 (1966:396).
31. Heinrich Zimmer (1951) suggests that the elephant in Indian mythology is equated to the clouds and is thereby given a celestial character. It is not convincing that this celestial character is present in Murukan̲'s elephant. One brāhmaṇ devotee at Tirupparaṅkun̲ram, who remains anonymous to me, scorned a suggestion that either the name *Devayān̲ai* or the elephant were intended to convey any celestial symbolism.
32. This was the suggestion of the chief priest of the Tiruchendur Temple. In fact, this was the only meaning he was willing to ascribe to the snake. Yet the notion of the snake's being 'left-over' from the *asura* like the two fowls must be an addition to the basic myth recorded in literature; in that myth, to my knowledge, no snake is to be found.
33. This myth was told me by the Malayali priest at the Kur̲iñci Āṇṭavar temple in Kodaikanal reading from a Malayalam text. Most Tamil priests to whom I mentioned it dismissed it as 'unauthentic'.
34. Basham suggests that the Śakas and Kuṣāṇas brought into Northern India the practices of the Seleucids and other Middle Eastern emperors. Not content as was Aśoka to be termed a *rāja*, they called themselves *mahārāja* (king of kings) after a Persian model, and *tratara*, equivalent to the Greek *Sotēr* (savior). Basham also suggests that the Kuṣāṇas, possibly under Chinese influence with their Son of Heaven, took the title 'Son of the Gods' (*devaputra*).
35. The Tamil word *vāraṇam* used in Pari. 8:1–5 to refer to the gift of Agni to Murukan̲ most

probably means shield, but it may also mean 'coat of armor', 'elephant', 'cock', or a number of other possibilities (*A Dictionary Tamil and English* 1933:866).

36. The Madurai Āṭīṉam insisted in a conversation with me on December 10, 1966, that the *vēl* was the only lance which could be associated authoritatively with Murukaṉ.
37. I have witnessed a dedicatory *apiṣekam* (Sanskrit: *abhiṣekam* – anointing) for a lance, which in that worship was intended to represent all that Murukaṉ himself represented. In fact, it is common on festival occasions for the lance to represent Murukaṉ.
38. This rather imaginative, yet reductionistic interpretation of the lance was suggested by Prof. A. S. Gnanasambandam of Madurai University.
39. Robert Bellah, (1970:20–50) has suggested in a manner not inconsistent with Mircea Eliade's conclusions that the religion of the 'primitives' envisions a world that is still undifferentiated, and that it is only with the coming of the 'historic religions', that religious man envisions a dichotomy between sacred and profane, sky and earth, church and state. The distinction between the religion of the Epic period and that of the *Caṅkam* period is worth pondering in these terms, even though we do not find the term 'primitive' appropriate to describe the early civilization and religion of Tamil Nadu.
40. The process by which Dionysos was incorporated into Greek religion is not dissimilar to that we have described in Murukaṉ. However, there are at least three stages to Dionysos' acculturation. In the first stage, the Dionysos of Phrygia and Thrace is a great deal like the Tamil Murukaṉ: He is nursed by the Maenaeds, is the son and consort of goddesses and son and consort of damsels. He is born in chthonic hills, is the leader of the Korybantes, hunters of the hill and forest. He is associated with the 'wet principle' in Phrygia – sap, wine or intoxicants, blood – and is thus lord of plants and herd. He was worshipped with frenzied dance, often by women who leave their looms at night and drunk with wine, experience *ecstasis* (standing outside oneself) and *enthusiasmos* (possession by the god).

    A second stage in Dionysos' history finds him in Delphi, together with the more orthodox and sedate Apollo. The worship of Dionysos is more subdued, occurring largely in the context of moonlight festivals and accepted in modified form, even by the classicists, as an opportunity for momentary immortality. Eventually, in a third stage, Dionysos and Apollo are virtually coalesced in the person of Orpheus. While Orpheus was seen in the pattern of Apollo in certain respects, he also expressed some Dionysian themes; for example, in the Orphic cult, man is seen as having been created from the ashes of Dionysos and thus having the capacity to be immortal. For more extensive description of the history of Dionysos, see, for example, W. K. C. Guthrie (1950:148ff.) or Walter F. Otto (1965).
41. We noted earlier that the name 'Skanda' can be ascribed a Sanskrit etymology and that there is little or no evidence that the word has a Greek origin.
42. The study of Dennis Hudson among the Vēḷāḷars of Tirunelveli District suggests a long-standing identity of many members of the community as devotees of Murukaṉ. The Vēḷāḷars are also recognized as the authors of considerable Tamil literature throughout the Medieval period including a significant portion of the literature of Śaiva Siddhānta. The Pillais and Mudaliars, quite noticeable in the Murukaṉ cultus today, share a *vēḷāḷar* heritage.
43. Charles Ryerson reported this impression to me after an interview with Ramaswamy Naicker.

References

A Dictionary Tamil and English. Third edition. Tranquebar, Evangelical Lutheran Mission Publishing House, 1933.

Agrawala, P. K. 'Skanda in the Purans', *Purāna*, VIII, No. 1 (January) 1966:135–58.

Agrawala, Vasudeva S. *Sparks From the Vedic Fire*, Varanasi, Tara Printing Works, 1962.

Aiṅkuṟunūṟu Madras, E. S. Rajam, 1957.

Aiyangar, Narayana, *Essays on Indo-Aryan Mythology*. Vol. II. Madras, Addison and Co., 1901.

Akanāṉūṟu. Madras, E. S. Rajam, 1958.

Allchin, Bridget and Allchin Raymond. *The Birth of Indian Civilization*. Hammondsworth, Middlesex, Penguin Books, 1968.

Allchin, F. R. *Neolithic Cattlekeepers of South India*. Cambridge, University Press, 1963.

'An Introduction to Sri Subramanyaswamy Temple, Tiruchendur'. Tiruchendur, Srī Subramanyaswamy Temple, n.d.

Arthavaveda Pariśiṣṭas. *Skanda–Yāga*. Oral translation rendered by V. Raghavan on January 25, 1967.

Aruṇakirinātar 'Kantaralaṅkāram' and 'Kantaranapūti'. *Murukavēl Tirumurai*. Introduction and commentary by V. S̱. Chengalvaraya Pillai. Tirunelveli, South India Saiva Siddhanta Publishing Works, n.d.

——— *Tirruppukal, selected stanzas*. Translated by J. M. Somasundaram Pillai and V. S. Chengalvaraya Pillai in: J. M. Somasundaram Pillai, *Palani– The Sacred Hill of Murugan*. Palanai Sri Dandayuthapani Swami Devasthanam, 1963; and by N. Subrahamiam (hand written).

Ayer, V. A. K. *Everyday Astrology*. Bombay, D. B. Taraporevala Sons and Co., Ltd., 1966.

Ayyar, Narayana. *The Origin and Early History of Saivism in South India*. Madras, University of Madras Press, 1936.

Ayyar, P. V. Jagadisa. *South Indian Festivals*. Madras, Higginbottams, Ltd., 1931.

Banerjea, Jitendra Nath. *The Development of Hindu Iconography*. Calcutta, University of Calcutta Press, 1956.

Banerjee, N. R. *The Iron Age in India*. Delhi, Munshiram Manohailal, 1965.

Banerjee, N. R. and Soundara Rajan, K. V. 'Sanur, 1950 and 1952: A Megalithic Site in District Chingleput', *Ancient India*, XV (1959):4–42.

Barnett, L. D. 'The Early History of South India', pp. 593–603 in *The Cambridge History of India*, Vol. I, ed. by E. J. Rapom. Cambridge, University Press, 1922.

Basham, A. L. *The Wonder That Was India*. Bombay, Orient Longams, Ltd., 1963.

Beck, Brenda. 'A Praise Poem for Murugan'. Translation and commentary, prepared for publication in *The Journal of South Asian Literature* (1973), (xeroxed).

Bellah, Robert. 'Religious Evolution', pp. 20–50 in *Beyond Belief.* New York, Harper and Row, 1970.

Bhandarkar, D. R. *Lectures on Ancient Indian Numismatics.* Calcutta, University of Calcutta Publications, 1921.

Bhandarkar, Ramakrishna G. *Vaishnavism, Śaivism, and Minor Sects.* Strassburg, K. J. Trubner, 1913.

Bharati, Agehananda. 'Pilgrimage in the Indian Tradition', *History of Religions* III (1) Summer 1963:135 ff.

Bhattacharya, H. D. 'Minor Religious Sects' pp. 435–45 in: *The History and Culture of the Indian People,* Vol. III. Bombay, Bharatiya Vidya Bhavan, 1954.

Bosch, Frederick. *The Golden Germ.* The Hague, Mouton, 1960.

Brown, Percy. *Indian Architecture (Buddhist and Hindu Periods).* Bombay, D. B. Taraporevala Sons and Co., Ltd., 1965.

Burrow, T., and Emeneau, M. B. *Dravidian Etymological Dictionary.* Oxford, Clarendon Press, 1961.

Campbell, Joseph. *The Masks of God: Oriental Mythology.* London, Secker and Warbing, 1962.

Champalakshmi, R., Kuppanna Sastri, T. S., Mahalingam, T. V., Subbaralu, Y, and Mani, V. R. 'Calendar in Hindu Tradition', *Bulletin of the Institute of Traditional Cultures.* Madras, University of Madras, 1968.

Chatterji, S. K. 'Race Movements and Prehistoric Culture', pp. 139–52 in: *The History and Culture of the Indian People,* Vol. I. Bombay, Bharatiya Vidya Bhavan, 1954.

Clark, R. T. Rundle. *Myth and Symbol in Ancient Egypt.* London, Thames and Hudson, Ltd., 1959.

Danielou, Alain. *Hindu Polytheism.* New York, Bollingen Foundation, 1964.

Das, Tarak Chandra. 'Religious Beliefs of the Indian Tribes', pp. 139–52 in: *The History and Culture of the Indian People,* Vol. I. Bombay, Bharatiya Vidya Bhavan, 1954.

Das Gupta, S. *A History of Indian Philosophy,* Vol. I. Cambridge, University Press, 1951.

Deshpande, V. V. (ed.). *Hindu Viṣva Pariṣad.* Patna, Souvenir Volume, 1969.

Devasenapati, V. A. *Of Human Bondage and Divine Grace.* Annamalai, Annamalai University Press, 1963.

Diehl, C. G. *Instrument and Purpose.* Lund, C. W. K. Gleenup, 1956.

———'The Goddess of Forests in Tamil Literature', *Tamil Culture* XI (1964):308–16

Dikshitar, V. R. Ramachandra. 'What is Tamil Culture?', *New Review* V (1937): 513–26.

——— (ed.). *Selected South Indian Inscriptions,* Madras, University Press, 1952.

Earhart, Byron. 'A Religious Study of the Mount Haguro Sect of Shugando: An Example of Japanese Mountain Religion'. Unpublished Ph.D. dissertation, Divinity School, University of Chicago, 1965.

Ehrenfels, V. R. *Kadar of Cochin.* Madras University Anthropological Series, No. I. Madras, University of Madras, 1952.

Eliade, Mircea. *The Myth of the Eternal Return.* Translated by Willard R. Trask. London, Routledge and Kegan Paul, 1955.

———*Yoga: Immortality and Freedom.* London, Routledge and Kegan Paul, 1958.

———*The Sacred and the Profane.* Translated by Willard R. Trask. First American edition. New York, Harcourt and Brace, 1959.

———'Methodological Remarks on the Study of Religious Symbolism', pp. 86–107 in: *History of Religions: Essays in Methodology,* ed. by Mircea Eliade and Joseph Kitagawa. Chicago, University of Chicago Press, 1959b.

———*Patterns in Comparative Religion.* Translated by Rosemary Sheed. New York, World Publishing Co., 1964.

——— 'Australian Religions: An Introduction, Part I', *History of Religions* VI (2) November, 1966:108–34.

Eliot, Charles. *Hinduism and Buddhism – an Historical Sketch.* London, Edward Arnold and Co., 1921.

Frankfort, Henri. *Ancient Egyptian Religion.* New York, Harper and Row, 1961.

Fürer-Haimendorf, Christoph von. 'New Aspects of the Dravidian Problem', *Tamil Culture* II (1953):126–35.

Gaster, Theodor H. *Thespis: Ritual, Myth and Drama in the Ancient Near East.* Garden City, N.Y., Doubleday-Anchor Books, 1956.

Getty, Betty. *Ganesa. A Monograph on the Elephant-Faced God.* Oxford, Clarendon Press, 1936.

Gnanasambandan, A. S. Conversations held periodically from July 1971 to April 1972.

Gonda, Jan. *Aspects of Early Viṣṇuism.* Utrecht, van Dishoeck's Uitg., 1954.

———*Some Observations on the Relations Between 'Gods' and 'Powers' in the Veda. A Propos of the Phrase 'sūnaḥ Sahasaḥ'.* The Hague, Mouton, 1959.

Goodwin, Charles J. 'The Skanda-Yāga, Text and Translation' *Journal of the American Oriental Society* XV (1893):v–xiii.

Gopinath Rao, T. A. *Elements of Hindu Iconography,* Vols. I and II. Madras, Law Printing House, 1916.

Gordon, D. H. 'The Stone Industries of the Holocene in India and Pakistan', *Ancient India* VI (1950):64–82.

Guthrie, W. K. C. *The Greeks and Their Gods.* London, Methuen and Co., 1950.

Heine-Geldern, Robert. 'Das Megalith Problem', Beitrage Oesterreichs zur Erforschung der Vergangenheit und Kulturgeschichte der Mensheit, Symposium, 1956. New York, Werner-Gren Foundation, 1956.

Heras, H. 'Light on the Mohenjo-daro Riddle', *New Review* IV (1936):1–15.

———'The Problem of Ganapati', *Tamil Culture* V (1956):151–213.

Hooke, S. H. *Babylonian and Assyrian Religion.* London, Hutchinson House, 1953.

Hopkins, Edward W. *The Religions of India.* Boston, Ginn and Company, 1895.

Ilango Adigal. *Shilappadikaram.* Translated by Alain Danielou. New York, New Directions, 1965.

'Information Bullettin', Paḻani, Sri Dandayuthapani Swamy Devasthanam, n.d.

Jensen, Adolph E. *Myth and Cult Among Primitive Peoples.* Translated by Mariana T. Choldin and Wolfgang Weisslader. Chicago, University of Chicago Press, 1963.

Joseph, P. 'The South Indian Megalithic Tombs', *New Review* XXIV (1946):214–20.

——'Ophir of the Bible-Identification', *Tamil Culture* X (1963):48–70.

Kalidāsa. *Kumārasambhava.* Introduction, translation, and commentary by M. P. Kale. Bombay, 1913.

Kandaswami Temple, Madras. Conversations with priests and devotees in November, 1966.

'Kantaṉ Karuṇai'. A film based on mythology of the Murukaṉ tradition and released in Madras on January 14, 1967.

Keith, Arthur Berriedale. *The Religion and Philosophy of the Vedas and Upanishads.* Harvard Oriental Series, Vol. XXXI, ed. by Charles Rockwell Lanman. Cambridge, Harvard University Press, 1925.

Keller, Carl A. 'A Study of the Tirumurukāṟṟuppatai', *Śaiva Siddhānta* II, Nos. 1 and 2 (January–June 1967):1–8.

Koppers, W. 'Bhagwan. The Supreme Deity of the Bhils', *Anthropos* XXXV-XXXVI (1940–41):265–325.

Kramrisch, Stella. *The Hindu Temple.* Calcutta, University of Calcutta Press, 1946.

Krishnamachari, C. 'Villudayanpati', *The Hindu* (Madras), January 14, 1967.

Krishnaswami, V. D. 'Changes of Prehistoric Man Near Madras', *Journal of Madras Geographical Association* XIII (1938):58–90.

——'Megalithic Types of South India', *Ancient India* V (1949):35–45.

Kumāragurupara Swamigal. *Kanta Kali Veṇpā.* Translated by H. Arunasalam. Madras, Bharati Vijayam Publishing, 1949.

'Kumara Vayalur', *Sunday Standard* (Madras), October 16, 1966.

Kuṉṟakkuṭittalavaralāṟu [Historical Details of Kuṉṟakkuṭi]. Kuṉṟakkuṭi, Tiṟuvannamalai Atinam, 1966.

Kuṟinci Āṇṭavar Temple, Kodaikanal. Conversations with Pūcāri and devotees in April and May, 1967.

Kurukkal, K. Kailasanatha. 'A Study of the Kārtikkeya Cult', *University of Ceylon Review* XIX (2) (October 1961):131–37.

Kuṟuntokai. Madras, E. S. Rajam, 1957.

Lal. B. B. *Indian Archaeology Since Independence.* Delhi, Motilal Banarsidass, 1964.

Lang, Andrew. *The Making of Religion.* London, Longmans, Green and Co., 1900.

Lèvi-Strauss, Claude. *Totemism.* Translated by Rodney Needham. Boston Beacon Press, 1963.

Long, Charles. 'The West African High God: History and Religious Experience', *History of Religions* III (2) (Winter 1964):328–42.

Madras, University of. Personal interview with Mr. Gururajarao, reader in South Indian archaeology. February 4, 1967.

Mahābhārata. *Vana Parva* (Book III), chapters 223–232; *Śalya Parva* (Book IX), chapters 46–47; *Anaśāsanu Parva* (Book XIII), chapters 130–133. Oral translation rendered by V. Raghavan on January 25, 1967.

Mahābhārata of Kṛṣṇa-Dvaipāyana-Vyāsa, The. Translated by Pratap Chandra Roy. Second edition. Calcutta, Oriental Publishing Co., 1966.

Maloney, Clarence. 'The beginnings of Civilization in South India', *Journal of Asian Studies* XXIX (3) (May 1970):603–16.

Marriott, McKim. 'Little Communities in an Indigenous Civilization', pp. 211–18 in: *Village India*, ed. by Marriott. Chicago, University of Chicago Press, 1955.

Maturai Ātīṉam. Personal interview in January 1967.

Meenakshirsundaram, T. M. P. 'Nakkirar, the Earliest Tamil Mystic', *Tamil Culture* VI (1957): 309–18.

———Personal interview on March 3, 1967.

Monier-Williams, Monier. *A Sanskrit–English Dictionary.* Oxford, Clarendon Press, 1951.

Mudaliar, N. Murugesa. Personal interview on December 15, 1966.

Mudaliar, S. Arumuga. 'Concepts of Religion in Sangam Literature and Devotional Literature', *Tamil Culture* XI (1964):252–71.

Mukhodyay, Manmatha. 'Some Notes on Skanda–Kārttikeya', *Indian Historical Journal* VII (1931):309–18.

Murti, M. Chitananda. *Samśōdhana Taranga.* Mysore, n.p., 1966.

Mus, P. 'Has Brahmā Four Faces?' *Journal of the Indian Society of Oriental Art*, AICC Volume (1937):60–73.

Naṟṟiṇai. Madras, E. S. Rajam, 1957.

Nayar, T. Balakrishnan. 'Where Did the Dravidians Come From?' *Tamil Culture* X (1963): 121–34.

O'Flaherty, Wendy. 'Ascetisism and Sexuality in the Mythology of Siva', *History of Religions* VIII (4) May 1969:300–37; and IX (1) August 1969:1–41.

Otto, Rudolf. *The idea of the Holy.* Translated by John W. Harvey. London, H. Milford, Oxford University Press, 1925.

Otto, Walter F. *Dionysos, Myth and Cult.* Translated by Robert Palmer. Bloomington, Indiana University Press, 1965.

Pallis, Marco. *The Way and the Mountain.* London, Peter Gwen. 1960.

Paripāṭal. Madras, E. S. Rajam, 1957.

Parker, H. *Ancient Ceylon.* London, Luzec and Co., 1909.

Parthasarathy, Sadhu. 'Life of Sri Vallimalai Sacchidanandan Swami', *The Indian Express*, November 26, 1970.

Paterson and Krishnaswami, V. D. 'Changes of Prehistoric Man Near Madras', *Journal of Madras Geographical Association* XIII (1938):58–90.

———'Prehistoric Man Around Madras', *Indian Academy of Sciences* (Madras), No. 3 (1938):32–35.

Pattupāṭṭu. Introduction, translation, and notes by J. V. Chelliah. Madras, South India Śaiva Siddhānta Works Publishing Society, Ltd., 1962.

Pettazzoni, Raphael. *The All-Knowing God.* Translated by H. J. Rose. London, Methuen and Co., Ltd., 1956.

———'Structure and Historical Development'. Translated by Lucio Chiaraviglio, pp. 59–67 in: *History of Religions: Essays in Methodology*, ed. by Mircea Eliade and Joseph M. Kitagawa. Chicago University of Chicago Press, 1959.

Piet, John H. *A Logical Presentation of the Śaiva Siddhānta Philosophy*. Madras, Christian Literature Society for India, 1952.

Piggott, Stuart. *Prehistoric India to 1000 B.C.* London, Cassell and Co., Ltd., 1962.

Pillai, J. M. *Tiruchendur: The Sea Shore Temple of Subrahmanya*. Madras, Addison Press, 1948.

———Somasundaram. *Palani – The Sacred Hill of Murugan*. Palani, Sri Dandayuthapani Swamy Devasthanam, 1963; 1970.

———*Two Thousand Years of Tamil Literature*. Madras, South India Śaiva Siddhanta Works Publishing Society, n.d.

Pillai, N. Gopala. 'Skanda. The Alexander Romance in India', pp. 955–97 in: *Proceedings of the All-India Oriental Conference*, Vol. IX. Trivandrum, Government Press, 1937.

Pillai, S. Satchidanandan. *Śaiva Siddhanta*. Annamalainagar, University Press, 1952.

———Reprint of 'Periya Purāṇam', *Tamil Literature*, 1962–1963.

———Reprint of 'The Significance of the Avatar and Form of Lord Subramanya', *Jyothi Manram*, Souvenir Issue (1963):15–16.

———Personal interview on December 15, 1966.

Pillai, S. Vaiyapuri. *History of Tamil Language and Literature*. Madras, Ganasakthi Press, 1956.

Pillai, V. S. Chengalvarya. Manuscript of radio address, entitled 'Murugan Tradition', delivered over All-India Radio, Madras on September 19, 1954 (Typewritten).

Pillay, K. K. 'Aryan Influence in Tamilaham During the Sangam Epoch', *Tamil Culture* XII (1965):159–69.

Puranāṉūru. Madras, E. S. Rajam, 1958.

Raghavan, V. 'Brahma-Śāstā. A Form of Subrahmanya', *Journal of the Indian Society of Oriental Art*, Vol. VII (1939).

———'Holy Water', *Vedanta Kesari* (Madras), November 1940:243–48.

——— 'Dīpāvali Down the Ages', *The Hindu* (Madras), November 7, 1961.

———'Festive India', Paper read at the University of Chicago in May, 1963 (typewritten).

——— Translation of an article published in Tamil as 'Subrahmanya Tattva', *Kuṇṭūci* VII (7), Deepavali Special Number (1964):37–42 (typewritten).

———Discussion in November 1966, February 1967, and July–August, 1967.

Rajamanickiniar, N. An untitled response to a paper presented by K. A. Nilakanta Sastri to the Archaeological Society of South India in Madras on September 22, 1964, entitled 'Murugan' (typewritten).

Raman, K. V. 'Distribution Patterns of Culture Traits in the Pre- and Proto-Historic Times in Madurai Region', *Araycci* I (4) (July, 1970):499–509.

———Conversations held from July 1971–June 1972.

Ramanujan, A. K. Discussions in February–March, 1967.

———*The Interior Landscape*. Bloomington, University of Indiana Press, 1969.

Rāmāyaṇa, Balakāṇḍa, chapters 36–37, Oral translation rendered by V. Raghavan on January 25, 1967.

Rea, A. 'Prehistoric Antiquities in Tinnevelly', pp. 11–40 in: *Archaeological Survey of India. Annual Report, 1902–1903.* Calcutta, Office of Government Printing, 1904.

Ricœur, Paul. 'The Hermeneutics of Symbols and Philosophical Reflection', *International Philosophical Quarterly*, Vol. II (May 1962):191–218.

Ross, F. Denison. *An Alphabetical List of the Feasts and Holidays of the Hindus and Mohammedans.* Calcutta, Superintendent, Government Printing, India, 1914.

Ryerson, Charles. Personal interview on March 2, 1967 and periodic conversations from July 1971–July 1972.

Sankalia, H. D. 'Animal Fossils and Paleolithic Industries from the Pravaṇa Basin at Nebasi, District Ahmednagar', *Ancient India* VI (1950):35–52.

——— *Prehistory and Prohistory in India and Pakistan.* Bombay, University of Bombay Press, 1962.

Sankaranarayanan, A. 'Saint Tāyumanuvar and the Spirit of His Age'. Unpublished Ph.D. Thesis submitted to the University of Madras in 1969.

Santaramurthi, T. K. *Tirupparankuṉṟat Talavaralāṟu* [Historical Details of Tiruppaṟankuṉṟam Maturai, Meenakshi Sundarar Temple Publishers, 1966.

Sastri, K. A. Nilakanta. *Development of Religion in South India.* Madras, Orient Longmans, Ltd., 1963.

———'Murugan'. Paper read before the Archaeological Society of South India in Madras on September 22, 1964, and later revised by the author (typewritten).

——— *A History of South India from Prehistoric Times to the Fall of Vijayanagar.* Third edition. London, Oxford University Press, 1966.

Sathianatharier, R. 'Dynasties of South India', pp. 265–66 in: *The History and Culture of the Indian People*, Vol. III Bombay, Bharatiya Vidya Bhavan, 1954.

Schmidt, Wilhelm. *The Origin and Growth of Religion.* Translated by H. J. Rose. London, Methuen and Company, Ltd., 1931.

Seligmann, C. G., and Seligmann, Brenda Z. *The Veddas.* Cambridge, University Press, 1911.

Seshandri, K. 'Śaiva Siddhanta as Religion and Philosophy', *Tamil Culture* VIII (1959):172–77.

Sircar, D. C. *Indian Epigraphy.* Delhi, Motilal Banarsidass, 1965.

Sivananda, Swami. *Hindu Gods and Goddesses.* Sivananda–nagar, Divine Life Society, 1963.

Sivaramamurti, C. 'Geographical and Chronological Factors in Indian Iconography', *Ancient India* VI (1950):21–64.

——— *Kalugumalai and Early Pandyan Rock-Cut Shrines.* Bombay, N. M. Tripathi Private, Ltd., 1961.

———'Early Eastern Chalukya Sculpture', *Bulletin of Madras Government Museum, General Section*, Vol. VII, No. 2 (1962).

Skanda Purāṇa. Sthāṇana Vaibhava Khāṇda, Jayantipura Māhatyma. Chapters VI–VIII: Translated by V. Raghavan from Sanskrit text copied from manuscripts in the Government Oriental Manuscripts Library, Madras (typewritten).

Söderblom, Nathan. 'Holiness', in: *Encyclopedia of Religion and Ethics*, ed. by James Hastings. Edinburgh, T. T. Clark, 1913.

——— *The Living God.* London, Oxford University Press, 1933.

Sörenson, S. *An Index to the Names of the Mahābhārata.* London, Williams and Norgate, 1904.

Soundararajan, K. V. 'Stone Age Industries Near Giddalur', *Ancient India* VIII (1952):64–92.

———'Early Temple Origins in Lower Deccan with Special Reference to Nagarjunakonda', *Journal of the Oriental Institute (Baroda)* XI (1) (September 1961):21–25.

——— Personal interviews on February 9, 1967 and on June 15, 1972.

Srinivasan, K. R. 'Some Aspects of Religion as Revealed by Early Monuments and Literature of the South', *Journal of the Madras University Section A: Humanities* XXXII (1) (July 1960):131–98.

———*Cave Temples of the Pallavas.* Kanpur, Job Press Private, Ltd., 1964.

Srinivasan, K. R., and Bannerjee, N. R. 'Survey of South Indian Megaliths', *Ancient India* IX (1953):103–14.

Sri Taṇṭāyutapāni Cuvāmi Tevastānam, Paḻani. Conversations with executive officer, K. K. Menon; with Tevastānam office personnel; and with devotees and townspeople on March 4, 1967; and with executive officer, G. Athimulam, priests, devotees, and townspeople from March 20th to March 30th, 1972.

———Personal interview with C. Ramanujan, lecturer in Srī Paḻani Āṇṭavar College of Oriental Studies on March 5, 1967.

Srī Subrahmaṇya Swamy Temple, Kuṉṟakkuti. Conversations with chief priest, *maṭam* staff, and devotees on March 23, 1967.

———Personal interviews with the Kuṉṟakkuṭi Aṭikal on March 23, 1967 and May 9, 1972.

Śrī Subrahmaṇya Swamy Temple, Tiruchendur. Conversations with executive officer, Mr. Sankaranarayanan; with chief priest; with assistant priests; resident swami, students and devotees on April 4, 1967.

———Conversations with executive officer; chief priest; assistant priests; devotees and townspeople, October 22–28, 1971.

Śrī Subrahmaṇya Swamy Temple, Tirupporur. Conversations with resident swami and attendant priests.

Śrī Subrahmaṇya Swamy Temple, Tiruttaṇi. Conversations with devotees and townspeople on December 31, 1966.

Śrī Vaṭapaḻani Āṇṭavar Temple, Vaṭapaḻani. Conversations with executive officer, Mr. Balasubramaniam; with temple office staff; with chief priests; assistant priests; and devotees during the period October 1966 to January 1967.

Stein, Burton. Research Report given at Annual Conference of Fellows of the American Institute of Indian Studies in Poona on January 14, 1967.

———Personal interview on February 10, 1967.

Stenzler, Adolf Friedrich. *Yajnavalkyas' Gesetzbuch.* Berlin, Ferdinand Dummler Buchandlung, 1894.

Stevenson, Mrs. Sinclair. *The Rites of the Twice-Born, The Religious Quest of India,* ed. by J. N. Farquhar and H. D. Griswold. London, Oxford University Press, 1920.

Subramania Sastri, P. S. *Reprint of Religion and Philosophy in Ancient Tamil Classics.* Madras, Dharma Thondu Sabha, n.d.

Subrahmaniam, N. Conversations held in February 1967, October 1971, and March 1972.

——— *Pre-Pallavan Tamil Index*. 'Madras University Historical Series', Vol. XXIII, ed. by K. K. Pillay. Madras, University of Madras Press, 1966.

——— *Sangam Polity*. Bombay, Asia Publishing House, 1966.

'Subramaṇya Bhujaṅga Stotra'. Translated by V. Raghaven (typewritten).

Tamil Lexicon. Madras, Madras Law Journal Press, 1928.

Temples of South India. Delhi, Publications Division, Ministry of Information and Broadcasting, Government of India, 1960.

Thangavelu, M. K. 'Study of the Concept of God Muruga in Sangam Literature'. Unpublished thesis for the M. Litt. Degree, University of Madras, 1963.

——— Personal Interview on February 18, 1967.

Thapar, B. K. 'Porkalam, 1948: Excavation of a Megalithic Urn–Burial', *Ancient India* VIII (1952):3–16.

——— 'Maski. 1954: A Chalcolithic Site of the Southern Deccan', *Ancient India* XIII (1957):4–142.

Thurston, Edgar. *Castes and Tribes of Southern India*, Madras, Government Press, 1909.

Tirumantiram. Stanzas 520, 1026, 2758. Translated by N. Subramaniam (hand-written).

Tirumurukāṟṟupaṭai. Pattupāṭṭu. Introduction, translation, and notes by J. V. Chelliah. Madras, South India Śaiva Siddhānta Works Publishing Society, Ltd., 1962.

Tolkāppiyar, Tolkāppiyam. Introduction, translation, and commentary by S. Ilakkivanar. Madurai, 'Kural Neri' Publishing House, 1963.

Tolkāppiyam. Porulatikāram. Introduction, translation, and commentary by E. S. Varadaraja Iyer. Annamalai, Annamalai University Press, 1948.

Tylor, Edmund B. *Primitive Culture*, Vol. 1. London, John Murray, 1903.

Underhill, Muriel M. *The Hindu Religious Year*. London, H. Milford, Oxford University Press, 1921.

Uṟcavaṅkalin vivaram [Details of Festivals], 1966–1971. Paḻani, S.R.K̄.V. Press, 1967–1971.

van der Leeuw, Gerardus. *Religion in Essence and Manifestation*. Translated by J. E. Turner. London, George Allen and Unwin, Ltd., 1938.

Veliah, T. S. 'Andarkuppam', *The Hindu* (Madras), January 8, 1967.

Venkataraman, K. R. 'Skanda Cult in South India', pp. 309–13 in: *The Cultural Heritage of India*, Vol. IV. Calcutta, The Ramakrishna Mission, 1956.

Venkata Ramanaya, N. *An Essay on the Origin of the South Indian Temple*. Madras, Methodist Publishing House, 1930.

——— *Rudra-Śiva*. Madras, University of Madras Press, 1941.

Venkatasubramaniam, E. V. (ed.). *Kantan Malar* [The Flower of Skanda]. Tinnevelly, South India Śaiva Siddhānta Works Publishing Society, Ltd., 1961.

——— *Tiruttaṇikai Murukaṉ Piḷḷaittamiḻ*. Madras, Śri Kumāra Taṉuvamas Tirúkkáit Tiruppukaḻs Caṅkam, 1964.

Vijayaragavachariar, Embar. A Hārikathā (story-telling) entitled 'Murukan's Marriage to Vaḷḷi.' Performed in the Music Academy, Madras on December 24, 1966.

Waddell, L. A. 'The Dharani Cult in Buddhism, its Origin, Deified Literature, and Images', *Ostasiatische Zeitschrift* I, Part II (July 1912):155–95.

Widengren, George. *The King and the Tree of Life in Ancient Near Eastern Religion*. Uppsala, Lundequistaka Bokhandeln, 1951.

Willetts, Ronald Frederick. *Cretan Cults and Festivals*. New York, Barnes and Noble, Inc., 1962.

Winternitz, Moriz. *A History of Indian Literature*. Translated by S. Ketkai and H. Kohn. Calcutta, University of Calcutta Press, 1959.

Wirz, P. *Kataragama, the Holiest Place in Ceylon*. Gunasena, Ceylon, 1966.

Zeuner, Frederick E., and Allchin, Bridget. 'The Microlithic Sites of Tinnevelly District, Madras State', *Ancient India* XII (1956):4–20.

Zimmer, Heinrich. *Myths and Symbols in Indian Art and Civilization*, by Joseph Campbell. New York, Pantheon Books, 1951.

——— *Philosophies of India*, by Joseph Campbell. New York: Pantheon Books, 1951.

Zvelebil, Kamil. Reprint of 'The Bull-Baiting Festival in Tamil India', *Annals of the Naprstek Museum* I (1962):191–99.

——— 'Harappa and the Dravidian – an Old Mystery in a New Light', *New Orient* IV (3) (June 1965):65–69.

——— 'Arunagirinathar – Confessor of Beauty', *New Orient* IV (5) (October 1965):155–56.

——— 'Aruṇakiri, The Great Formalist'. A lecture given at the University of Chicago on May 7, 1966.

——— 'Caṅkam Literature'. Lecture given at the University of Chicago on April 2, 1966.

——— Conversations held periodically from October 1965–May 1966.

——— 'The Tamil *Bhakti* Poets'. A lecture given at the University of Chicago on April 16, 1967.

Index

Religion and Society

1. *Ibn Taimīya's Struggle against Popular Religion.*
With an Annotated Translation of his Kitāb iqtiḍā' aṣ-ṣirāṭ al-mustaqīm mukhālafat aṣḥāb al-jaḥīm,
by Muhammad Umar Memon (University of Wisconsin, Madison)
1976, XXII + 424 pages. Clothbound
ISBN 90-279-7591-4

2. *Tibetan Religious Dances.*
Tibetan Text and Annotated Translation of the 'chams yig,
by René de Nebesky-Wojkowitz
With an Appendix by Walter Graf
Edited by Christoph von Fürer-Haimendorf
1976, VIII + 320 pages, with illustrations. Clothbound
ISBN 90-279-7621-X

3. *Johann Christian Edelmann.*
From Orthodoxy to Enlightenment,
by Walter Grossmann (University of Massachusetts at Boston)
1976, XII + 210 pages. Clothbound
ISBN 90-279-7691-0

4. *Shahrastānī on the Indian Religions,*
by Bruce B. Lawrence (Duke University)
With a Preface by Franz Rosenthal (Yale University)
1976, 300 pages. Clothbound
ISBN 90-279-7681-3

5. *The Precarious Organisation.*
Sociological Explorations of the Church's Mission and Structure,
by Mady A. Thung (University of Leiden)
With a Preface by C. J. Lammers (University of Leiden)
1976, XIV + 348 pages. Clothbound
ISBN 90-279-7652-X

7. *Divine Word and Prophetic Word in Early Islam.*
A Reconsideration of the Sources, with Special Reference to the Divine Saying or *Ḥadîth Qudsî*,
by William A. Graham (Harvard University)
1977, XVIII + 266 pages. Clothbound
ISBN 90-279-7612-0